Henry VIII
and the
English Nobility

Henry VIII
and the
English Nobility

HELEN MILLER

Basil Blackwell

© Helen Miller 1986

First published 1986

First published in paperback 1989

Basil Blackwell Ltd
108 Cowley Road, Oxford OX4 1JF, UK

Basil Blackwell Inc.
432 Park Avenue South, Suite 1503
New York, NY 10016, USA

British Library Cataloguing in Publication Data

Miller, Helen
  Henry VIII and the English nobility.
  1. England—Nobility—History
  I. Title
  305.5'223'0942   HT653.G7
  ISBN 0-631-13836-6
  ISBN 0-631-16863-X Pbk

Library of Congress Cataloging in Publication Data

Miller, Helen.
  Henry VIII and the English nobility.
  Bibliography: p.
  Includes index.
  1. Great Britain—Nobility—History—
16th century.
  2. Henry VIII, King of England,
1491-1547—Relations with nobility.
  3. Great Britain—History—Henry VIII,
1509-1547.   I. Title.
  DA332.M55   1986 942.05'2   85-26712
  ISBN 0-631-13836-6
  ISBN 0-631-16863-X

Typeset by Freeman Graphic, Tonbridge, Kent.
Printed in Great Britain by TJ Press Ltd, Padstow

Contents

Abbreviations

APC	*Acts of the Privy Council*
BL	British Library
Bull.IHR	*Bulletin of the Institute of Historical Research*
Cambridge HJ	*Cambridge Historical Journal*
CCR	*Calendar of Close Rolls*
CPR	*Calendar of Patent Rolls*
CSPSp.	*Calendar of State Papers, Spanish*
CSPVen.	*Calendar of State Papers, Venetian*
DKR	*Reports of the Deputy Keeper of the Public Records*
DNB	*Dictionary of National Biography*
EHR	*The English Historical Review*
GEC	*The Complete Peerage* by G.E.C.
HJ	*The Historical Journal*
HMC	*Historical Manuscripts Commission*
LJ	*Journals of the House of Lords*
LP	*Letters and Papers, Henry VIII*
PPC	*Proceedings of the Privy Council*
Rot.Parl.	*Rotuli Parliamentorum*
SP	*State Papers, Henry VIII*
TRHS	*Transactions of the Royal Historical Society*
VCH	*The Victoria History of the Counties of England*

Biographical information, unless otherwise noted, is taken from GEC.
Manuscripts references, unless otherwise noted, are to documents in the
Public Record Office, Chancery Lane.

Introduction

As Henry VIII celebrated his accession to the throne, Edmund Dudley, prisoner in the Tower of London, reflected on the power of the devil, the world and the flesh. They 'contynuallie fighte and make battell ayenst all mankynd, and peradventure more farventlie ayenst a prince then a pore man'. In a guarded reference to his late master, Dudley admitted that Henry VII had been insatiable in his financial demands, although he was 'in maner withowt faulte, saving only that'. He rejoiced to hear that Henry VIII was determined to see his father's will performed to the relief of his soul.[1] Like many lesser men, Henry VII had asked in his will for restitution to be made to any he had wronged, and Dudley for his part compiled for two of the king's executors a list of 'such persons as I thincke were hardlie intreated and much more sorer then the causes required'. He also reminded them that Henry VII had often bound his subjects in large sums of money, without intending to enforce payment, in order to have them 'in his danger at his pleasure'.[2] Henry VIII's methods were not those of his father and some, at least, of the noblemen named by Dudley were freed from their bonds in the early years of the new reign.[3]

The management of relations between the crown and the nobility was a major aspect of the art of government. In essence, the relationship was a personal one and Henry VIII had no interest in continuing a policy which was already counter-productive, especially in creating an aggrieved and resentful nobility.[4] Instead, he allowed the death of

[1] *The Tree of Comonwealth. A Treatise written by Edmund Dudley*, ed. D. M. Brodie (Cambridge, 1948), pp. 23–4, 28–9.
[2] C. J. Harrison, 'The petition of Edmund Dudley', *EHR*, lxxxvii (1972), 86.
[3] See below, pp. 207–8.
[4] J. R. Lander, 'Bonds, coercion, and fear: Henry VII and the peerage' in *Florilegium Historiale: Essays Presented to Wallace K. Ferguson*, ed. J. G. Rowe and W. H. Stockdale (Toronto, 1971), p. 353.

Henry VII to expose his ministers to the vengeance of their enemies: Sir Richard Empson and Edmund Dudley, with no one to protect them, were cast as scapegoats for Henry VII's financial controls and immediately arrested.[5] Henry VIII's dramatic disavowal of the former regime evoked a chorus of rejoicing summed up by William Blount, lord Mountjoy, in a letter to Erasmus: 'All is milk and honey and nectar.'[6] The special relationship between the king and the nobility was stressed in the indictments. Empson was charged with having conspired to seize control of the government at the accession of Henry VIII and to remove all the noblemen and other magnates from the favour and council of the king; Dudley with conspiring to deprive Henry of his royal liberty and to move discords, divisions and dissensions amongst his magnates and councillors.[7] Yet the king's gesture had ominous implications, not least for the nobility. The response to it might have given Henry, in his turn, cause for concern. Did the euphoria conceal an intention, by at least some nobles, to make a bid to recover lost political ground? The new regime opened up more than one possibility of a fresh start. The interaction between Henry VIII and the nobility, unfolding down the years, was to form a significant part of the history of the reign, and one that has not, so far, been systematically explored.

The nobility in the sixteenth century was a clearly defined status group, the lay members of the house of lords. At an earlier period a writ of summons to attend parliament did not ennoble the recipient. Even by 1509 a personal summons to parliament did not necessarily create a prescriptive right. Nevertheless, custom had crystallized to the point where it had become generally binding in practice and, with few exceptions, a family was summoned consistently or not at all. But the nobility was always in need of renewal. In the fourteenth and fifteenth centuries on average over one-quarter of all noble families had become extinct every 25 years.[8] The wastage rate from all causes in the early sixteenth century was equally high. The first strand of any royal policy towards the nobility had to be the selection of men to keep

[5] E. W. Ives, *The Common Lawyers of Pre-Reformation England. Thomas Kebell: A Case Study*, Cambridge Studies in English Legal History, ed. D. E. C. Yale (Cambridge, 1983), pp. 235–6.

[6] *Collected Works of Erasmus*, ii, *The Correspondence of Erasmus. Letters 142 to 297: 1501 to 1514*, trans. R. A. B. Mynors and D. F. S. Thomson, annotated W. K. Ferguson (Toronto, 1975), no. 215.

[7] *DKR*, iii, Appendix ii, pp. 226–8.

[8] K. B. McFarlane, *The Nobility of Later Medieval England* (Oxford, 1973), pp. 172–6. McFarlane included all families whose head at any time received a writ of summons and counted them as extinct when a head died leaving only a female heir or heirs or a male heir or heirs whose claim came through a female.

it in corporate existence. The king might also promote men within the peerage. The barons always outnumbered the high nobility – the viscounts, earls, marquesses and dukes who in each degree took precedence over those beneath them. Rank mattered more than birth and promotions could be as significant as new creations. Part I covers Henry VIII's policy towards both, as well as the parallel process by which noblemen were removed from the peerage by treason trials and acts of attainder.

The role of the nobility is discussed in Part II. Few family archives have survived from the early sixteenth century. Even for the greatest noblemen there is rarely enough known to sustain a full biography: nevertheless, many episodes in their lives are well documented. The danger is that these high noblemen may be taken as typical of the nobility as a whole. Henry VIII's reign is the first for which evidence survives in the central records in sufficient quantity – patchy though it is – to form the basis for a study of the nobility in certain key areas of political activity. How important for noblemen was attendance at court, in council and parliament, in war? What did Henry VIII expect of them? Did his views or their attitudes change in the course of the reign? Finally, how generous – or otherwise – was Henry VIII in his rewards to the nobility? Part III reconstructs the pattern of the king's grants of offices and lands.

PART I

The Changing Membership of the Nobility

CHAPTER 1

Creations and Promotions

On All-hallow-e'en, 1494, Henry VII's second son was created duke of York in the parliament chamber at Westminster. The heralds recorded the ceremony. The king stood wearing his crown under his cloth of estate accompanied by the dukes of Bedford and Buckingham, the marquess of Dorset, the earls of Arundel, Oxford, Essex and Kent, 'with dyversse other erlles all in their robes of astate, and also the substance of all the barons of the realme in their robis'. A procession entered, led by Garter king of arms; the earl of Derby bore the cap of estate, the earl of Northumberland the rod of gold, and the earl of Suffolk the sword, 'the pomell upwardes'. The earl of Shrewsbury carried the three-year-old prince 'tyll they were somwhat enteryd the parleament chambre', when the child was led to the king. The patent was read out and Henry VII invested his son and gave him £1,000 p.a. After divine service Shrewsbury again carried the prince who now wore the cap of estate and held in his hands his letters patent and the gold rod. During the celebratory dinner which followed his style was proclaimed. It included not only his title but also the offices with which his father had previously invested him: 'duc de York, lieutenant generall d'Irland, conte mareschall d'Angleterre et guardien de cincq portz.'[1] The future Henry VIII had made his formal entry into the ranks of the English nobility. In 1502 he became duke of Cornwall on the death of his elder brother and when parliament was next in session, in 1504, Henry VII created him prince of Wales and earl of Chester.

[1] BL, Harl. 6074, ff.48–50. Alternative text in BL, Cotton Julius B.XII, ff.91–3, part of a longer account printed *Letters and Papers Illustrative of the Reigns of Richard III and Henry VII*, ed. James Gairdner, Rolls Series 24, 2 vols (London, 1861, 1863), i, Appendix A, vi.

When he became king on 22 April 1509, two months before his eighteenth birthday, there were 42 noblemen. Since Jasper Tudor, duke of Bedford, had died without an heir in 1495, Edward Stafford, duke of Buckingham, was the sole duke. He was 31 years old and had been mentioned by 'grett personages' during an earlier illness of Henry VII as a suitable king.[2] The only marquess – Thomas Grey, marquess of Dorset – was thé same age, the son of the old marquess who had assisted at Henry's creation as duke of York. Another participant in that ceremony, though physically alive, was legally dead. Edmund de la Pole, earl of Suffolk – also favoured as a possible successor to Henry VII – had been attainted in his absence abroad by the parliament of 1504 and returned to England two years later by the archduke Philip. De la Pole remained in the Tower. Of the ten surviving earldoms, one hovered on the brink of extinction. Sir William Courtenay, son and heir of Edward earl of Devon, had been imprisoned as an adherent of Suffolk and attainted with him in 1504. He was still under attainder when his father died a few weeks after Henry VIII's accession, and the earldom became forfeit. John de Vere, earl of Oxford, was 66 years old, Thomas Howard, earl of Surrey, not much younger. The earl of Arundel was in his late fifties, the earl of Shrewsbury in his early forties, the earls of Kent, Essex and Northumberland in their thirties, the earl of Derby in his mid-twenties. Only Ralph Neville, earl of Westmorland, was a minor, aged 11. There were 27 barons of full age and three – Ferrers, Daubeney and Grey of Powis – who were under 21.[3]

Henry VIII soon demonstrated his willingness to restore to favour all those who had fallen foul of his father apart from the former earl of Suffolk and his brothers, although he excepted from the general pardon of 30 April 1509, as well as the de la Poles, Sir William Courtenay, the marquess of Dorset and Thomas lord Dacre of the north.[4] Dacre's troubles with the crown were financial, represented by bonds and recognizances whose justice he contested. Henry VIII did not allow the dispute to create personal difficulties between them and in July he reappointed Dacre warden of the west march against Scotland.[5] In July, also, the king recalled the marquess of Dorset from Calais, where he was being held in the custody of the deputy.[6] Although he was never attainted, his Yorkist blood had taken him as

---

[2] *Letters and Papers of Richard III and Henry VII*, i, 233.
[3] See below, Appendix, for a list of all the noblemen of the reign of Henry VIII.
[4] *LP*, i(i), 11 g.10.
[5] ibid., 131, 132 g.5. Having paid only £200, Dacre was released in 1516 from a debt of £1,333 6s 8d acknowledged by indenture of 17 July 1506: *LP*, ii(1), 2555.
[6] *HMC, Various Collections*, ii, 304.

well as Courtenay to the Tower, and the two prisoners had been transferred to the castle of Calais by Henry VII six months before his death.[7] On 26 August 1509 Henry VIII authorized the issue of letters patent of general pardon to Dorset whenever he like to sue for them.[8] The rehabilitation of Courtenay was more complicated. His wife, the king's aunt, Katherine, daughter of Edward IV, was given an annuity of 200 marks in August 1509 during the king's pleasure. Courtenay himself remained in the keeping of the deputy of Calais for the time being.[9] It took until April 1511 for Henry VIII to negotiate with them both an indenture which covered the restoration of title and a settlement of lands. The king, with the advice of his council, undertook to issue letters patent enabling Courtenay to receive grants, notwithstanding his attainder, to grant him specified lands and to create him earl of Devon, all before Michaelmas, and to reverse his act of attainder when parliament next met.[10] The clumsy procedure was made necessary by the king's inability to reverse a parliamentary attainder by prerogative.[11] Henry VIII issued the enabling letters patent on 9 May 1511 and on the following day created Sir William Courtenay earl of Devon.[12] Although he died before he had been invested with the title, he was, at the king's command, buried with the honours due to an earl.[13] Parliament assembled in February 1512, but it was not until the second session, opening in November 1512, that the petition of the earl's young son, Henry, for the annulment of his father's attainder was passed and he was enabled by the act of repeal to inherit the older earldom of his grandfather as well as the more recent title.[14] In the first session of this parliament the attainder of James Tuchet, lord Audley, for taking part in the Cornish rising of

---

[7] The Chronicle of Calais, ed. J. G. Nichols, Camden Soc., xxxv (London, 1846), p. 6.

[8] LP, i(1), 158 g.75. Dorset's pardon was already drawn up, dated 20 August: ibid., 438(3), m.21.

[9] ibid., 158 g.20, 170. GEC under Devon states that Courtenay bore the third sword at the coronation of Henry VIII, but see below, p. 93.

[10] LP, i(1), 749 g.23.

[11] In 1504 Henry VII had been authorized by statute to reverse attainders by letters patent, but only for his lifetime: 19 Henry VII, c.28.

[12] C82/364 (LP, i(1), 784 gg.14, 16). By the letters patent of 9 May Henry VIII annulled the attainder as far as he could: 'concedimus pro nobis et heredibus nostris quantum in nobis est . . .'

[13] College of Arms, I.11, ff.74–5 describes the funeral, with Courtenay's body remaining 'in his chamber in the cowrt' at Greenwich until it was taken by river to the Black Friars in London. I am grateful to the College of Arms for permission to make use of this and other MSS.

[14] 4 Henry VIII, c.9. On 26 March 1512 the bill of restitution was respited in the house of lords, Courtenay and his mother having been called to further discussions with the king: LJ, i, 17.

1497 was also repealed and his son, John, succeeded to the barony.[15] In the third session, early in 1514, the attainder of Edward Plantagenet, earl of Warwick, was repealed on the petition of his sister Margaret, the widow of Sir Richard Pole. She was restored in blood, title and estate, and became countess of Salisbury.[16] There seems little doubt that Henry VIII intended from the start of his reign to make these restorations. The delay stemmed from the need first to devise satisfactory arrangements about the lands: Henry VIII's approach in this respect was not as different from his father's as he may have liked his people to suppose.[17]

Margaret Pole's grown-up son and heir, Sir Henry Pole, was known as lord Montagu from the date of his mother's restoration. Families of the higher nobility often held lesser titles as well, one of which could be used by the eldest son. Margaret's right to the barony of Montagu – tenuous though it might seem under modern peerage law – was no doubt the justification for her son's use of that title. Men with courtesy titles were often grouped with the nobility, for example on state occasions, but they had no place in the house of lords and enjoyed none of the legal privileges of the nobility. Sir Henry Pole was not a peer until he was summoned to parliament and took his seat on 1 December 1529.[18]

There were, of course, a number of heirs to peerages in the reign of Henry VIII who succeeeded to their titles but did not live long enough to receive a writ of summons. There is no doubt about their noble status. There were others whose rights to succeed were less clear. Patents of creation generally limited the inheritance to heirs male, but few baronial titles were granted by patent or charter before the sixteenth century.[19] Baronies created by writ – or, in reality, more probably by word of mouth followed by a writ of summons to parliament – had no such limitation and could therefore be inherited by a woman. Yet the right of the heir general in such cases had not always prevailed over that of the heir male. In 1497 two claimants to a barony could each cite recent examples proving their contradictory assertions that baronies had or had not descended through a female.[20]

[15] 3 Henry VIII, c.17.
[16] 5 Henry VIII, c.12.
[17] See below, pp. 209–10.
[18] College of Arms, 2 H.13, f.398v, printed GEC, ix, Appendix B. GEC under Montagu argues that he was created a baron in 1514 by word of mouth, but neither there nor in a discussion of the evidence in ix, Appendix E offers any explanation for the 15-year interval before he was summoned to parliament.
[19] GEC, vii, Appendix A.
[20] J. Enoch Powell and Keith Wallis, *The House of Lords in the Middle Ages. A History of the English House of Lords to 1540* (London, 1968), Appendix A.

The right, if any, of the husband of an heiress to sit in the house of lords was even more contentious. Yet the issue of a writ of summons could be a casual business. It was the duty of the chancery clerks to keep up to date the list of peers summoned to each parliament. But news sometimes travelled slowly, and the clerks were not infrequently left in ignorance or doubt. In the fifteenth century there were many examples of several parliaments assembling before the death of a nobleman was followed by the issue of a writ of summons to his heir.[21] In November 1511 the clerks sent a writ of summons to Richard lord Lumley 18 months after his death, their misgivings expressed only in a marginal entry, *mortuus est, ut dicitur*.[22] They felt no overwhelming need to establish the facts. In October 1509, when they sent out the writs for the first parliament of Henry VIII's reign, to be held in January 1510, they entered on the list of those summoned no fewer than five peers for whom they had no christian name.[23] Moreover, the chancery clerks were not even consistent: Robert lord Willoughby de Broke was summoned to the parliament of 1512 but not to those of 1510 and 1515, and Robert lord Ogle was summoned to the parliament of 1539 but not to those of 1536, 1542 and 1545.[24]

Hidden behind the direction of a writ of summons to '– Scrope' to attend the parliament of 1510 lay a writ of summons to a peer in his wife's barony as well as his own. As it happened, the effects of this summons were short-lived. The barony of Scrope of Upsall or Masham had devolved upon Alice, the sole heiress, in 1493. She married Henry, son and heir of Henry lord Scrope of Bolton, and he assumed her title.[25] After he succeeded to his father's barony he was known by different combinations of his titles which he was careful to itemize when he sued out the general pardon in May 1509: Henry Scrope of Bolton, lord Scrope, alias Henry Scrope, lord Scrope of Upsall, alias lord Scrope of Bolton and Upsall.[26] He was summoned to the parlia-

---

[21] J. C. Wedgwood, *History of Parliament: Register of the Ministers and of the Members of Both Houses 1439–1509* (London, 1938), p. lxi.

[22] C54/379 (*LP*, i(1), 963).

[23] C54/377 (*LP*, i(1), 205). Gaps in the record were filled, not always correctly, by Sir William Dugdale, *A Perfect Copy of all Summons of the Nobility to the Great Councils and Parliaments of this Realm* (London, 1685).

[24] Lists of those individually summoned are on the close rolls (C54) for the parliaments of 1510, 1512, 1515, 1536 and 1542 or the parliament pawn (C218/1) for the parliaments of 1539 and 1545, or on both, for the parliament of 1529. There is no extant list for the parliament of 1523.

[25] He was described as Henry lord Scrope of Upsall in his father's inquisition post mortem: DUR3/3, f.lv.

[26] *LP*, i(1), 438(2), m.7.

ment of 1512 as Henry Scrope, lord Scrope and Upsall.[27] However, by the end of 1512 Alice was dead leaving no children and her barony had gone to her uncle Ralph, brother of the former lord Scrope of Upsall.[28] When the writs went out in November 1514 for a new parliament to meet in 1515, he was summoned as lord Scrope of Upsall and Henry as lord Scrope of Bolton.[29] The baronial title had followed the line of descent of the manors of Upsall and Masham.[30] It was for this reason, perhaps, that the issue of the writs of summons seems to have been treated as a matter of routine, within the competence of the clerks of chancery, although the link between a barony and the land from which its name was derived was not indissoluble.

Two other heiresses took their titles permanently to new families in the early part of the reign of Henry VIII. When Edmund Ros, lord Ros, died childless in 1508, his coheirs were his two sisters or their heirs. One sister died without issue, leaving as sole heir to the barony the other sister's son, Sir George Manners. On 21 November 1512, while parliament was in session, Henry VIII issued a warrant for his summons to parliament as George Manners, knight, lord Ros.[31] Henry Lovel, lord Morley, in 1489 left as sole heir his sister, Alice Lovel. She married, as her first husband, Sir William Parker. Unlike Sir Henry Scrope he was never summoned to parliament in her barony, but after his death in December 1518 their son, Henry Parker, became lord Morley. He served on the panel of peers which tried the duke of Buckingham in 1521 and was present in (or expected at) the parliament of 1523.[32] By coincidence, neither Henry Lovel, who had been killed in Flanders shortly after coming of age, nor Edmund Ros, judged incapable of looking after himself, had been summoned to parliament. This had not affected the descent of their titles and the precedence of the ancient baronies was accorded to their heirs.[33] The Clinton family, more remarkably, survived a 50-year intermission in its summons, lasting two generations. No writ was issued to the head

[27] C54/379 (LP, i(1), 963). GEC under Scrope (of Masham or Upsall) wrongly assigns the writ of summons to the parliament of 1512 to Ralph's elder brother Henry.

[28] The first reference to Ralph as lord Scrope comes late in 1512 when he and Henry lord Scrope were named as subsidy commissioners for the North Riding of Yorkshire in the schedule to the subsidy act: 4 Henry VIII, c.19.

[29] C54/382 (LP, i(2), 3464(2)).

[30] VCH, Yorkshire North Riding, i, 324–5, ii, 41–2.

[31] LP, i(1), 1494 g.45.

[32] DKR, iii, Appendix ii, p. 233; College of Arms, Muniment Room 6/41 (Garter's roll, 1523).

[33] George's son, Thomas Manners, lord Ros, was ranked first of the barons after the prior of St John's in Garter's roll of 1523, and Henry Parker, lord Morley, tenth.

of the family between the death of John lord Clinton in 1464 and the succession of Thomas lord Clinton in 1514. The intervening barons continued to be known as lords Clinton, or Clinton and Say, and if (as has been suggested) poverty caused their non-summons, there is no sign that Thomas lord Clinton in 1514 was in any better financial state.[34] However, he was married to an illegitimate daughter of Sir Edward Poynings, a royal servant well placed to further the interests of his family of bastards. The first writ to Thomas was addressed to '– Clynton de Clynton *chevalier*'.[35] The chancery clerks evidently knew no more than that the barony had passed to the heir. When he arrived to take his seat in the house of lords in the second session of parliament, in November 1515, he was allotted his place of sitting in parliament, saving the right of anyone else, in the middle of the bench of barons.[36] From his entry, therefore, he was treated as present in right of an old barony, not as a new creation. Although not quite in the same category as those who inherited their peerages in a more regular fashion, Ralph Scrope, Manners, Parker and Clinton were peers by inheritance, not new men picked by Henry VIII for elevation to the peerage. Other noblemen, by contrast, were clearly new creations in spite of their possible claims to peerage titles. It was the king's decision that ennobled them, not the acceptance of any right of inheritance vested in them.

Henry VIII advanced to the peerage friends, relatives and servants. Sometimes the reason for his choice is obvious. Sometimes it is not clear why he chose one man rather than another with apparently similar qualifications, although clues may be found in the timing of the grant of a peerage or the title selected. But every grant served one basic purpose: to project the image of a munificent prince, glorified in the distribution of honours. The investiture focused attention upon the king as the source of nobility. The ceremonies for the award of the higher titles were great occasions carefully stage-managed by the heralds and attended by as many noblemen as could be gathered together. This was one reason for Henry VIII's choice of parliament time for many of his peerage creations.[37] It also provided the oppor-

[34] Poverty was the reason for the non-summons of John lord Clinton (d.1488) given by J. C. Wedgwood, *History of Parliament, Biographies of the Members of the Commons House 1439–1509* (London, 1936), p. 196.

[35] C54/382 (*LP*, i(2), 3464(2)). GEC under Clinton wrongly assigns this writ to John lord Clinton, father of Thomas, who had died on 4 June: C142/32/50.

[36] *LJ*, i, 46.

[37] From at least the reign of Edward II to the end of Henry V's reign most peerages were actually conferred in parliament, but investiture in one of the royal residences then became the norm: Sir Anthony Wagner and J. C. Sainty, 'The origin of the introduction of peers in the house of lords', *Archaeologia*, ci (1967), 119–50.

tunity to create a peer 'with the assent of parliament', presumably as a way of associating the commons as well as the lords with the cele- brations.[38] The opening of parliament itself was an impressive ritual performed by Henry VIII for the first time on 21 January 1510. The sword was carried before him by lord Henry Stafford, brother of Edward duke of Buckingham.[39] Stafford's initial experience of the new reign had been less pleasant. According to Edward Hall he had been sent to the Tower with Empson and Dudley 'upon suspicion of treason laied unto hym', although quickly released.[40] The rapid reversal of fortune which was to mark so many careers at the court of Henry VIII worked happily in his case and he soon became a favourite of the king. His rise was probably helped by the fact that his two sisters were resident at court from the beginning of the reign.[41] Henry VIII created Stafford earl of Wiltshire with the assent of parliament on 28 January 1510.[42] The investiture was held in the palace of Westminster on the following Sunday, 3 February. The king, in his great chamber, had 'the great parte of his lordis both spirituall and temporall aboute him'. Lord Henry Stafford was led in by the earls of Northumberland and Shrewsbury, wearing their robes of estate, preceded by the earl of Derby bearing the sword. After the king had girded him with the sword the new earl gave humble thanks for the great honour done him and went to dinner in the council chamber, where he was proclaimed as earl of Wiltshire, 'fitz et frere des ducs de Bokyngham'.[43] The title itself emphasized this noble ancestry, since the earldom of Wiltshire had been granted to a younger son of Humphrey Stafford, first duke of Buckingham, but had become extinct in 1499.

No high birth could be claimed by the next new peer to be created, Charles Brandon. In 1509 he sued out the general pardon as Charles Brandon, esquire, of London and Bishop's Lynn, Norfolk.[44] But he was one of Henry's closest friends, some five years older than the king, an esquire of the body at the beginning of the reign and knighted in

[38] The assent of parliament, or a similar phrase, was often included in charters of creation up to 1414, but implied no limitation on the king's right to create peers by prerogative alone: Sir Harris Nicolas, *Report of Proceedings on the Claim to the Earldom of Devon* (London, 1832), pp. clxxxvi–clxxxvii.

[39] BL, Add. 5758, ff.8–9, printed Powell and Wallis, *The House of Lords*, pp. 543–4, where lord Henry Stafford is wrongly identified as Buckingham's eight-year-old son.

[40] *Hall's Chronicle*, [ed. Henry Ellis] (London, 1809), pp. 505, 512.

[41] Henry's interest in one of them was to upset the queen and enrage the duke of Buckingham in May 1510: *CSPSp.*, *Supplement to volume i and volume ii*, i, 8.

[42] C82/344 (*LP*, i(1), 357 g.37).

[43] BL, Harl. 6074, ff.54–5. His reward to Garter king of arms was an annuity of £2, with 10 marks 'for recompense of his gown and his apparell that he ware the same daie that he put on him the robys of an erle'.

[44] *LP*, i(1), 438(3), m.4.

1512. In May 1513, as Henry prepared to lead an invasion of France, he appointed Brandon marshal of his army.[45] A few days earlier, doubtless in order to give him the status appropriate to that role, Henry VIII had created him viscount Lisle, with remainder to his heirs male by his wife, Elizabeth Grey, baroness Lisle.[46] This was indeed special treatment. The wardship and marriage of Elizabeth, daughter and heir of John Grey, late viscount Lisle, had recently been sold for £1,400 to Brandon.[47] He had announced his intention to marry her, but she was only a child and no wedding was in immediate prospect. In fact, the wedding never took place. In 1515, after his marriage to Henry VIII's sister, Brandon resigned the wardship, which was then sold for £4,000 to Katherine countess of Devon.[48] The title of viscount he retained even longer, only surrendering it in 1523 for Henry VIII to bestow on Arthur Plantagenet, who was married to the next heiress, also Elizabeth, aunt of Brandon's former ward.

The war brought a limited victory for the army royal in France and a spectacular triumph over the Scots. Immediately after the battle of Flodden in September 1513 Thomas Ruthal, bishop of Durham, suggested to Wolsey that the king should advance the earl of Surrey, the victorious commander, to the honour of duke.[49] The thought probably occurred to Thomas Howard himself, restored to the earldom of Surrey by Henry VII, but never yet allowed his father's title of duke of Norfolk. On 1 February 1514, after the reassembly of parliament, Henry VIII issued four patents of creation. The warrant for each grant was a signed bill in the form of a petition. 'Please it your highnes of your most habundaunt grace to graunte your gracious lettres patentes in due forme under your grete seale to be made according to the tenor ensuyng' introduced the text of the letters patent creating Surrey duke of Norfolk.[50] The younger Thomas Howard, the lord admiral, who had joined in the action against the Scots, was created earl of Surrey for life, his father relinquishing the title for his benefit.[51] In each case the letters patent declared that the peerage,

[45] *LP*, i(2), 1948 g.93.

[46] C82/392 (*LP*, i(2), 1948 g.68).

[47] *LP*, i(1), 1804 g.57; E36/215, f.669 (*LP*, ii(2), p. 1485).

[48] *LP*, ii(1), 660, 696; E36/215, f.689 (*LP*, ii(2), p. 1487). Elizabeth married Henry Courtenay, earl of Devon, but d.s.p. in 1519, aged about 14.

[49] SP1/5, f.39 (*LP*, i(2), 2284).

[50] C82/401 (*LP*, i(2), 2684 g.1). Signed petitions cannot therefore be taken as proof that the initiative lay with the petitioner. In these instances, they were clearly no more than a convenient way of putting into effect decisions reached by the king. This conflicts with the view that 'signed petitions meant exactly what they said' expressed by G. R. Elton, 'Thomas More, councillor (1517–29)' in *St Thomas More: Action and Contemplation*, ed. R. S. Sylvester (New Haven, Conn., and London, 1972), p. 90.

[51] C82/401 (*LP*, i(2), 2684 g.2), text recited in 5 Henry VIII, c.11.

accompanied by grants of land, was in reward for outstanding service in battle. No specific reason was given for the creation of Charles Brandon as duke of Suffolk. The patent mentioned his services in general terms, but stressed rather the liberality that became a king, opening with a sonorous: 'Cum equidem nichil sit quod principem magis deceat quam ut munifiçum et liberalem se exhiberet . . .'[52] The high dignity may have been given to Brandon to make him a suitable husband for Margaret of Savoy, regent of the Netherlands, as the Venetian ambassador in London supposed.[53] The courtship had begun at Tournai and Lille the previous autumn, with much flirtatious play encouraged by Henry VIII.[54] When news of it leaked out, however, Henry disowned the project, writing to Margaret's father, the emperor, to denounce the *mauvais esprits* who had started the rumours.[55] Nevertheless, in May 1514 the English ambassador in Flanders still expected Margaret to agree to the marriage.[56] He was wrong, as it turned out, but the grant of this particular dukedom still had political implications. The war against France had brought death to the imprisoned Edmund de la Pole, who had once been duke of Suffolk.[57] Before embarking for France Henry VIII had ordered him to be beheaded, but his brother, Richard, was accepted as the rightful duke in succession by Henry's enemies abroad.[58] Charles Brandon as duke of Suffolk would confront the counterfeit duke across the Channel and signal the final eclipse of the de la Poles in England.

Henry VIII had perhaps delayed his letters patent for practical reasons: the large gifts of lands to the Howards must have taken some time to arrange.[59] But, parliament being in session, he could again cite its assent to the grant of a title, to the fourth man to be honoured on the same day: Charles Somerset, lord Herbert, now created earl of Worcester.[60] Besides being the king's chamberlain, he had distinguished himself at the siege of Tournai, adding to a record of military service going back to the battle of Stoke in 1487. The celebrations

---

[52] C82/401 (*LP*, i(2), 2684 g.5), text recited in 5 Henry VIII, c.10 and printed *Foedera, Conventiones, Literae* [etc.], ed. Thomas Rymer, 3rd edn, 10 vols (The Hague, 1735–45), vi(1), 55.

[53] *CSPVen.*, ii, 371.

[54] BL, Cotton Titus B.I, ff.145–54 (*LP*, i(2), 2941), printed *The Chronicle of Calais*, pp. 71–6.

[55] *LP*, i(2), 2701.

[56] ibid., 2940.

[57] By indenture with Henry VII Edmund had exchanged his dukedom of Suffolk for the earldom because, it was said, he lacked the revenues needed 'to maynteyn honorably and convenyently the astate of a duke': 11 Henry VII, c.39.

[58] *CSPVen.*, ii, 248; *LP*, i(2), 2934.

[59] See below, pp. 211–12.

[60] C82/401 (*LP*, i(2), 2684 g.3).

came opportunely, too, as the cost of the war was counted. It was stupendous.[61] Parliament voted taxes to help pay for it, the preamble to the subsidy act reminding everyone of the king's 'great victories' in France, 'where his grace of his valyaunt courage was in his most royall persone', capturing Tournai and taking prisoner the duc de Longueville and other noblemen, as well as his 'pollytyk provision' for the defence of the kingdom which secured the victory over the Scots.[62] The investiture reinforced the message. It was held on Candlemas day, 2 February, in the archbishop of Canterbury's palace at Lambeth. Newly created peers were normally introduced by noblemen of the rank they were joining, but the duke of Buckingham played no active part in the proceedings.[63] The herald noted that 'for defaute of great astates accordying to ther astates the oon duke was created after the toder', first Norfolk, then Suffolk. Each was led in by the earl of Kent bearing the cap and the earl of Derby the gold rod, while the earl of Essex carried the sword. The king received them under his cloth of estate, 'gretely accompanied with noblemen', girded them with the swords, placed the caps of estate on their heads and gave them their gold rods. The two earls were created next, led in by earls. The four then processed to the gatehouse for dinner, during which their styles were proclaimed. They each made Garter king of arms a gift in recompense of the gowns they had worn before donning their new robes. Norfolk had been dressed in a comparatively sober garment of crimson velvet furred with black, but Suffolk's gown was magnificent and Garter wore it all day after the duke's creation. Estimated to be worth £200 and more, it was of violet velvet furred with sables, 'ramplisshed with scriptures of fyne gold inameled wheryn was wrytten *Loyalte me oblige*'.[64] Another witness noticed among the spectators the duc de Longueville as well as the queen and ladies of the court, and observed that, although the doors were guarded, 'the presse was sumwhat gret' because it was parliament time.[65] Some weeks after the dissolution of parliament Henry VIII ennobled another leader of the army against the Scots, Sir Edward Stanley, who had commanded the left wing at Flodden. He was the second son of the first earl of Derby and uncle of the current earl, and was created a baron on Sunday, 21 May at the bishop of London's palace beside St Paul's, during a

---

[61] J. J. Scarisbrick, *Henry VIII* (London, 1968), p. 54.

[62] 5 Henry VIII, c.17.

[63] He may have stood with the king as he had done in 1494 during Henry's creation as duke of York.

[64] BL, Harl. 6074, ff.51–2 (*LP*, i(2), 2620(2)). Suffolk redeemed his gown by giving Garter another one, of black velvet, £10 in angels and an annuity of £4.

[65] BL, Add. 29,549, f.1 (*LP*, i(2), 2620).

festival at court to mark the reception by Henry VIII of a cap and sword sent by the pope. The king himself chose the title of Monteagle for him in recognition – as one account had it – of his 'valiant actes' when he 'wan the hill or mounte ageinst the Scottes and overcam all that cam ageinst hym . . . And also in consideracion that his awncestors bare in their crest an egle.' A week later, on Whitsunday, the heralds proclaimed his title in the king's presence.[66]

Apart from Monteagle's, the peerage titles granted by the young Henry VIII were all titles of the higher nobility. These carried with them gifts of annuities: £40 for a duke, £20 for an earl, 20 marks for a viscount, to be paid out of the revenues of designated counties. This might cause problems. The £20 p.a. out of Worcestershire granted to the new earl of Worcester in 1514 had to be charged instead to the city of Bristol, since it could not be raised from the county.[67] Henry Percy, earl of Northumberland, sued a succession of Northumberland sheriffs for failing to pay his annuity.[68] However, annoying though such hitches must have been to the frustrated noblemen, nothing could detract from the dignity of their rank. In the first five years of his reign Henry VIII had enhanced the splendour of his court by adding to the number of the high nobility. He had underlined his achievements as a war leader by rewarding military service above all other. He had made most of his grants in parliament time, but only Charles Brandon brought new blood into the house of lords; the other three new peers were all sons of noblemen. Henry VIII had shown himself generally content with the noble families he had inherited.

He found no need to make further peerage grants in the years of peace which followed, creating no more new peers until 1523, when another large-scale invasion of France was in preparation. Again the awards were linked with an assembly of parliament; again the choice of men was dominated by thoughts of war. But there were differences. With one exception, only baronial titles were given, and one man was almost certainly ennobled to give him a place in the house of lords. On 9 April 1523, six days before the opening of parliament, the king issued letters patent making Sir Henry Marney a baron.[69] He had been a member of the king's council since the beginning of the reign, chancellor of the duchy of Lancaster, vice-chamberlain and captain of the king's guard. Although he had gone to war in 1513, he was primarily an administrator and in February 1523 he was appointed lord privy

---

[66] BL, Harl. 6074, f.55v (*LP*, i(2), 2931); College of Arms, L.12, ff.46–7 (*LP*, i(2), 2929), printed GEC, ix, Appendix F; *LP*, ii(2), p. 1464.
[67] C82/401 (*LP*, i(2), 2684 g.3).
[68] C1/552/60–1.
[69] *Foedera*, vi(1), 211–12.

seal.[70] The grant of a barony gave him a seat in the house of lords where Henry VIII's previous lords privy seal, being bishops, had been accustomed to sit. The ceremony of creation – which for a baron consisted of a formal investment with his parliament robe – took place on Sunday, 12 April at the king's palace at Richmond, lord Ros and lord FitzWalter leading Marney into the king's presence and lord Mountjoy carrying his robe.[71] Although he was in his mid-sixties, Marney's recent appointment as lord privy seal suggests that he was in reasonable health at that time, but he died on 24 May at his London home and the barony went to his son. On 25 April, ten days after the beginning of parliament, Sir Arthur Plantagenet, illegitimate son of Edward IV, was created viscount Lisle, with remainder to the heirs male of his wife Elizabeth, sister and heir of Sir John Grey, viscount Lisle, Charles Brandon having surrendered the title for this grant to be made.[72] Although known in his youth as Arthur Wayte, he had long been acknowledged at court as a royal kinsman, and Henry VIII by this advancement gave him a status befitting his birth. His ceremony was held on 26 April at Bridewell, the herald's orders noting that he should have 'the preeminence as a bride' at the dinner afterwards 'for th 'onour of his newe criacion'. All was done according to plan, the earl of Devon and lord Ros leading him into the king's presence and lord Ferrers bearing his robe.[73]

At the same time Henry VIII created three barons: Sir Maurice Berkeley, Sir William Sandys and Sir Nicholas Vaux.[74] Berkeley was lieutenant of Calais, Sandys treasurer there, and Vaux lieutenant of Guisnes. Vaux was actually in London, but ill: he died in the hospital of St John of Jerusalem in Clerkenwell on 14 May, leaving a son of 14. The grant of a barony to him was in the outcome his reward for a lifetime of service as a courtier and soldier. Berkeley and Sandys, too, were old servants of the crown. They had both taken part in the raid into France launched from Calais in 1522 and were expected to resume the offensive later in 1523.[75] As it happened, though, Berkeley died in September, shortly before the invasion began. His pleasure in the

---

[70] *LP*, iii(2), 2830.

[71] BL, Add. 6113, f.127 (*LP*, iii(2), App. 41), printed Powell and Wallis, *The House of Lords*, pp. 557–8.

[72] C82/531 (*LP*, iii(2), 2979). Elizabeth (who had formerly been the wife of Edmund Dudley) must by this time have become sole heiress to her brother through the death of her sister Anne without children.

[73] BL, Add. 6113, ff.64–5.

[74] John Stow, *Annales*, ed. Edmund Howes (London, 1631), p. 519 (dating all four creations 27 April); *The Chronicle of Calais*, pp. 32–3. Both quoted GEC, ix, Appendix B.

[75] *The Chronicle of Calais*, pp. 31–3.

grant of a peerage had been tempered by the discovery that he was expected to take his seat at the bottom of the bench of barons, not in the precedence of the ancient barony formerly enjoyed by his family. Neither he nor his father had been considered as other than commoners, but Maurice's uncle had been lord Berkeley as well as marquess of Berkeley and earl of Nottingham. The higher titles became extinct when he died in 1492 leaving no children, but the barony might have passed to his brother. It did not, perhaps because he had alienated to the king most of his estates, including Berkeley castle. Many of the lands had been recovered by the family by 1523, but the castle was still in the hands of the crown. Sir Maurice Berkeley had to decide whether to accept the baronial title as it was offered, or to try for the higher precedence. John FitzJames, chief baron of the exchequer, and two other friends gave their advice: 'Sir, wee all will advise you to take the honor; and howbeit that as yet yee have not the roome in the parliament chamber that the lord Berkeleys have had of old time, yet wee will advise you to take this roome appointed to you at this time, and to make noe labor of the higher roome at this time, for causes to longe to write ... peradventure yee shall have more convenient time hereafter then now. And for your farther spede in this matter, wee have caused your name to bee enterid into the parliament roll, with your writt, and have desired the lord Mountgoie to appier there for you, and to give his voice for you in like manner as in time passide hath bene usied one lord to doe in the absence of another. So that you stand now by matter of record in the full estate and degree of a baron.'[76] But Berkeley had no legitimate son. Only if the title were acknowledged as the revival of an earlier creation would the barony be inherited by his brother. He kept up the pressure and, when Garter king of arms added his name to the list of peers for this parliament, it was inserted between the names of two holders of baronies created in the fifteenth century.[77] The Berkeley title was in fact much older, but its future had been secured.

The names of viscount Lisle and lord Marney were also added to Garter's list, but not those of Sandys or Vaux, nor that of Boleyn, included in another report of the new barons created in April 1523.[78] Sir Thomas Boleyn was at that time in Spain, about to return from an embassy to Charles V. He was rising in favour at court, his daughter Mary probably already the king's mistress, but there is no confirming

---

[76] John Smyth, *The Lives of the Berkeleys*, 2 vols (Gloucester, 1883), ii, 208, reprinted GEC, ix, Appendix B, and Powell and Wallis, *The House of Lords*, p. 559.

[77] College of Arms, Muniment Room 6/41.

[78] SP1/27, f.260 (*LP*, iii(2), 2982), quoted GEC, ix, Appendix B.

evidence of his ennoblement and he continued to be known as Sir Thomas Boleyn, even in official documents, until 1525. Then he become one of the beneficiaries of a distribution of honours which surpassed even that of 1514. As on the earlier occasion the grants followed a military success, not England's this time – the campaign of 1523 had been a failure and there was no action in 1524 – but the emperor's famous victory at Pavia, where the French king had been taken prisoner. Henry VIII received the news with great excitement early in March, expecting to embark upon a partition of France with Charles V. Instead, Charles repudiated his promise to marry Henry's daughter Mary, and in June Henry reopened negotiations with France for a peace treaty.[79] It was in that month that he made his peerage grants. The last great hope of the Yorkists, Richard de la Pole, had been killed at Pavia, but an imperial victory which had already turned sour was no real cause for rejoicing, although it may have been the published reason.[80] Henry VIII was looking forward, not back, trying to secure the future. His lack of a son and heir had assumed an oppressive importance and he began to pave the way for various alternative solutions to the succession problem. Despite the underlying anxiety, the ceremony itself was a joyful occasion. All Henry VIII's investitures took place on a Sunday or holy day, and this one was held on the feast of Corpus Christi, the great summer festival of the church, which in 1525 fell on 18 June. Henry VIII opened the proceedings by ennobling his young son by Elizabeth Blount, Henry FitzRoy, his 'worldly juell', creating him earl of Nottingham and duke of Richmond and Somerset.[81] The court was at Bridewell, and FitzRoy was led into the king's chamber there by the earls of Arundel and Oxford, with the earl of Northumberland bearing the sword; these three were the senior earls in order of precedence and were no doubt selected for that reason to do honour to the king's son. FitzRoy knelt before Henry VIII, who was standing under the cloth of estate attended by Cardinal Wolsey and other lords spiritual and temporal. Henry commanded his son to stand up and Sir Thomas More read out the letters patent granting the earldom. FitzRoy knelt again for his father to gird him with the sword. He then retired to the long gallery and returned between the dukes of Norfolk and Suffolk, with Arundel and Oxford now carrying the cap of estate and the gold rod, the marquess of Dorset bearing the sword and the earl of Northumberland a duke's robes of estate. Henry invested

---

[79] Scarisbrick, *Henry VIII*, pp. 136–40.
[80] As in College of Arms, Vincent 31, quoted GEC under Cumberland.
[81] *LP*, iv(1), 1431(1) and (2); SP1/55, ff.14–15 (*LP*, iv(3), 5807). FitzRoy was probably born in 1519.

him with the dignity of duke.[82] Richmond, Somerset and Nottingham all had royal connotations and the new duke was granted pre-eminence over all other dukes except the king's legitimate issue.[83] Henry VIII, it is clear, had in mind the possibility of making FitzRoy heir to the throne.

Another potential successor was the king's nephew, Henry Brandon, his sister's son by the duke of Suffolk. Henry VIII created him earl of Lincoln. (The title had been held by the son and heir of John de la Pole, duke of Suffolk, killed at the battle of Stoke.) Another kinsman, the king's cousin, Henry Courtenay, earl of Devon, was made marquess of Exeter.[84] A different way ahead was suggested (at least with hindsight) by the creation of Sir Thomas Boleyn as viscount Rochford: the king's interest had probably already switched from Mary to her sister Anne. At the same time three peers were promoted: Thomas Manners, lord Ros, became earl of Rutland, Henry lord Clifford became earl of Cumberland and Robert Radcliffe, lord FitzWalter, was created a viscount.[85] Ros, Clifford and FitzWalter were the three senior barons in order of precedence.[86] They were also, all three, friends of the king. Their promotion served to balance the grants he was making for dynastic motives with rewards to the representatives of the ancient nobility.

Henry VIII had also been ready to create one new baron. On 9 June Sir John Arundell of Lanherne wrote to Wolsey in answer to a letter he had received two days before. In it Wolsey had informed him that it was the king's pleasure to make him a baron on the feast of Corpus Christi, when he would create his son duke and earl. Arundell felt he would be unwise to accept: 'if his grace knew the moche unworthenes and lake of abilite in me many waies, as well for to receve suche honnour as to the contynuall maintenaunce of the same to his honnour and my poor honeste, I know well his grace wuld not offere hit to me.'

---

[82] BL, Add. 6113, ff.62–3 (*LP*, iv(1), 1431(8)), an account of all the creations of 18 June 1525; printed Powell and Wallis, *The House of Lords*, pp. 561–2.

[83] *LP*, iv(1), 1431(4).

[84] *LP*, iv(1), 1432. Courtenay was led in by the duke of Suffolk and the marquess of Dorset, with Northumberland carrying the sword and Oxford the cap.

[85] BL, Add. 6113, f.63, where a reference to 'the lorde Bulleyne' being created viscount has been corrected to 'Sir Thomas Bulleyne'. His supporters were not named, but FitzWalter, the other new viscount, was led in by the earl of Shrewsbury and lord Bergavenny, his mantle borne by lord Dacre of the north. On f.66 a note recorded that 'all their patentes' were presented to the king by Garter during the ceremony. The patents were enrolled only for FitzRoy and Courtenay. Signed bills, not delivered, survive for Clifford and Radcliffe: *LP*, iv(1), 1433, 1444.

[86] The point is made by Powell and Wallis, *The House of Lords*, p. 561.

Anyway, he had not been given enough warning.[87] Sir John Arundell was receiver-general of the duchy of Cornwall and brother-in-law of Thomas Grey, marquess of Dorset; perhaps more significantly in this context, his second son was a valued servant of Wolsey.[88] The choice of Arundell, unexceptionable in itself, may have been made at Wolsey's instigation: the short notice suggests that it did not form part of the king's original plan. The lack of time to prepare for the honour, although disconcerting, would hardly have been an insuperable obstacle. Sir John could have managed to get to court in 11 days, but presumably preferred his role as one of the leading Cornish families to the unfamiliar duties of a nobleman. Although wealthy, he may genuinely have considered his income insufficient to sustain a higher rank.

However, the new peers created by Henry VIII were not all owners of exceptionally large estates. As the reign moved towards the crisis of the Reformation the king's policy reflected his changed priorities. In 1529 he created no fewer than seven new barons and promoted three peers. As often before, the awards were made in parliament time, but now more clearly for a political purpose. The seven additional peers reversed the numerical balance of those summoned to the house of lords and for the first time the lords spiritual were outnumbered. A writ of summons did not necessarily produce attendance in parliament; the change had most meaning as a symbol. It fitted the mood established by Henry VIII's appointment of Sir Thomas More as the first lay chancellor since 1455. Moreover, it came in the middle of an outburst of anti-clericalism in the house of commons which had exposed the divisions between clergy and laity in the upper house. The grievances on which the commons concentrated were those notoriously exemplified by Wolsey and may well have been picked for this reason, as part of a campaign to obtain his permanent exclusion from power.[89] Significantly, the new barons, probably created by word of mouth, began to take their seats in the lords on 1 December, the day on which the leading lords temporal produced their 44 articles of complaint against Wolsey.[90] Henry VIII was not prepared to take any

---

[87] SP1/35, f.1 (*LP*, iv(1), 1399).

[88] S. T. Bindoff, *The House of Commons 1509–1558*, The History of Parliament, 3 vols (London, 1982), i, 337–9.

[89] S. E. Lehmberg, *The Reformation Parliament 1529–1536* (Cambridge, 1970), pp. 87–9; Christopher Haigh, 'Anticlericalism and the English Reformation', *History*, 68 (1983), 391–407. In 1535 Henry VIII planned to make barons in Ireland 'for the encrease of the number of temperal lordes of his parlament there': *SP*, i, 439–42.

[90] College of Arms, 2 H.13, f.398v, printed GEC, ix, Appendix B. For the articles against Wolsey see below, pp. 107, 111.

further action against his former chancellor, but he gave this public sign of support for the lay nobility.

One name probably came readily to mind as he pondered his choice of men to ennoble: that of Henry Pole, son and heir of the countess of Salisbury, who had been known as lord Montagu since 1514. On 1 December 1529 he was, as the herald phrased it, 'restored and admitted' to the house of lords. Sir Thomas Burgh of Gainsborough, Lincolnshire, admitted on 2 December, had some claim to a barony. His grandfather – although never, it seems, called lord Burgh – had been summoned to parliament by Henry VII. His father, who had sat in the commons as MP for Lincolnshire, succeeded to the family estates in 1496 but was never summoned to the house of lords even before he was found a lunatic, 'distracted of memorie', in 1510. After his father's death in 1528, Sir Thomas Burgh may have expected a writ of summons to the next parliament, but his name was not included when the writs went out in 1529 for a parliament to meet on 3 November and the low precedence accorded him in the house of lords after his summons shows that his barony was deemed to be a new creation. Sir Edmund Bray, who took his seat on 4 December, was the nephew of Sir Reginald Bray, Henry VII's minister. He was a courtier and presumably a friend of Henry VIII, although never appointed by him to any high office.[91] The other four new peers had all been elected to the house of commons. Two of the earlier barons made by Henry VIII had previously sat in the house of commons – Marney in 1491 and Vaux in 1515 – but never before had Henry removed anyone from the lower house to the upper. Sir John Hussey and Sir Gilbert Tailboys, elected as knights of the shire for Lincolnshire, took their seats in the lords on 1 December, with Sir Andrew Windsor, returned as a royal nominee for Buckinghamshire, followed the next day by Sir Thomas Wentworth, a knight of the shire for Suffolk: they all took their baronial titles from their surnames.[92] Windsor was an old servant of the crown, keeper of the great wardrobe since 1506. Hussey was about the same age – they had both been born in the 1460s – and had been comptroller of the household to Henry VII and master of the wards from 1503 to 1513; in July 1529 he had been sworn in as a witness against the validity of the dispensation exhibited by Katherine of Aragon in defence of her marriage. The other two were younger men. Tailboys, one of the king's chamber in the mid-1520s,[93] had married Elizabeth Blount, the king's ex-mistress, and was thereby stepfather to the duke of Richmond. Wentworth had recently been a

[91] He was a cupbearer to Henry VIII: E36/130, f.199.
[92] Biographical references here and below from Bindoff, *The House of Commons*.
[93] E179/69/2.

member of the duke of Suffolk's household and may have owed his barony to the duke's patronage at a time when Suffolk was enjoying a political influence he had not known since the early years of the reign.

On 8 December Henry VIII completed his grants by raising three of his friends to the status of earl. Robert Radcliffe, viscount FitzWalter, became earl of Sussex, Thomas Boleyn, viscount Rochford, became earl of Wiltshire in the peerage of England and earl of Ormond in that of Ireland, and George lord Hastings was made earl of Huntingdon.[94] The investiture was held the same day, the feast of the Immaculate Conception, at York Place, Wolsey's former residence taken over by the king.[95] As in 1525 the rejoicing was perhaps in part contrived, designed to prove that all was well in spite of Wolsey's failure to obtain the annulment of the king's marriage. Three years later Henry VIII at last gave notice of his solution to the problem when he created Anne Boleyn marchioness of Pembroke and, with the assent of his chief noblemen and councillors, gave her precedence over all others 'in statu marchionisse'.[96] The creation and the investiture took place on the same day, Sunday, 1 September 1532, at Windsor castle. Henry VIII was accompanied by the dukes of Norfolk and Suffolk and other noblemen, with the French ambassador. Anne was led into his presence by Eleanor countess of Rutland and Margaret countess of Sussex. The king invested her with the coronet and a crimson velvet mantle furred with ermines, carried in by her cousin Mary, Norfolk's daughter. Henry gave her two patents, one for her ennoblement, the other for £1,000 a year 'to maynten hir astate'. She thanked him and returned to her chamber.[97]

Never again was Henry VIII to grant so many peerage titles at one time as in 1529. Instead he made noblemen more frequently, creating new titles in most of the remaining years of his reign. On 4 May 1532, a few days before the end of the third session of the Reformation parliament, Sir John Mordaunt of Turvey, Bedfordshire, took his seat

---

[94] C82/622 (*LP*, iv(3), 6084, 6085, 6086). The earldom of Wiltshire had been held by one of Boleyn's maternal ancestors who had died in 1461; through his mother, also, he was one of the heirs general to the Irish earldom, which Henry VIII had induced the heir male to surrender in February 1528.

[95] BL, Add. 6113, f.66v (note of creations). *Hall's Chronicle*, p. 768 also notes the creations without describing the ceremony.

[96] C82/660 (*LP*, v, 1370 gg.1, 2). The Latin consistently employed the female form of the title, making it clear that Anne was created a marchioness, not a marquess, although she was generally referred to as 'the lady marquess', the usual form of address for a marquess's wife.

[97] BL, Add. 6113, f.70 (*LP*, v, 1274(3)). Christian names of countesses corrected.

in the house of lords as lord Mordaunt.[98] He was a councillor and a courtier who had in his youth attended upon Prince Arthur, and must have been known to Henry VIII since childhood. His ennoblement, with that of Bray in 1529, gave to Bedfordshire two resident peers in replacement of Richard Grey, the late earl of Kent, the only nobleman with extensive lands in the county in the previous reign.[99] Henry VIII's perception of local needs was not a strong feature of his policy in creating peers, but it probably played some part in his selection of men to honour. His decision to ennoble three Lincolnshire knights in 1529 had shown little care for geographical balance within the kingdom, but it raised the status of these men in a large county whose greatest noble landowner, William lord Willoughby de Eresby, had died in 1526 leaving rival claimants to his lands in his daughter and his brother.[100] However, Henry was generally moved by more immediate considerations. The fourth session of the Reformation parliament opened on 4 February 1533 to carry through the break with Rome. The following day Henry VIII ordered the issue of a writ of summons to George Boleyn, Anne's brother, to be present as a baron in parliament that very day.[101] (Since his father had been made an earl, Boleyn had been known as viscount Rochford or lord Rochford. This was the courtesy use of the subsidiary title vested in his father.)[102] Henry VIII also summoned two heirs to more ancient earldoms to attend this meeting of parliament: his godson and former page, the 20-year-old Henry lord Mautravers, only son of William FitzAlan, earl of Arundel, at the same time as Boleyn, and, on 17 February, Francis lord Talbot, in his early thirties, son and heir to the lord steward, George Talbot, earl of Shrewsbury.[103] All three were in effect made peers for the lifetime of their fathers, as the younger Thomas Howard had been in 1514. It was

---

[98] College of Arms, 2 H.13, f.398v, printed GEC, ix, Appendix B. The sessions of the Reformation parliament are variously counted; I follow Lehmberg's numbering, which ignores short prorogations.

[99] For the earldom of Kent see below, pp. 38–9, 209.

[100] G. A. J. Hodgett, *Tudor Lincolnshire*, History of Lincolnshire, ed. Joan Thirsk, vi (Lincoln, 1975), pp. 6, 151–3.

[101] C82/665 (*LP*, vi, 123 i). Rochford was actually admitted to the house of lords on 7 February: College of Arms, 2 H.13, f.398v, printed GEC, ix, Appendix B.

[102] GEC under Ormond believes that his signature as George Rochford among those of the *Barones* on the letter to the pope of July 1530 means that he had been ennobled by then, but the evidence is not convincing. cf. the list of lords receiving new year's gifts in 1532 which included, besides Rochford, Stafford (Buckingham's son) and Curson (sometimes called baron Curson), neither of whom was a lord of parliament: *LP*, v, 686.

[103] C82/665 (*LP*, vi, 123 ii, iii).

an act of grace on the king's part which Henry VIII only accorded to these four men during his reign: after Surrey had succeeded his father as duke of Norfolk, even his son, though styled earl of Surrey, never received a writ of summons.

The fall of Anne Boleyn ended her brother's life and her father's career. The king's marriage to Jane Seymour in its turn brought a peerage to her brother, Sir Edward Seymour, created viscount Beauchamp on 5 June 1536, three days before the opening of the parliament called to empower Henry VIII to settle the succession as he judged best.[104] Beauchamp's name was added to the list of those summoned on 27 April to attend this parliament, with that of Walter lord Hungerford of Heytesbury.[105] Hungerford was admitted to the house of lords 'by writ' on 8 June, the first day of the parliament.[106] He had been a royal ward and was an esquire of the body by 1523, when he had livery of his lands. The local and court connections between Hungerford, the Seymours and the king might account for his ennoblement. Sir Edward Seymour's father and uncle had been returned to the house of commons in 1529 as MPs for Heytesbury, Hungerford's borough, and in June 1536 Hungerford granted the uncle an annuity of £6 13s 4d.[107] However, he also had links with Cromwell. Hungerford's new father-in-law, lord Hussey, had written in August 1532, at his request, introducing him and sending Cromwell Hungerford's patent for an annuity of 4 marks, with the promise that 'herafter for suche matters as he shall desyre your ffavour in, he shall more largely deserve your peynes'.[108] Two months later Hussey wrote again, to thank Cromwell for his goodness to Hungerford and to ask 'if it might be possible by your help that he might be the sheriff of Wilshire this yere'.[109] Hungerford was picked for sheriff the following year, in November 1533. The aim was modest for the head of a once significant house. Sir Walter Hungerford (he was knighted between 1530 and 1532) was the heir male to the Hungerfords of Farleigh in Somerset and Heytesbury in Wiltshire, a family ennobled in 1426 and destroyed by attainder in 1461. Sir Walter's grandfather had successfully petitioned in 1485 for the reversal of his father's attainder and the

---

[104] C82/713 (*LP*, x, 1256 g.4). A fourteenth-century ancestor had been coheir to the barony of Beauchamp. Garter reported the king's choice of title to Cromwell: *LP*, x, 1017.

[105] C54/406 (*LP*, x, 736 ii), printed *Foedera*, vi(3), 4.

[106] College of Arms, 2 H.13, f.398v, printed GEC, ix, Appendix B.

[107] Bindoff, *The House of Commons*, i, 224, iii, 293–5.

[108] SP1/70, f.226 (*LP*, v, 1238).

[109] SP1/237, f.239 (*LP, Addenda*, i, 795).

restoration of all titles, dignities and estates.[110] The main estates went to him, but the barony descended to the heir general, the daughter of the last lord Hungerford's eldest son. It was probably her death in 1533 which suggested the possibility of a peerage for Sir Walter Hungerford. Although his barony was a new creation, it gave him back the noble status of his forefathers.

The king granted two more peerage titles before he dissolved this parliament. Thomas Cromwell was created lord Cromwell by letters patent of 9 July, but he did not take his seat in the upper house until 18 July, the last day of the parliament, when he was admitted to the lords 'by writ and patent'.[111] Cromwell's presence in the commons was deemed more important in the short term, but he could hardly be indefinitely denied ennoblement. The co-ordination of the court faction which removed Anne Boleyn, no longer desired by Henry VIII, was his most recent service to the king.[112] Moreover, on 2 July Cromwell had replaced Thomas Boleyn, earl of Wiltshire, as lord privy seal.[113] This in itself would probably have persuaded Henry to make him a baron, following the precedent set by the ennoblement of Marney in 1523: Marney having been succeeded in turn by a bishop and a peer, the office had never yet been held in this reign by anyone who was not a member of the house of lords. The size of the house was not increased by the other grant. The 65-year-old John Bourchier, lord FitzWarin, who had been summoned to the lords since 1492, was made earl of Bath.[114] No record survives of any ceremony for the new peers, but the earldom was conferred on lord FitzWarin with the usual ritual on the day of his creation, Sunday, 9 July, at the palace of Westminster. He was led in by his kinsman, Henry Bourchier, earl of Essex, and the earl of Sussex, preceded by the earl of Huntingdon bearing the sword.[115] Although FitzWarin was a councillor earlier in the reign, he was not a member of the reorganized council of 1536, nor was he ever given high office. The grant of an earldom to him was perhaps intended to set up a counter-balance in the west country to the power of Henry Courtenay, marquess of Exeter, already suspected of disloyalty although still from time to time in attendance at court.[116] FitzWarin's promotion also

---

[110] CPR, Henry VII, i, 149.

[111] C82/714 (LP, xi, 202 g.14); College of Arms, 2 H.13, f.398v, printed GEC, ix, Appendix B.

[112] E. W. Ives, 'Faction at the court of Henry VIII: the fall of Anne Boleyn', History, 57 (1972), 169–88.

[113] LP, xi, 202 g.3.

[114] C82/714 (LP, xi, 202 g.15).

[115] BL, Harl. 6074, f.62.

[116] See below, pp. 64–5.

served to honour the established nobility at the same time as new men were ennobled, as in 1525, 1529 and 1533. The following year Henry VIII celebrated the birth of Prince Edward by advancing Edward Seymour, viscount Beauchamp, to the earldom of Hertford and creating Sir William FitzWilliam earl of Southampton.[117] The investiture was held at Hampton Court on the day their patents were issued, 18 October, the feast of St Luke. Beauchamp was invested first: the earl of Sussex carried the sword before him but he was led in by the duke of Norfolk and the marquess of Exeter rather than by the customary two earls. The ritual was repeated for FitzWilliam 'for defawte of astates present in their robes' to accompany them both at once. The new earls moved to the council chamber for dinner. Their styles, when they were proclaimed, included not only their titles but also Hertford's status as uncle of the prince and brother of the king and Southampton's as admiral of England.[118] His high office and long record of service to Henry VIII doubtless earned FitzWilliam this exceptional advancement from commoner to earl in one move, but – with no legitimate son to succeed him – the earldom was in effect no more than a life-grant.

The next promotion in the peerage was ascribed by one hostile observer to the corrupt influence of the earl of Hertford. In June 1538 John Husee, the London agent of Arthur Plantagenet, viscount Lisle, the deputy of Calais, informed lady Lisle that Henry lord Daubeney 'wyll be an erlle in all hast', adding that 'whensoever he take his creacion he shall losse his discression'. In July Husee reported to Lisle that Daubeney had come to London with 80 horses and all his men in new liveries to complete a land deal and to be made an earl; that he 'gapithe to be avauncyd to his desyred erldome'; and finally, on 18 July, that it had been agreed 'by the measnes of the erlc of Hartford that the lorde Dawbnye shalbe creatyd on Sonday next erlle of Brydgewater and therfor the sayde erlle of Hartford shall have aftre his dycesse a C and vii^li land to him and his eyers'.[119] The king's privy seal for the grant was dated 17 July 1538 and the letters patent were issued two days later.[120] On the afternoon of Sunday, 21 July Henry VIII

[117] C82/731 (LP, xii(2), 1008 gg.21, 22). The text of the letters patent in Beauchamp's signed bill left a blank for the name of his present wife (on whose heirs male, or those of any future wife, the earldom was entailed to the exclusion of his sons by his first wife). He seems unlikely, therefore, to have been personally involved in drafting the bill, although it is in the form of a petition. A signed petition was also the warrant for FitzWilliam's creation as earl.

[118] BL, Add. 6113, ff.87–8 (LP, xii(2), 939).

[119] SP3/12, ff.14–15, SP3/4, ff.35–7 (LP, xiii(1), 1286, 1333, 1389, 1407), printed The Lisle Letters, ed. Muriel St Clare Byrne, 6 vols (Chicago and London, 1981), v, 1176, 1179, 1188, 1193.

[120] C82/742 (LP, xiii(1), 1519 g.61).

held the investiture at his manor of Woking. Hertford carried the sword before Daubeney, who was accompanied by the earls of Derby and Sussex; after the ceremony his style was proclaimed in the king's hall. The formal business completed, the king and the noblemen went into the park 'to shoght the popyngaey'. Fortunately the new earl of Bridgwater hit it with his first shot and was rewarded by the king with a popinjay's wing made of gold.[121] Husee's allegation that Daubeney had bought his earldom from Hertford may well be true. It evidently stemmed from his knowledge of an indenture agreed between the two on 19 July, the date of the patent of creation. By it Daubeney sold lands to Hertford to be held in reversion and fee farm until Daubeney's death, until which time Hertford would pay him each year, at his manor of South Perrott, Dorset, the annual value of the lands, some £175 (not £107, as Husee supposed). No purchase price was specified: the transfer was in return 'as well for dyvers sommes of money' paid to Daubeney 'as also for many greate benefittes and kyndnesses shewed and doon to hym by the said erle and by his meanes and labour'.[122] Daubeney, son of Sir Giles Daubeney, made a baron by Henry VII, was brother-in-law to FitzWarin, whose creation as earl of Bath perhaps stirred his own ambition to rise higher. He was a younger man, in his mid-forties, and never, so far as is known, even a member of the unreformed council, but, like the earl of Bath, he was a significant landowner in the west country. His earldom could have been represented to the king as a further reinforcement to the prestige of the nobility in a region which was increasingly regarded as a potential threat to the security of the realm. In retrospect, the two promotions may be seen to have been linked in yet another way. FitzWarin was the last representative of the pre-Tudor nobility to be advanced in the peerage and Daubeney the last of a family ennobled by Henry VII. After 1538 Henry VIII promoted only men whom he had himself ennobled: it no longer seemed necessary to distribute such honours with an eye to a balance between the old and the new nobility.

Sir Thomas Audley was the next to be ennobled. As lord chancellor Audley could preside over the house of lords, although no peer; but he could not act as high steward for the trials of the marquess of Exeter and lord Montagu. On 29 November 1538 Henry VIII created him a baron of parliament as lord Audley of Walden and at once appointed him lord high steward for both trials.[123] Clearly the king's choice was

---

[121] BL, Harl. 6074, f.62 (*LP*, xiii(1), 1431).

[122] C54/417, quoted in part by M. L. Bush, 'The Lisle-Seymour land disputes: a study of power and influence in the 1530s', *HJ*, ix (1966), 271.

[123] C82/746 (*LP*, xiii(2), 967 g.52); *DKR*, iii, Appendix ii, pp. 255–7.

determined by Audley's legal expertise and his proven service in earlier state trials – of Sir Thomas More and the Carthusians, among others.[124] Audley tried to make even more of this turn of events by obtaining his barony on exceptional terms. He had had no children by his first wife, who had died in January 1538. He had already re-married, but, in case he should still have no son, he included in the bill drawn for the king's signature a remainder to the heirs male of his brother. Henry VIII signed the bill and it was delivered into chancery on 29 November, but then immediately surrendered for the patent to be made out differently. An alternative warrant, also signed by the king, which made no reference to any remainder, was delivered on the same day and Audley was granted the barony in tail male.[125] (As he had feared, it died with him in 1544.) The executions of Exeter and Montagu, following those of Darcy and Hussey in 1537, perhaps suggested to Henry VIII that it would be politic to make some more new peers before parliament reassembled. On 1 March 1539 the writs went out for a parliament to meet on 28 April. On 9 March the king conferred three baronies by letters patent: on Sir William Paulet, Sir John Russell and Sir William Parr.[126] At Westminster on the same day, a Sunday, after High Mass, he created them respectively lord St John, lord Russell and lord Parr, in that order. There were too few barons present for each to be attended by three of their new rank, two to lead him in and one to carry his parliament robe, and the ceremony was shorter than usual – only one obeisance as the procession entered, the patents not read out – 'bicawse the daye was far spent'. The new barons then went to dinner, during which their styles were pro-claimed.[127] Russell and Paulet were in their mid-fifties. Paulet was treasurer of the household and Russell its comptroller, but both were now replaced in these offices, which during this reign were never held by peers. Russell was about to be appointed president of a new council in the west, Paulet was – and remained – master of the wards. Sir William Parr, by contrast, was a young man of 25, son of Sir Thomas Parr of Kendal, who had been a prominent courtier at the beginning of the reign. He was already known at court by October 1537, when John

[124] S. E. Lehmberg, 'Sir Thomas Audley: a soul as black as marble?' in *Tudor Men and Institutions. Studies in English Law and Government*, ed. A. J. Slavin (Baton Rouge, La, 1972), p. 8, where Anne Boleyn is mistakenly listed among those tried by Audley.

[125] C82/746 (*LP*, xiii(2), 967 g.52).

[126] C82/750 (*LP*, xiv(1), 651 gg.18, 19, 20): signed bills delivered on 9 March for Russell and Paulet, undated charter for Parr, all three enrolled.

[127] BL, Harl. 6074, ff.56v–7 (*LP*, xiv(1), 477). The barons taking part in the ceremony were Cobham, Dacre of the south and Clinton (for Paulet), Stourton and Windsor (for Russell) and Wentworth (for Parr).

Husee mistakenly informed Lisle that he was to be made a lord in the distribution of honours following the christening of Prince Edward.[128] His father being dead, he presumably owed his advancement to the duke of Norfolk, who recommended him to the king in March 1537, and to his uncle, also Sir William Parr, former chamberlain to the duke of Richmond, who, early in 1538, asked Cromwell to find him a place in the king's privy chamber.[129] It seems that the younger Parr found favour with Henry VIII and was chosen for a peerage as a consequence, although he also had some claim to a barony through his father, one of the coheirs of George lord FitzHugh, who had died childless in 1513. Indeed, John Husee at first wrongly reported to lady Lisle in 1539 that Sir William Parr had been created lord FitzHugh, a title which the father had years before tried to obtain for himself, only to provoke counter-arguments from the other coheir, Thomas Fiennes, lord Dacre of the south.[130] Any revival of that altercation was avoided by the choice of a different title for Sir William Parr.

A year later the instability of life at court was once more illustrated by the promotion of lord Cromwell to an earldom two months before his fall from power. The signed bill (in the form of a petition) was delivered on 17 April 1540. The following day, a Sunday, in his chamber of presence in the palace of Westminster, Henry VIII invested Cromwell with the earldom of Essex 'to hym and his heyres masles for ever'. The ceremony, taking place soon after the start of the parliamentary session, was probably well attended. It was certainly not hurried through. Cromwell was led in by the dukes of Norfolk and Suffolk, an unprecedented honour for a new earl: the two dukes had performed this service together only once before, at the creation of Henry's son as duke. The lord admiral, the earl of Southampton, carried the sword. After they had made their three obeisances, the patent was read, Cromwell kneeled down and the king girded him with the sword. Cromwell gave thanks in the usual way and then listened to a second patent being read out, appointing him great chamberlain of England for life. After the ceremony the noblemen went to the council chamber to dine and during dinner heard Cromwell's style proclaimed in full: 'Seigneur Thomas Crumwell conte D'essex, vicegerent et grande chamberlain D'angleterre, gardien du privey seale, chauncellier de la chequier et justicier de forestes et de chascis de la ryver du Trent vers north.'[131] This particular earldom had only

---

[128] *The Lisle Letters*, iv, 1024.

[129] *LP*, xii(1), 713; SP1/241, f.285 (*LP, Addenda*, ii. 1297).

[130] *The Lisle Letters*, v, 1364a; Powell and Wallis, *The House of Lords*, p. 579.

[131] C82/765 (*LP*, xv, 611 g.37); BL, Harl. 6074, ff.57v–8 (*LP*, xv, 541).

become vacant on 13 March, when Henry Bourchier, earl of Essex since 1483, had died after a fall from his horse, leaving a daughter and heiress, married to William lord Parr. Cromwell already had some lands in Essex, but it was not until one week before his creation as earl that he became a major landowner in the county with the king's grant to him of the abbey of St Osyth and a large number of other properties.[132] The fortuitous death of the old earl of Essex must have given a new focus to Cromwell's efforts to procure for himself an unmistakable sign of the king's favour with which to bolster his position. The death of the great chamberlain, Oxford, on 21 March was the clinching stroke of fortune: if Cromwell were to be granted one of the great offices of state, formerly the hereditary possession of the earls of Oxford, an earldom would be almost a necessity.[133] The two promotions went together in the most spectacular success of Cromwell's career, making his fall, when it came, even more dramatic. However, it may also have eased the way for Henry VIII to do something for Cromwell's son, Gregory, married to a sister of Jane Seymour. There was no question of restoring him to his inheritance, but the king created him lord Cromwell in December 1540, granting him the dignity which, as the son of an earl, he had for a few months been entitled to use as a courtesy title.[134]

Another death – that of Arthur Plantagenet, viscount Lisle – opened the way into the nobility for Sir John Dudley. Lisle, sent to the Tower on suspicion of treason in 1540, died there on 3 March 1542, on the eve of his release. The title had been granted to him and his heirs male by his first wife, baroness Lisle, but he had had no son by her. Her son by Edmund Dudley, her first husband, made his way at court as a commoner until, on 12 March 1542, the king created him viscount Lisle.[135] Sir John Dudley thus became the third person to be granted this title by Henry VIII. He was invested the same day in the king's privy chamber at the palace of Westminster, Henry VIII under his cloth of estate being accompanied by 'all his noble men of his coun-sell'. Dudley was led in by the earl of Hertford wearing his robes of estate and the lord admiral, Russell, in his more ordinary parliament robe. Lord La Warre carried the viscount's mantle, with its two-and-a-half bars of ermine. At dinner afterwards, in the chamber of the lord great chamberlain, the new viscount – like Arthur Plantagenet before

---

[132] See below, pp. 242, 247.

[133] See below, pp. 164–5.

[134] C82/775 (*LP*, xvi, 379 g.34), printed *Foedera*, vi(3), 62–3.

[135] C82/792 (*LP*, xvii, 220 g.46). The patent was entered on the patent roll for 1543: *LP*, xviii(1), 346 g.25.

him – was given pre-eminence 'as a bride'. His style was proclaimed, as usual, after the second course. As Lisle held no high office it recited the landed titles to which he laid claim: 'baron de Malpas, seigneur de Bassett, de Draton et de Tiasse.'[136] Dudley had been returned as knight of the shire for Staffordshire to the parliament which had opened in January; on Monday, 13 March he took his seat in the house of lords.[137] The earldom of Essex, too, was soon to be granted again. Katherine Parr, widowed in March 1543, married Henry VIII in July. On 23 December her brother, William lord Parr, was created earl of Essex with the precedence in parliament of his late father-in-law, Henry Bourchier, earl of Essex.[138] (He had in fact repudiated his wife earlier in 1543 and obtained an act of parliament to bastardize her children, but this was evidently reckoned no obstacle to his advancement to her father's earldom.) His uncle, now chamberlain to Katherine Parr, was created lord Parr of Horton.[139] The investiture was held on the same day, a Sunday, at Hampton Court, after the king had heard High Mass. The new earl was led into the chamber of presence by the marquess of Dorset and the earl of Derby, with viscount Lisle bearing the sword, the new baron by lords Russell and St John; their patents were read out and Henry invested them in turn. During the dinner which followed in the council chamber 'in the gallery' they heard their styles proclaimed, stressing the relationship of each to the queen.[140]

Kinship with the royal family was one clear way to a peerage – if also, on occasion, a highway to destruction. The return to war in the 1540s reopened another main route to nobility. Sir Thomas Wriothesley, one of the king's principal secretaries, was treasurer for the wars against France. On 1 January 1544 Henry VIII made him lord Wriothesley.[141] He was invested with his parliament robe the same day at Hampton Court, with Russell and St John again acting as supporters and the newest baron, lord Parr of Horton, carrying his robe. This time dinner was taken in the great chamber before the queen's lodging. Garter proclaimed his style: 'Thomas seigneur Wryothesley et seigneur de Tichefelde et une de la estroict councell du roy notre souveraine seigneur.'[142] A few weeks later the king issued letters patent granting baronies to two veterans of the northern front,

---

[136] BL, Add. 6113, ff.89–90. Lisle's right to these titles was dubious: GEC, v, Appendix F.

[137] *LJ*, i, 184.

[138] C82/817 (*LP*, xviii(2), 529 g.26).

[139] C82/817 (*LP*, xviii(2), 529 g.27).

[140] BL, Add. 6113, f.113 (*LP*, xviii(2), 516).

[141] C82/818 (*LP*, xix(1), 80 g.1).

[142] BL, Add. 6113, f.114 (*LP*, xix(1), 1(2)).

Sir William Eure, deputy warden of the east march, and Sir Thomas Wharton, deputy warden of the west march, the commander of the army which had defeated the Scots at Solway Moss in November 1542. Both were now made full wardens.[143] Hertford took the patents of creation with him when he went north as lieutenant-general. He formally presented them to Eure and Wharton at Newcastle on 18 March 1544 and, as he reported, took the opportunity to stress the king's liberality towards those who served him 'honorably, trulye and honestly'.[144] Henry VIII, when he made his last nobleman the following year, preferred to emphasize the effect the honour would have on the recipient. Sir Thomas Poynings, illegitimate son of Sir Edward Poynings, was created a baron on 30 January 1545 and the next day appointed lieutenant of Boulogne, the army's one prize in the war against France.[145] Hertford was again chosen to convey the king's decisions to Poynings, who was serving as one of the council of Boulogne. His instructions set out Henry's reason for the elevation of Poynings to the peerage: it was 'as well for sum declaration of our goodnes towardes him, as also to encourage him to serve us the better' in his new appointment.[146] In the eyes of Henry VIII a grant of nobility was as much a call to further effort as a reward for past services.

The timing of his grants indeed shows how frequently they were his response to a particular situation. The men whom he ennobled might well have been raised to the peerage in other circumstances, but often it was the needs of the moment which precipitated the king's action. The holding of office, especially, was a direct way to nobility. Although he sometimes insisted on the undoubted duty of all subjects to obey any man to whom he gave authority, Henry VIII generally accepted the practical necessity for certain offices to be held by noblemen. Yet he would not confine his choice to the existing nobility. In these instances the selection of commoners for office was the crucial decision and a patent of nobility the consequence. Henry VIII did not often bestow the higher titles for this reason. Of the ten men and boys whom he introduced into the peerage with the rank of viscount or above, only Charles Brandon, created viscount Lisle in 1513, was ennobled to equip him for office. But for a quarter of the 28 new barons, a new office was fairly clearly the proximate cause of ennoblement (Marney, Thomas Cromwell, Audley, Russell, Wharton, Eure

---

[143] For the wardenship of the marches see below, pp. 192–6.
[144] *The Hamilton Papers*, ed. Joseph Bain, 2 vols (Edinburgh, 1890, 1892), ii, 189, quoted GEC, ix, Appendix B.
[145] C82/833 (*LP*, xx(1), 125 gg.29, 30).
[146] *State Papers*, x, 250–3.

and Poynings). A further three men (Berkeley, Sandys and Vaux) owed their baronies to the military leadership expected in wartime of office-holders in Calais and the marches – a leadership which in Henry's view could best be provided by noblemen.[147] Office-holding in fact ennobled more military men than civilian administrators, at least in this directly observable correlation. But too much should not be made of the distinction. The holders of office in the north and in Calais were not merely soldiers but governors with administrative and often diplomatic duties. On the other side, the administrators were not exempt from military service in time of war. Even Cromwell in the late 1530s was anxious to establish his credentials as a leader of armed men ready to defend the kingdom.[148] There was no sharp division between a *noblesse d'epée* and a *noblesse de robe*.

Henry VIII had inherited a nobility depleted in numbers by his father's failure to create enough noblemen to replace the noble families which died out or were attainted during his reign. The number of attainders in Henry VIII's reign, supplementing the natural wastage, meant that even a comparatively generous policy did not produce an exceptionally large peerage. Nevertheless, it ensured that a significant proportion of the nobility at the end of the reign of Henry VIII was of his own creation. When he died on 28 January 1547 there were 51 noblemen, nine more than at his accession. Of the 34 barons (four or five of whom were under age), 16 were men ennobled by Henry VIII himself, or their heirs, and one (John Tuchet, lord Audley) a man restored to the peerage by him. Half the barons therefore owed their noble rank to Henry VIII. For the higher nobility the debt was even more striking: of the 17 surviving peers of the rank of viscount or above, only six did not owe their title to Henry VIII (Dorset, Arundel, Derby, Oxford, Shrewsbury, Westmorland). Norfolk had been removed from the peerage by act of attainder.[149] There remained therefore one duke, as in 1509 (the 11-year-old son of Charles Brandon), one marquess (Dorset, as in 1509), one viscount (John Dudley) and 14 earls (two of them of Henry VIII's creation and promotion, and seven of his promotion). Yet Henry VIII shortly before his death was said to have been dissatisfied with his nobility, considering it 'greatly decayed', and ready to create ten new barons and to promote six peers. That, at least, was the deposition of Sir William Paget to the council after the accession of Edward VI.[150] It was transparently the pro-

---

[147] See below, chapter 5.
[148] See below, p. 91.
[149] See below, pp. 72–3.
[150] *APC*, ii, 15–22.

gramme of the new regime, but it was not a total fabrication.[151] A state paper almost certainly composed before Henry died revised the list of creations, reducing the new barons to six and the promotions to four.[152] Plans were also being made to create Edward prince of Wales: he himself later noted that the preparations had been interrupted by his father's death.[153] His investiture would have been a suitable occasion for the distribution of honours to those whom Henry VIII – in Paget's words – 'mynded to place' about his son. But Henry was reluctant to assist any one faction to power after his death. He had not chosen to give a dukedom to Edward Seymour, earl of Hertford, although he was the uncle of the heir to the throne. He had not promoted his brother-in-law, William Parr, beyond an earldom, nor given John Dudley, in spite of his war services, any higher title than that of viscount. His liberality, extolled in public by Hertford, had its limits. The fact that the fourth man to be promoted in 1547, Thomas lord Wriothesley, was the lord chancellor suggests that for him an earldom was the price of acquiescence in a scheme to which Henry VIII had not been fully committed. The delay in implementing it should perhaps be seen as the rearguard action of a dying king determined to keep control of the nobility to the end.

The creation of peerages was indeed an area of political activity in which the monarch was exceptionally free from constraint. The number of creations was absolutely within his discretion; no material considerations limited him as they did in his exercise of other forms of patronage. The creation policies of rulers are therefore important indicators of their attitude towards the nobility. Henry VIII showed himself willing to make peers – with none of the reluctance exhibited by his daughter Elizabeth as well as by his father – but also for the most part careful. In his youth his policy was at its most conventional. At least once it may have been the fruit of impulse. The election of Sir Edward Stanley to the order of the Garter in April 1514 had all the appearance of being the due reward for his services at Flodden, coming as it did nearly 12 weeks after the distribution of peerage titles to four other military leaders of the previous year's campaigns. Yet in May the arrival of a papal embassy became the occasion of Stanley's creation as lord Monteagle. The victory over the Scots was celebrated

---

[151] Helen Miller, 'Henry VIII's unwritten will: grants of lands and honours in 1547' in *Wealth and Power in Tudor England: Essays Presented to S. T. Bindoff*, ed. E. W. Ives, R. J. Knecht and J. J. Scarisbrick (London, 1978), pp. 87–105.

[152] SP10/1/11.

[153] *Literary Remains of King Edward the Sixth*, ed. J. G. Nichols, 2 vols, Roxburghe Club (London, 1857), ii, 210.

once more at court, this time in the presence of envoys from the peace-making successor to Julius II, the pope who had invested Henry VIII with the kingdom of France and promised him a coronation when he had defeated Louis XII.[154] The collapse of that dream could be partially obscured by diverting attention to Henry's triumph over James IV. The king was glorified again in his gift of honour.

The grant of titles to victorious commanders was both the simplest and the most traditional use of the king's prerogative. In his maturity Henry VIII preferred to make his creations serve a more complex political purpose, combining reward and display with the solution of a specific problem. The multiple grants of 1525 and 1529 in particular revealed a wide-ranging appreciation of future possibilities. For most of his reign, too, he took care to balance the creation of new noblemen with the promotion of men already of noble rank. The rapid rate of change within the peerage cannot have been easy to assimilate, but the new noble families were a sign of Henry VIII's commitment to the nobility. By his readiness to increase its size he demonstrated his belief in its value. By refusing to make an excessive number of grants he preserved its status. Whatever they thought of the new peers as individuals, the noblemen who took part in their investiture or witnessed their entry into the house of lords were also celebrating the power and prestige of the nobility as a whole.

[154] Scarisbrick, *Henry VIII*, pp. 33–4.

CHAPTER 2

Treason Trials and Acts of Attainder

Henry VIII in 1509 inherited a nobility made up of 12 high noblemen and 30 barons, to which four barons were added by the restoration or revival of titles in the early years of the reign.[1] Only one of the high noble families died out by 1547 through failure to leave a male heir. However, the earldom of Essex, escheating to the crown on the death of Henry Bourchier in 1540, was not the only high title to come to an end without being extinguished by attainder. When Richard Grey, earl of Kent, died in 1524 his half-brother, Sir Henry Grey, did not succeed him as earl. In the seventeenth century the heralds declared that Richard Grey's dissipation of his inheritance had led Henry VIII to suspend the earldom for want of a competent estate to maintain it. The family adopted an alternative view – that Sir Henry had chosen not to assume the title – and in the 1570s successfully petitioned for recognition as earls of Kent.[2] The heralds' version was nearer the truth. Henry VIII had refused to accept Sir Henry Grey as earl, influenced, Sir Henry believed, by those who had acquired the family estates. He admitted that he had inherited only 'the bare honor of an earldome', his lands being worth no more than 200 marks a year. But the crucial fact was that he was 'destytute of all fryndes, ye, havinge the kynge, the noblemen and almoste all in greatest favor in courte (who shoulde have byn his beste fryndes by meanes of his ryght to the earledom and the landes devyded amongeste them) utterly agaynste

---

[1] Clinton has been counted among the barons of 1509, although he was never summoned to parliament by Henry VII or Henry VIII, because he was treated as a peer, being one of the panel for the trial of the earl of Warwick in 1499.

[2] Helen Miller, 'Attendance in the house of lords during the reign of Henry VIII', *HJ*, x (1967), 327–8.

hym'.[3] To hinder his succession his enemies persuaded the king that Grey was mad. When Henry VIII was told that the claim to the earldom was not good, he took no further interest in the matter.[4] A baron, on the other hand, could survive in the peerage without being summoned to parliament. Like lord Clinton at the start of the reign, John Sutton, lord Dudley, retained his title although he never received a writ of summons. The debts of his father, which he inherited with the barony in 1532, added to his own, forced him to mortgage his inheritance to his cousin, Sir John Dudley. His poverty, allied to doubts of his mental capacity, kept him off the list of those to be summoned. The omission may not have worried him, but his son when he inherited the title in Mary's reign exerted himself to regain the family lands; once he had recovered them he was regularly summoned to parliament.[5] During the reign of Henry VIII six baronial families died out through natural causes.[6] In all, therefore, only 16 per cent of the noble families inherited by Henry VIII or accepted by him soon after his accession failed in the male line before the end of the reign.

Among the nobility created by Henry VIII the survival rate was lower. Henry VIII promoted two men whom he had earlier ennobled as barons (Cromwell and Parr) and granted titles of high nobility to ten others who had not previously been peers. Five of the 12 left no son to succeed them, failing in the male line before the king died.[7] However, the new baronial families fared better than the high nobility. Of the 26 barons (besides Cromwell and Parr) created by Henry VIII, three were in effect made barons for their lifetime only – as Thomas Howard had been made an earl in 1514 – since they stood to inherit the higher titles of their fathers.[8] Only four of the remaining 23 families died out in the male line before 1547.[9] The new nobility, taking all ranks together, thus experienced a natural wastage rate of 26 per cent during the reign. By definition, the new families had fewer years to surmount than the pre-existing nobility and might have been expected

---

[3] Quoted G. W. Bernard. 'The fortunes of the Greys, earls of Kent, in the early sixteenth century', *HJ*, xxv (1982), 684. Dr Bernard has corrected the earl's date of death, hitherto assigned to 1523: ibid., 679.

[4] ibid., 684–5.

[5] Miller, 'Attendance in the house of lords', 328.

[6] Bourchier (lord Berners), FitzHugh, Ormond, Scrope of Upsall, Willoughby (de Broke), Willoughby (de Eresby).

[7] Brandon (earl of Lincoln), FitzRoy, FitzWilliam, Plantagenet, Stafford (earl of Wiltshire).

[8] See above, p. 25.

[9] Audley (of Walden), Marney, Poynings, Tailboys.

to survive in greater numbers to the end of the reign. But their titles, if limited to the heirs male of their body, could not (in the first generation) go to brothers or more distant heirs, as those of the longer established nobility could. Moreover, Henry VIII ennobled two boys – his own son and Charles Brandon's – and four middle-aged men – Arthur Plantagenet, William FitzWilliam, Thomas Audley and Thomas Poynings – who had no sons: they all died without leaving heirs to their titles.

The higher natural wastage rate of the new nobility was not offset by any markedly greater immunity to destruction by attainder. Five new families foundered with the first peer, an extinction rate comparable with that of the somewhat larger group of old nobility, which suffered the loss of seven families. The immediate victim was not always the nobleman himself. The families of Percy, Lumley and Boleyn disappeared from the peerage following the attainder of the heir to the title, only one of whom, George Boleyn, was a peer. But it was the execution of noblemen which above all reminded contemporaries of one of the truths of life in early Tudor England: no one was so exalted that he might not be brought down. The combined effect of natural and artificial causes reduced the old nobility by 33 per cent between 1509 and 1547 and removed 41 per cent of the noble families created by Henry VIII.

One of the privileges of nobility was trial by peers – in the exact sense of trial by fellow nobles. Did the privilege include trial in parliament, by all the peers assembled there? Littleton in the reign of Edward IV believed that it did. When a lord is indicted of treason or felony at the king's suit 'the case shall be brought into parliament, and there the seneschal of England shall put him to reply, and he shall plead that he is not guilty, and he shall be tried by his peers, etc., and then the lords spiritual who cannot consent to the death of a man shall appoint a procurator in the parliament etc., and then the steward must ask first the junior lord present if he is guilty, and so on separately all the lords who are there'.[10] Thomas Courtenay, earl of Devon, was indeed accorded such a trial in 1454 – and was acquitted.[11] But it was the last trial under this procedure. In 1478 the duke of Clarence was brought into parliament to answer the charge against him but he was

[10] Year Book, Easter term 10 Edward IV, cited in this translation L. W. Vernon Harcourt, *His Grace the Steward and Trial of Peers* (London, 1907), p. 393.

[11] *Rot.Parl.*, v, 249–50.

[12] *Ingulph's Chronicle of the Abbey of Croyland with the continuations by Peter of Blois and anonymous writers*, trans. Henry T. Riley (London, 1854), pp. 479–80; *Rot.Parl.*, vi, 193–5.

not tried by his peers: he was convicted by act of attainder passed by king, lords and commons.[12] Parliamentary attainder, except in his instance, never involved the presence of the victim. In 1485 the attainder of the supporters of Richard III at Bosworth rehearsed their crime in levying war against the king and enacted that they 'be convicte and atteinte of high treason'.[13] However, neither the earl of Surrey nor John lord Zouche, the only defeated noblemen to be taken prisoner, was executed. Ten years later John Radcliffe, lord FitzWalter, whose trial had proceeded no further than the indictment, was attainted for 'favouryng and helpyng' Perkin Warbeck.[14] But his life too was spared and he was sent as prisoner to Guisnes – although he was eventually executed, in November 1496, after trying to escape.[15] For James Tuchet, lord Audley, leader of the Cornish rebels in 1497, an alternative procedure was used: trial under the law of arms. In time of war noblemen, as other men, were subject to the summary jurisdiction of the court of chivalry.[16] Only for Edward Plantagenet, earl of Warwick, was the common law trial by peers revived in the reign of Henry VII.

But it was revived with a difference. Warwick was to be tried not by all his peers in parliament, only by a selected panel of peers. There was a precedent for this procedure. In 1415 Thomas duke of Clarence was commissioned by Henry V to summon the peers of Richard earl of Cambridge and Henry lord Scrope to give immediate judgment on them 'per vestrum et eorumdem parium communem assensum'. Clarence at once summoned his brother Humphrey duke of Gloucester, Cambridge's brother Edward duke of York – who was however to be represented by Thomas earl of Dorset – and 17 other peers, including Dorset acting in his own right, 'ibidem presentibus, et pro viagio domini regis ultra mare intendentibus'. The two men were found guilty and executed at once. The need for swift punishment of traitors discovered as the king prepared to embark for France ruled out recourse to parliament, but when parliament met in November 1415 the lords spiritual and temporal adjudged the proceedings to have been 'bona, justa et legalia judicia'.[17] The circumstances must also have limited the choice of peers to act as lords triers. Only those who

[13] *Rot.Parl.*, vi, 275–8.

[14] ibid., 503–7.

[15] *Chronicles of London*, ed. C. L. Kingsford (Oxford, 1905), p. 212.

[16] G. D. Squibb, *The High Court of Chivalry. A Study of the Civil Law in England* (Oxford, 1959), pp. 26–7; M. H. Keen, 'Treason trials under the law of arms', *TRHS*, 5th series, 12 (1962), 86, 92–4.

[17] *Rot.Parl.*, iv, 64, 66, 67.

were in Southampton could be chosen and the inclusion of York – in form at least – suggests that Clarence interpreted his commission literally, as meaning that all who were available should be called. Yet when the earl of Oxford was appointed high steward for the trial of Warwick he was instructed to summon not all the peers but 'tot et tales' – such and so many – peers of the accused, by whom the truth might be known. And no mention was made of their 'common assent'.[18]

Warwick pleaded guilty and so was condemned to death without any discussion of the evidence, although not – as the chronicler misleadingly worded it – 'without eny processe of the lawe'.[19] The 22 peers summoned by the high steward were spared the responsibility of deciding the fate of the young man whose life was briefly summarized in his sister's petition for the repeal of the attainder which followed his conviction: he 'was alweis frome his childehode beyng of th'age of viij yeres untill the tyme of his decease remaynyng and kepte in warde and restrayned from his libertie as well in the Towre of London as in other places, havyng none experience nor knoulege of the worldely polices nor of the lawes of this realme, so that if any offence were by hym done concernyng such matiers specified in the said acte of atteynder yt was rather by innocencye then of any maliciouse purpose'.[20] Nevertheless, his trial set the precedent. In 1503 when Edward Sutton, lord Dudley, was indicted of felony in Staffordshire, Henry VII commissioned Thomas Howard, earl of Surrey, to act as high steward, authorizing him to summon for the trial such and so many lords – the formula of 1499.[21] When Edward Stafford, duke of Buckingham, was charged with treason in 1521 there was apparently some expectation that parliament would be called to deal with his case and the affairs of Ireland, but the evidence suggests that parliament's role would have been simply to pass an act of attainder on the duke after his trial.[22] At all events, Buckingham was tried by a selected panel of peers and attainted by parliament when it was next summoned, nearly two years after his execution.

---

[18] Records of the trial in KB8/2 (*DKR*, iii, Appendix ii, pp. 216–18), printed Harcourt, *His Grace the Steward*, pp. 460–7.

[19] *Chronicles of London*, p. 227.

[20] 5 Henry VIII, c.12.

[21] *Foedera*, v(4), 206, also printed Harcourt, *His Grace the Steward*, pp. 467–8. The commission, undated, is entered on the first part of the patent roll for 19 Henry VII: *CPR, Henry VII*, ii, 360. The trial apparently never took place.

[22] BL, Cotton Vit.B.IV, f.84v, printed *LP*, iii(1), 1204 with part translated pp. cxix–cxx.

This trial, and all those of Henry VIII's reign, followed the pattern set in 1499. The high steward appointed for the occasion sent his precepts to the special commissioners to return the indictments found before them, to the serjeant at arms to summon the lords triers and to the constable of the Tower to bring the prisoner before him at a specified date and place. The serjeant at arms returned the precept with a schedule annexed listing the names of the peers summoned. At the end of a trial where a plea of not guilty had been entered the high steward asked each peer for his verdict, starting with the most junior, and wrote the response against each name on the list. He then gave his judgment. The original documents and the record of pleas were brought into the king's bench by the high steward and remained there in the baga de secretis. The indictment was given in full, but nothing of the trial proceedings beyond the formal plea of guilty or not guilty and the verdict. Legal and other commentators, however, sometimes filled out the picture. In 1521 the novelty of trial by peers was no doubt responsible for the year book entry detailing the correct procedure.[23] In most respects the description tallied with the documentary evidence but there was one discrepancy. The high steward was described as sending his precept to the serjeant at arms 'pour faire venir xx seigneurs ou xviij a tiel jour'. Nineteen peers (including the prior of St John of Jerusalem) were indeed summoned in 1521, the same number as in 1415, but more had been summoned for the trial of Warwick, and in later trials of Henry VIII's reign the number was to vary between 17 and 27. On another procedural point, however, the year book is revealing. The evidence having been given, the prisoner was removed and the peers retired to confer together. They returned to their places 'quand ils touts, ou le grand part est agree', and gave their individual verdicts, after which the prisoner was brought back to hear the verdict and judgment. This proceeding by majority vote in cases tried by a panel of peers may have been based on a precedent forged to safeguard the crown against a divided panel at Warwick's trial, although the evidence is not conclusive.[24] Nevertheless, in these circumstances the possible use of a majority decision – perhaps acceptable when all the lay lords in the upper house had been asked their verdict – clearly upset some legal opinion and in 1572 the judges themselves resolved at the trial of the duke of Norfolk that 'the peers ought to continue

---

[23] *Les Reports des Cases en les Ans des Roys Edward V, Richard III, Henrie VII et Henrie VIII, touts qui par cy devant ont este publies* (London, 1679), Easter term 13 Henry VIII; also printed Harcourt, *His Grace the Steward*, pp. 469–70.

[24] Harcourt, *His Grace the Steward*, pp. 416–35, criticized L. Owen Pike, 'The trial of peers', *The Law Quarterly Review*, xxiii (1907), 442–7.

together (as juries in case of other subjects ought to do) until they be agreed of their verdict'. Coke, who recorded this decision, was also at pains to point out that no peer could be convicted by the verdict of less than 24 men, that is to say of 12 freeholders or more at his indictment and 12 peers or more at his trial.[25] In practice, no minority voice was recorded at any trial by peers in the sixteenth century. One reason for this was the crown's choice of peers to sit as lords triers; the serjeant at arms issued the formal summons, but he did not select the men to sit on the panel. And the peers so summoned could not be challenged by the prisoner.[26]

During the reign of Henry VIII the court of the high steward was convened six times, to try eight noblemen and one woman, Anne Boleyn, marchioness of Pembroke. The panel of lords triers generally included fewer than half the peers. The northern barons were less often summoned than those who lived in more accessible parts of the kingdom. John lord Lumley was called to none of the six trials, John Nevill, lord Latimer, John lord Scrope and Robert lord Ogle to none of the five held during their lifetimes. However, the first three were involved in the pilgrimage of grace and, although they were pardoned, their tarnished record might in any case have prevented their summons to the later trials. The only noblemen within easier reach of London to be consistently omitted from five trial panels were John Sutton, lord Dudley, who was never summoned to parliament either, and Thomas lord Vaux of Harrowden in Northamptonshire. Vaux took his seat in the house of lords in 1531 and is known to have attended two later sessions of the Reformation parliament, but after its dissolution in April 1536, although regularly sent writs of summons, he never again appeared during Henry VIII's reign, nor during the reign of Edward VI. Only with the accession of Mary did he resume attendance.[27] The pattern suggests a commitment to Roman Catholicism strong enough to alienate Vaux from the Henrician regime – and perhaps Henry VIII from Vaux.[28]

On the other extreme, a few noblemen were consistently summoned to sit on trial panels. The only peer to attend all six trials (out of 11 who might have done so) was Henry Parker, lord Morley, the author

[25] Sir Edward Coke, *The Third Part of the Institutes of the Laws of England*, 4th edn (London, 1669), p. 30.

[26] ibid., p. 27: 'in case of a tryal of a nobleman, lord of parliament, he cannot challenge at all any of his peers'.

[27] See below, p. 125.

[28] Godfrey Anstruther, *Vaux of Harrowden. A Recusant Family* (Newport, Mon., 1953), p. 43 judged the absence of Vaux from parliament 'eloquent enough' of his religious views, for which there is no direct evidence.

and translator, who dedicated a number of his works to Henry VIII.[29] Two men (out of a further 25) took part in all five trials for which they were eligible: George Brooke, lord Cobham, and John lord Mordaunt, both noblemen, like Morley, of minor political significance, living, like him, in the home counties. All three were probably called upon as reliable men, easily available when needed. Mordaunt, it is true, came temporarily under investigation in 1538, when he had the misfortune to make his Lenten confession to Friar Forrest shortly before Forrest's arrest and execution. But Mordaunt denied any conversation with his confessor about the religious situation and no action was taken against him.[30] The summons to take part in the trial of the Catholic peers Montagu and Exeter in December 1538 must have come to a man more anxious than most to prove his unbroken allegiance to Henry VIII. Andrew lord Windsor attended four of the five trials, as did Henry Bourchier, earl of Essex, Henry FitzAlan, lord Mautravers, and Thomas lord Burgh. George lord Hastings (later earl of Huntingdon), Thomas Manners, lord Ros (later earl of Rutland) and Robert Radcliffe, lord FitzWalter (later earl of Sussex) attended four or, in the case of Radcliffe, five of the six trials held during their lifetimes. Henry Courtenay as earl of Devon and marquess of Exeter, Henry Pole, lord Montagu, and Thomas Fiennes, lord Dacre, served on the panel of every trial for which they were eligible before each appeared at his last trial as the prisoner at the bar. Darcy and Hussey were each summoned to one trial before 1537. Buckingham likewise had attended the only trial to precede his: one of the allegations against him in 1521 was that he had been heard to inveigh against Warwick's execution and to see God's vengeance in the death of Henry VIII's baby son.[31] The political convulsions of the reign took many by surprise and, of all the noblemen condemned by their peers, only George Boleyn, lord Rochford, had no experience of any trial but his own.

Although courtiers and noblemen living near London served more frequently than other peers, the selection of lords triers was as much related to the specific circumstances of each case as to any general considerations. Sometimes lack of time for preparation may have affected the composition of the panel, but not in the first trial of the reign: the fall of the duke of Buckingham moved slowly to its crisis. The action began with allegations against the duke by his dismissed surveyor, Charles Knyvet. A letter informing Wolsey was sent to him

[29] Morley is wrongly described in both GEC and *DNB* as a gentleman usher to the king, the MS. cited (*LP*, ii(i), 2735) being misdated.

[30] *LP*, xiii(1), 880, 1043(2).

[31] BL, Harl. 283, f.70 (*LP*, iii(1), 1284(3), printed in full pp. cxxix–cxxxi).

at The More – probably in September 1520[32] – by a royal servant (never since identified) who followed up his initial report with an unsigned letter suggesting a strategy of 'good awaite and espiel', as favoured by Henry VII, while pressure was put on Knyvet to reveal everything he knew.[33] It seems to have been this developing story which induced Henry VIII to write in his own hand to order Wolsey to 'make good wache' on the duke of Suffolk (the king's brother-in-law), on the duke of Buckingham and the earls of Northumberland and Wiltshire (Buckingham's brother-in-law and brother), on the earl of Derby 'and on others whyche yow thynke suspecte'.[34] Suffolk and Derby were not long under suspicion and both were ultimately selected to sit in judgment on Buckingham; for Derby this was to be his last service to the king, for he died ten days after the trial. Still the nightmare vision grew of a conspiracy against the crown by Buckingham and the powerful families with which he was allied, until at last the decision was taken to move against the duke. On 8 April 1521, at Thornbury, he received a letter from the king calling him to London. He set off at once and was at Westminster a week later.[35] He was sent to the Tower the same day.[36] The formal proceedings began with indictments of high treason found against him by three sets of special commissioners sitting in Kent and Surrey on 6 and 7 May. On 10 May the high steward was appointed for the trial and the same day sent his precept to the serjeant at arms to summon 'such and so many' peers to be at Westminster three days later.[37] The short notice means that earlier warning must have been given to the noblemen summoned; the four-week interval between the duke's arrest and his trial gave ample opportunity to consider the selection of the panel.[38] Early in May it was being reported at the French court that George Nevill, lord Bergavenny, and Henry Pole, styled lord Montagu, had been arrested as well, that the earl of Northumberland had been sent for and the earl of Wiltshire had fled. The report was only partially accurate, but Bergavenny, a son-in-law of Buckingham, had been sent

[32] Wolsey was at The More on 21 September 1520: *LP*, iii(1), 1016.

[33] SP1/22, f.57 (*LP*, iii(1), between 1283 and 1284, printed in full pp. cxiii–cxiv).

[34] Facsimile of BL, Add. 19,398, f.44 in Scarisbrick, *Henry VIII*, plate 4; printed in full *LP*, iii(1), 1 (under 1519).

[35] E36/220, f.15 records payments on 8 April to the king's messenger bringing letters and on 15 April to 'my lord cardinales cookes . . . at his place besidis Westmynster' (*LP*, iii(1), 1285(4), first reference misprinted 18 April).

[36] *CSPVen.*, iii, 187.

[37] Records of the trial in KB8/4/5 (*DKR*, iii, Appendix ii, pp. 230–4).

[38] No reference to this aspect of the trial is made by Mortimer Levine, 'The fall of Edward, duke of Buckingham' in *Tudor Men and Institutions. Studies in English Law and Government*, ed. A. J. Slavin (Baton Rouge, La, 1972), pp. 32–48.

to the Tower with his son-in-law Montagu, who was also brother-in-law to Buckingham's only son.[39] Montagu was soon released, but Bergavenny was kept in the Tower for almost a year. He was brought into king's bench in February 1522 and there confessed to misprision in concealing Buckingham's treason.[40] He had to surrender his offices, sell his manor of Birling, Kent, to the king and bind himself to pay a fine of 10,000 marks (less the price of Birling), but in return he was pardoned.[41] Wiltshire and Northumberland remained at liberty, yet powerless to help the duke. They were not summoned to take part in his trial; neither were his brothers-in-law George lord Hastings and Robert Radcliffe, lord FitzWalter, nor his son-in-law and former ward, Ralph Neville, earl of Westmorland. Another son-in-law, Thomas earl of Surrey, was in Ireland and not available. Of all the peers connected to him by blood or marriage only one was called to attend Buckingham's trial: Surrey's father, Thomas duke of Norfolk, earl marshal and treasurer of England, was nominated high steward for the occasion, as he had been for the projected trial of lord Dudley in 1503.

Family connection does not guarantee friendship, but these men – with the exception of Surrey – were Buckingham's friends. That relations with Surrey had been strained appears from his allegation, 25 years after the event, that Buckingham at his trial 'confessed openly at the bar, my father sittyng as his judge, that of all men lyvyng he hated me most, thynkyng I was the man that had hurt hym most to the kynges maieste – which now, quoth he, I perceyve the contrary'.[42] Surrey had been sent to Ireland as deputy in 1520 in place of Gerald FitzGerald, earl of Kildare, whose son Thomas was Buckingham's ward.[43] But there is no sign that Buckingham was in any way involved in Irish affairs and if he had (before the day of his trial) supposed that Surrey was the man who had 'hurt him most' to Henry VIII his suspicions probably went back to the period before Surrey's appointment as deputy, when he was at court and more easily capable of influencing the king. The actual evidence against Buckingham was supplied by three of his own servants – Charles Knyvet, Robert Gilbert and John Delacourt. They cited conversations designed to show that the duke had intended to kill the king and take the crown for himself, and suspicious acts interpreted as attempts to win adherents

[39] LP, iii(1), 1268, 1293.

[40] Hall's Chronicle, p. 630.

[41] SP1/22, f.154 (LP, iii(1), 1290); C82/514 (LP, iii(2), 2140).

[42] BL, Cotton Titus B.I, ff.99–101 (LP, xxi(2), 554), printed Gilbert Burnet, The History of the Reformation of the Church of England, ed. Nicholas Pocock, 7 vols (Oxford, 1865), vi, 274–8.

[43] LP, iii(1), 497, iii(2), 2145 g.14.

for his cause.[44] Buckingham fought hard for his life, got his accusers into court and answered the indictment which he described as a false accusation.[45] According to the year book report he denied everything, 'in effect'; presumably contesting the construction put upon any words or deeds he could not totally deny. Any hopes of acquittal were dashed by chief justice Fineux, who intervened to advise the court that in cases of treason no overt act was necessary: words were enough.[46] After long deliberation Buckingham's peers one by one declared him guilty and Norfolk delivered judgment on him, weeping as he did so.[47]

Treason by words was indeed an offence at common law.[48] Nevertheless, Buckingham's conviction seemed unjust, whatever the law might say. Even the year book reporter was moved to describe the duke as 'tres noble prince et prudent, et mirror de tout courtoisie', while Londoners, still more extravagantly, lauded him as 'a saynte and a holy man' and declared that he died guiltless.[49] When the law of treason was under discussion in the 1530s Thomas Cromwell, who wanted to make treason by words a statutory offence, reminded himself of 'the boke wherin the report of the duke of Bukkyngham's arreyng[ment] for treson ys pryntyd and what woordes be ther to be notyd'.[50] Cromwell's proposal was thought too drastic early in 1534 but was accepted in the autumn session of parliament.[51] Contemporary comment showed that the idea of treason by speech alone was still unfamiliar. The new act was assumed to be introducing a novel concept, feared for its potential scope, and Montagu voiced a general reaction when he reflected that it would be 'a strange worlde, saying wordes be made treason'.[52] The earl of Northumberland was not the only peer likely to have been 'pensyve' at the events of May 1521.[53]

[44] The charges are discussed by Levine, 'The fall of Edward, duke of Buckingham', pp. 36–41.

[45] *Hall's Chronicle*, p. 623.

[46] Year Book Easter term 13 Henry VIII, printed Harcourt, *His Grace the Steward*, pp. 469–70.

[47] *Hall's Chronicle*, pp. 623–4. Hall has Norfolk asking the verdict of the peers starting with the duke of Suffolk, but the most junior baron (in precedence) was always asked first.

[48] John Bellamy, *The Tudor Law of Treason. An Introduction* (London and Toronto, 1979), pp. 31–2.

[49] Quoted Helen Miller, 'London and parliament in the reign of Henry VIII', *Bull.IHR*, xxxv (1962), 140. Popular acclaim of earlier political victims is noted by Joel T. Rosenthal, *Nobles and the Noble Life 1295–1500*, Historical Problems: Studies and Documents, ed. G. R. Elton, no. 25 (London, 1976), pp. 39–40.

[50] BL, Cotton Titus B.I, f.453v (*LP*, vi, 1381).

[51] G. R. Elton, 'The law of treason in the early Reformation', *HJ*, xi (1968), 221–3.

[52] SP1/139, ff.30–2 (*LP*, xiii(2), 829iii(2)).

[53] SP1/22, f.203 (*LP*, iii(1), 1356, where Northumberland is wrongly called duke).

Henry VIII discovered then how easy it was to destroy even the greatest nobleman. The king's expectation – noted by Pace[54] – that the lords would find Buckingham guilty was fulfilled, helped by the careful selection of the trial panel and by Fineux's guidance on the crucial point of law, which must have served to quieten consciences. It would perhaps be unduly harsh to suggest that some of the panel hoped for a tangible reward for their co-operation, but it is a matter of fact that Henry VIII made grants of Buckingham's lands to seven of the 20 peers who had tried and condemned him.[55]

In sharp contrast was the fate of Charles Knyvet, who had provided the most damaging evidence in his allegation that Buckingham had, on 4 November 1519, put his hand on the hilt of his sword and sworn to kill the king if he should be ordered to the Tower for the illegal retaining of Sir William Bulmer. Knyvet drafted numerous petitions to the king and Wolsey begging for restitution to his lost offices and fees as some compensation for having revealed Buckingham's offences, an act of loyalty to the king which had earned him 'the most extreme sclaunder, hate and dysdayne'. When he heard that his old offices had nevertheless been granted to others he asked for two manors in Suffolk instead and the keepership of two of Buckingham's parks in Kent.[56] The manors went to the duke of Suffolk, the keeperships to other men until the parks themselves were granted in 1531 to Thomas Boleyn, by then earl of Wiltshire.[57] All Knyvet obtained was a special protection for one year from April 1521 and, when that ran out, a place for a further year in the retinue of lord Berners, deputy of Calais. By December 1523 Knyvet had been recruited for war service in the retinue of a ship's captain.[58] Eventually, according to Buckingham's son, he met a miserable death, 'eaten with vermen' – which showed the judgment of God on the man who had wrongfully accused the duke of 'certein wordes which he tooke upone his deathe he nevere spake'. Henry lord Stafford in his petition to Mary, soon after her accession, gave Knyvet's motive as revenge for his dismissal by Buckingham for deceiving him 'in one matire of C C markes', but laid more blame upon Wolsey for inducing him to make the false accusation. The cardinal, Stafford declared, 'threatynde my fathire he wolde be even with him or hit were longe' after he defended Katherine of Aragon against Wolsey's insolent charge that she had shamed Henry VIII by

---

[54] In the memorandum cited in n. 22 above.
[55] See below, pp. 214–16.
[56] SP1/22, ff.102–36 (*LP*, iii(1), 1289(2)).
[57] *LP*, iii(2), 3162, v, 506 g.16.
[58] C82/501, 518, 539 (*LP*, iii(1), 1262 g.21, iii(2), 2297 g.21, 3677 g.1).

failing to go out to welcome Francis I at the meeting of the two kings in the summer of 1520. He rammed the moral home: the tragedy had been precipitated by his father's 'hartie love to that moste noble queene youre mothire'.[59]

Stafford was only adding circumstantial detail to the generally accepted story. Wolsey was universally blamed for Buckingham's fall, although if it had been achieved by procuring false witnesses they had not been rewarded for their perfidy. Wolsey had established himself in the king's mind as the guardian of his security. Henry had praised his special concern for his safety in April 1518 after Wolsey had written to him 'touchynge greate personagis', apparently including the duke of Buckingham; before his council he had declared that 'ther is no man lyvyng that ponderth mor the seurty of his parson, and the comon welth of this his reame'.[60] However, Wolsey had made at least one attempt to steer Buckingham into safer paths. In 1516, according to the duke, he had sounded him on his plans for his son: 'he brake with me that I shuld let my sone come se the kyng and the quen, and to be aquynted.' When Buckingham replied that he had only the one son and was unwilling to let him come to court for fear of infection, at all events until he was married and had a child, they talked of the boy's marriage. Two possible brides were discussed, the daughters of the countess of Salisbury and the earl of Shrewsbury. It was the latter alliance which Wolsey recommended: 'hit where bothe to the kynges honowre and surty to see you to knett togeyder.' Buckingham had suggested this very match years before, but Shrewsbury complained that he had asked too large a dowry then and was still demanding more than he could afford.[61] So in October 1518 Buckingham signed indentures for the marriage of his heir to the daughter of the countess of Salisbury – Warwick's sister and the niece of Edward IV and Richard III.[62] It might indeed have been for the duke's surety, as well as for the king's, to have followed Wolsey's prompting. But Buckingham would not tread warily. His provocative retaining of Bulmer in 1519 could not be ignored and precipitated an open break with the king. His attempt to obtain a licence to visit his lordships in Wales in February 1521 with 300 or 400 armed men – in spite of the rejection of his earlier requests – was all too reminiscent of his father's preparations for

[59] SP11/1, ff.37–8.

[60] SP1/16, ff.209–11 (*LP*, ii(2), 4057); BL, Cotton Vesp. C.XIV, ff.229–30 (*LP*, ii(2), 4124).

[61] Lambeth Palace Library, MS.3206, ff.13, 11 (*LP*, ii(1), 1893, 1970).

[62] *HMC, Seventh Report*, p. 584; *HMC, Hastings*, i, 308. The marriage was to take place early in 1519.

rebellion in 1483.[63] If Wolsey proved his downfall, Buckingham had played into his hands.

Henry VIII was personally threatened by the treasons alleged against Buckingham – his 'great enemy' as he described him after his execution.[64] The charge against William lord Dacre of the north, warden of the west marches, was of traitorous dealings with the Scots; a serious enough matter but without the same implication for the king's own safety. The affair erupted in the spring of 1534 at a time of great political activity, with Scottish ambassadors in London negotiating a peace treaty and preparations being made throughout England and Wales to swear all the king's subjects to the act of succession. Dacre himself had not returned home after attending the session of parliament which passed the act when royal commissioners arrived at Naworth to attach his goods and search for incriminating papers. They went on from there to his other residences at Greystoke, Kirkoswald and Morpeth, making inventories of all his possessions.[65] The commissioners were Ralph Neville, earl of Westmorland – who thanked Cromwell for this sign of the king's favour – and Henry earl of Cumberland and his brother Sir Thomas Clifford, the leading rivals to the Dacre interest in Cumberland. They were manifestly disappointed at finding so few letters of any significance, and apologetic: 'howe that shulde happen we doo not well knowe.' At any rate it was not their fault, they assured the king from Naworth on 17 May. They had travelled north as unobtrusively as possible, taking different ways to avoid notice, but it seemed likely that, even so, the Dacres had had 'some coniecture of this busynes or ever we cam to thies parties'. However, they sent the inventories made by Cromwell's servant, John ap Rice, and such letters as he had found; the bearer was Sir Thomas Clifford, 'which was at all our doinges', who would report 'howe studiously we did endeavour ourselfes to accomplish your graces pleasure in every behalf'.[66]

But Dacre was not without friends. The earl of Shrewsbury, who had hoped – or so he said[67] – to marry all his daughters with the dowry required by Buckingham for one of them, had married the youngest to

---

[63] *The Marcher Lordships of South Wales, 1415–1536. Select Documents*, ed. T. B. Pugh, Board of Celtic Studies, University of Wales, History and Law Series, xx (Cardiff, 1963), pp. 260–1.

[64] Miller, 'London and parliament', 140.

[65] Inventory of Dacre's goods: SP1/84, ff.33–50 (*LP*, vii, 676).

[66] SP1/84, ff.60, 66 (*LP*, vii, 679, 687).

[67] Lambeth Palace Library, MS.3206, f.11 (*LP*, ii(1), 1970).

him; and Dacre's sister was married to Shrewsbury's son and heir.[68] Shrewsbury wrote on 29 May to ask Cromwell to be 'good maister' to his daughter when she came to see the king: 'she hathe nat ben accustomed or brought upp in any suche affayres or uncomfortable besyness, but after the homely facyon of the cuntrey.' The earl believed that Dacre would declare himself 'an honourable man and the kinges true subiect' and 'so as his trought tryed by your good helpe he maye the soner optayne the kinges most gracyous favour, and his accusers may be ordred according to theire demerettes'.[69] But soon Shrewsbury himself was in trouble. On 10 June, still at Sheffield castle, he wrote two letters to Cromwell. One concerned an office in Wales in which Cromwell was interested; the earl was sending his son to consult him about it. The other – more confidential – referred to a matter never openly named, but which had 'somwhat perplexid' him since Cromwell had informed him of it. Shrewsbury would have come in person 'to have made my owen declaracion in any thyng that cowde be leede to my charge' had not Cromwell assured him that the king himself was 'makyng aunswere for me towchyng suche thynges as was spoken of me'. Moreover, although he had no knowledge of what the allegations were, 'yet myn assured trowith shall dyscharge me according to the dutie of my elegens, what so ever any man say to the contrarye'. Shrewsbury was relying on his son to find out from Cromwell whether the king would like to see him, in which case he would come with all possible speed.[70] By this time, in spite of the shortage of documentary evidence against Dacre, the legal machinery had been set in motion to bring him to trial. The instigator of the proceedings was another of his enemies, Sir William Musgrave, constable of Bewcastle in Cumberland. Cromwell instructed him to make sure that the indictments were fully substantiated. Musgrave promised that 'the day and tym of every indyctment shalbe perfytly knowyn': he was confident that 'the kynges grays shall have every thyng sett so furth in so playn a wys and with so substancyall wyttness on my behalf that yt shalbe undenyable anything that I have alegyd'.

---

[68] A draft agreement was prepared in December 1517 for William's marriage to Mary, another daughter of the earl, who eventually married Northumberland's son and heir; by May 1519 a marriage between William Dacre and one of Shrewsbury's daughters was finally agreed: *LP*, ii(2), 3819, 3820, iii(1), 238. His marriage to Elizabeth, the youngest daughter, probably took place soon after. Francis Talbot was married to Mary Dacre by 1523.

[69] SP1/84, f.100 (*LP*, vii, 727). In Dacre's indictment he was said to have been warden of the west march up to 8 May 1534, which was presumably the date of his arrest.

[70] SP1/84, ff.189, 190 (*LP*, vii, 818, 819).

Nevertheless, he told Cromwell, 'your mastershyp and I speshally beryth all the blame in thys mater towchyng the lord Dacre and Sir Christofer hys unkle, and therefor, sir, I pray you stand styfly in thys mater and that I may have your gentyll ayd', particularly as 'dyvers of thys cuntrey . . . as mych as they dar and may' continue to support lord Dacre. But once 'they see he shall go dowyn I dowt not but they will say *Crucefige*, for the cuntrey hath ben so overlayd with the lord Dacres that they thowght her was non other kyng'.[71]

For the moment, Musgrave seemed in little need of assistance. Westmorland, Cumberland and Sir Thomas Clifford had already been appointed to receive indictments of treason in Cumberland, together with two more of Dacre's enemies, Henry earl of Northumberland and Sir Thomas Wharton; two lawyers completed the commission.[72] On 15 June at Carlisle the indictment was presented by two grand juries dominated by Clifford, Percy and Wharton servants and relatives.[73] Dacre was formally charged with having betrayed his allegiance by making secret agreements with the king's enemies. Most of the charges were indeed specific: on 8 November 1532 lord Dacre, through his uncle Sir Christopher, agreed with certain Scots of Liddesdale that neither should harm the other – and Sir William Musgrave's men, excluded from this treaty, were attacked by the Scots on 1 July 1533 without reprisal by Dacre; on 5 December 1532 Dacre agreed with the laird of Buccleuch that neither should harm the other – and Dacre allowed Buccleuch to invade the east marches of England, defended by the earl of Northumberland, on 20 December; on 1 October 1532 lord Dacre and Sir Christopher agreed with Robert lord Maxwell that neither should harm the other, Dacre warning Maxwell on 10 December of his intended invasion of Scotland – and when Maxwell in his turn invaded England he spared Dacre's lands and spoiled the possessions of Musgrave's men; on 28 March 1533, at his tower of Rockcliff in Cumberland, Dacre met Maxwell and agreed that neither should harm the other – and at the same time Maxwell attacked the earl of Northumberland and Sir William Musgrave. But Dacre was also alleged to have had secret meetings with Robert Charteris, laird of Hempsfield, for which no date nor place was given. The details of the charges made clear the motives for this case of march treason (and for

---

[71] SP1/84, f.199 (*LP*, vii, 829). 'Dyverse variances' between Dacre and Musgrave were depending in star chamber from 1530–1: STAC2/19/127.

[72] Records of the trial in KB8/5/6 (*DKR*, iii, Appendix ii, pp. 234–6, where Wharton is misprinted Walton).

[73] M. E. James, *Change and Continuity in the Tudor North. The Rise of Thomas first lord Wharton*, Borthwick Papers, no. 27 (York, 1965), p. 18.

the treason, if they were true): they lay in the feuds which had for years riven the border country. The indictment was found *billa vera* and the action moved to London.

Thomas duke of Norfolk, earl marshal and treasurer of England, as his father had been in 1521, was appointed high steward for the trial on 26 June and four days later sent his precept to the serjeant at arms to summon peers to be at Westminster on 9 July. The noblemen who were to be called were evidently expected to be in attendance two days before the trial: lord Mordaunt received a signet letter from Henry VIII dated 30 June, calling him to come to London on 7 July, 'there to tarry and demeur until ye shall know farther of our pleasure, which shall be declared unto you on our behalf by the mouth of our chancellor'.[74] On the day appointed 21 peers sat on the trial panel; the name of one of them – Thomas lord Berkeley – was inserted into the list, which may mean that he was not summoned at the same time as the rest. Shrewsbury, who had been on Buckingham's panel, was not called upon this time, but his son, lord Talbot, already at court, was summoned to attend. Thomas lord Darcy, who had been warden of the marches in the early years of Henry VIII's reign, was the only other northern peer among the lords triers. The earls of Northumberland, Westmorland and Cumberland all attended the trial, but only to present the indictment. Although they were omitted from the panel and his brother-in-law was included, Dacre was reluctant to trust to the verdict of his peers, according to the account of the case in the law reports of John Spelman, a justice of king's bench.[75] The day before the trial opened all the justices met to decide two legal questions which they thought might be raised. Could Dacre refuse to be tried by his peers and ask to be tried instead 'by the country'? All the justices were agreed that he could not, citing Magna Carta. If the peers could not agree, would a majority verdict suffice? Most of the justices thought that it would, so long as at least 12 peers were agreed on it.

Spelman went on to describe the trial itself. Norfolk as high steward sat in Westminster hall under the cloth of estate, with 20 lords, half sitting on one side of him, half on the other.[76] The justices also sat on each side, at the feet of the peers; the clerk of the crown sat at the feet of the high steward. After the prisoner was brought in the clerk of the crown read the indictment and asked Dacre how he answered to the

[74] Robert Halstead, *Succinct Genealogies of the Noble and Ancient Houses of . . . Mordaunt of Turvey* (London, 1685), p. 556.

[75] *The Reports of Sir John Spelman*, ed. J. H. Baker, Selden Soc., 93, 94 for 1976, 1977 (London, 1977, 1978), i, 54–5.

[76] Spelman's reference to 20 lords triers reinforces the impression that only that number was originally summoned.

charge of treason. He asked for respite on the ground that the indictment was long and contained 'many things'. He was told that if he would not plead, judgment would be given against him. He pleaded not guilty. Then he was asked how he wished to be tried. Again he asked for time, and would not put himself upon his peers. The high steward told him that if he refused to say that he would be tried by his peers, judgment would be given against him. He said he would be tried by his peers. The evidence against him was produced and witnesses, including Sir William Musgrave, were examined. According to Chapuys, Dacre defended himself for seven hours.[77] He was then removed to the exchequer chamber and the lords triers began to consider their verdict. After two hours they sent to ask for a conference with the high steward. Norfolk called all the justices to advise him and was informed that he could not confer with the panel except in the prisoner's presence. The peers then asked for Sir Christopher Dacre to be brought from the Tower. They wanted to interrogate him on one specific point: whether or not lord Dacre had ordered him to treat with Maxwell in favour of the Scots. The high steward was advised by the justices that this could not be allowed either since all the evidence had been given – and because Sir Christopher, being uncle to the prisoner, would not willingly give evidence against him. When the peers had considered this, they returned to give their verdict. The high steward asked each in turn, starting with lord Mordaunt, the most junior baron: each said he found Dacre not guilty. Dacre was recalled to hear Norfolk report this verdict and give the order for his discharge. When the 'common people' who were in Westminster hall realized that Dacre had been acquitted, Spelman reported, they all clapped and shouted with joy. The justices, more soberly, discussed the case among themselves. It was clear that the evidence of Musgrave and the others had been dismissed as proceeding from malice. But, if the peers had not been able to agree at once, could the trial have been adjourned to the next day? They thought it could have been; some considered that the peers would have had to be kept together overnight, but others reckoned the precaution unnecessary 'because they were not sworn – on account of the trustworthiness that is presumed in them'. And could the peers who had been commissioned to hold the initial inquiry also have sat on the trial panel? Many of the justices said that they could have done so.

It was fortunate for Dacre that they did not. The three northern earls who had returned the indictment had an interest in the outcome beyond their personal antagonism to the Dacres. In any treason trial it

<hr>

[77] *CSPSp.*, v(1), 75.

was assumed that the evidence would be incontrovertible. Coke gave this as the main reason why the prisoner was allowed no counsel to defend him: 'the testimonies and the proofs of the offence ought to be so clear and manifest, as there can be no defence of it.'[78] Dacre's acquittal discredited those who had accused him. It also, inevitably, reflected upon Cromwell, known to have been closely involved in the case. But the trial was not the end of the matter. Although discharged by the high steward, Dacre was not allowed to go home. On 27 July Chapuys reported a rumour that he was being kept in the Tower because he refused to sign a petition for pardon.[79] Why should a man found innocent require a pardon? On 25 July, more than two weeks after his acquittal, Dacre had signed a confession. In the presence of the lord chancellor, Sir Thomas Audley, Norfolk, Exeter, Thomas Cromwell, the lieutenant of the Tower, Sir Edmund Walsingham, and the solicitor general, Richard Rich, 'without any maner of coaccion', Dacre had confessed to misprision of treason. He acknowledged that he had, contrary to his allegiance, concealed two letters sent to him by his uncle Sir Philip Dacre and by Robert Charteris – no doubt the letters found by the commissioners who searched his houses. (The evidence of contact with Charteris explains his inclusion in Dacre's indictment despite the lack of specific knowledge of when they might have met.) Dacre for his concealment begged the king's pardon and put himself in his hands 'as most humble and obedient subgiet'. The price of forgiveness was high: Dacre had to pay £10,000 for his pardon. Seven thousand marks were paid within three months – the greater part of it (£4,066 3s 4d) being the plate and ready money attached by the commissioners, retained by the king. The rest of the £10,000 was to be paid in instalments by 1541. Dacre had to bind himself in 10,000 marks to pay the sum in full, not to go more than 10 miles from London without the king's special licence in writing, not to vex any man for 'his late acwsacion, indictment or arraynment' or for seizing his goods to the king's use, and to give up all letters patent and leases that he had of the king's grant so that they could be annulled. The recognizance, acknowledged on 17 October 1534, referred to 'dyvers mesprisions and crymynall offensys' confessed by lord Dacre on 25 July, 'over and besydes the offense of high treason wherof the said lorde was lately arrayned'.[80] The pardon for his misprision was issued in December.[81] Three months later Dacre was at last given a licence to

---

[78] Coke, *Third Institute*, p. 29.

[79] *CSPSp.*, v(1), 75.

[80] SP2/Q/14 (*LP*, vii, 1270, where Cromwell's name is omitted). Inventory of Dacre's plate and money: *LP*, *Addenda*, i, 933.

[81] *LP*, vii, 1601 g.1.

leave London – provided that he returned by 1 November.[82] He went home in disgrace, deprived of his offices, to face a future burdened with debt.

Nevertheless, Dacre had some reason to be thankful. No other nobleman was acquitted by his peers in the reign of Henry VIII. Chapuys ascribed his comparative good fortune to the fear of Norfolk and others that if Cromwell began to lay his hands on noble blood, he would follow Wolsey to complete dominance.[83] Cromwell did indeed consolidate his power by the destruction of noble families, although the blood of most of the victims was of no great antiquity and the responsibility for shedding it was not confined to Cromwell. The next trial of peers was the outcome of court faction rather than local feud, the product of a temporary alliance early in 1536 between Cromwell and the enemies of Anne Boleyn, who included Henry Courtenay, marquess of Exeter, and Henry Pole, lord Montagu.[84] Rumours had been circulating for weeks of the king's desire to rid himself of Anne. The method chosen was cruelly damaging to the king's reputation, but necessary in order to destroy her faction in the privy chamber. If Henry VIII believed the charges brought against her, few others did. According to Chapuys an acquittal was expected at least for her brother, lord Rochford, accused of incest: as no witnesses were produced against him, some of those present at his trial were prepared to bet that he would be found not guilty.[85] This story was repeated by George Constantine, a servant of Henry Norris and friend of William Brereton: 'there were that sayed that moch money wold have byn layed that daye, and that great oddes, that the lorde Ratchforde shulde have byn quytte.' Constantine also 'hearde saye' that Rochford would have escaped 'had it not byn for a letter'; but he was found guilty by a panel which included 'almost all the lordes that were in the realme'.[86] That was an exaggeration, but the 26 peers called to try Anne Boleyn and her brother did outnumber those who were not summoned.[87] The

---

[82] *LP*, ix, App.1. On the same day Sir Christopher Dacre was granted a general pardon: *LP*, viii, 481 g.5.

[83] *CSPSp.*, v(i), 75 (better translated in *LP*, vii, 1013).

[84] Ives, 'Faction at the court of Henry VIII', 169–88. Montagu, Exeter and his wife kept Chapuys in touch with developments at court: *CSPSp.*, v(2), 43, where the marquess is wrongly identified as Dorset.

[85] *CSPSp.*, v(2), 55.

[86] 'Memorial from George Constantyne to Thomas lord Cromwell', ed. Thomas Amyot, *Archaeologia*, xxiii (1831), 64–6.

[87] Records of both trials in KB8/9 (*DKR*, iii, Appendix ii, pp. 243–5), printed, with the proceedings against the commoners, Charles Wriothesley, *A Chronicle of England during the Reigns of the Tudors from A.D. 1485 to 1559*, Camden Soc., new series, xi, xx (London, 1875, 1877), i, Appendix.

intention was doubtless to secure as many voices as possible in condemnation of the queen.

Proceedings began on 24 April 1536 with the appointment of special commissioners of oyer and terminer for Middlesex and Kent. They included the dukes of Norfolk and Suffolk, the earls of Oxford, Westmorland, Wiltshire and Sussex, and lord Sandys, all of whom except Suffolk had been with the king the previous day attending the Garter meeting at Greenwich.[88] On 10 and 11 May indictments were found in the two counties citing dates on which the queen was alleged to have committed adultery with Rochford, Norris, Brereton, Sir Francis Weston and Mark Smeaton. They were already in the Tower, arrested after the king's sudden and ominous departure from the May day jousts. On 12 May the four commoners were tried and found guilty by the commissioners and Norfolk was appointed high steward for the trial of the queen and lord Rochford, his niece and nephew. The next day he sent his precept to the serjeant at arms to summon the peers, who were presumably already assembling. On 15 May the trial began in the Tower of London. Norfolk sat under the cloth of state on a scaffold made in the king's hall there, holding the long white staff of the high steward, while his son sat at his feet with the golden staff which belonged to Norfolk as earl marshal. Sir Thomas Audley, lord chancellor, present as an adviser, sat on his right, opposite the duke of Suffolk. The rest of the peers were ranged in order of precedence.[89] The noblemen who had been named as special commissioners for the earlier trial were also present at this one, with a single exception: Thomas earl of Wiltshire was not called to pass judgment on his children. Henry Parker, lord Morley, was summoned as usual, although on this occasion he had to decide the fate of his son-in-law. William FitzAlan, earl of Arundel, was present at this one trial out of the five held during his lifetime. Ralph Neville, earl of Westmorland, also found himself for the only time in his life acting as a lord trier, although he was eligible for a summons to all six trials of the reign; the Garter meeting which had presumably brought him to London involved him in these more memorable events. Northumberland, too, had been present at the St George's day chapter, when he had been appointed to preside at the feast of the order to be held on 21 May. He also was summoned to this one trial – to give his verdict on the woman

---

[88] *The Register of the Most Noble Order of the Garter*, ed. J. Anstis, 2 vols (London, 1724), i, 398–401.

[89] Wriothesley, *Chronicle*, i, 35–42 gives an account of events from 1 to 19 May. The editor's comment (i, 38n.) that only 26 peers were present at the trial out of 53 then in England ignores the fact that four peers were children and two more, Mountjoy and Dorset, only 19 years old.

he had once hoped to marry. Exeter had missed the Garter meeting but attended the trial. Henry Bourchier, earl of Essex, who was present at every other trial of peers between 1499 and his death in 1540, was absent from this one in spite of the king's letter sent on 9 May commanding him immediately, 'setting all other affaires apart', to come to treat of 'suche greate and weightie mattres as wheruppon dothe consist the suertie of our person, the preservacion of our honour and the tranquilytie and quietnes of youe and all other our loving and faytheful subgiettes'.[90]

The queen was tried first. After the peers had one by one recorded their verdicts of guilty and Norfolk had passed sentence, she was removed and Rochford was brought in. One of the charges in his indictment was not read out in court but was handed to him, with instructions that he should answer it without making it public. It contained an allegation that Anne had told his wife that the king was impotent. Rochford denied spreading any such rumour. But he read the charge aloud – to a court packed with spectators, including the lord mayor and representatives of the leading crafts of London.[91] This is perhaps the origin of Constantine's story of a letter which tipped the scales against Rochford. But it was naïve to suppose that he might have been allowed to go free. The panel which had condemned the queen was hardly likely to find her brother innocent, and again the peers, one by one, declared their verdict of guilty: all, that is, except the earl of Northumberland, who had suddenly been taken ill and was absent from the court. Two days before the trial Northumberland had written to Cromwell, denying once again that there had ever been any contract or promise of marriage between him and Anne Boleyn, 'wheruppon I was not oonly hertofore examined uppon myn othe before the archebusshoppes of [Canterbury] and Yorke, but also receyved the blessed sa[crament] uppon the same before the duke of Northfolk [and] other the kinges highnes counsaill lernyd [in the] spirituall lawe'.[92] Nevertheless, on grounds of a pre-contract or some other impediment to which she was said to have confessed, Anne's marriage to Henry VIII was dissolved before her execution.[93] On the day of the annulment of his sister's marriage lord Rochford was executed on Tower hill; when his father died in 1539 the earldom of Wiltshire became extinct.

[90] BL, Cotton Titus B.I, f.415 (*LP*, x, 833).

[91] *CSPSp.*, v(2), 55; Wriothesley, *Chronicle*, i, 39.

[92] BL, Cotton Otho C.X, f.224 (*LP*, x, 864), printed Burnet, *History of the Reformation*, vi, 167.

[93] The grounds of nullity were never officially revealed and remain uncertain: Henry Ansgar Kelly, *The Matrimonial Trials of Henry VIII* (Stanford, Calif., 1976), pp. 243–59.

Mary's supporters expected that, as the elder daughter of a king with no legitimate child, she would be named heir apparent, although early in June Chapuys reported that the earl of Sussex in the privy council, with Henry VIII present, argued for the male bastard, Richmond, in preference to a female. Mary herself apparently believed that her troubles were over until Henry VIII insisted that she should swear obedience to the laws of the realm and thus acknowledge both the royal supremacy and her own illegitimacy. Chapuys advised her that it was a sacrifice she ought to make to save her life for the future of the kingdom. She eventually agreed to submit, signing the paper without reading it in a vain attempt to placate her conscience.[94] The hopes of her party collapsed. The defeat of the conservative faction at court removed any alternative to direct action in the country.[95] Darcy and Hussey had already discussed this possibility, having assured each other in the summer of 1534 that would never become heretics 'for we woll die Cristen men'.[96] Hussey, who had lost his office as Mary's chamberlain when her household was dissolved in 1533, left London in September 1534. He had a secret interview with Chapuys before going, at which he urged Charles V to declare war as soon as possible. The people of England would then rise and remedy the grievances of the kingdom with the aid of the nobility and clergy. He referred the ambassador to Darcy, an experienced soldier, for details of the military operation. Darcy explained that Charles V would need to send only a small contingent to the mouth of the Thames and a band of hackbut men to the north; his major role would be to procure a supporting invasion by the king of Scots. Darcy himself was ready to take the field with 8,000 men. He claimed to be one of the most loyal servants of Henry VIII, but as a man of honour and a Christian he could not consent to the current outrages against God and reason.[97] He had some difficulty in obtaining a licence to leave London, but in May 1535 he sent word to Chapuys that he was going home immediately and would lose no time in the advancement of his plans.[98] Richmond's death in July 1536 might have been expected to add urgency to the preparations of Darcy and Hussey, but the Lincolnshire rising evidently took them by surprise. Hussey, his hope of support from the earl of Shrewsbury disappointed, refused to commit himself to the rebellion. Darcy, on the other hand, after a show of resistance,

[94] *CSPSp.*, v(2), 61, 70. The text of Mary's submission is in *LP*, x, 1137.

[95] G. R. Elton, 'Politics and the pilgrimage of grace' in *After the Reformation: Essays in Honor of J. H. Hexter*, ed. Barbara C. Malament (Manchester, 1980), pp. 25–56.

[96] SP1/118, f.123 (*LP*, xii(1), 899).

[97] *LP*, vii, 38; *CSPSp.*, v(1), 257.

[98] *CSPSp.*, v(i), 157.

yielded the king's castle at Pontefract to the rebels and joined the pilgrimage of grace. Nevertheless both men, for all the militancy reported by Chapuys, in the event adopted the role of mediator between the rebels and the king. Darcy backed Robert Aske in curbing those leaders, including lords Latimer and Lumley, who sought a violent end to the confrontation at Doncaster, and worked for a negotiated settlement, relying on the duke of Norfolk to present a list of their grievances to Henry VIII.[99] Each rising ended with the grant of a general pardon to the participants, which all individuals (with a few specified exceptions) were entitled to sue out of chancery without charge.[100] Hussey apparently felt no need to obtain an individual pardon, but Darcy sued out his, and it was issued on 18 January 1537.[101]

By then Sir Francis Bigod was assembling the commons for an attack on Scarborough. Immediately the news had reached him Darcy had written to Aske and Sir Robert Constable, urging them to calm the people.[102] On 21 January he advised his deputy at Knaresborough to warn his friends and neighbours there to keep within the king's pardon and take no part in the new rising. They should all put their trust, as he did, in the 'free' parliament promised by Henry VIII, where rich and poor alike would 'have justice agaynst all that was naymed in the byll of the comons at Doncaster'.[103] But nothing could save Darcy now. On 7 February, within a week of his return to the north as the king's lieutenant, Norfolk cast renewed doubt on his loyalty.[104] When Darcy was arrested, early in April, the privy council instructed Norfolk to spread the word that he and the others taken into custody were to stand trial only for offences committed since the pardon.[105] Attempts were made to prove Darcy's traitorous intent after that date, especially in his enthusiasm for a free parliament, but he was mainly questioned about his part in the pilgrimage of grace and in particular his surrender of Pontefract.[106] It proved impossible to frame a convincing charge without referring to the earlier events. When Norfolk received the text of the indictment of Darcy and others

---

[99] M. E. James, 'Obedience and dissent in Henrician England: the Lincolnshire rebellion 1536', *Past & Present*, 48 (1970), 52–65 and *English Politics and the Concept of Honour 1485–1642*, Past & Present Supplement 3 (1978), pp. 37–9.

[100] *LP*, xi, 1061, 1062, 1063, 1224(2), 1276.

[101] *LP*, xii(1), 134.

[102] ibid., 115.

[103] E36/122, f.1 (*LP*, xii(1), 184).

[104] *LP*, xii(1), 362.

[105] ibid., 846.

[106] ibid., 848, 900.

in Yorkshire he explained to Cromwell how he intended to make sure that 'the matier shalbe fownd according to the kinges pleasure'. He would impanel two grand juries, one to include 'the best frendes thiese men have', in order 'to prove their affections'; 'and if they woll not fynd, then they may have thankes according to their cankered hertes'. For the other he would 'appoynte suche, that I shall no more doubte then of my selff'.[107] Darcy was charged with conspiring to deprive the king of his title of supreme head of the church and to compel him to hold a parliament and assembling to levy war against him in October 1536 – and with persevering in these treasons after the pardon. On 9 May at York each inquest duly found that Darcy had aided and abetted the rebellion of Sir Francis Bigod. In Hussey's case the pardon was simply ignored. On 12 May the grand jury at Sleaford, Lincolnshire, found that he had conspired to deprive Henry VIII of his title of supreme head on 1 October 1536 and aided those who had levied war on the king during the subsequent four days. On 15 May in Westminster hall each man in turn pleaded not guilty and put himself upon his peers.[108]

For the first time in the reign, the earl marshal was not appointed high steward for the trial; Norfolk was still busy in the north. The duke of Suffolk was not summoned, and the two highest-ranking noblemen to take part in the trials were the marquess of Exeter and the 20-year-old Henry Grey, marquess of Dorset. Exeter was chosen as high steward, partly perhaps because of this seniority, but also in all likelihood because, although he had led a contingent against the rebels, he was known to be sympathetic to Mary's interests and could in this way be put under further pressure to demonstrate his loyalty to Henry VIII. Henry Clifford, earl of Cumberland, just elected a knight of the Garter in recognition of his services during the rebellion, attended this one trial out of the five to which he might have been called. George Talbot, earl of Shrewsbury, first in the field against the rebels the previous October, appeared as a lord trier for the first time since 1521. Henry Percy, earl of Northumberland, who had had to defend himself against suspicion of treason for allowing Aske the use of his castle at Wressle, was at Newington Green, near London, but seriously ill.[109] He was not called to sit on the trial panel; neither was Westmorland, Darcy's stepson. Lord Sandys, Darcy's brother-in-law, was away at Guisnes. Edward Seymour, viscount Beauchamp, and

[107] BL., Cotton Calig.B.I, f.341 (*LP*, xii(1), 1156), printed *The Priory of Hexham*, ed. J. Raine, Surtees Soc., 44, 46 for 1863, 1864 (Durham, 1864,1865), i, Appendix cvi.
[108] Records of both trials in KB/8/10/2 (*DKR*, iii, Appendix ii, pp. 247–9).
[109] *LP*, xii(1), 1062.

Thomas lord Cromwell took part in these trials, the first for which they were eligible. Cromwell, the most recently created baron, was last on the list of 21 lords triers and must have given his verdict first. According to lord La Warre he encouraged the hope that Darcy would escape with his life, even though the lords found him guilty, by promising them that he would do all he could to save both his life and his goods. After they had convicted Darcy (and Hussey), La Warre, Cobham and others visited Henry VIII at Hampton Court, presumably making their pleas directly to him.[110] Darcy sent a petition through Cromwell and Hussey also petitioned the king, but neither pleaded for his life.[111] Hussey before his trial had rejected Cromwell's offer to be 'good lorde unto me, and to be meane for me that I shulde have my pardon of my lyffe, landes and goodes' if he made a full statement of everything he knew; he had sworn then that he was no traitor – 'and that will I take my dethe uppon when it shall plese God and his highnes'.[112] The rest of those put to death for their part in the Lincolnshire rising had been executed in March 1537.[113] Hussey's excuse that he could not trust his men to oppose the rebels seemed to have been accepted. Whatever he had once intended, Hussey had much less to answer for than the northern barons – Scrope of Bolton as well as Latimer and Lumley – against whom no legal action was taken. But as Darcy's friend and Mary's former chamberlain his fate was sealed once the decision was taken to proceed against Darcy. Henry VIII ordered him to be executed in his home county in the presence of a number of gentlemen who were to be informed of the king's clemency in remitting the full penalty of hanging, drawing and quartering. Hussey was delivered to the duke of Suffolk and beheaded at Lincoln. Darcy was executed on Tower hill on 30 June. Northumberland's brother and heir, Sir Thomas Percy, and George Lumley, son and heir of lord Lumley, also found guilty of treason, were hanged at Tyburn.[114] Three baronies were eventually extinguished, therefore, and the earldom of Northumberland.

Darcy had focused his opposition on Cromwell, abusing him in the discussions at Doncaster in a manner he later regretted – since, after all, 'every man had a begynyng'.[115] During his interrogation he was said to have charged Cromwell to his face with being 'the verey

---

[110] SP1/138, f.211 (*LP*, xiii(2), 803).

[111] *LP*, xii(2), 1, 2.

[112] SP1/118, f.123 (*LP*, xii(1), 899).

[113] James, 'Obedience and dissent', 78n.

[114] *LP*, xii(2), 156, 228, App.31; Wriothesley, *Chronicle*, i, 64–5. All noblemen executed for treason during Henry VIII's reign were beheaded.

[115] SP1/111, ff.139–43 (*LP*, xi, 1086).

originall and chif causer of all thies rebellyon and myschif' and of 'the apprehension of us that be noble men', aiming 'to bryng us to our end and to strik of our heddes'.[116] After the executions Cromwell assured the English ambassador to Charles V that 'as ferr as we can perceyve all the cancered hertes be wyded awaye'.[117] Yet, in spite of its effect on public opinion at home as well as abroad, the struggle for power at court continued. The supporters of Mary had become a political faction, adhering to a cause which went beyond self-interest.[118] The stakes were high: for Catholic noblemen of royal descent survival itself. Henry Courtenay, marquess of Exeter, once the king's favourite, tried desperately to retain his favour in the early 1530s. In July 1531 Chapuys reported that he had been temporarily forbidden to appear at court, accused of recruiting men in Cornwall and neighbouring counties.[119] It was evidently at this time that Exeter was put out of the privy chamber – and according to his wife nothing grieved him so much in all his life.[120] Two months later Chapuys informed Charles V that one of Exeter's servants had been sent to the Tower for trying to persuade his fellows to rally to their master, saying he could not fail to be king of England in time.[121] The servant was William Kendall, who had apparently retained men for the marquess in order to support Exeter's father-in-law, lord Mountjoy, in a private dispute; another servant rashly tried to encourage recruitment by proclaiming that the marquess of Exeter was 'heyr apparent, and in case the king shuld dye or marye, the marquis shuld be king', foreseeing that 'if the king's grace marye my lady Anne there wolbe nede of suche good felowes'.[122] Henry Pole, lord Montagu, believed that his friend was hardly dealt with since he had 'a juste suytt depending in the lawe for that mater'.[123] Exeter was indeed vindicated in the courts in the cases he brought against one of the informers, Peter Coryngton or Coryton of South Newton in Cornwall. In the Easter term of 1534 he was awarded damages of £3,000 against Coryngton in king's bench for malicious words uttered at South Newton on 1 May 1530. Coryngton had publicly declared that 'the lord marques of Exeter hath onlaufully reteigned a gret nomber of men what so ever he meanyth therby'. Further, he had said to John Amadas and another of the king's

---

[116] E36/119, f.82 (*LP*, xii(1), 976).
[117] BL, Harl. 282, f.205 (*LP*, xii(2), 228).
[118] Ives, 'Faction at the court of Henry VIII', 180–1.
[119] *CSPSp*, iv(2), 765, where the marquess is wrongly identified as Dorset.
[120] SP1/138, f.210 (*LP*, xiii(2), 802).
[121] *CSPSp.*, iv(2), 788, where the marquess is again wrongly identified.
[122] SP1/140, ff.3–8 (*LP*, xiii(2), 961).
[123] SP1/138, ff.218–19 (*LP*, xiii(2), 804(6)).

servants that he would not be a servant to the marquess 'for he hath made to many ffrendys in this contre allredy howe so ever the worlde happyn and what chaunge so ever shall combe – and ye bothe be the kynges servauntes wherfor I charge you and requyre you informe the kynges grace and his counsell of this'. In consequence, Exeter declared, Henry VIII had conceived such suspicion of him that he could no longer enter the royal presence and for three months he had been shunned by the rest of the nobility. In an action of *scandalum magnatum* in common pleas Exeter cited a similar allegation of illegal retaining made by Coryngton at Launceston on 12 June 1530 and proved his case.[124] But Henry VIII's mistrust was not permanently allayed. According to Chapuys, Exeter was dismissed from the council in June 1536 for his support of Mary.[125] Although he was back in the council by October, and appointed to lead the west country men against the rebels, he was soon afterwards made to give up his office of constable of Windsor castle.[126] The signs of conflict at court naturally bred rumours and in mid-December 1536 a Somerset butcher related how the marquess had drawn a dagger on Cromwell who had then ordered him to the Tower; the butcher and his friends agreed that they would soon have had him out again, if it had indeed come to that.[127]

Exeter played his part in the condemnation of Darcy and Hussey, but in 1538 he himself was the prisoner, accused with lord Montagu of adhering to Cardinal Pole, seeking to deprive the king of his title of supreme head of the church and desiring his death.[128] The earliest evidence put in against Exeter referred to his saying, at his house in West Horsley, Surrey, on 24 July 1536, 'I lyke well the procedyng of the Cardynall Pole'. Then on 25 August he said to Montagu, knowing him to be a traitor: 'I trust ones to have a faire day upon these knaves which rule abowte the kyng; and I trust to se a mery woreld oone day.' The next year he suited the action to the words as he traitorously shook his clenched fist and looked forward to giving the knaves a 'buffett'. The evidence against Montagu was more extensive. All of it came from his younger brother, Sir Geoffrey Pole, who was also the witness to Exeter's approval of Cardinal Pole's doings. On 12 May 1535 at Lordington in Sussex Sir Geoffrey had heard Montagu say that he would rather he lived in the west country, 'for yn the west parties the lord marques of Excettor is strong'. He also lamented the

---

[124] KB27/1091, m.39; CP40/1077, m.504; *The Reports of Sir John Spelman*, ii, 245.
[125] *CSPSp.*, v(2), 70.
[126] See below, pp. 203, 234–5.
[127] *LP*, xii(2), 51.
[128] Records of both trials in KB8/11/2 (*DKR*, iii, Appendix ii, pp. 255–7).

death of his father-in-law, lord Bergavenny, 'for if he were alyve, he were abyll to make ten thowsand men'. In July 1537 Montagu declared that Darcy had 'playd the fowle, he went abowte to pluck awey the counsell, he shuld first have begonne with the hedd: but I beshrew hym for levyng of so sone'. Earlier in 1537 in London he had spoken of dreaming that Henry VIII was dead, and forecast that the king's leg would suddenly kill him one day, 'and then we shall have joly styrryng'.

Montagu was tried first, on 2 December. Although both Norfolk and Suffolk attended, neither was chosen as high steward: Suffolk was never selected for this duty, Norfolk never again after 1536. Henry VIII turned instead to the hierarchy of legal office. The lord chancellor, Sir Thomas Audley, who had presided over the trials of More and Fisher, among others, was created a baron and appointed high steward for both trials. The panel of peers numbered 27, over half the nobility. One more peer, who would have been the most junior – Walter lord Hungerford – was summoned, but was not present: his name was crossed off the list. John lord Mordaunt, as in 1534, was then the most junior baron since Cromwell, a more recent creation, sat in his precedence as lord privy seal below the two dukes. The 26 lords triers besides Cromwell were drawn in equal numbers from the higher nobility and the barons. The barons had been in a greater majority on all previous occasions except at Buckingham's trial, where the prior of St John of Jerusalem, like Cromwell, had just tipped the balance in their favour. The desire for a substantial number of high noblemen to try the marquess, as well as the west country connection, probably accounted for the presence of Henry Daubeney, promoted to the earldom of Bridgwater earlier in 1538, who as a baron had attended none of the previous trials. William FitzWilliam, earl of Southampton since October 1537, was also a lord trier. He and the bishop of Ely had interrogated Montagu's mother, the countess of Salisbury, before the trial, dealing with her, as they described it, 'sometyme with doulx and myld wordes, now roughly and asperly, by traytring her and her sonnes to the ixth degree'. She had then been removed from her home at Warblington in Hampshire to Southampton's house at Cowdray.[129] But the panel included some friends of the accused, including Charles Blount, lord Mountjoy, Exeter's brother-in-law, and the earl of Huntingdon, whose son and heir was married to Montagu's daughter. According to Sir Geoffrey Pole, Huntingdon as well as Montagu 'did always murmur and grudge' against the decisions of parliament,

[129] *Original Letters Illustrative of English History*, ed. Henry Ellis, 11 vols in 3 series (London, 1824–46), 2nd series, ii, 110–13; *LP*, xiii(2), 838.

castigating the 'knaves and heritickes that gave over' out of fear.[130] There had also been talk of 'a grete confederacy' between Exeter and Montagu and the lord chamberlain, Sandys, lord La Warre, and possibly the earl of Oxford.[131] Sandys and Oxford were on the trial panel, but La Warre came near to joining his friends as prisoner at the bar. He was said to have spoken openly against various statutes and to expect the punishment of God 'for the plucking down of abbeys and for reading off thies new Englisshe bookes.'[132] The privy council reported to Henry VIII on 1 December that 'as yet' they had found no sufficient cause to commit him to the Tower, warning of the effect on the king's reputation of an unjustified committal.[133] But the next day, the day of Montagu's trial, La Warre was sent to the Tower, presumably on Henry's order.[134] It was rumoured that La Warre was imprisoned because he had refused to be 'the fforeman off the quest to my lord Montagew'[135] – which would seem to refer to Montagu's indictment in Sussex on 30 November rather than to his trial, in spite of the coincidence of dates. Whatever the cause, he was released before Christmas.[136] After Montagu had been found guilty by his peers Exeter was tried on 3 December and also condemned. They were executed on Tower hill on 9 December.[137]

A few days later Hugh Latimer ended a letter to Cromwell with a note of congratulation: 'I herde you say wons, after you hade sene that furyows invectyve of Cardynall Pooll, that you wold make hym to ete his owne hartt, which you have now [I trow] browght to passe.'[138] The French ambassador remembered Henry VIII himself saying that he intended to exterminate the Pole family, which was of the white rose.[139] Anxiety for the succession had not been removed by the birth of Prince Edward. After the death of Jane Seymour there was a rumour that the baby had died too, and the king's death was widely reported at the end of 1537 and in the early months of 1538.[140] In

---

[130] SP1/138, ff.218–19 (*LP*, xiii(2), 804(6)).

[131] SP1/139, ff.25–8 (*LP*, xiii(2), 829).

[132] SP1/139, f.5 (*LP*, xiii(2), 821).

[133] *Original Letters*, 1st series, ii, 124–5.

[134] *The Lisle Letters*, v, 1299.

[135] SP1/140, f.107 (*LP*, xiii(2), 1062).

[136] See below, pp. 228–9.

[137] Wriothesley, *Chronicle*, i, 92. GEC mistakenly gives 9 January 1539 under Devon, Exeter and Montagu.

[138] BL, Cotton Cleo. E.IV, ff.320–3 (*LP*, xiii(2), 1036), printed *Three Chapters of Letters relating to the Suppression of the Monasteries*, ed. Thomas Wright, Camden Soc., xxvi (London, 1843), pp. 148–50.

[139] *LP*, xiii(2), 753.

[140] G. R. Elton, *Policy and Police. The Enforcement of the Reformation in the Age of Thomas Cromwell* (Cambridge, 1972), pp. 73–8.

December 1537 the abbot of Reading heard the alarming news that Henry VIII and the marquess of Exeter were both dead.[141] Exeter was undoubtedly seen as a possible successor by others besides his servants. His power in Devon and Cornwall made him a potential danger in the event of a Catholic invasion, a threat brought nearer by the truce agreed by Charles V and Francis I in June 1538. The destruction of Exeter and Montagu was the logical sequel to the defeat of the pilgrimage of grace, a pre-emptive strike against any challenge to the new regime from the southern half of the kingdom. It was completed by action against their families. In November 1538 Exeter's wife and 12-year-old son were imprisoned in the Tower, where Edward Courtenay remained until Mary's accession. Montagu's young son disappeared into the Tower and died there before the end of the reign of Henry VIII.[142] The countess of Salisbury was moved to the Tower in 1539 and beheaded in May 1541.

No trial had been accorded the countess. She had been convicted and attainted by act of parliament in 1539, with Exeter's widow and others who had never been brought to trial, Cardinal Pole and others who had been indicted but not tried, and Darcy, Hussey, Exeter, Montagu and others who had been convicted at common law and executed.[143] Attainder for treason, without trial, had not been used in Henry VIII's reign until early in 1534. Even then, Elizabeth Barton and those attainted with her had, the act declared, confessed their offences before the council.[144] But in each of the next six sessions of parliament prisoners who might have been produced in a court of law were attainted instead by statute.[145] At some stage Henry VIII sought reassurance from the judges on the legality of the procedure: could a man able to appear in person be attainted of high treason by parliament without being called to answer the charge? Sir Edward Coke recorded the answer of the judges as it had been relayed to him by Sir Thomas Gawdy. They had replied 'that it was a dangerous question, and that the high court of parliament ought to give examples to inferiour courts for proceeding according to justice, and no inferiour court could do the like; and they thought that the high court of parliament would never do it'. But finally, at the king's command and

---

[141] *LP*, xii(2), 1205.

[142] He was still alive in September 1542, but probably died soon after.

[143] House of Lords, Original Acts, 31 Henry VIII, no. 15. The marchioness of Exeter was not put to death; her attainder was reversed after Mary's accession.

[144] S. E. Lehmberg, 'Parliamentary attainder in the reign of Henry VIII', *HJ*, xviii (1975), 681–3; 25 Henry VIII, c.12.

[145] The statutes are discussed by Lehmberg, 'Parliamentary attainder', 680, 685–97.

pressed by the earl of Essex to give a direct answer, they had said 'that if he be attainted by parliament, it could not come in question afterward, whether he were called or not called to answer'. Coke noted that the judges were right – the act of attainder passed by parliament against the man was never challenged – and that the next victim was the earl of Essex himself.[146] The notion that parliament 'would never do it' conflicts with the date implied by the rest of Coke's account, which must be 1540, when the difficulty foreseen by Cromwell in convicting Giles Heron of treason in a court of law was circumvented by introducing a bill of attainder against him in parliament.[147] It passed both houses by 10 May, the day before parliament was prorogued for a fortnight.[148] The next person to be attainted by parliament was Thomas Cromwell, earl of Essex.

He had been caught in the same trap as Wolsey. To help the king to escape from his marriage would be to free him to marry a niece of the duke of Norfolk. After years of enforced semi-retirement Norfolk had moved on to the offensive in 1539 and again, more decisively, in February 1540, when he saw an opportunity to use the religious unrest in Calais to engineer Cromwell's fall on a charge of heresy.[149] During the parliamentary recess Cromwell realized that the trap was closing and lashed out in a counter-attack, bringing down viscount Lisle, the deputy of Calais, arrested on 19 May as a confederate of Cardinal Pole.[150] But on 10 June he himself was arrested in the council chamber at Westminster. Henry VIII at once sent to inform the French ambassador that Cromwell had plotted to force the new religious doctrines on him. On the same day the council elaborated the charge in a common letter to the English ambassadors to Francis I, Charles V and the duke of Cleves: Cromwell had not only secretly opposed the king's policy in religion but had 'most traitorously' threatened to defend his own opinions with force of arms.[151] Allegations of heresy may have served, therefore, to persuade Henry VIII to order Cromwell's arrest, but from the start it was clear that treason was also imputed. Indeed, it was for treason that he was arrested. Cromwell appealed to the privy councillors present to search their consciences as to whether he was in truth a traitor. Unmoved, Norfolk and Southampton stripped him of his Garter and he was led prisoner to the

---

[146] Sir Edward Coke, *The Fourth Part of the Institutes of the Laws of England*, 5th edn (London, 1671), pp. 37–8.
[147] Elton, *Policy and Police*, p. 308.
[148] *LJ*, i, 136.
[149] *The Lisle Letters*, vi, pp. 215, 227–31.
[150] *LP*, xv, 697.
[151] ibid., 766; *SP*, viii, 349–50.

Tower.[152] When he obeyed the king's order to write 'suche thinges as I thought mete', Cromwell concentrated on the Cleves marriage and the question of treason: 'Sholde any faccyon or any affeccyon to any poynt make me a traytor to your mageste, then all the devylles in hell conffounde me'; truly, 'I never thought treson to your highnes, your realme, or posteryte, so God helpe me, ayther in woorde or dede'.[153] But both heresy and treason were laid to his charge.

Given the recent precedents for parliamentary attainder it was almost inevitable that Cromwell would be denied trial by his peers. The number of noblemen involved was nevertheless substantial: as many peers gave their voices against him in the house of lords as were likely to have been summoned to a trial. The difference was that they condemned him without hearing either him or the witnesses against him. The bill was introduced in the house of lords on 17 June and was passed two days later, *nemine discrepante*, with 30 lay peers present. Of the high nobility, 12 were there – including Norfolk and Southampton, now lord privy seal in place of Cromwell – and four absent. Sussex, the only one of the four who was a privy councillor, was seeing to affairs at Calais. Huntingdon and Worcester were absent throughout the session, but Derby, otherwise a regular attender, was not there to give his assent to this bill. Neither was Sandys, the only baron who was a member of the privy council: he had gone to his post at Guisnes. On 29 June 24 lay peers were present to give their assent to a new bill sent up from the commons to replace the original text.[154] The redrafting was probably decided upon to incorporate extra points in the bill: it clearly made no difference to its effect.[155] In the form of a petition from lords and commons, the final text of the bill listed the charges against Cromwell, as in an indictment. They were said to be based on the depositions of a large number of witnesses – not named, but described as 'personages of great honour, worship and discrecion' – which proved him 'the moost false and corrupte traytor, deceyvor and circumventor ayenst youre moost royall persone and th' emperiall crowne of this youre realme that hathe bene knowen, seen or hard of in all the tyme of youre moost noble reigne'. Among the charges were allegations that, being a person of as low degree 'as fewe be' in the realm, he pretended to have such a 'stroke' about the king as to be 'sure of you', and, being 'a detestable heretyke', he found no fault in

[152] *LP*, xv, 770, 804; *LJ*, i, 143.

[153] *Original Letters*, 2nd series, ii, 162–9.

[154] *LJ*, i, 145–6, 149. The two archbishops and 14 of the bishops were marked as present on 19 and 29 June; presumably they also voted for the bills.

[155] The bill is discussed by G. R. Elton, 'Thomas Cromwell's decline and fall', *Cambridge HJ*, x (1951), 177–82.

books undermining faith in the sacrament of the altar, saying that 'yt was as leefull for every Christen man to be a mynyster of the saide sacrament as well as a preest'. But only two of the alleged offences were pinned down to specific dates. On 31 March 1539 he refused to condemn the preaching of such as Robert Barnes, saying that 'yf the kyng wolde turne frome yt, yet I wolde not turne', holding up his arm as if he held a sword while he affirmed his intention to fight in its defence, and on 31 January 1540, being reminded of other noblemen guilty of treason, he traitorously declared that 'yf the lordes wolde handle hym so, that he wolde gyve them suche a brekefaste as never was made in Englonde'. For these and other misdeeds 'overlonge here to be rehersed', it was enacted that Thomas Cromwell, earl of Essex, should be 'convycted and atteynted of herysie and high treason'.[156] Three days later the house of lords moved to another attainder bill, to convict a vicar of Bradford, Wiltshire, for calling Henry VIII a heretic at the time of the pilgrimage of grace, and Walter lord Hungerford for nevertheless taking him into his service as a chaplain for three months, for getting others to 'coniure' in order to discover how long the king would live, and for buggery. The bill was passed by the lords without dissent on 14 July, when 18 lay peers were present, and was returned, approved by the commons, two days later.[157] The lords turned next to a bill to attaint Arthur Plantagenet, viscount Lisle, and others. It was read for the first time on 17 July, again on 19 July and then once more on 21 July – with Lisle's name removed.[158] The king had decided to spare his elderly uncle, although Lisle remained in the Tower. At the dissolution of parliament on 24 July Henry VIII gave his assent to all the bills of attainder and the bill to annul his marriage with Anne of Cleves. Four days later Cromwell and Hungerford were executed on Tower hill.[159] Henry VIII and Katherine Howard were married the same day at Oatlands.[160]

Before the end of 1541 Katherine Howard's disgrace, swiftly followed by the arrest of Norfolk's stepmother, his half-brother William and his wife, and his half-sister the countess of Bridgwater, had brought Norfolk into 'the grettest perplexite that ever poure wretche was in', as he confided to the king, begging him to continue his 'gode and gracious lord'.[161] Norfolk survived, seemingly unscathed. But in the

---

[156] House of Lords, Original Acts, 32 Henry VIII, no. 52. Text printed, from the parliament roll, Burnet, *History of the Reformation*, iv, 415–23.

[157] *LJ*, i, 150, 155–6, 157; House of Lords, Original Acts, 32 Henry VIII, no. 72.

[158] *LJ*, i, 158–9.

[159] Wriothesley, *Chronicle*, i, 120.

[160] *DKR*, iii, Appendix ii, p. 264.

[161] *SP*, i, 721.

last weeks of Henry VIII's reign, when the struggle for power after
the king's death reached its climax, the duke's destruction was crucial
to the success of the faction led by Edward Seymour, earl of Hertford.[162] It was achieved by means of an attack on his son, Sir Henry
Howard, styled earl of Surrey. Richard Devereux, son of lord Ferrers,
hinted in the summer of 1546 at a move to abate Surrey's pride: Henry
VIII would be informed that he had called Norfolk the most suitable
man to govern Prince Edward if the king should die. Surrey was
detained early in December and depositions were taken alleging this
and other indiscreet remarks as well as the use of the arms of Edward
the Confessor.[163] Norfolk was arrested when he arrived in London on
12 December and deprived of his staff of office and his Garter. Father
and son were then sent separately to the Tower.[164] Norfolk wrote to
the king protesting that he could no more guess the charge against him
than a new-born baby. Nevertheless, to recover Henry's favour he put
all his lands and goods at the king's disposal.[165] He was examined by
William Paulet, lord St John, and Sir William Paget, but remained, it
seems, in doubt as to the charge, writing afterwards to the council: 'I
thynk seuerly ther is som fals men that have layd som gret cause to my
charge . . . humble I beseche you to fynd the meanys, if they and I may
not be broght fase to fase, yet let me be made prevy what the causes
ar.' He added that he had had great enemies throughout his life. The
duke of Buckingham had hated him above all men. Cardinal Wolsey
had confessed to him at Esher that he had tried for 14 years to destroy
him at the instigation of Suffolk, Exeter and Sandys, who warned
Wolsey that Norfolk would 'undo' him if he were not put out of the
way. Cromwell in 1538 had examined the marchioness of Exeter 'more
streitle' about him than about any other man, as she had sent word to
him through her brother, lord Mountjoy. The malice towards him of
his two nieces whom it had pleased Henry VIII to marry was well
known. Yet 'who tried out the falshod of the lord Darcy' and others,
'but only I? . . . Who can thynk that I, havyng be[en] so long a trew
man, shuld now be fals to his maieste?'[166]

He was not left in suspense for long. On 7 January 1547 an
indictment was found against Surrey alleging infringement of the act
of succession of 1536 by his use of the king's arms with his own on 7

[162] Miller, 'Henry VIII's unwritten will', pp. 87–105.

[163] *LP*, xxi(2), 555.

[164] *CSPSp.*, viii, 364.

[165] Edward lord Herbert of Cherbury, *The Life and Reign of King Henry the Eighth*
(London, 1672), pp. 629–30.

[166] BL, Cotton Titus B.I, ff.99–101 (*LP*, xxi(2), 554), printed Burnet, *History of the
Reformation*, vi, 274–8.

October 1546 at his father's house at Kenninghall. He was found guilty at his trial on 13 January.[167] Norfolk had the previous day confessed to high treason in concealing his son's use of the royal arms and in having himself, since the death of his father, borne in the first quarter of his coat of arms the arms of England with a difference which pertained only to Prince Edward. 'Without compulsion, without force, without advice or counsel', Norfolk signed his confession in the presence of Chancellor Wriothesley, St John, Hertford, Lisle and others.[168] Surrey was executed on 19 January. A bill in the form of a petition to attaint both him and his father received its second reading that day in the upper house. The lords passed it on 20 January, when 21 lay peers were present, and received the bill back from the commons four days later. It referred to Norfolk's confession to the charge contained in Surrey's indictment and attainted both men for their acts committed on 7 October 1546. On 27 January the chancellor informed parliament that Henry VIII – too ill to attend in person – had appointed commissioners to give his assent to this one bill. The commission was read and the royal assent pronounced.[169] Whether or not Henry VIII really authorized the action taken in his name the day before he died, he had earlier read and amended a paper on the legal implications of the use by a subject of the arms of England in the first quarter – the crime to which Norfolk confessed.[170] The king's death made the duke's execution unnecessary since it removed any chance of a royal pardon. Norfolk, like some earlier victims of parliamentary attainder, was allowed to live, albeit a prisoner in the Tower.

Although after the trials of Exeter and Montagu no nobleman was tried for treason, the court of the high steward was convened once more during the reign of Henry VIII, to try a case of felony. Thomas Fiennes, lord Dacre of the south, a young man in his twenties, was indicted in 1541 for his part in the murder of a gamekeeper fatally wounded in the course of an illegal hunting expedition. Lord Audley of Walden was again appointed high steward, as in 1538, and 17 peers were impanelled to try Dacre on 17 June.[171] There were lengthy discussions before the trial, as Sir William Paget recounted in a letter to Sir Thomas Wriothesley. Audley, with Sussex, Hertford, Russell and St John – all lords triers – and the attorney-general, Sir John Baker, conferred in the star chamber about the case. They 'made gret

[167] *DKR*, iii, Appendix ii, pp. 267–8.
[168] Herbert, *Henry the Eighth*, pp. 631–3.
[169] *LJ*, i, 285–7, 289–90; House of Lords, Original Acts, 37 Henry VIII, no. 32.
[170] *SP*, i, 891–2.
[171] Records of the trial in KB8/12 (*DKR*, iii, Appendix ii, pp. 259–60).

conscience' over finding Dacre guilty of murder, sending two or three times for the indictment, and trying to discern instead 'sum meanes to induce hym to confesse'. Paget himself later heard all 17 peers discussing the points at issue with the chief justices and others of the king's learned counsel, 'and albeit I was excluded yet they spake so lowde, sum of them, that I myght here them notwithstanding two doores shut betwene us. Among the rest that could not agre to wilful murdre, the lord Cobham, as I tooke hym by his voyce, was very vehement and stiff. Sodenly and softlye they agreed, I wot not how, and departed to the kinges bench togeders.' Dacre at first pleaded not guilty, declaring 'with long circumstances' that he had intended no murder, but – after hearing that his companions had already confessed – he changed his plea to guilty, which Paget reckoned 'he did not without sum insinuacion'. The same day, after dinner, the council attended upon Henry VIII to declare Dacre's humble submission, 'hoping therby to move his majesty to pardone hym'. Henry refused.[172] Dacre was hanged at Tyburn two days later.[173]

The French and imperial ambassadors both commented on the shameful death of a young nobleman of high birth and great riches.[174] Although the barony came to an end, the king's lawyers soon advised that the lands were entailed and ought not to be forfeited, so that Henry VIII would only have the profit from them until Dacre's baby son came of age.[175] The king was forced to accept that Dacre had had no more than a life interest in his lands and the whole estate, valued at £1,000 p.a. or more, came into the temporary possession of the court of wards.[176] The ambassadors perhaps saw a sinister connection between Dacre's wealth and his execution, but, whatever Henry VIII's motive in resisting the appeal to clemency, justice was done: Dacre was an accessory to murder, whether or not he had intended it. Harsh though his fate was and dubious the pressure put upon him to confess, Dacre was condemned by due process for a crime he had in fact committed. Of none of the other nobles could a similar claim be made without reservation. The three noblemen and two women convicted by act of parliament were denied due process of the law. The six noblemen and one woman found guilty of treason by the court of the high steward were the victims of political trials, where reasons of state were more compelling than the right of the accused to impartial justice. If Henry VIII himself believed their removal necessary, that was enough, it

---

[172] SP1/166, ff.73–4 (*LP*, xvi, 932).
[173] Wriothesley, *Chronicle*, i, 126.
[174] *LP*, xvi, 941; *CSPSp.*, vi(1), 168.
[175] *LP*, xvi, 978.
[176] WARD 9/148 and 152 (entered each time under Sussex, 37 Henry VIII).

seems, not only for the king but for everyone called to participate in their conviction. The precedent set in the first weeks of the reign held good to the very end. Empson and Dudley were condemned for crimes of which they were innocent because their death suited both the king's purposes and the needs of their enemies. Henry VIII all his life remained vulnerable to manipulation where his own interests were at stake. For some noblemen the chance to condemn a rival might be welcomed, even sought after; for others it meant the sacrifice of a friend. Yet there was no easy alternative to collaboration when the king was personally involved in the case. The law of the kingdom was the king's law, responsive to his wishes, as the common lawyers themselves recognized.[177] The noblemen called to pass judgment on their peers in the court of the high steward or in parliament showed that they understood that fact, and accepted it.

Their compliance set the pattern of the relationship of the nobility to Henry VIII. The king's right to create peers was matched by his power, in practice, to destroy them. Henry's reputation suffered in the process: each execution increased the toll of lives claimed by his regime. His own interests were often served in the short term only. He himself might even come to regret the bloody solution to an immediate problem. Yet, his mind made up, perhaps by factional pressure, his will prevailed. Service on a trial panel inexorably tested the 'affections' of the noblemen selected. Jurymen of lesser status might be punished in Tudor England for reaching verdicts deemed to be perverse. No retribution was visited on the noblemen who acquitted lord Dacre of the north, but it was made quite clear after the event that their judgment was displeasing to the king, even though his own security had not been at risk. To have returned a verdict of not guilty on the duke of Buckingham, Anne Boleyn or her brother, Darcy or Hussey, Exeter or Montagu would have called for an independence of mind hardly to be expected of the nobility. Even in the house of lords, where the members gave their voices individually, as in a trial by peers, it was not the practice to vote against a major government bill.[178] Not one nobleman, it seems, dared to raise the question of the legality of proceeding by act of parliament against an alleged traitor untried at common law. The series of treason trials and acts of attainder revealed the actual balance of power within the kingdom by asserting the personal authority of Henry VIII over the nobility.

---

[177] Ives, *The Common Lawyers of Pre-Reformation England*, pp. 193, 222–4.
[178] See below, pp. 123–4.

PART II

The Nobility's Service

CHAPTER 3

Attendance at Court

The Tudor court was the centre of political life, 'the true seat of power, profit and policy'.[1] It existed wherever the king happened to be and naturally reflected his style of kingship. Henry VIII was concerned to show that his accession marked a new beginning, signalled by the arrest of Empson and Dudley. Everyone at court had to reassess their own position. Lord Darcy, vice-chamberlain to Henry VII, was sufficiently confident of his influence with the young king to promise Dudley's friends that he would obtain a pardon for him if they gave him £300. Edmund Dudley himself remitted £100 which Darcy owed him and Richard Dudley handed over £100 and a bond for the remaining £100; somewhat insensitively, Darcy started an action of debt on the bond after Dudley's execution.[2] Darcy overestimated his powers of persuasion in this instance, but he was right to count himself among those in whom Henry VIII trusted at the start of his reign. Although he was the only nobleman to be removed from office at court in 1509, he was appointed to an exceptionally wide range of offices in Yorkshire and the far north.[3] He still reckoned himself high in the king's favour along with Surrey and Shrewsbury, Henry Marney (the new vice-chamberlain) and Charles Brandon.[4] But, away from the court, his influence eventually faded.

Darcy did not help his cause by refusing in 1511 to reside on the border rather than at home in Yorkshire. Nevertheless, he blamed Wolsey for his political decline, just as he later ascribed to Cromwell a

---

[1] G. R. Elton, 'Tudor government: the points of contact, iii. The court', *TRHS*, 5th series, 26 (1976), 228.
[2] C1/303/62.
[3] See below, pp. 187, 201.
[4] *LP*, i(1), 157.

determination to destroy the nobility.[5] Although himself a peer by creation, he shared the simple interpretation of their misfortunes favoured by noblemen of ancient lineage such as Buckingham. There is no doubt that Darcy's career, as other careers, waned and waxed with the rise and fall of the two chief ministers. Wolsey and Cromwell each tried to control or repress all potential rivals, whatever their rank. But no more than Henry VIII did they follow a policy against the nobility as such.[6] Often it was in their interest to be obliging, for example when Wolsey supported Suffolk in the crisis following his marriage in 1515 and Cromwell helped Norfolk to obtain monastic lands in 1537.[7] Such actions secured an ally, if only temporarily, and made manifest the power of the minister. Cromwell indeed clearly indicated his wish to be the sole mediator between a nobleman and Henry VIII.[8] Norfolk, for one, was prepared to accept this condition in his pursuit of land. Expressions of loyalty flowed freely from even the highest noblemen. Suffolk in 1518 assured Wolsey that, next to the king, he bore him 'a trewe herte planted and sett withowt dissimulacion, crafft or untrowthe'.[9] Norfolk sent Cromwell 'a myllion of thankes' in 1536 for the pains he had taken on his behalf and the next year bound himself 'by this my writyng duryng my liff to be your poure assewred frend'.[10] The writers may even have meant what they said – at the time. Yet their subservience was itself a cause of resentment. Ambitious noblemen moved in for the kill when the ministers lost the king's confidence: Wolsey as well as Cromwell was brought down by a coalition of peers.[11] In the last analysis, it was only the relationship with Henry VIII which mattered.

The court was the forum for the power struggle. As John Husee described it in the 1530s it was a 'quesy' world, 'unstable', 'besy'. 'It is hard trustying this wyllye worlde', he sighed; 'every man here is ffor himsylff.'[12] The conventional criticisms of court life ring true enough, even if genuine political issues were also at stake. Yet the court at the same time acted as an image of unity expressed through ceremonial. The king's daily life was itself an aspect of government projecting his

---

[5] See above, pp. 63–4 and below, p. 188.

[6] The argument is developed in G. W. Bernard, *The Power of the Early Tudor Nobility. A Study of the Fourth and Fifth Earls of Shrewsbury* (Brighton, 1985), pp. 199–208.

[7] See below, pp. 213, 231–2, 237.

[8] *The Lisle Letters*, ii, 375.

[9] SP1/232, f.81 (*LP, Addenda*, i, 216).

[10] SP1/106, f.183, SP1/121, f.131 (*LP*, xi, 470, xii(2), 101).

[11] J. A. Guy, *The Public Career of Sir Thomas More* (Brighton, 1980), pp. 31–2, 98.

[12] SP3/5, f.3, SP3/4, f.101, SP1/240, ff.38–9, 144, 195 (*LP*, vii, 1581, viii, 178, *Addenda*, i, 1090, 1116, 1144), printed *The Lisle Letters*, ii, 298, 323, iii, 753a, 776, 792.

power in the ways which appealed most to him. Henry VII by choice had kept his distance from his courtiers and never attended court entertainments except as a spectator. Henry VIII led the jousts and revels.[13] His most intimate friends among the nobility in his early years were to be found in the select band who shared these pastimes with him. Henry Bourchier, earl of Essex, captain of the spears, in his forties, was the oldest in the group, which included Thomas Grey, marquess of Dorset, George Nevill, lord Bergavenny, Robert Radcliffe, lord FitzWalter, George lord Hastings and Walter Devereux, lord Ferrers, who was still under age at Henry VIII's accession. Other close companions of the king were three men whom he soon ennobled – Charles Brandon, Henry Stafford and the younger Thomas Howard – and Sir Thomas Boleyn, to be created a viscount in 1525.[14] The familiar relationship with Henry was the foundation on which they built their lives. They needed the king, but he needed them too, or others ready to fill their role. His splendour could not be adequately portrayed without the demonstration of courtly and martial skills.

The early Henrician tournaments and spectacles fed the king's desire for reputation. The birth of his longed-for son on 1 January 1511 was celebrated in February by a magnificent court festival at Westminster. Henry VIII led the challengers at the tilt and Charles Brandon the answerers; Dorset, Wiltshire, Howard and Boleyn all took part. A banquet followed in the White hall, to which foreign ambassadors had been invited. The king's clothes were decorated with pieces of gold in the shape of the letters H and K, many of which were lost when Henry, having arranged for the ambassadors to pluck them from him as a gesture of liberality, found himself under general attack.[15] (Sadly, before the end of the month the revellers were to parade as mourners at the prince's funeral.)[16] Such entertainments, with the young king at the centre of the action, were resounding triumphs, acclaimed by foreign observers and remembered for generations.[17] Some noblemen took part year after year. Suffolk and Essex were the challengers with Henry VIII at the jousts of honour for the visit of the king's sister, the queen of Scots, in 1516; Henry VIII led the challengers again in June 1517, when there were a number of foreign ambassadors at court, and Suffolk the answerers, supported by

[13] David Starkey, 'From feud to faction: English politics circa 1450–1550', *History Today*, xxxii (1982), 17–18.

[14] *LP*, ii(2), pp. 1490–1510.

[15] Sydney Anglo, *The Great Tournament Roll of Westminster* (Oxford, 1968), pp. 51–8, 83–107, 112–15.

[16] *LP*, i(1), 707.

[17] Anglo, *Tournament Roll*, pp. 15–18.

Dorset, Essex and Surrey.[18] At the field of cloth of gold the feats of arms were dominated by Suffolk, Dorset and Henry Courtenay, earl of Devon, now in his early twenties. When Charles V visited England in 1522 it was again Suffolk, Dorset and Devon who led the jousting. Two years later Suffolk almost killed the king in a tilt, when Henry forgot to close his visor, and swore·he would never run against him again. Dorset was perhaps more to blame since he had handed the king his weapon before he was ready to use it in comparative safety, but Henry was magnanimous about the whole incident.[19] The following Christmas he and Suffolk once more led the feats of arms, this time with Devon, Thomas Manners, lord Ros, and Henry Pole, styled lord Montagu, who had been part of the royal household since the beginning of the reign.[20] Henry VIII continued to joust for a few more years, but less and less frequently. Although a tournament was held in November 1527 to entertain ambassadors from France, he contented himself with arranging for the performance of a Latin play, to include such characters as *Ecclesia* and *Veritas* ranged against False Interpretation, *Corruptio Scriptoris* and the heretic Luther with his wife 'lyke a frowe of Spyers in Almayn, in red sylke'.[21] By the end of the 1520s court festivals were past their peak, mere shadows of their former glory.[22]

The jousters and revellers also provided the attendance at other court occasions, together with some of the less physically active peers. Thomas Howard, duke of Norfolk, too old for jousting, was present at three of the major, though still intimate ceremonies of the early years: the reception of a cap and sword sent to Henry VIII by the pope and the proxy marriage of the king's sister to Louis XII of France in 1514 and the christening of Princess Mary in February 1516.[23] The duke of Buckingham, by contrast, attended only the proxy marriage. He visited Henry VIII at other times but was evidently not particularly anxious to come to court. When Henry appointed him to be an answerer in the May day jousts he wrote to Wolsey from Thornbury declaring that he could rather go to Rome than run against the king, although he was ready to take part on Henry's side.[24] Worcester, the king's chamberlain, and Shrewsbury, the lord steward, were present at both the proxy marriage and the christening; Thomas Stanley, earl of

---

[18] *LP*, ii(2), p. 1507; *Hall's Chronicle*, pp. 591–2.

[19] *Hall's Chronicle*, pp. 611–18, 635, 674.

[20] Anglo, *Tournament Roll*, p. 71.

[21] Sydney Anglo, *Spectacle, Pageantry and Early Tudor Policy* (Oxford, 1969), pp. 232–3.

[22] Anglo, *Tournament Roll*, p. 73.

[23] *LP*, i(2), 2929ii, 3146, ii(1), 1573. There is no record of the full attendance at the christening of Prince Henry in 1511.

[24] *Original Letters*, 3rd series, i, 214–18.

Derby, attended only the christening. The rest of the high noblemen and the barons, apart from those involved in the disguisings and pageants, attended none of the three ceremonies. Henry VIII sometimes complained that Wolsey was better attended than he was himself. Indeed, more noblemen turned out for the reception of the cardinal's hat in November 1515 than for the arrival of the papal cap and sword.[25] However, Wolsey's readiness to take young noblemen or heirs to titles into his house might also swell the numbers at court. Henry Percy, eldest son of the earl of Northumberland, was one of Wolsey's household in the early 1520s when he visited the court and fell in love with Anne Boleyn. As recounted by Cavendish, when the attachment was discovered he claimed that he had 'gone so far before so many worthy witnesses that I know not how to avoid myself nor to discharge my conscience' – a difficulty which Wolsey quickly resolved by calling Northumberland to London to put an end to the affair.[26]

Some noblemen were catered for at court besides those with household appointments, but the privilege seems to have been confined to a small circle of the king's close friends. In October 1519 daily liveries were assigned to Worcester and Shrewsbury and to Mountjoy, the queen's chamberlain, and also to the dukes of Norfolk and Suffolk, the marquess of Dorset, the earls of Surrey and Devon, and lords Hastings and Bergavenny; in November lord Ferrers was added to the list.[27] Norfolk was lord treasurer, but the others were not at this time holders of high office in either the household or the administration. Friendships were fragile and even these noblemen could be out of court and out of favour, but throughout the first half of the reign the continuity of service was striking. Early in 1526 the noblemen lodged at court, besides the lord steward and the chamberlains, were the former earl of Surrey, now duke of Norfolk, the duke of Suffolk, the marquesses of Dorset and Exeter (the former earl of Devon), with the earl of Rutland (formerly lord Ros) and lord Sandys, soon to be appointed deputy to Worcester, the king's chamberlain.[28] When Wolsey was away in France in July 1527 Sir William FitzWilliam reported that Henry VIII was keeping 'a verrey greate and a chargeable house' at Beaulieu in Essex. Lodged there with him were Norfolk and his wife, Suffolk, Exeter, Essex, Rutland and the earl of Oxford (a leading landowner in the county), with viscount FitzWalter and Thomas Boleyn, viscount

[25] LP, ii(1), 1153.

[26] Two Early Tudor Lives: The Life and Death of Cardinal Wolsey by George Cavendish, The Life of Sir Thomas More by William Roper, ed. Richard S. Sylvester and Davis P. Harding (New Haven, Conn., and London, 1962), pp. 32–6.

[27] LP, iii(1), 491, 528.

[28] LP, iv(1), 1939(6).

Rochford.[29] Yet two comparable lists of those assigned lodgings at court in the 1540s show no group of king's friends. All the noblemen then fed at court held high office except Henry's brothers-in-law, Hertford (on the first list) and William Parr, the new earl of Essex (on the second).[30] The development was due largely to Henry VIII's promotion of his friends, but the shift to an overwhelmingly official presence at court also reflected the change in the king's lifestyle. Ill and rapidly ageing, he preferred the company of men whom he had known from his youth, such as the lord privy seal, Russell, noted by the Venetian ambassador in 1545 as one of his closest companions.[31] The opportunities for advancement offered by the court diversions of earlier years died a natural death.

But Henry VIII always needed men to attend upon him. Russell himself had come to his notice through service as a gentleman usher of the king's chamber.[32] Noblemen by inheritance might achieve the same end by similar means. Thomas Manners, lord Ros, early in his career was a cupbearer, one of those on duty at Christmas 1521 to serve the king in his privy chamber under the direction of the gentlemen ushers, or elsewhere as ordered by the lord chamberlain or vice-chamberlain.[33] The king's chamber regularly included a few noblemen. Men came from all over the kingdom to staff it and a book – the writing now badly faded – recorded the names 'of the kynges servauntes of the shyres of England sworne to the kyng by th'erle of Worcester lord chamberleyn'.[34] The noblemen whose names are legible mostly served as cupbearers. They included, besides Ros (entered under the county of Surrey), lord Daubeney (Middlesex), lord Clifford (listed under Northumberland and Yorkshire) and John lord Lumley (Yorkshire). Lord Grey of Powis, from North Wales, was the only nobleman down as a sewer. Ralph Neville, earl of Westmorland, was named in a list of knights with the annotation, 'sworne the kynges servaunt'. He, Daubeney, Lumley and Grey of Powis had all succeeded to their titles as minors, Ros to his shortly after coming of age; Clifford was brought up at court during his father's lifetime. Service in the king's chamber was a fitting start to the career of a

[29] SP1/42, f.255 (*LP*, iv(1), 3318).

[30] 'Excerpts from the manuscript of William Dunche, no. 3', ed. A. G. W. Murray and E. F. Bosenquet, *The Genealogist*, new series, xxx (1914), 18–19, 23 (headed 31 Henry VIII, but dating from after Cromwell's fall); BL, Lansdowne 2, ff.34–5 (*LP*, xx(2), App.2).

[31] *CSPVen.*, vi(3), App.118.

[32] *HMC, Various Collections*, ii, 307.

[33] College of Arms, M.8, f.1. Also BL, Add. 21,116, f.1 (*LP*, iii(2), 1899).

[34] E36/130, ff.165–227 (*LP*, iii(1), 578).

young nobleman, even for an heir to a great title: Henry FitzAlan, son to the earl of Arundel, was taken on as a page of honour when he begged Henry VIII to accept his 'younge and grene habilitye of service'.[35] Such attendance could be advantageous to the father as well. Arundel himself very rarely appeared at court; Shrewsbury was equally reluctant to reside there, in spite of holding high office in the household, and in 1523 put pressure on his heir to move to court after his marriage.[36] In 1540 or 1541 Norfolk's son, styled earl of Surrey, and Huntingdon's son were cupbearers and Cumberland's son was a carver to the king. By the mid-1540s the last two had succeeded to their earldoms and no longer served at court, but Surrey was still a cupbearer and Edward lord Clinton – who had been a royal ward but was then in his early thirties – was a carver.[37] These appointments kept noblemen in touch with Henry VIII: the carver, sewer and cupbearer selected to attend upon him sat at the end of his table.[38] Yet they gave no independent right of access to the king.

The lord chamberlain in the fifteenth century had been in charge of both the public ceremonial of the court and the king's private service, but from the 1490s the privy chamber began to acquire its own staff and its own head officer, the groom of the stool. By 1520 the development was complete and the privy chamber was almost independent of the chamber, which retained only the public ceremonial. The gentlemen of the privy chamber – instituted in 1518 in imitation of the French court – attended to the king's personal needs throughout the day and guarded him at night.[39] This small group of body servants surrounding the king had continuous access to him and, with access, near certainty of influence. They were mostly recruited from gentry families, but Henry VIII liked to have one or two noblemen at their head. His cousin, Henry Courtenay, earl of Devon, was one of the privy chamber by July 1520.[40] Thomas Grey, marquess of Dorset, was admitted to membership in 1523 as he was about to go north to lead an army against the Scots. He thanked the king in extravagant terms for choosing to admit him 'at my departing from your grace'; 'it was more

[35] 'The life of Henrye FitzAllen, last earle of Arundell of that name', [ed. J. G. Nichols], *The Gentleman's Magazine*, ciii, pt 2 (1833), 12.

[36] *LP*, iii(2), 3604.

[37] As n. 30 above.

[38] BL, Add. 21,116, f.7v.

[39] David R. Starkey, 'Representation through intimacy: a study in the symbolism of monarchy and court office in early modern England' in *Symbols and Sentiments. Cross-Cultural Studies in Symbolism*, ed. Ioan Lewis (London, 1977), pp. 197, 203–4.

[40] *LP*, iii(1), 894, 901. Dr Starkey has kindly given me a list of all the upper servants of the privy chamber, to which this paragraph is much indebted.

to my comfort then [if] your grace had geven me either fee, lande, gold or silver.'[41] The timing of his appointment illustrates the wider significance of the privy chamber. Dorset was admitted at the very moment when he could not actually attend upon Henry, but when his membership would usefully augment his authority by giving him the special status of an intimate royal servant, with something of the charisma of the king himself.[42] He did not keep the appointment long. The Eltham ordinances of January 1526 insisted that in future only 15 named men should be admitted to the privy chamber: Henry Courtenay, now marquess of Exeter, 'who is the king's neer kinsman, and hath been brought up of a childe with his grace in his chamber', six gentlemen of the privy chamber, who included Sir John Russell, two gentlemen ushers, four grooms, a barber and a page.[43] Sir George Boleyn was a gentleman of the privy chamber by the end of the decade.[44] The number of gentlemen had doubled by then and in the early 1530s they were divided into two teams of six, to serve alternately, one under the marquess of Exeter, the other under George Boleyn, lord Rochford, 'so that the kinges highnes shall never be unpurvaide of syx gentlemen of hys chamber at oones an[d] oon lord to serve hym'.[45] In March 1536 Sir Edward Seymour was admitted to the privy chamber.[46] However, he does not appear to have remained a member once he had been ennobled. After Rochford and Exeter (and their friends) had been condemned as traitors, Cromwell placed his own men in the vacant posts. By the beginning of 1539 it seems that he himself was the nobleman who headed the privy chamber.[47] In April 1540, through his appointment as great chamberlain, Cromwell gained control over both chamber and privy chamber, though it was not enough to keep him in power. The peers in the privy chamber after 1540 were, besides Russell, William FitzWilliam, earl of Southampton, William Parr, earl of Essex, who served with the privy chamber retinues in the French campaign of 1544, and John Dudley, viscount Lisle, who was listed among the gentlemen of the privy chamber in 1544 or 1545.[48] Henry Courtenay and the marquess of Dorset, therefore, were the only

---

[41] BL, Cotton Calig.B.VI (Pt 2), f.325 (*LP*, iii(2), 2955).
[42] Starkey, 'Representation through intimacy', pp. 197–200.
[43] *A Collection of Ordinances and Regulations for the Government of the Royal Household* (London, 1790), pp. 154–7.
[44] *LP*, iv(3), 6073.
[45] BL, Add. 9835, ff.24, 26 (*LP*, v, 927, the marquess wrongly identified as Dorset).
[46] *LP*, ii(1), 2735 (dated March/April 1536 by Dr Starkey), x, 495.
[47] SP1/142, f.1 (*LP*, xiv(1), 2). The MS. has no heading but all the men listed have been identified by Dr Starkey as members of the privy chamber.
[48] Starkey, 'From feud to faction', 20; *LP*, xvi, 394(6), xix(1), 275(4), xx(2), App.2.

noblemen by birth to be members of the privy chamber in the reign of Henry VIII.

The Eltham ordinances required at least some of the gentlemen of the privy chamber to be good linguists, able to carry the king's messages to foreign courts. Sir John Russell, fluent in French and Italian, was frequently employed on diplomatic missions in the 1520s. Sir William FitzWilliam, not a member of the privy chamber before his ennoblement but a knight of the body to Henry VIII, was often sent on embassy to France. His French, too, was good, but it was his knowledge of hunting that impressed Francis I on his first embassy, in February 1521: 'they well perceyved that he that taught me was a maister.' As he reported to Henry VIII, FitzWilliam was able to transfer the compliment to him by telling Francis that Henry himself had been his teacher 'as it was in dede, for sithens I was ten yeres of age I have ever been with your grace'.[49] FitzWilliam also used his ability at hawking to gain access to the admiral of France.[50] The sporting accomplishments fostered by the style of education traditional to the aristocracy could be as useful to an' ambassador as any more formal learning, apart from a knowledge of foreign languages. When his clerk fell ill in October FitzWilliam lost the use of a skill he did not possess and clearly did not intend to acquire: 'and ye wold gyf me all thow goud in thow world, I canot lerne to make thes syfers.'[51] But after their ennoblement neither Russell nor FitzWilliam was sent abroad again as ambassador. Sir Thomas Boleyn, on the other hand, another fluent French-speaker, and his son were sent on embassies both before and after they became peers. Sir John Dudley, too, appointed chief trencher to Henry VIII in February 1537, went as ambassador to Spain the following October and, as viscount Lisle, to France in 1546, when the young earl of Rutland was attached to his embassy.

Service abroad on any negotiating embassy was likely to be a testing experience and the noblemen called to undergo it were all men close to Henry VIII, if not actually members of his household. Besides those who went on their first mission as commoners, they included Worcester, the king's chamberlain, frequently employed in this way; Suffolk, dispatched to France at the time of Mary's marriage to Louis XII and again in 1529; the younger Thomas Howard, sent abroad on a number of embassies as earl of Surrey and duke of Norfolk; and, ambassador to Charles of Spain for some months in 1518, John Bourchier, lord Berners, a friend of the king who was later to win enduring fame as the

---

[49] SP1/21, f.204 (LP, iii(1), 1160).

[50] LP, iii(1), 1278.

[51] SP1/23, f.98 (LP, iii(2), 1710).

translator of Froissart's *Chronicles*. Noblemen were more likely to be selected when the main purpose of the mission was ceremonial. While Suffolk grappled with the political negotiations in 1514, Norfolk led the escort which accompanied Mary to France. He took with him his wife and eldest son, Dorset and his wife, Thomas West, lord La Warre, Edward Stanley, recently created lord Monteagle, and lord Berners, chosen to be Mary's chamberlain, presumably because of his facility in the language. (However, much to Mary's disgust, Norfolk soon acquiesced in a French demand for the dismissal of all her men servants, including Berners, and Henry Courtenay, earl of Devon, was appointed by Louis XII to attend upon her instead.)[52] Henry Parker, lord Morley, was commissioned in 1523 to take a knighthood of the Garter to Charles V's brother, Ferdinand. Morley probably could not speak German, although he knew French, but he observed events with interest. In particular he reported from Cologne on the alarming spread of Luther's books and the open mockery of the pope – although he was in the 1530s to congratulate Henry VIII on his break with Rome which 'hath set the Englysshe nation at fredoome and lybertie'.[53] Arthur Plantagenet, viscount Lisle, another French-speaker, led a similar mission to Francis I, investing him with the Garter in 1527.

Lisle had the additional merit of being himself a knight of the Garter and so able to wear the robes and insignia for the occasion. The order united its 26 members into a confraternity, bound to each other in a common observance of the patronal feast and in a commitment to pray for the soul of each knight when he died.[54] A knighthood of the sword or of the Bath came the way of most noblemen in the reign of Henry VIII. The Garter was an exceptional honour, making the recipient the companion of kings. Charles V, elected as a child in 1508, made a point of sitting in his stall on his visit to England in 1522.[55] When Henry VIII visited France in 1532 he held 'a most glorious chapter' of the order at Calais, attended by Francis I, at which the great master and the admiral of France were elected knights of the Garter. The king of Portugal in 1510, the brother of the pope in 1514, and Henry's nephew, the king of Scotland, in 1535, were also made KGs by Henry VIII, but the knights who believed, in April 1540, that the duke of Cleves and the duke of Bavaria would be diplomatic choices proved not to have the backing of the king, who preferred two Englishmen. No

---

[52] *LP*, i(2), 3321, 3325, 3348(3), 3355, 3357.
[53] *LP*, iii(2), 3275, 3390, 3391, 3546, 3619, iv(1), 89; quotation in GEC.
[54] Maurice Keen, *Chivalry* (New Haven, Conn., and London, 1984), pp. 181–2.
[55] *Hall's Chronicle*, p. 641.

more foreigners were put forward for election while Henry lived.

The king as sovereign of the order had the absolute right of choice. Henry VIII, 'out of the love that he now hath, and ever hath had, to the military state', clarified the procedure in 1522. Having received the nominations of all the knights present, the king 'shall pronounce him elected who is supported by the most votes or whom the sovereign himself shall judge more worthy, more honourable, more useful, and more fit for his kingdom and crown'. Each knight of the order nominated nine men for election, three in each category of foreign prince or high English nobleman, baron or banneret, and knight bachelor. Stalls were not always immediately filled and in 1542, 'after a long and grave debate', the king and all the knights present decided not to proceed to an election. In 1516 and 1546 no one was elected although full lists of nominations were drawn up. In the course of his reign Henry VIII gave the dignity to 19 men in the first category, but as seven of them were foreigners the 12 Englishmen of the high nobility whom he so honoured were outnumbered by the 17 men in the second category and the 17 ordinary knights whom he made knights of the Garter.[56] At his accession the duke of Buckingham, the marquess of Dorset and eight earls had been knights of the Garter; only the two youngest earls – Derby and the 11-year-old Westmorland – were not members of the order. There were many more high nobles who were not knights of the Garter in 1547: the marquess of Dorset and eight earls, besides the duke of Suffolk and the earl of Rutland, who were not yet of age. All were from families ennobled before 1509, and some may have felt themselves ill-used. Edward Stanley, earl of Derby, like his father before him had been nominated many times for election but never chosen by Henry VIII. Thomas earl of Derby had actually received more votes in 1518 than either of the men chosen by the king; Edward's support fluctuated but rarely collapsed altogether. Henry Grey, marquess of Dorset, succeeded his father, who had been a knight of the Garter, in 1530. He began to appear in the nominations in 1537 and was put forward in every election thereafter to the end of the reign, collecting more votes than any other nobleman in 1546, when no election was made. There was no constitutional ground for complaint since the king was acting within the correct procedure. Nevertheless, immediately after Henry VIII's funeral, without waiting for St George's day, the knights of the Garter assembled in the king's chamber, in the presence of Edward VI, and both Derby and Dorset were elected into

[56] All references to proceedings of the order are from the English translation in *The Register of the Most Noble Order of the Garter*. The numbers given include two men with courtesy titles, Thomas lord Howard (1510) and his son, styled earl of Surrey (1541).

the order, with Protector Somerset's brother Thomas and Sir William Paget. The earl of Worcester had also been nominated many times since he succeeded his father in 1526, but for him the change of regime brought no change of fortune. The earls of Cumberland and Sussex – like Worcester, sons of KGs – and the earl of Huntingdon had received some nominations in the 1540s. No one at any time had been moved to suggest the election of the three remaining Garterless earls of January 1547: Henry Daubeney, a baron since 1508 and earl of Bridgwater since 1538, John Bourchier, who had succeeded his father as earl of Bath in 1539, and John de Vere, earl of Oxford since 1540.

Henry VIII did not use the order to extend his familiar circle so much as to reward those who were already part of it. The men elected in the non-noble category were, without exception, members of the royal household or close friends of the king. They included six men whom Henry later ennobled: Sir Henry Marney, vice-chamberlain, elected in 1510, and Sir Charles Brandon, chosen in 1513; Sir Edward Stanley and Sir William Sandys, knights for the body, elected in 1514 and 1518; and Sir Thomas Boleyn and Sir William FitzWilliam, each treasurer of the household when elected in 1523 and 1526. The noblemen chosen by Henry VIII to be knights of the Garter were also most often his friends and household officers, or his relatives. Henry VII's death meant the postponement of the chapter due to be held on 23 April 1509, and the two men elected in May – Darcy and Edward Sutton, lord Dudley – may have been his choice rather than Henry VIII's; Dudley, at all events, took little part in political life in the new reign. Thomas West, lord La Warre, elected in 1510, was a former member of the royal household.[57] Henry VIII's jousting companions, Bergavenny and Ferrers, were elected in 1513 and 1523 as each was about to leave for active service in France. The king elected his young cousin, Henry Courtenay, earl of Devon, in 1521, his uncle, Arthur Plantagenet, viscount Lisle, in 1524 and his son FitzRoy, named among the barons, at a special chapter in June 1525, shortly before creating him duke of Richmond. Ralph Neville, earl of Westmorland, the king's sworn servant, was elected with FitzRoy. Two courtiers who were to be promoted in June 1525, FitzWalter and Ros, were made knights of the Garter in 1524 and April 1525. (No one realized that Ros was not eligible for election since he was not a knight bachelor. When the error was revealed the next day, presumably by Ros himself, Henry VIII reassembled the chapter, declared the election void, knighted Ros with his sword, ordered a new election and chose him again.) John de Vere, described as Henry's 'old trusty servaunt' when

[57] *LP*, i(1), 438(2), m.21.

he succeeded to the earldom of Oxford in 1526,[58] was elected in 1527.
Mountjoy was chamberlain of the queen's household at the time of his
election in 1526 and William Paulet, lord St John, was the newly
appointed chamberlain of the king's household at his election in 1543.
Edward Seymour, earl of Hertford, was elected to the order in 1541 as
he was beginning his rise to power.

John lord Russell had been ennobled a few weeks before his election
in 1539: the honour helped to prepare him for his future responsibilities in the west country. Charles Brandon's election in 1513,
immediately before his ennoblement, was also linked with an impend-
ing appointment, as marshal of the army against France; in 1544 the
new earl of Arundel (Henry VIII's former page) was elected to the
order before being given the same post later in the year. Another old
courtier, Henry Clifford, earl of Cumberland, was made a knight of the
Garter in 1537 for his services against the northern rebels, although he
was at the same time removed from his office of lord warden. He was
the only nobleman chosen explicitly for his military service, but other
wardens of the marches against Scotland were made knights of the
Garter by Henry VIII: Thomas lord Dacre in 1518, the earl of
Northumberland in 1531 and William lord Parr a few days before his
departure for the north in 1543. Probably only Parr would have been
sure of election in any other circumstance. He had been named by no
more than half the knights present but was already reaping the benefit
of Henry VIII's determination to marry his sister. John Dudley,
viscount Lisle, elected with him, was the retiring lord warden and
recently appointed lord admiral. Francis Talbot, earl of Shrewsbury,
was also elected to the order after a period on the borders, in April
1545, when his commission as lieutenant of the north came to an end.

Anne Boleyn tried to obtain the honour for her brother in 1536: her
failure was noted as an ominous sign.[59] While Henry VIII was
doubtless subjected to other pressures, only one nobleman is known to
have been admitted to the order at the suit of a patron. William
FitzAlan, earl of Arundel, was a friend of the king – Henry personally
stood godfather to his son, named after him, in 1512 – but he thanked
Wolsey in 1525 for 'your most favyrable reporte the wyche ye have
made of me unto the kynges highnes, by reason whereof hit hath
pleasyd his grace to prefer me to be on of the numbre of the noble
ordre of the Garter, the wyche I know well ys by your good remem-
brans and procurement'. He promised Wolsey 'my true harte and
servys, my eleygens exceptyd, before all men'.[60] The chapter had not

[58] See below, p. 165.
[59] *CSPSp.*, v(2), 47.
[60] SP1/34, f.204 (*LP*, iv(1), 1335).

been well attended – there were only six knights present – but every one had voted for Arundel; they may have had foreknowledge of Henry VIII's decision to elect him, as they obviously did two months later when FitzRoy, never before nominated, was also named by every knight. An honour of such prestige was inevitably sought by men whose background was neither aristocratic nor military, but it was not until 1537 that Henry VIII made a significant break with tradition. After Darcy's execution he called a special chapter at Windsor on 5 August, attended by five knights. Six was the minimum attendance enjoined by the statutes of the order, but the king went ahead and announced the election of Cromwell, which the knights present agreed to, 'extolling him for his merits, as much as they were able'. Cromwell's merits were hardly in the chivalric mode, although he had sent a company of men to fight against the rebels the previous year and continued to do what he could to project a military image of himself, notably in 1539, when he provided an impressively large contingent of armed men for the march of the London musters from the city to Westminster, where they were viewed by the king.[61] Military service was still, indeed, expected of all the nobility.[62] Nevertheless, the election of the lord privy seal, followed by that of two successive chancellors – lord Audley of Walden in 1540 and lord Wriothesley in 1545 – was at odds with the martial ethos of an order of chivalry. A knighthood of the Garter was becoming more clearly a political honour, divorced from the chivalric culture which had retained its hold into the early sixteenth century.[63]

In the world of the Henrician court it would have been unrealistic to expect the knights of the Garter to feel bound to each other in the sort of relationship forged by more humble lay confraternities. Yet Henry VIII made little attempt to create any bond of companionship or even to exploit the opportunities for pageantry provided by the order. He freely excused the attendance of knights at the St George's day chapter, which met at court, although he himself attended every recorded meeting except that of 1544, when the nine knights who had assembled waited for him three hours before receiving word that weighty affairs of the kingdom kept him from joining them. The annual feast, held at Windsor some weeks after the April meeting, was probably even less well attended. Year after year the king appointed a noble member of the order to preside over it as his deputy. Only once is he known to have been present at the feast, in 1519; then, apart from the foreigners, every knight was there as well except Dacre, Monteagle

[61] *LP*, xi, 831; *The Lisle Letters*, v, 1406.
[62] See below, chapter 5.
[63] Keen, *Chivalry*, p. 238.

and Sir Rhys ap Thomas. The festivities began on Friday, 27 May, when Henry VIII ordered noblemen and others to attend him from Richmond to Windsor. Dukes were allowed to bring 60 horses, a marquess 50, earls 40, barons 30 and ordinary knights of the Garter 20; every one else was restricted to 16 horses. Henry was accompanied by Garter king of arms and Richard Fox, prelate of the order. The queen and her ladies stood in the fields to watch them all pass by, then crossed by ferry to Windsor. The next day was taken up with the feast itself. On the Sunday, after the procession to Mass, Henry kept his royal estate at dinner, with his style – and largesse – being proclaimed after the second course and trumpets sounding throughout except when the minstrels were playing. The French hostages for the performance of the Tournai agreement were present, sitting at the lord steward's board with men of rank who were not knights of the Garter; they included Buckingham's son, the earls of Devon, Oxford and Westmorland, four barons and two heirs to earldoms. The private feast was made the occasion for a public celebration.

Henry VIII must have been particularly anxious to create an impression abroad at this time, when he had just decided to enter the imperial election. But throughout his life the splendours of his court were directed as much at foreign observers as at his subjects. Comparatively few noblemen were courtiers or knights of the Garter; how far did the nobility as a whole fulfil a courtly role? The answer lies in the records of the great state occasions, of which the first was the coronation of Henry VIII and Katherine of Aragon on midsummer day, 24 June 1509. The nobles who 'did their dewtie and homage' at the coronation included the duke of Buckingham, four earls, the prior of St John of Jerusalem and 23 barons.[64] Only seven barons were missing from the list, including Grey of Powis who was a child, and Walter Devereux, lord Ferrers, who was also under age, although he was not far from his majority and had been a mourner before the corpse of Henry VII at Richmond. John lord Clinton, who was never summoned to parliament, was not listed, nor lord Darcy, who was no longer vice-chamberlain and captain of the guard as he had been when he took part in Henry VII's funeral. The northern lords Latimer and Ogle were also omitted, with John Brooke, lord Cobham, a man of about 60 whose experience of coronations went back to that of Richard III. However, omission from the list cannot be taken as proof of absence since the attendance of the high nobility was certainly not limited to the five named as doing homage: Edward duke of Buckingham, great constable of England for the day preceding the coronation

---

[64] BL, Add. 6113, f.72 (*LP*, i(1), 82(5), number of barons understated).

and great steward for the day itself, Thomas earl of Surrey, marshal of England for both days, Thomas earl of Arundel, butler, John earl of Oxford, great chamberlain, and Henry earl of Northumberland. Shrewsbury, steward of the king's household, as one might expect, was also present. He and Buckingham rode into Westminster hall on great horses at the start of the dinner which followed the religious service.[65] For the rest of the high nobility the only source for reconstructing attendance is the 'device' for the coronation drawn up by the heralds in preparation for the ceremonies.[66] Unfortunately, they did not consistently update the model from which they worked, the order for the coronation of Henry VII.[67] Two viscounts were therefore expected to carry the sceptre and ivory rod in the queen's procession, as in 1485, regardless of the fact that there were no English viscounts in 1509, and the six-year-old lord Grey of Powis was put down to lead the horses of the queen's litter as his grandfather had been in 1485. Where the heralds made changes, however, they may presumably be trusted as evidence at least of the intended presence of the men named; and some noblemen retained from the earlier plan probably served again. The duke of Buckingham took precedence over the rest of the nobility in the procession to Westminster abbey bearing the crown, the honour reserved to the king's uncle, Jasper Tudor, duke of Bedford, in 1485. Where the earl of Derby had been appointed to carry the king's sword at the coronation of Henry VII, the earl of Essex was given this part to play in 1509. The earl of Surrey replaced the former duke of Suffolk as bearer of the king's sceptre, while the earl of Arundel was down to carry the rod of gold on each occasion. Three earls together were to carry swords in the procession; the earl of Shrewsbury the sword *curtana* in 1509 as in 1485, flanked on one side by the earl of Kent, in place of Henry VII's earl of Nottingham. The other sword was to be entrusted at both coronations to the earl of Devonshire, according to these devices, although in 1509, after the death of the old earl on 28 May, there was no earl of Devon until his attainted son was given the title in 1511. No earl was put down to carry the queen's crown in 1509, the space for the name being left blank in the device: it was probably carried by the earl of Derby, whose countess was appointed to attend upon the queen.[68] The absentees among the high nobility seem therefore to have been – not surprisingly – the 11-year-old earl of

---

[65] *Hall's Chronicle*, p. 509.

[66] BL, Cotton Tiberius E.VIII, ff.90–100 (*LP*, i(1), 81). Also College of Arms, Vincent 25, ff.144–52, I.18, ff.54–66.

[67] *Rutland Papers*, ed. William Jerdan, Camden Soc., xxi (London, 1842), pp. 2–24. This device wrongly assumed that Henry VII's queen would be crowned with him.

[68] *LP*, i(1), 82.

Westmorland and Thomas Grey, marquess of Dorset, excepted from
the general pardon and still in custody at Calais.

The coronation was no doubt a memorable occasion for all the
noblemen present, and not least for the half-dozen barons who were
made knights of the Bath in honour of the occasion.[69] The 15-year-old
lord Daubeney was the youngest of them to receive this order of
knighthood, which tended to be conferred on young men; FitzHugh,
FitzWalter and Scrope of Bolton were in their twenties, William
Blount, lord Mountjoy, and Robert lord Willoughby de Broke in their
thirties. Sir Henry Clifford, the teenage son and heir of lord Clifford,
was also made a knight of the Bath and three others out of the total of
26 men so honoured were later to be raised to the peerage: Maurice
Berkeley, Andrew Windsor and Thomas Boleyn.

The other major ceremonial occasions of the reign were Henry
VIII's meetings with Francis I in 1520 and 1532, the visit of Charles V
to England in 1522, Anne Boleyn's coronation in 1533 and the
reception of Anne of Cleves in 1540. The field of cloth of gold in the
summer of 1520 became a byword for princely magnificence and for
the wasteful expenditure it demanded. Bishop Fisher was one of the
first to make the point publicly, in a sermon printed in 1532: 'great
money was spent, many great mennes coffers were emptied and many
were brought to a great ebbe and poverty' – and for no lasting good.[70]
Polydore Vergil declared that the nobles 'everywhere' were summoned
to attend.[71] It is true that, on the most detailed list of those appointed
to attend upon the king and queen, every one of the high nobility was
named except the duke of Norfolk, who stayed in London as the
leading councillor, the earl of Surrey, the king's deputy in Ireland, and
the 70-year-old earl of Arundel, whose son and heir was ordered to be
present. But only 15 barons were commanded to attend, according to
this source.[72] Another list, in *The Chronicle of Calais*, includes one
additional name.[73] (In the event, two barons – Berners and Darcy –
remained with the council in London.)[74] Lumley was the only northern baron besides Darcy to be listed, probably as a result of his service

[69] Names of knights of the Bath 'in order as they were made' at the beginning of the
device.

[70] Joycelyne G. Russell, *The Field of Cloth of Gold. Men and Manners in 1520* (London,
1969), Appendix D.

[71] *The Anglica Historia of Polydore Vergil A.D. 1485–1537*, ed. Denys Hay, Camden Soc.,
3rd series, lxxiv (London, 1950), p. 263.

[72] Russell, *Field of Cloth of Gold*, Appendix A ('the lord fferrers' wrongly identified as
Dorset's son – aged three at the time – instead of as Walter Devereux, lord Ferrers).
Another version is printed in *Rutland Papers*, pp. 29–38.

[73] *The Chronicle of Calais*, p. 20.

[74] *LP, Addenda*, i, 286, 288; *The Chronicle of Calais*, pp. 90–4.

at court, which left seven absentees from Lancashire, Yorkshire and further north. Five barons from the south of England were also omitted. Three of them were in their sixties and one – John Bourchier, lord FitzWarin – within a few weeks of his fiftieth birthday; but FitzWarin's daughter was present. The last absentee, John Tuchet, lord Audley, was only in his thirties, but deep in debt to the crown, still struggling to pay the 6,500 marks which his restitution to his title in 1512 had cost him.[75] These noblemen, at least, were spared the expense, although they missed a spectacle which even Fisher admitted was 'as great as mennes wyttes and studyes coulde devyse and ymagyn'.

It was to have no comparable sequel. The field of cloth of gold had depended entirely for its success on lavish expenditure: an encounter of rival kings for the most part in open country, where everything had to be provided, and honour was judged solely by physical prowess and external display. When Charles V came to England two years later, the court festivities were part of a more balanced programme. The young emperor was taken by Henry VIII to see over his new ship, the *Henry Grace à Dieu*, at Dover, and stayed in the archbishop's palace in Canterbury and the king's palace at Greenwich on his way to London, where he was lodged in the Black Friars. He heard High Mass at St Paul's cathedral on Whitsunday and evensong at Westminster abbey. He was shown Westminster hall and was suitably impressed by its size. The most elaborate of the ceremonies was the entry into London, for which the city prepared a magnificent pageant. Three days were set aside for political discussions. Throughout, noblemen were in constant attendance.[76]

However, the lists of those summoned to take part reveal that barons from the northern counties were not called upon.[77] With full-scale war imminent against the Scots, even Darcy and Lumley remained in the north. On the other hand, of all the barons resident in the southern half of the kingdom only three were omitted: lord Audley again and Edward Sutton, lord Dudley (also absent in 1520) and William lord Willoughby de Eresby. But one of those named initially – George Nevill, lord Bergavenny – was crossed off the list of men to accompany Henry VIII; unless he was ill, this must have been a deliberate slight to a leading nobleman in Kent, demonstrating that he had not recovered the king's favour lost at the time of Buckingham's fall. Every high nobleman was summoned, apart from the earl of

---

[75] *LP*, iv(3), App.245.

[76] *Hall's Chronicle*, pp. 634–42.

[77] *Rutland Papers*, pp. 70–6, 81; amended lists in SP1/24, ff.161–3, 165–6, 167 (*LP*, iii(2), 2288 (1–3)).

Derby, a minor. His London residence was used to help lodge the emperor's entourage; the earl of Kent's house at Greenwich, too, was pressed into service as extra accommodation.[78] The duke of Suffolk was given the honour of entertaining Charles V at his house in Southwark, where the company hunted in the park. The serious business of the visit ended with the signing of a treaty against France, ratified by the two monarchs in the chapel of Windsor castle on 19 June in the presence of witnesses who included the duke of Suffolk, the marquess of Dorset, seven earls and lord Hastings.[79]

Ten years later Henry VIII's second meeting with Francis I also included the signing of a treaty – against the Turks – and was an altogether more sober affair than the first, suiting the dominance of Thomas Cromwell as the field of cloth of gold had reflected the taste of Wolsey. Henry had sworn to a new alliance with France at Windsor, in the presence of the French ambassador, on 1 September 1532, immediately after creating Anne Boleyn marchioness of Pembroke. The imperial ambassador surmised that the meeting with Francis had less to do with the threat from the Turks than with Henry's need to gain the support of France for his divorce, a view shared by Edward Hall, who linked it with the interview expected to take place soon between the French king and the pope.[80] Hall gives the fullest list of those in attendance as Henry was first entertained by Francis at Boulogne and then welcomed him as his guest at Calais; a few more names may be added from an account derived from a French source.[81] Henry VIII took Anne Boleyn with him instead of Katherine, and she was treated almost as though she were the queen. The plan for the meeting required the number of attendants to be kept comparatively low.[82] Nevertheless, most high noblemen were in attendance. Sussex was left (with lords Darcy and Windsor) as part of the council in London.[83] Shrewsbury, the lord steward, did not attend, but his son did. Apart from the northern earls – Cumberland, Northumberland and Westmorland – the rest of the high nobility were present. However, only nine barons attended. Sandys, the king's chamberlain, was there, with Montagu and Bray, ennobled in 1529, and Mordaunt, created a peer earlier in 1532. Sandys was an old man, Bray and Mordaunt middle-aged, but Montagu was probably still in his thirties, like Cobham and Daubeney, who were also present. Three younger

---

[78] *Rutland Papers*, pp. 82, 91.
[79] *LP*, iii(2), 2333(6).
[80] *LP*, v, 1429; *Hall's Chronicle*, pp. 789–90.
[81] *Hall's Chronicle*, pp. 790–4 (wrongly including Sussex); *LP*, v, App.33.
[82] *LP*, v, 1373.
[83] ibid., 1421.

barons travelled with them: the second lords Monteagle and Vaux, and Edward lord Clinton, almost out of wardship and soon to marry the widowed Elizabeth Blount, the king's former mistress. The youthful element was strengthened by the inclusion of Richmond, Henry's son by her, and four heirs to peerages under the courtesy titles of Rochford, Mautravers, Talbot and FitzWalter. Not everyone who crossed to France proved to be a supporter of the king's proceedings. Indeed, Montagu's distaste for Henry's actions apparently dated from this visit.[84] Yet the following year the king's favour was shown above all to those whose presence had seemed to give tacit approval to his marriage plans. Three of the heirs to peerages were summoned in February 1533 to sit in the house of lords during the lifetime of their fathers. The fourth, FitzWalter, was made a knight of the Bath on the eve of Anne's coronation, with Monteagle and Vaux, the 15-year-old marquess of Dorset and the earl of Derby. The eldest sons of Huntingdon and Mordaunt were also made knights of the Bath, as well as the heirs to three noblemen who had not attended Henry and Anne to France: Cumberland, Morley and Windsor.[85]

Preparations for the coronation had begun well before Cranmer's formal pronouncement of the validity of Henry VIII's marriage to Anne. On 25 April 1533 the king instructed lord Mordaunt to get ready to be present 'in such wise furnished as to your degree, and that solemnity, shall be convenient and agreeable ... wherein ye shal do unto us very acceptable pleasure'.[86] A paper once in Cromwell's possession, but now lost, recorded the names of the noblemen sent for, no doubt by similar letters.[87] On 31 May Anne Boleyn rode from the Tower of London to Westminster, greeted by a series of pageants put on by the city, for her coronation on Whitsunday, 1 June. In the procession to the service the marquess of Dorset carried the gold sceptre, the earl of Arundel the rod of ivory and the earl of Oxford, great chamberlain of England, the crown. The dowager duchess of Norfolk carried the queen's long train. The duke of Suffolk was great constable on the eve and great steward on the day of the coronation, as Buckingham had been in 1509, and lord William Howard deputized as marshal of England for his brother, the duke of Norfolk, who was on embassy to France. After the ceremony Anne was supported on her

[84] *LP*, xiii(2), 804(6).

[85] *The Noble Triumphant Coronation of Queen Anne* (London, 1533), from reprint in Edward Arber, *An English Garner*, 8 vols (London, 1895–7), ii, 41–51; this includes lord Berkeley among the new KBs but his name is not found in other accounts, e.g. *Hall's Chronicle*, p. 800, nor in the order for the ceremony in *LP*, vi, 562.

[86] Halstead, *Succinct Genealogies*, p. 553.

[87] *LP*, vii, 923 (xxxiv).

right hand by her father, the earl of Wiltshire, and on her left by lord Talbot, standing in for his father, the earl of Shrewsbury. At the dinner which followed five earls performed the traditional services: Essex as carver, Sussex as sewer, Derby as cupbearer, Arundel as butler and Oxford as great chamberlain. Arthur Plantagenet, viscount Lisle, was pantler, Henry Nevill, lord Bergavenny, chief larderer and Edmund lord Bray almoner. Thomas lord Burgh, appointed chamberlain to the queen, was also present, as was the earl of Rutland who brought up the surnap as the long ceremony drew to a close.[88] Few barons were mentioned, but the references to the high nobility leave only four who may have been absent, besides Norfolk and Shrewsbury. Three were the northern earls who had stayed in England the previous autumn – Cumberland (whose son was present), Northumberland and Westmorland – and the fourth was Henry Courtenay, marquess of Exeter. Katherine of Aragon had seen the hand of Anne Boleyn in Exeter's exclusion from court in 1531, ascribing her malice to his loyalty to herself.[89] The marchioness, too, was one of Katherine's closest friends and if Exeter was indeed absent from the coronation, as seems likely, he presumably made an excuse not to attend, as Shrewsbury must have done. Two of Buckingham's children also seem to have shown some respect for Katherine's feelings. His daughter, the duchess of Norfolk, is said to have refused to attend out of love of Katherine, although Anne was her husband's niece.[90] His son, styled lord Stafford, a brother-in-law of Henry Pole, lord Montagu, paid a fine of £20 'to be excusid to be knyhte of the bathe'.[91]

None of Henry VIII's other queens was crowned, although Jane Seymour would have been if she had lived; her coronation had been arranged for 28 October 1537.[92] But noblemen and others were deputed to receive Anne of Cleves at every stage of her journey to England.[93] Again Henry VIII's letter to lord Mordaunt survives, dated 24 November 1539, informing him that he had been appointed to attend the reception with 20 of his servants.[94] A detailed account of Anne's progress is extant as well as a private letter which described her formal meeting with Henry VIII at Blackheath.[95] Anne was met at

---

[88] *Hall's Chronicle*, pp. 802–5. Sussex as lord FitzWalter had been given £20 for serving at the king's table after Henry VIII's coronation and was now appointed sewer at coronation dinners in tail male: *LP*, ii(2), p. 1442, vii, 588 g.1.

[89] *CSPSp.*, iv(2), 765 (the marquess wrongly identified as Dorset).

[90] *LP*, vi, 585.

[91] SP1/72, f.113 (*LP*, v, 1608).

[92] Blank letters missive for the creation of knights of the Bath: *LP*, Addenda, i, 1262.

[93] *LP*, xiv(2), 572(3); *The Chronicle of Calais*, pp. 167–71, 173–9.

[94] Halstead, *Succinct Genealogies*, p. 568.

[95] SP1/157, ff.5–10 (*LP*, xv, 14); BL, Cotton Vitellius C.XVI, ff.271–2 (*LP*, xv, 18), printed *The Lisle Letters*, vi, 1634.

the entrance to the Pale of Calais on 11 December 1539 by the deputy of Calais, Arthur Plantagenet, viscount Lisle, and, a mile from the town, by the lord admiral, the earl of Southampton, with a large entourage which included lord Grey of Wilton and the young lord Tailboys, Southampton's ward. When she reached Kent on 27 December she was received by the duke and duchess of Suffolk and their train, to which lord Cobham had been assigned. The duke of Norfolk, with many knights from Norfolk and Suffolk, met her on new year's eve at Rochester, with lords Mountjoy and Dacre of the south also in attendance. The king visited her in secret the following day, with some of the privy council, but the official encounter took place on 3 January, when Anne was attended by Norfolk and Suffolk and the household officers assigned to her, headed by the earl of Rutland, her chamberlain. The French ambassador reported that the public crier had called on all who loved the king to turn out to meet the lady who was soon to be their queen. Henry VIII was accompanied by a mounted escort numbering at least 5,000, but the ambassador dismissed the spectacle as less impressive than any of 20 entries made for Charles V on his recent progress through France – great occasion though the English thought it.[96] He himself took part, paired with the imperial ambassador in a long procession which included lord Cromwell walking with the lord chancellor, Audley of Walden, the earl of Southampton with duke Philip of Bavaria, and the marquess of Dorset carrying the sword before Henry VIII. However, of the high nobility, eight earls seem to have been absent: Derby (who had been expected to attend), Shrewsbury, Bath and Bridgwater and four who were represented by their eldest sons – Cumberland, Westmorland, Worcester and Huntingdon. The 11 barons who did not attend included some habitual absentees from such occasions: Latimer and Ogle (who apparently never, in any generation, attended any one of these six state functions), Audley (who is never known to have come to anything himself, but whose son was ordered to be present in 1540), and John Sutton, lord Dudley, William lord Dacre of the north and lord Scrope of Bolton (whose fathers had made the sole recorded contribution of their families to these great occasions by attending Henry VIII's coronation). Edward lord Grey of Powis, who had inherited his barony as an infant in 1504, still, it seems, did not attend any of the three functions held after he came of age. The other absentees in 1540 were Monteagle and Vaux, who had taken part in the two state occasions of 1532 and 1533 and Lumley and Zouche, whose families had been present at the coronation in 1509 and at least one other of these functions.

There was perhaps a certain weariness by 1540, with even the king's

[96] *LP*, xv, 22, 23.

enthusiasm beginning to flag as he approached his fourth marriage. The reception of Anne of Cleves was the last major state function of the reign. Absence from any particular event was sometimes unavoidable, but the noblemen who consistently failed to appear were neglecting a duty performed by most of the nobility. It was not in normal circumstances an unduly heavy burden. Although Henry VIII demanded this show of allegiance on formal occasions he did not set out to create a courtier nobility. There is no evidence for the assertion that the Stanley earls of Derby spent long periods performing ceremonial duties under the king's supervision, let alone for any royal plan to divorce the magnates from local power and influence by insisting on their attendance at court.[97] The two earls of Derby of Henry VIII's reign – as other noblemen – certainly appeared at court at other times than the great state occasions, but they cannot be detected there at all frequently. It was in their interest as well as in that of the king that they should be seen at court from time to time. The ceremonial which promoted the image of royal magnificence also worked to reinforce the prestige of the nobility. Henry VIII surrounded by his noblemen appeared as the embodiment of authority, made visible in splendour and power. Display came naturally to the nobility and only in 1520 was the expense clearly excessive. Court activities may even have been enjoyable: most of them were, after all, designed as celebrations. No doubt the underlying reality was less pleasant, but that was the necessary concern only of the few noblemen who were indeed courtiers, in regular attendance on the king. The majority of noblemen, no more than intermittently involved, could become part of the spectacle without being engulfed by the 'queasy' world of the court.

Henry VIII never exploited to the full the court's potential for bringing him into close contact with the nobility. He did not keep under his own supervision even high noblemen who succeeded to their titles as minors. The wardship of Edward Stanley, earl of Derby, was sold to the duke of Norfolk for £2,333 6s 8d, the wardship of Henry Grey, marquess of Dorset, to the duke of Suffolk for 4,000 marks, in each case without any land, and the wardship of Henry Brandon, duke of Suffolk, with 200 marks p.a. for his keep, to his mother, the dowager duchess, for £1,500.[98] The king occasionally stayed a few days with a noble family, as for example in August 1519 when the duke of Buckingham gave him 'excellent chere' at Penshurst.[99] Such visits did

---

[97] As argued by Barry Coward, *The Stanleys Lords Stanley and Earls of Derby 1385–1672. The Origins, Wealth and Power of a Landowning Family*, Chetham Soc., 3rd series, xxx (Manchester, 1983), p. 148.

[98] WARD9/149, ff.28, 40v, 136.

[99] *Original Letters*, 3rd series, i, 195–6.

not necessarily engender lasting sympathy: before the end of October Buckingham was in serious trouble for the retaining of Sir William Bulmer, while two other noblemen who offered hospitality to Henry VIII – lord La Warre in 1538 and lord Windsor some three years later – were shortly afterwards induced to give up to the king the very houses in which they had done their best to entertain him.[100] The opportunity to act as host to royalty was nevertheless a high honour, not usually accompanied by ill effects. Henry VIII preferred the pleasures of the chase to the elaborate progresses favoured by Elizabeth. Although he regularly left the neighbourhood of London in the summer, he rarely moved further away than the good hunting country of the midlands.[101] In 1535 he visited Buckingham's former castle at Thornbury, near Bristol: this seems to have been the limit of his travels to the west. His progress to York in 1541 to meet James V of Scotland (who failed to turn up) was his sole excursion into the north. Noblemen who lived at a distance from London never saw him in their localities, where their own power found its most natural expression. By its life of ceremony the court created no more than a superficial unity focused upon the king. For Henry VIII that was apparently enough.

[100] See below, pp. 228–9, 248–9.
[101] OBS1/1419. I am grateful to Mr Neil Samman for bringing to my notice this itinerary of Henry VIII compiled in the PRO.

CHAPTER 4

Attendance in Council
and Parliament

Temporal lords were the king's counsellors born, wrote Sir John Fortescue, 'and therfor awghton to counsell hym at all tymes when he woll'.[1] He was clearly describing a duty, not a right. By the reign of Henry VIII an individual writ of summons to advise the king in parliament had become almost – but not quite – a formality, although it never conferred an absolute right to be present in the house of lords.[2] The king's choice of councillors was governed by no similar convention, yet the idea persisted into the seventeenth century, among noblemen, that they had a right to sit in the council in star chamber.[3] The misapprehension perhaps stemmed from a distorted memory of earlier practice. In Henry VII's reign at least two-thirds of the peers had been present at one or more meetings of the king's council.[4] Most of their names were found in extracts copied from the council registers, since lost, in the Ellesmere MSS. These were also the source for the membership of Henry VIII's council between 1509 and 1527 discussed and tabulated by W. H. Dunham.[5] Ellesmere 2655 contains 48 meetings at which those present are listed; Ellesmere 2654 includes the presence at one additional meeting.[6] This evidence needs to be supplemented by documents in the British Library and Public Record

---

[1] Sir John Fortescue, *The Governance of England*, ed. Charles Plummer (Oxford, 1885), p. 147.

[2] See above, pp. 10–12 and below, pp. 118–19, 125.

[3] John Hawarde, *Les Reportes del Cases in Camera Stellata 1593 to 1609*, ed. W. P. Baildon (London, 1894), p. 171.

[4] *Select Cases in the Council of Henry VII*, ed. C. G. Bayne and W. H. Dunham, Selden Soc., 75 for 1956 (London, 1958), p. xxx.

[5] W. H. Dunham, 'The members of Henry VIII's whole council, 1509–1527', *EHR*, lix (1944), 187–210.

[6] I am most grateful to Dr J. A. Guy for lending me his transcripts as well as the microfilm of these two Ellesmere MSS. in the Huntington Library, California.

Office.[7] The most important is Lansdowne 639, another collection of extracts from the first register of Henry VIII's reign, which covered the years up to 1527, including the names of noblemen present at ten council meetings not entered in the Ellesmere MSS. as well as the admission to the council of George Nevill, lord Bergavenny, on 18 May 1512, when he took the ·councillor's oath.[8] Lansdowne 1 notices the presence of noblemen on two further days.[9] In addition the presence on 30 June 1526 is known from another extract of which the British Library owns a photocopy.[10] In the Public Record Office a pocket book belonging to Richard Eden, clerk of the council, contains notes of the presence at four meetings in June and July 1525.[11] Records of ten further meetings of the council before the end of January 1527 with the names of noblemen present are to be found in the proceedings of star chamber and among the state papers.[12] The information from all these sources, supplementing that used by Dunham, makes a new table necessary to set out the known attendance during these years of those councillors who were noblemen. (Dunham's figures are given in brackets for the sake of comparison.)

49	Thomas Howard senior, earl of Surrey, duke of Norfolk	(34)
32	Thomas Howard junior, earl of Surrey, duke of Norfolk	(18)
26	Thomas Grey, marquess of Dorset	(13)
24	George Talbot, earl of Shrewsbury	(14)
17	George Nevill, lord Bergavenny	(12)
13	Charles Brandon, duke of Suffolk	(9)
13	Charles Somerset, lord Herbert, earl of Worcester	(9)
7	Henry Bourchier, earl of Essex	(6)
7	Edward Stafford, duke of Buckingham	(5)
7	George lord Hastings	(1)
6	Thomas lord Darcy	(6)
6	Thomas Boleyn, viscount Rochford	(3)
5	Arthur Plantagenet, viscount Lisle	(1)
4	William Blount, lord Mountjoy	(4)
4	Henry Percy, earl of Northumberland	(2)
4	Robert Radcliffe, viscount FitzWalter	(2)

[7] Described in detail in J. A. Guy, 'The court of star chamber during Wolsey's ascendancy', Ph.D. thesis (Cambridge, 1973).

[8] BL, Lansdowne 639, ff.27, 33, 40v, 43, 44v, 45, 46v, 47, 48v, 49.

[9] BL, Lansdowne 1, f.108.

[10] BL, RP 152(5).

[11] STAC 10/4/Pt 2.

[12] STAC 2/17/406 (date probably 26 January 1527), STAC 2/21/232, STAC 2/24/130, STAC 2/29/Fragments, f.47, STAC 10/4/Pt 2; *LP*, iii(1), 365(2), iv(1), 1082, *Addenda*, i, 160, 206, 430.

3   John de Vere, earl of Oxford (2)
3   John Bourchier, lord Berners (2)
3   Thomas Stanley, earl of Derby (1)
3   William lord Sandys (–)
2   Richard Grey, earl of Kent (2)
2   Henry Stafford, earl of Wiltshire (2)
2   William FitzAlan, earl of Arundel (–)
1   Henry Clifford, earl of Cumberland (–)
1   Thomas lord Dacre of the north (–)

The addition of four noblemen to the table is noteworthy, yet in general it is reassuring to observe that the order of precedence based on attendance is not greatly changed. The actual figures of attendance can never be more than a rough guide, since so much of the evidence is lost. The first known attendance in council of Charles Brandon was on 25 April 1516, but he was referred to as a councillor in May 1513, the month in which he was created viscount Lisle.[13] The younger Thomas Howard was called councillor in September 1514, well before his first documented presence in council on 12 February 1516, and Mountjoy, first known to have been present on 20 February 1517, was described as a councillor in January 1515.[14] Worse, the council records so far used make no reference to Henry Courtenay, marquess of Exeter, who was named as one of the council in the Eltham ordinances of January 1526 and listed on 5 February 1526 among those councillors who might particularly attend to matters of law, nor to William lord Dacre of the north, also named on the February list.[15] However, Dacre had only succeeded to his title in October 1525 and Exeter was young – in his mid-twenties – and unlikely to have been a member of the council much before 1526. Exeter and lord FitzWarin – never recorded as present in council – were included in the list of 'Counsellors sworn to the king *anno regni Regis Henrici VIII decimo octavo*' which was entered at the beginning of the new council register started in 1527, and copied, with notes and extracts from a few of the early entries, in Lansdowne 160.[16] This list – the only one extant of the members of Henry VIII's council before 1540 – included 14 noblemen.[17] Even so it was far from complete. It omitted the earls of Arundel, Cumberland and North-umberland (who had been present in council in 1525), the earl of

[13] *LP*, i(2), 1880.
[14] ibid., 3294(2), ii(1), 41.
[15] *A Collection of Ordinances*, p. 159; *LP*, iv(3), App.67, amended *Addenda*, i, 481.
[16] BL, Lansdowne 160, ff.309v–12.
[17] The list was amended in or after December 1529 since Hussey and Windsor appear as barons, although Windsor is also listed among the knights. Neither has been counted here.

Oxford (present in November 1526 and January 1527) and lords Darcy and Mountjoy, both certainly councillors, besides lord Dacre of the north. Thomas Manners, earl of Rutland, not on the list either, was a member of the council by 1529, if not before.[18] The copyist in Lansdowne 1 also used the second council register. He transcribed from it only one extract of a meeting with the presence, but it was an exceptionally important one,' held on 19 October 1529, shortly after Wolsey's resignation of the great seal.[19] It was attended by 12 peers including Henry Percy, earl of Northumberland since May 1527. Finally, original council papers record the presence at three council meetings in 1530, three in 1534 and one on 5 May 1536.[20] The last meeting was attended by two noblemen not otherwise known as councillors: Edward Stanley, who had inherited the earldom of Derby as a boy in 1521, and Ralph Neville, earl of Westmorland throughout the reign of Henry VIII, although under age until 1519.

The surviving records of attendance in council between 1527 and 1536 are too few to support even a rudimentary statistical survey. Nevertheless, the sources for Henry VIII's reign from 1509 to 1536, patchy though they are, form an adequate basis for a general view. They provide evidence of membership of the council for all the dukes and marquesses and for almost all the earls. The first meeting of Henry VIII's council for which the attendance is known was on 11 October 1509, too late for any reference to Edward Courtenay, earl of Devon, who died in May; the one presence list surviving for the few weeks in 1511 when his son was earl of Devon does not contain his name. The earl of Oxford who died in 1513 is not recorded as present at any meeting of Henry VIII's council although he had been one of Henry VII's most influential councillors.[21] The next earl, who died at the age of 26, is not known to have been a councillor.[22] But his cousin

[18] BL, Lansdowne 160, f.310v, dated 16 April 21 Henry VIII [1530], but, as Wolsey headed the presence, presumed to be 1529. Dacre of the north was also present at this meeting.

[19] BL, Lansdowne 1, f.108v.

[20] STAC 2/17/399, STAC 2/17/405, STAC 10/4/Pt 2. The last paper, headed 'Veneris quinto die Maii in Camera Stellata', must date from 1536 (rather than 1531, when 5 May was also a Friday) since it included Sir John Baldwin as chief justice of common pleas.

[21] Margaret Condon, 'Ruling elites in the reign of Henry VII' in *Patronage, Pedigree and Power in Later Medieval England*, ed. Charles Ross (Gloucester, 1979), p. 121 and n.

[22] G. R. Elton, *The Tudor Revolution in Government. Administrative Changes in the Reign of Henry VIII* (Cambridge, 1953), pp. 347–8 argues that the 'lord chamberlyne' on the list of councillors in the Eltham ordinances of January 1526 ought to be Oxford, the great chamberlain, since Sandys is also listed; but Worcester was lord chamberlain until his death in April 1526, with Sandys authorized to act for him – without using the title – only from February 1526: see below, p. 175.

and heir, a man in his forties when he succeeded as earl of Oxford in July 1526, was present at a council meeting four months later. Thomas FitzAlan, earl of Arundel, another of Henry VII's councillors, appears not to have attended a council meeting in Henry VIII's reign although he lived until 1524. Henry Somerset, earl of Worcester from 1526, does not seem to have been a councillor. All the viscounts were members of the council, viscount Rochford first attending as Sir Thomas Boleyn. Eight of the barons created before 1536 were already councillors when they were made peers: Marney, Berkeley, Sandys and Vaux, Hussey and Windsor, Mordaunt and George Boleyn.[23] Nine barons not of Henry VIII's creation were also members of the council: Herbert and Hastings (before their promotion to earldoms), Darcy, Berners, William Blount, lord Mountjoy, George Nevill, lord Bergavenny, Thomas lord Dacre of the north and his son William, the next baron, and John Bourchier, lord FitzWarin (created earl of Bath in 1536). The council in the years up to 1536 thus provided many noblemen with an opportunity to participate in government at the centre. By meeting the needs of the king's most important subjects the unreformed council filled an important political function.[24]

Yet the role of individual peers was often little more than formal, as it had been for many councillors even in the reign of Henry VII.[25] In 1509, when Buckingham and Oxford had led a debate at court on how to treat the young Henry VIII – 'whether the kyngs majestie should be brought up in worldly knowledge, or els in pleasure and liberty, leaving the care to his counsell' – it was too easily assumed that the council by itself could take over the rule of the kingdom. As Sir William Paulet recorded many years later, 'it was agreed best to bringe him up in all pleasure, for otherwise he should growe to hard among his subjects as the king his father did'; but Henry VIII, 'delighting in pleasant life, was forced to apoint the cardinall to call his counsell togethers and sett forth the order and governement of the realme'.[26] Henry VII had taken an active part in council meetings, although in his last years he may not have regularly attended the council in star chamber. In the early years of Henry VIII's reign it seems that the king was never present at a council meeting. Warham as chancellor presided over the council in star chamber which dis-

[23] The evidence for George Boleyn being a councillor comes from Cavendish's *Metrical Visions*, cited GEC under Ormond.

[24] G. R. Elton, 'Tudor government: the points of contact, ii. The council', *TRHS*, 5th series, 25 (1975), 200–1.

[25] *Select Cases in the Council of Henry VII*, p. xxiii.

[26] *Original Letters*, 3rd series, iii, 369–72. I am grateful to Mr Henry James for giving me this reference.

cussed all matters of state and, sitting as a court, heard many cases, almost all at the suit of private persons. The main work of the council was done by an inner ring – developing naturally as it had done in the previous reign – which included three of Henry VII's most trusted councillors, the lord treasurer, Surrey, the lord steward, Shrewsbury, and the lord chamberlain, Herbert. The members of the inner ring acted as the link between the council and Henry VIII.[27] It might have lasted longer if Henry's idea of the pleasant life had not included an invasion of France. By complicating the work of the council and assisting the rise to power of Wolsey the war doomed to frustration any nobleman with political ambitions.

The council continued to be a real governing institution during the chancellorship of Wolsey, but it was his emphasis on its judicial function that enabled it to flourish. The inner ring was eclipsed. The council still exercised some executive authority but its advisory role was reduced to a minimum, with discussion confined almost entirely to domestic affairs and dominated by Wolsey.[28] In their 44 articles of complaint against the chancellor in 1529 his opponents, all councillors, moved from the offences he had committed against the king to his sins against themselves – to his arrogant demeanour in the council chamber, letting no man speak 'but one or two great personages, so that he would have all the words himself'.[29] Wolsey also used the council more publicly to abase individual councillors whenever they gave him the chance. His weapon was simply a policy of law enforcement. The first to suffer appears to have been Thomas Stanley, earl of Derby, who was fined £1,000 'for a riot' and bound to pay the whole sum in ten annual instalments, starting in November 1515.[30] But the policy was formally announced by the chancellor in an 'elegant oration' in the presence of Henry VIII and the council on 2 May 1516 in which he dwelt on 'the enormityes usuallye exercised' in the realm and the remedies devised by the councillors. The king, remembering the oath he had taken at 'his moste triumphant coronacion', replied that he was determined to see 'th' indifferent ministracion of justice to all personnes as well heighe as lowe, which be to him in semblable regarde'. If his officials were prevented by 'sinister meanes' from enforcing the law, the councillors were to inform him and he would 'addresse his moste terrible power yf neede sholde, as God forbid, for

[27] J. A. Guy, *The Cardinal's Court. The Impact of Thomas Wolsey in Star Chamber* (Hassocks, 1977), pp. 23–6.

[28] ibid., pp. 29–30.

[29] Coke, *Fourth Institute*, p. 91.

[30] BL, Add. 21, 481, f.341; C54/383.

the subduinge and repressinge of th' enemyes of justice yf anye suche be founden'.[31] The occasion was stage-managed to publicize the fate of Wolsey's noble victim. The earl of Northumberland had been ordered by the council to appear before it either to answer certain charges laid against him or to submit 'pietate domini Regis'. On 16 April he appeared, submitted and asked the lord chancellor and all the council to intercede for him with Henry VIII.[32] On 2 May he was examined before the king in star chamber and committed to the Fleet prison 'for diverse contemptes'.[33] Buckingham, Norfolk and Suffolk, Surrey and Worcester, Bergavenny and Darcy were present to witness his humiliation.

Yet the clear message was not picked up by all the councillors. The next day Henry VIII's sister, Margaret queen of Scots, arrived in London. George lord Hastings and his stepfather, Sir Richard Sacheverell, made the mistake of attending the reception for her with too many men wearing their livery. Wolsey at once started an investigation. Both men were examined and evidently laid charges against the marquess of Dorset, leader of the faction which challenged their power in Leicestershire. The three of them were bound over to appear in star chamber. Information was also laid against them and against lord Bergavenny and Sir Edward Guildford in king's bench and they were all thought to be in great danger for illegal retaining. Thomas Alen, sending the news to his master, Shrewsbury, added an urgent warning: 'at the reverens of God, my lord, take heed to hit.' Another man sent to the Fleet had been wearing the earl's badge until a friend noticed it and got him to remove it.[34] As Alen reported it, Surrey as well as Dorset and Bergavenny had been 'putt out of the counsell chambre' before the end of May, 'whatsoever that did mean'; but no further action was taken against him. On the other hand, Buckingham, returning home, 'hath all his desires with gret thankes of the kyng'. Suffolk and his wife had left as well. 'Her be so many thynges out of ordre', Alen told Shrewsbury, that Henry VIII and Wolsey were more than ever anxious for him to come to court, especially since he was one of the king's household officers. But Shrewsbury preferred to distance himself from the 'gret snerling'. Even Wolsey was concerned to shift

---

[31] Huntington Library, Ellesmere 2655, f.10.

[32] BL, Lansdowne 639, f.45v.

[33] Lambeth Palace Library, MS. 3192, f.31 (*LP*, ii(1), 1861), printed *Illustrations of British History, Biography, and Manners, in the Reigns of Henry VIII, Edward VI, Mary, Elizabeth, and James I*, ed. Edmund Lodge, 3 vols, 2nd edn (London, 1838), i, 11–15; BL, Cotton Vesp. C.XIV (Pt 2), f.266v.

[34] Guy, *Cardinal's Court*, p. 31; Lambeth Palace Library, MS. 3192, f.41 (*LP*, ii(1), 2018), printed *Illustrations of British History*, i, 26–30.

the blame for it, openly accusing Sir Henry Marney of having 'done mor displeasur' to the king, 'by the reason of his cruelnesse ayenst the gret estates of this realme, then any man lyving'.[35]

Henry VIII, it seems, had been hardly more prepared than the nobility for such a sequel to his speech. Wolsey had launched an unprecedented attack on noble councillors who were, unlike Northumberland, the king's friends. Dorset, Surrey, Hastings and Bergavenny all took part in the jousts of honour at Greenwich on 19 and 20 May to entertain the Scottish queen.[36] Henry's relationship with them survived the upset, although it must have revived memories of Bergavenny's earlier brush with the law for infringing the statute of liveries of 1504.[37] The act had expired with Henry VII; in the euphoria of a new reign the nobility had perhaps forgotten that the statute of liveries of 1468 was still in being, if not in force. Yet three years after the dramatic reminder, Buckingham openly flouted the law. Again Henry VIII sat with his council in a formal display of his commitment to justice. He heard another 'notable oration' by Wolsey on 27 October 1519 and the next day, personally affronted this time, himself gave 'a lesson to be remembred' to Sir William Bulmer, his own sworn servant, for 'putting himselfe in the duke of Buckinghams service', contrary to his oath, and wearing the duke's livery in his presence. Buckingham's brother, Wiltshire, was there on each day, together with the earl of Kent – the only meetings of the council either is known to have attended. Norfolk and Suffolk were present as well, with Dorset, Surrey, Worcester, Darcy and Bergavenny.[38] Buckingham was in the neighbourhood, but did not attend. He had been at his house at Bletchingley, Surrey, in September, grumbling to Bergavenny (so it was said) about the king's councillors. By early November he was at East Greenwich in Kent, where he was alleged to have reacted to the king's displeasure by making the threat laid to his charge 18 months later – to kill Henry VIII as his father had been ready to kill Richard III.[39]

The judicial murder of Buckingham in 1521 profoundly disturbed Sir Thomas More, to whom it seemed all too reminiscent of the reign of Richard III.[40] It was indeed the first indication of the lengths to which Henry VIII could be driven by fear for the future of his dynasty.

[35] Lambeth Palace Library, MS. 3192, f.39 (*LP*, ii(1), 1959), printed *Illustrations of British History*, i, 21–4.

[36] *LP*, ii(2), pp. 1507–8.

[37] C54/373, quoted W. C. Richardson, *Tudor Chamber Administration 1485–1547* (Baton Rouge, La, 1952), p. 149.

[38] Huntington Library, Ellesmere 2655, f.15, Ellesmere 2654, ff.14v–15.

[39] KB8/4/5.

[40] Alistair Fox, *Thomas More. History and Providence* (Oxford, 1982), pp. 100–4.

Wolsey, credited with the duke's destruction, seemed at the height of his power. The restricted scope of conciliar activity kept all the councillors in subjection to him. Even in 1525, when the 'amicable grant' was causing widespread unrest, Norfolk and Suffolk apparently failed to persuade Henry VIII to call a meeting of the council to decide how to tackle the problem.[41] But the king himself eventually began to resent the lack of councillors around him and Wolsey included in the Eltham ordinances a proposed reform of the council. The 20 men nominated to attend upon the king included seven peers: the two dukes – Norfolk, the lord treasurer, and Suffolk, at that time marshal of England – the two marquesses – Dorset and Exeter – and two earls – Shrewsbury, steward of the household, and Worcester, the lord chamberlain – with one baron, lord Sandys. Yet Wolsey's real intentions were betrayed by the next ordinance, which whittled down the 'honourable presence of councellors about his grace' to two, if more could not be spared to attend at court.[42] No council attendant would be tolerated while Wolsey was chancellor. Nor was Wolsey prepared to relax his pressure on disorderly noblemen. Thomas lord Dacre had in February 1525 been brought to confess 'the bearinge of theaves and his remysnes and negligens in ponyshement of them' and been committed to the Fleet.[43] In December 1528 his son, William lord Dacre, bound himself in £100 to pay a fine imposed upon him for riots in Cumberland, following a complaint laid by the earl of Cumberland. In the same month Walter Devereux, lord Ferrers – a member of the council in the marches of Wales – acknowledged a recognizance of 1,000 marks binding him to pay any fine Wolsey and the council might impose for his retaining of men 'as he hath confessed to have made contrarie to the kinges lawes'.[44] Wolsey's determination to assert his authority never faltered until his failure to free Henry VIII from Katherine of Aragon gave his enemies the chance to overthrow him.

His fall allowed an inner ring to revive, made up of those councillors to whom Henry VIII turned for advice on the divorce. As the struggle for influence raged between his advisers, official and unofficial, Henry VIII began to summon councillors to court for policy meetings.[45] When Darcy in July 1529 had prepared articles against Wolsey, listing his offences against God and the king, he had noted sadly that Wolsey's first line of defence would be to create divisions among the nobility.[46] Against his expectation, a coherent group emerged at the

[41] *LP*, iv(1), 1329.
[42] *A Collection of Ordinances*, pp. 159–60.
[43] BL, Lansdowne 1, f.105.
[44] C54/397; *LP*, iv(2), 4855.
[45] Guy, *More*, pp. 98–9.
[46] *LP*, iv(3), 5749.

critical moment and held firm until it had achieved its immediate aim. When the council met on 19 October 1529 to debate the succession to Wolsey, there were 12 noblemen present: Norfolk and Suffolk, Dorset and Exeter, the earls of Oxford, Northumberland and Shrewsbury, viscounts FitzWalter and Rochford, and lords Mountjoy, Darcy and Sandys.[47] On 1 December the same 12 councillors signed the 44 articles preferred in the house of lords against Wolsey, petitioning the king to take such action against him 'that he never have any power, jurisdiction or authority hereafter to trouble, vex and impoverish the common-wealth of this your realm as he hath done heretofore'.[48] But this unity forged by hatred of Wolsey soon disintegrated. Even as they combined to destroy him, Norfolk resisted an attempt by Suffolk to succeed Wolsey himself. Norfolk was soon clearly identified as the leading lay councillor in spite of his statement to Chapuys in October that the government was to be managed by the council, not by any individual. Henry VIII was for a time more inclined to see to affairs himself and early in 1530 Chapuys was told that he had appointed Suffolk president of the council to assist him when Norfolk and the new chancellor, More, were kept from attending on him by their official duties.[49] The post of president had been reinstated by act of parliament in 1529, presumably at Suffolk's request. The statute added the president of the council to the law-enforcing tribunal set up in 1487, whose members already included the chancellor, treasurer and keeper of the privy seal, making him a high officer of state. As president Suffolk would also be able to attend ceremonies such as the swearing-in of sheriffs and justices of the peace from which he had previously been excluded.[50] But he did not in fact play the political role which this appointment seemed to herald, perhaps because, as the Venetian ambassador reported, he preferred his own amusements to close attention to conciliar business.[51] No evidence survives of any official use of his new title until late in 1536.[52] By then the reform of the council needed to make it an effective instrument of government had been carried through by Cromwell, who was careful not to make Wolsey's mistake of concentrating the appearance of power in himself as well as the reality. Henry VIII at last acquired what he had wanted in 1526 and 1530, a council permanently attendant upon himself.

[47] BL, Lansdowne 1, f.108v.
[48] Coke, *Fourth Institute*, pp. 89–95.
[49] *CSPSp.*, iv(1), 194, 211, 257 (Suffolk miscalled Norfolk).
[50] 21 Henry VIII, c.20; Guy, *Cardinal's Court*, pp. 132–3.
[51] *CSPVen.*, iv, 694.
[52] *LP*, xi, 1224(2).

The privy council in 1536–7 numbered 19 men and included nine peers: all those on the list in the Eltham ordinances of 1526 who were still alive (Norfolk, Suffolk, Exeter, Shrewsbury, Sandys), with the earls of Oxford and Sussex, Edward Seymour, viscount Beauchamp, and Thomas lord Cromwell.[53] For the higher nobility, in particular, the loss in prestige was substantial. Yet a working council almost half made up of noblemen was hardly a blow at the concept of noble rule, and Henry VIII was indignant when the Yorkshire rebels compared it unfavourably with his first council. 'As touching the begynnyng of our reigne, where ye say so many noblemen were counsaillours, who were then counsaillours I well remember, and yet of the temporaltee I note non but 2 worthie calling noble, the one treasourer of Englonde [Surrey], the other high stewarde of our house [Shrewsbury]; others, as the lorde Marney, and Darcye, but scant well borne gentilmen, and yet of no grete landes till they were promoted by us, and so made knightes and lordes.'[54] The king had expunged from his memory such undoubted noblemen as Buckingham and Northumberland, but he gave an accurate enough description of the status of the leading councillors of his youth: Surrey and Shrewsbury, Darcy, a baron only since 1504, and Henry Marney, made a knight and a lord by Henry VIII, were – with Charles Brandon – the men in most favour (by Darcy's estimation) early in the reign.[55] Nevertheless, Henry was disingenuous in the contrast he made with the 'many nobles indede both of byrth and condicyon' in the council of 1536. The king included in his count not only those of noble birth – Norfolk, Exeter, Shrewsbury 'when he may com', Oxford and Sussex – but also Suffolk and Sandys and Sir William FitzWilliam and Sir William Paulet, the 1530s equivalents of the 'scant well born gentlemen' of the early years of the reign. The membership of the council in 1536 in fact perpetuated the same balance between old nobility and new men that had been usual in the inner ring of Tudor councillors and in the unreformed council as a whole. Yet when the reform of the council was completed by the appointment of a clerk in August 1540, after Cromwell's fall, Norfolk and Sussex were the only noblemen by birth remaining, although there were eight noblemen on the council.[56] Sussex died two years later and on the king's death, with Norfolk under attainder, Arundel, admitted in 1546, was the sole nobleman of ancient family on the privy council. No government imaginable in sixteenth-century England could have excluded the nobility from power at the centre, but the

[53] Elton, *Tudor Revolution*, pp. 339–40.
[54] *SP*, i, 506–10.
[55] *LP*, i(1), 157.
[56] *PPC*, vii, 3–4.

terms on which power might be achieved had been transformed.

Unless noblemen were to be content with a personal or merely ceremonial role at court, they had to be members of the privy council. Membership was possible, but it normally had to be attained through office. Ennoblement might even mean loss of office and so of council membership, as it did for Sir William Paulet in 1539, when he was created lord St John and gave up his office of treasurer of the household. Sir John Russell, the comptroller of the household, ennobled with Paulet, also gave up his office and probably ceased to be a privy councillor, although by August 1540, as the newly appointed lord admiral, he was a member of the privy council.[57] The importance of office-holding was made crystal clear by the act 'for the placing of the lordes' in parliament and council. The chancellor introduced it in the house of lords on 5 May 1539 as a bill drawn at the king's command 'concernentem assignationem locorum quorundam procerum et capitalium officiorum hujus regni Anglie, videlicet, vicegerentis domini regis in spiritualibus, domini cancellarii, domini thesaurarii, et aliorum in eadem billa declaratorum'. The immediate problem was evidently the place to be assigned to Cromwell, who had not taken his seat in the upper house until the last day of the previous parliament in July 1536, and the precedence of Audley, ennobled in 1538. On the opening day, 28 April 1539, they were entered in the lords' journal almost at the bottom of the list of barons, with only the three barons created the previous month below them. As vicegerent Cromwell exercised the king's authority as supreme head of the church and took precedence over all other subjects. On 10 May 1539, immediately after the bill had passed the lords and without waiting for the views of the commons, the clerk amended the list he had prepared and moved Cromwell to his rightful place heading the bench of bishops.[58] Audley had until 1539 presided over the lords, as More had done before him, without being listed among those present; it was clearly thought inappropriate, when as a member of the house he had to be included, that he should appear, even on paper, among the most junior barons. The act listed the great lay offices of state in order of precedence. The first four – the lord chancellor, lord treasurer, lord president of the

[57] St John and Russell (and lord Mordaunt) were nevertheless present in star chamber on 23 February 1540 and Russell again on 28 April: BL, Add. 4521, ff.120, 122v. St John (and lord Windsor) also signed letters from the council in London to the council with the king in July and October 1541: *LP*, xvi, 978, 1028, 1261. They were presumably in the category described by Henry VIII in October 1540 as 'of our counseil, thoughe not of our pryvie counseil': *SP*, viii, 455–6.

[58] 31 Henry VIII, c.10; *LJ*, i, 104–7. The amended entry in the MS. lords' journal for 10 May 1539 is reproduced in Powell and Wallis, *The House of Lords*, plate XXIII.

council and lord privy seal – if they were of the degree of baron or above were to sit above all dukes except those of the king's own family. Audley was absent from parliament on 10 May, but on 12 May he headed the list of temporal peers. The position of the two dukes was unchanged: Norfolk, the lord treasurer, came next, followed by Suffolk in the place to which he was entitled as president of the council, although when he was described – in later sessions of parliament – it was always by the title of his other office, as great master of the household. Under the act the great chamberlain, the constable, marshal and admiral of England, the great master or steward of the king's household and the king's chamberlain were to sit in that order above all others of their own degree; the chief secretary, if a baron, was to sit above all other barons except any holders of the previously named offices. As Cromwell was lord privy seal and chief secretary, neither of these titles appeared in the lords' journal of 1539; neither did the (non-existent) constable, nor the marshal of England, already present in the person of Norfolk. But Oxford, great chamberlain, and Southampton, lord admiral, were moved up the list on 10 May to give them precedence over all other earls. For Southampton, a peer of less than two years' creation, it was a dramatic rise. In June 1540, after he became lord privy seal, he was moved higher still, above the marquess of Dorset; Russell, the new lord admiral, formerly next to the bottom, headed the list of barons. From 12 July 1540 Sussex, an earl only since 1529, as great chamberlain took precedence over all the earls except Southampton.[59]

The act of 1539 pinpointed the offices which would bring membership of the privy council. When Cromwell gave up being secretary, before he was created earl in April 1540, the office was granted to two commoners, with a diminished status. The king's warrant for their appointment placed them in council lower than any nobleman and below the treasurer, comptroller, master of the horse and vice-chamberlain of the household.[60] These office-holders, all commoners, with the chancellors of augmentations and of first fruits, made up almost half the privy council in August 1540, eight knights balancing the eight noblemen with three clerics bringing the total membership to 19. After the death of Sandys, the lord chamberlain, in December 1540, there were seven noble councillors, reduced to six by the death of Southampton in mid-October 1542. The appointment of Russell to succeed Southampton as lord privy seal enabled Henry VIII to grant the office of lord admiral to his brother-in-law, Edward Seymour, earl

[59] *LJ*, i, 146–61.
[60] *SP*, i, 623–4.

of Hertford, the only lay privy councillor in 1540 without high office. The number of noble privy councillors was raised to seven again by the admission of William Paulet, lord St John, 'admitted and sworne in to the nomber off the privye cownsell' on 19 November 1542, the day before he was appointed master of the new court of wards and liveries.[61] The death of the earl of Sussex later in November 1542 reduced the noble privy councillors to six once more until the pro- motion of Hertford to take his place as great chamberlain left a vacancy as lord admiral filled by John Dudley, viscount Lisle, an appointment which brought Lisle council membership.[62] The number rose again with the elevation to the peerage of one of the secretaries, Sir Thomas Wriothesley, on 1 January 1544 – but only briefly, since the lord chancellor, Audley of Walden, died at the end of April. William Parr, earl of Essex, was a councillor by March 1544, no doubt admitted by virtue of his status as the king's new brother-in-law.[63] In contrast to Hertford, he was never given high office by Henry VIII. Finally, the death of Suffolk in 1545 brought further promotion to St John and – almost a year later – the admission of Arundel to the privy council on his appointment as lord chamberlain.[64] The number of noble privy councillors then remained at eight until the arrest and attainder of Norfolk in the last weeks of the reign.

The privy council could not satisfy the ambitions of any significant number of men, as the unreformed council had done, but it also undermined the position of the one, dominant minister, now no longer indispensable. Henry VIII, it is true, came to look back on Cromwell as the most faithful servant he had ever had, just as he had rounded on his councillors in 1530, comparing them unfavourably with Wolsey.[65] Nonetheless, whatever the quality of its advice and actions, the privy council from the fall of Cromwell to the end of the reign acted as a governing board, meeting regularly to discharge a wide range of business. The surviving registers record its activities from August 1540 to May 1543 – apart from a short gap in April and May 1542 – and from July 1545 to January 1547.[66] Until the summer of 1546 the council met on over half the days of each month covered by the registers except in July 1542, when it held only 12 meetings. But from August 1546 until the death of Henry VIII recorded meetings were less frequent, dropping to nine in September, seven in October and six

[61] *APC*, i, 54; *LP*, xvii, 1154 g.72.
[62] *APC*, i, 118.
[63] *LP*, xix(1), 162.
[64] *APC*, i, 495.
[65] *CSPSp.*, iv(1), 509; *LP*, xvi, 590.
[66] *PPC*, vii and *APC*, i, passim.

in November, although picking up to 15 in December, when the council began to meet at Ely Place in Holborn. However, the council in these months was divided, some councillors being with the king and some in London. When this was the case – as, for example, in 1541, when Henry VIII went on progress to York – the register recorded only the business of the main group. At nearly every meeting entered in the registers the presence was recorded – no doubt with less than perfect accuracy, but giving some indication of the pattern of attendance.

Henry VIII was never recorded as present. He and the council might give audience together, as they did to the imperial ambassador on 21 December 1540, but the king did not attend the meeting of the council which immediately followed in the council chamber. Lord Sandys was at Guisnes until October 1540, but attended the council in November, within a fortnight of his death. Southampton attended two-thirds of the council meetings held before his death in October 1542 and Sussex over three-quarters of those held before he died the following month. The lord chancellor had other duties which might make it difficult for him to be present and lord Audley of Walden attended fewer than half the council's meetings in the three years from August 1540. He did not travel north with Henry VIII in 1541 and from April to the end of August 1542, when the king was for the most part away from London, although in its vicinity, Audley was never entered in the register as present. However, his successor as chancellor, lord Wriothesley, attended well over half the council meetings of 1545–7, including most of those held at Portsmouth in July 1545, when Henry VIII inspected the navy assembled to resist a French invasion. Wriothesley had a special interest in Hampshire, his home county, and acted as host to the king and council at his home at Titchfield on 31 July, but he was also more politically involved than Audley had been; in the crucial last three months of the reign he attended every council meeting entered in the register, wherever it was held.

Suffolk, lord president of the council until his death in 1545, attended slightly over a quarter of its meetings. He had some long breaks at home, yet the charge of idleness, probably justified in 1530, seems out of place in the 1540s. Suffolk attended the council in concentrated bursts. He was more often than not present at council meetings from mid-November 1540 to the end of January 1541 and attended almost every meeting in August and September 1541 as he accompanied Henry VIII to York. He was called to court again in November and attended the council regularly for the next four months, combining this with attendance in the parliament which opened in January 1542. A few days after the prorogation of parliament on 1

April, Suffolk went home. The following September he was sent north with the army. In December, as in the preceding two years, he was at court, although neither he nor anyone else had to attend a council meeting on Christmas day, as they had done in 1540 and 1541. In January 1543 he was back in the north, where he served until March 1544; early in July he joined the army in France. When the council register resumes in the summer of 1545, Suffolk was sometimes present, sometimes away attending to military matters. Early in August when he was at Portsmouth trying – among other things – to raise the *Mary Rose*, he was recalled to court and appointed to command the army in Boulogne, a commission he never lived to carry out. His final days were spent attending 11 consecutive council meetings at Guildford, the last on 21 August, the day before he died. (Henry VIII paid for a grand funeral in St George's chapel, Windsor, as befitted a knight of the Garter, although Suffolk had asked in his will to be buried at Tattershall in Lincolnshire, 'yf if so convenyently may be, without any pompe or outwarde pryde of the worlde'.)[67] Norfolk attended rather more council meetings than Suffolk: about one-third of those for which the presence is known. He also was away in the north at intervals – in 1541 and 1542 – but he had as well to withdraw from the council on a number of occasions while it dealt with members of his family: in December 1541 (when the council sent to the Tower the dowager duchess and lord William Howard and committed lady Bridgwater to ward); in July and August 1542 and again in April 1543 (when Surrey was sent to the Fleet for disorderly behaviour and eating meat in Lent); and in May 1546 (when his younger son, lord Thomas Howard, was warned to stop disputing over the scriptures). In 1545 Norfolk was responsible for raising men for the war during the summer, but he was regularly present in council in September and October and, once parliament was in session, in November and December. Yet in 1546 his attendance declined sharply. He was present at nine meetings in August, but after that attended only once more, on 1 November. In the late 1520s and the 1530s Norfolk had been kept away from the council by Wolsey and Cromwell. Now it was either the influence of Hertford or his own feeling that he had lost favour with his fellow councillors as well as with the king which kept him at home – until he was called to London in December and lodged in the Tower.[68]

---

[67] *Wills from Doctors' Commons*, ed. J. G. Nichols and J. Bruce, Camden Soc., lxxxiii (London, 1863), pp. 28–41.

[68] Norfolk's mistress deposed that he had said that 'none of the king's council loved him because they were no noblemen born themselves' and that 'the king loved him not because he was too much lov'd in his country': Herbert, *Henry the Eighth*, p. 627.

Hertford himself attended slightly over one-third of the council meetings between 1540 and 1547 and John Dudley, viscount Lisle, just under one-third of those held after he was admitted to the council. Both were often absent on active service and it was not until December 1546 that they were recognized by the imperial ambassador as the dominant figures at court.[69] St John was present at about half the recorded council meetings held after November 1542, in spite of an extended absence in the summer and autumn of 1545 when he was first at Portsmouth seeing to the victualling of the navy and then seriously ill. Essex attended nearly two-thirds and Arundel almost exactly two-thirds of the meetings held after they had been admitted to the privy council. (For all their diligence, Essex and Arundel – the two most recently admitted councillors – were omitted from the regency council named in Henry VIII's will: they headed the list of assistant councillors, to give their advice only when called upon.)[70] But the nobleman with the best record of attendance, maintained over a long period, was Russell. In the years covered by the registers he attended over three-quarters of the council meetings, missing only two complete months – July and August 1545, when he was reviewing the coastal defences of the west country. If the register had survived for 1544, when Russell was one of the commanders in the French war, his record would have been less striking. Nevertheless, by his regular attendance in council Russell helped to give some stability to Henry VIII's last years – without ever being an outstanding figure.[71] In his lack of distinction he was typical of the noblemen who most frequently attended the council between 1540 and 1547. They were not the men with the greatest reputation – Norfolk and Suffolk – nor the most ambitious – Hertford and Lisle. Henry VIII himself did not treat attendance in council as the highest service. He often diverted his councillors to other duties; in the case of the noblemen, above all to military service. War was still the priority for the king, and for the nobility the surest way to the top.

The full complement of noblemen was most likely to be present in council when a parliament was in session. At such times the privy council generally met at Westminster or St James's palace, if necessary waiting until the day's business in parliament – normally confined to the morning – was over. Yet Henry VIII did not feel it essential to make sure that all the noblemen on the privy council were free to

[69] CSPSp., viii, 370.

[70] Foedera, vi(3), 142–5.

[71] The judgement of Diane Willen, John Russell, First Earl of Bedford. One of the King's Men, Royal Historical Society Studies in History Series, no. 23 (London, 1981), p. 129.

attend the house of lords. Sandys, who was captain of Guisnes as well as lord chamberlain, was at Guisnes for the whole of the 1539 session and part of the 1540 session of parliament; Sussex was a commissioner at Calais for part of the session in 1540; Suffolk, away in the north throughout the session of 1543, was recalled during the next session, in 1544, but could attend only the closing weeks of the parliament; Hertford, sent to replace him as lieutenant of the north, had to leave in mid-session; in 1544, too, the lord admiral, Lisle, preoccupied with naval business, left for Harwich before the dissolution. Nevertheless, no privy councillors except Sandys and Suffolk missed an entire session and most of them attended regularly, being present in each session on at least three-quarters of the days for which the attendance was entered.[72] The journals surviving in the house of lords note the daily attendance in the upper house for the two sessions of parliament in 1515, for one session (opening in January 1534) of the Reformation parliament and for every session of parliament from June 1536 to the end of the reign.[73] The printed lists in the *Lords' Journals* are not entirely reliable. Suffolk, for example, is entered as present in the house of lords on three days in 1543, when the manuscript journal never marks him present.[74] The clerks, too, may have made mistakes. However, the evidence will support some conclusions. The session of 1544 was clearly exceptional: no privy councillors were present for as many as three-quarters of the days on which the lords met, although Norfolk attended regularly for the first six weeks and again during the last two weeks, when he presided over the house in the absence of the chancellor, Audley, who was near to death. Audley had not attended regularly in 1543 either, but Wriothesley, when he became chancellor, presided over the upper house every day during the sessions of 1545 and 1547. Except in 1544 – and during the second session of 1515 (as earl of Surrey) – Norfolk was always a regular attender; so were Seymour and Russell after their ennoblement, except in 1544, and William FitzWilliam, earl of Southampton, up to his death. By contrast, Robert Radcliffe as lord FitzWalter and earl of Sussex, although present at some time in every session, only attended regularly in the sessions of June–July 1536 and 1539. He apparently thought attendance in council was more worthwhile since during the parliamentary

---

[72] The criterion of regular attendance used in Miller, 'Attendance in the house of lords'.

[73] *LJ*, i, 18–291. For a descriptive analysis of the MS. lords' journals of the reign see G. R. Elton, 'The early journals of the house of lords', *EHR*, lxxxix (1974), 481–512.

[74] *LJ*, i, 209, 217, 231 (21 February, 14 March, 9 May), checked with House of Lords, Lords' Journals, i. For the need to use the attendance lists with reservations see M. A. R. Graves, 'The two lords' journals of 1542', *Bull.IHR*, xliii (1970), 182–9.

session of January–April 1542 he missed only four meetings of the privy council but was present at only 30 of the 52 meetings of the house of lords. St John was likewise more often present in council than in parliament in 1543, although in other sessions, apart from that of 1544, he was a regular attender. Even for privy councillors, it seems, regular attendance in the house of lords was a matter of choice: no more than Henry VIII did they treat it as an overriding duty.

Nevertheless, in each session of parliament from June 1536 to the end of the reign (except the session of 1544) the majority of the noblemen who were privy councillors attended regularly in the house of lords. In 1539 every privy councillor, apart from the absent lord Sandys, was regularly present. The sessional pattern of attendance of the privy councillors reflected that of the nobility as a whole: the percentage of the nobility attending regularly was at its highest (55 per cent) in 1539 and its lowest in 1544 (4 per cent).[75] The poor level of regular attendance in 1544 was not caused by any fall in the number of noblemen attending at some time during the session. Indeed, a slightly higher percentage of the nobility than in the previous session made an appearance in the house of lords in 1544, although fewer than in the first session of this parliament, in 1542. Preparations for the coming invasion of France perhaps helped to divert the attention of the nobility during a session which was not notable for the quantity or quality of its legislation.[76] The high level of regular attendance in 1539, on the other hand, was built on the presence of 88 per cent of the nobility. It was on both counts the best attended session of the reign, and not only by the nobility: a higher percentage of the bishops and abbots also appeared and attended regularly in 1539 than in any other session.

The attendance of the lay nobility in June–July 1536 was almost as striking, with regular attendance showing a marked improvement on that of January–March 1534. However, 84 per cent of the nobility had been present in early 1534 for some part of the session. The real contrast was with the two sessions of 1515, when under 60 per cent of the nobility appeared at all and under 20 per cent attended regularly. More noblemen had attended parliament in 1512. An original paper, now in the British Library, records the presence of 66 per cent of the nobility on 2 or 3 March 1512, although there is no way of knowing

[75] Percentages, here and below, from Miller, 'Attendance in the house of lords', 337, table 2.
[76] S. E. Lehmberg, *The Later Parliaments of Henry VIII 1536–1547* (Cambridge, 1977), p. 191.

how regularly they attended during the session.[77] But generally in the early years of the reign of Henry VIII attendances probably conformed to the slack and haphazard pattern of the late medieval house of lords.[78] However, the opening of parliament never had to be put off for lack of a sufficient presence to grace the occasion. The ceremony gave a special opportunity for display to a number of the noblemen. At the opening of Henry VIII's first parliament, in 1510, Oxford as great chamberlain bore the king's train, supported by lord Herbert, the lord chamberlain, while the duke of Buckingham carried the cap of maintenance. The sword was entrusted to Buckingham's brother, lord Henry Stafford.[79] This honour, exceptionally bestowed on one who was not a member of the house of lords, foreshadowed the grant of an earldom to Stafford a week later. The bearers of the cap and sword are not known for every one of Henry VIII's parliaments, but it is clear that to be chosen to carry either was a sign of royal favour. Henry Courtenay as earl of Devon and marquess of Exeter bore the cap in 1523 and the sword in 1529, Dorset the cap in 1529, Richmond the cap and Sussex the sword in 1536, Suffolk the cap in 1539, Francis Talbot, earl of Shrewsbury, the sword in 1539, 1542 and 1545 and Henry Grey, marquess of Dorset, the cap in 1542 and 1545.[80]

Proceedings in parliament itself began with a speech by the lord chancellor which was entered in the lords' journal, where it was followed by the names of receivers and triers of petitions. Their appointment has justly been described as an archaic survival without practical meaning.[81] Yet to be named a trier – especially of petitions

[77] BL, Harl. 158, ff.140–2, printed N. H. Nicolas, *Report of Proceedings on Claims to the Barony of L'Isle* (London, 1829), pp. 418–21. BL, Harl. 158, f.143 (*LP*, x, 244) records the presence on 4 and 5 February 1536, when 19 peers were noted as present.

[78] J. S. Roskell, 'The problem of the attendance of the lords in medieval parliaments', *Bull.IHR*, xxix (1956), 153–204.

[79] BL, Add. 5758, ff.8–9, printed Powell and Wallis, *The House of Lords*, pp. 543–4 (lord Henry Stafford wrongly identified).

[80] Accounts of the opening of parliament in College of Arms, 2 H.13, f.396 (1523), f.403 (1529, printed GEC, ix, Appendix B and Powell and Wallis, *The House of Lords*, pp. 563–4), f.404 (1539, printed Dugdale, *A Perfect Copy of all Summons of the Nobility*, pp. 502–3, lord chancellor mistranscribed lord chamberlain), f.406v–7 (1542), ff.410v–11 (1545); Wriothesley, *Chronicle*, i, 44–8 (1536).

[81] Elton, 'The early journals', 505. The names of triers of petitions for the parliaments of 1510, 1512, 1515 and 1536, 1539, 1542 and 1545 are entered in the lords' journals, but the names as printed for the parliament of 1545 rightly belong to Edward VI's first parliament: *LJ*, i, 4, 10–11, 18–19, 84–5, 103, 165, 267. The names for the parliaments of 1523 and 1529 are printed from the parliament rolls ibid., lxxvi, cli–clii. House of Lords, Lords' Journals, i, f.643 gives the triers of petitions for 1545, amended for 1547.

from England, Ireland, Wales and Scotland – was also a mark of distinction. The triers of petitions from Gascony and other parts of the continent (including Tournai and Thérouanne in 1515) were headed by a bishop or, in the 1540s, the archbishop of York, and typically included noblemen of less importance than those named as triers of petitions from England, always in this reign headed by the archbishop of Canterbury. In 1529, for example, the triers of petitions from England included Norfolk and Suffolk, Dorset and Exeter, the earl of Shrewsbury, viscounts Lisle, FitzWalter and Rochford and lord Bergavenny, while the earls of Arundel, Northumberland and Rutland and lords Audley, Mountjoy and Sandys were triers of petitions from Gascony. In 1536 Edward Seymour, just created viscount Beauchamp, was a trier of petitions from Gascony, but for the next parliament, in 1539, as earl of Hertford, he was transferred to the English list, which included every nobleman who was a privy councillor, except the chancellor. In 1542 all the noble privy councillors except the chancellor were again triers of petitions from England, with William Paulet, lord St John, a former privy councillor soon to be readmitted to the council. The pre-eminence of the privy councillors in the house of lords was clearly recognized in these lists, formal though they were.

In a similar development, lay proxy votes came to be almost entirely concentrated in the hands of noble privy councillors. Throughout the reign noblemen were absent from parliament without (it seems) obtaining a licence, but in the early years those who were licensed to be absent always appointed spiritual and lay peers to represent them, acting together.[82] By the 1520s 'mixed' proxies were out of favour with the nobility; in 1523 and 1529 each nobleman for whom proxies survive named one or two other lay peers.[83] Councillors were frequently chosen as proctors in these years, but often jointly with a neighbour or friend of the absent nobleman. As late as 1536, writing to his master, viscount Lisle, deputy of Calais, John Husee took friendship for the relevant criterion, suggesting as Lisle's proctors Montagu and La Warre, 'whom I thought your lordship loved wele'; and these two were named in the proxy.[84] However, after the imprisonment of La Warre in December 1538 and the execution of Montagu, Lisle adopted a more politic approach. He named Hertford as his sole proctor in 1539.[85] Other noblemen, more alert to the ways of the world, made the adjustment earlier. William FitzAlan, earl of Arundel, was said by Chapuys to have been the only one out of 30 lay peers not

[82] *LJ*, i, 11–12, 19–20, 22, 25, 33, 43–4.
[83] SC10/50, no. 2481, SC10/52, no. 29–31, 46.
[84] SP3/4, ff.118–19 (*LP*, x, 994), printed *The Lisle Letters*, iii, 705; *LJ*, i, 83.
[85] *LJ*, i, 103.

to have voted for the bill in restraint of annates in 1532; for the next session, in 1533, he obtained a licence to be absent and authorized Thomas Boleyn, earl of Wiltshire, to act for him, 'knowing your honor, wysdome and good consciens'.[86] A year later, in the session which opened in January 1534, George Boleyn, lord Rochford, held four proxies, including one from La Warre.[87] Sometimes noblemen simply gave up their right of nomination to the king. In the last session of the Reformation parliament, early in 1536, Rochford's name was inserted into blank proxies sent in by La Warre and Lumley, and Wiltshire's name into another, made out by Northumberland; with Arundel now naming both Wiltshire and Rochford as his proctors, father and son between them held four proxies in this session.[88] Lumley, sending Cromwell £5 in September 1535 as the second instalment of his yearly fee, had made plain his expectation that when parliament was called 'it may please your maistershipp to be myne excuse enempste the kynges highnes fore apperaunce at the same'.[89] His confidence was justified then, but in May 1536, when he again sent Cromwell his fee and asked him to obtain the king's 'especyall pardon ffor all parlia- menttes' as he had promised, Lumley had no success and had to come up to London in spite of the pain he suffered in his throat and mouth and the 'boollyng heeytt' upon his stomach.[90] Licences of absence were hard to obtain in the summer of 1536 and in 1539 and few proxies were entered: in 1536 lord Daubeney sent in a blank proxy which remained unfilled and in 1539, besides Hertford, St John held one proxy, Cromwell and Audley of Walden shared one from lord Mordaunt, and Latimer and Windsor one from the prior of St John of Jerusalem. From 1540 to the end of the reign Edward Stanley, earl of Derby, and John lord Conyers, each holding one shared with Russell, and Henry Radcliffe, earl of Sussex, and Thomas lord Burgh, with one each, were the only noblemen to hold proxies without being privy councillors.[91] Nevertheless, the collection of proxies had no more practical signifi- cance than the naming of triers of petitions. It reflected the prestige of leading noblemen rather than any plan to use proxy votes, which – so far as it is known – were never cast in the reign of Henry VIII. Indeed, voting itself was a rare occurrence, first recorded in the surviving lords' journals in 1542, the noble dissentients never mustering more

---

[86] *CSPSp.*, iv(2), 922; SC10/52, no. 41.

[87] *LJ*, i, 58.

[88] SC10/52, no. 43, 45; BL, Harl. 158, f.144; SP1/101, f.131 (*LP*, x, 145).

[89] SP1/97, f.71 (*LP*, ix, 489).

[90] SP1/103, f.260 (*LP*, x, 826). Lumley was present in the house of lords from 12 June 1536.

[91] *LJ*, i, 83, 103, 128, 164, 266–7, 291.

than four, and never on a bill of major importance.[92] Moreover, it was not unusual for blank proxies to be left unfilled: their assignment was evidently not a matter of great moment. Privy councillors themselves did not always bother to send in proxies when they had to be away. Sandys named St John as his proctor in 1539,[93] but Suffolk apparently appointed no one to represent him in 1543. In the following session neither Suffolk nor Hertford arranged for proctors to act for them while they were in the north.

The high attendance rate in the house of lords in the 1530s was not maintained after 1539, although attendance seldom dropped back to the level of 1515: only once – in 1545 – did fewer than 60 per cent of the nobility appear at a session, while regular attendance fell below 20 per cent twice, in 1543 and 1544. Cromwell's influence had undoubtedly been one reason for the good attendance. He handled almost all the requests for leave of absence and, although the full effects of the policy were not seen until the summer, he had reminded himself early in 1536 to advise the king 'to graunt fewe licences for any to be absent from the parlyament'.[94] If the intention was to get noblemen to commit themselves either to acceptance of the main government bills or to overt opposition, it was successful. Darcy stoutly maintained his conviction that all matrimonial cases belonged to the ecclesiastical jurisdiction when Norfolk asked a group of influential men for their views on the king's divorce during the parliamentary session of 1532.[95] In the house of lords itself he made a parallel point: anything concerning the spiritual authority ought to be dealt with by convocation, as in the past, not in parliament.[96] But when he realized that he had no chance of influencing events in parliament, Darcy disengaged himself from its proceedings. Chapuys believed that he had been instructed by Henry VIII not to attend the session which began in January 1534, but there is no supporting evidence; by the autumn Darcy certainly wanted to get away. He sent his son to petition the king for a licence of absence from all future parliaments on grounds of age and illness, and made arrangements to send two doctors to give Cromwell details of his diseases. The licence was granted and Darcy never again appeared in the house of lords.[97] Hussey also stayed away in January 1534, but he returned to the house in June 1536, perhaps hoping to speak in favour

[92] ibid., 185, 225, 260, 272, 277, 279, 281. The vote on the annates bill reported by Chapuys cannot be substantiated since the journal for 1532 is lost.

[93] ibid., 103.

[94] SP1/102, ff.5–9 (*LP*, x, 254).

[95] *CSPSp.*, iv(2), 899.

[96] 'Aske's examination', ed. Mary Bateson, *EHR*, v (1890), 568.

[97] *CSPSp.*, v(1), 8; *LP*, vii, 1142, 1143, 1426, viii, 291 g.20.

of Mary. Thomas lord Vaux of Harrowden attended the sessions of January 1534 and February 1536 but then withdrew completely until Mary came to the throne.[98] So far as is known, every nobleman took the oath to the act of succession in 1534, when both houses of parliament were sworn. But for a few that represented the limit of their acquiescence.

Yet they were a tiny minority. From June 1536 to the death of Henry VIII most noblemen, on the evidence of the lords' journals, generally attended parliament. Of those noblemen who never became privy councillors, 22 might have attended all the eight sessions of parliament held in these years. Two of them in practice could not: William lord Grey of Wilton, lieutenant of Hammes, and George Brooke, lord Cobham, deputy of Calais, had to stay at their posts. Ten of the remaining 20 appeared at every session and a further six attended between four and seven sessions. Only three noblemen besides Vaux attended less than half the eight sessions, for reasons which remain obscure but were not, it seems, political. John lord Mordaunt, created a baron in 1532, was licensed to be absent in 1539 because of illness, but attended regularly in 1540; he never sat again in the house of lords in the reign of Henry VIII – nor in the reigns of Edward VI, Mary and Elizabeth, although he remained active in local affairs.[99] Ralph Neville, earl of Westmorland, laid up with gout in 1539, was allowed to be absent then but attended in 1540; his next appearance was in January 1547, although for only one session (that of 1542) was he instructed to remain at home in the north.[100] Henry Somerset, earl of Worcester, son of the old lord chamberlain, was present in 1536 and 1539 but during the rest of the reign attended only the session of 1543. There were 30 other noblemen, apart from the privy councillors, who were eligible to attend two or more sessions but not all eight. Three of them were not free to attend without licence: Arthur Plantagenet, viscount Lisle, the deputy of Calais, and Wharton and Eure, wardens of the northern marches from 1544. Of the remainder only five missed more parliamentary sessions than they attended. Like the former group of absentees, they came from both old and new families. Three were the sons of peers of Henry VIII's creation or promotion: John Bourchier, earl of Bath from 1539, was present in three sessions out of a possible seven, but Thomas lord Sandys, who succeeded his father in 1540, was never marked as present in any of the five sessions he might have attended during the reign and Henry

[98] *LJ*, i, passim; BL, Harl. 158, f.143v.

[99] *LP*, xiv(1), 845; *LJ*, i, 103, 541; Michael A. R. Graves, *The House of Lords in the Parliaments of Edward VI and Mary I. An Institutional Study* (Cambridge, 1981), pp. 38–9.

[100] *LP*, xiv(2), 251; *PPC*, vii, 285.

Clifford, earl of Cumberland from 1542, was credited with only one day's attendance in one of four possible sessions.[101] William lord Parr of Horton, ennobled by Henry VIII, took his seat in 1544 but did not attend in 1545 or 1547. The fifth absentee came from an old northern family which, so far as is known, never appeared at all in the house of lords during the reign of Henry VIII. Indeed, when Robert lord Ogle succeeded to the barony in the early 1530s, the chancery clerks found it hard to remember to send him a writ. When he did receive one, in 1539, he ignored it.

The noblemen who took little account of parliament effectively opted out of political life at the centre. The house of lords was the one institution which most noblemen could attend at will. The reform of the mid-1530s having removed from the higher nobility the almost certain prospect of council membership, a seat in the house of lords became all the more valuable. Four high noblemen who were not privy councillors attended every one of the last eight sessions of parliament in the reign of Henry VIII. One of them – Henry Daubeney, earl of Bridgwater – died at the age of 54 in 1548, but the other three went on to become privy councillors in the reign of Edward VI, when the council was more open to the nobility: Francis Talbot, earl of Shrewsbury, was a member of the privy council by January 1549 and Henry Grey, marquess of Dorset, by November 1549, while Edward Stanley, earl of Derby, was admitted on 9 August 1551 (in effect as a member for one day only). Of the six barons who attended all eight sessions of parliament, three also became privy councillors: Thomas lord Wentworth by August 1549, Walter Devereux, lord Ferrers, in January 1550 and Edward lord Clinton in May 1550. The only other non-conciliar noblemen of Henry VIII's reign to be sworn of the privy council in the reign of his son were George Brooke, lord Cobham, who attended every session of parliament for which he was eligible before he became deputy of Calais in 1544, and Francis Hastings, earl of Huntingdon from 1544, who attended the sessions of 1545 and 1547. It is not claimed that their attendance in the house of lords brought them council membership. Shrewsbury, Huntingdon and the four barons made their reputations first as commanders in war, Dorset was admitted to the privy council for his reformed religious views and Derby (briefly) as a leading Catholic whose support had to be obtained.[102] Nevertheless, the attention these noblemen gave to parlia-

---

[101] Sandys is wrongly marked in *LJ*, i as present on 17 March 1544, but Cumberland's presence on 18 January 1547 correctly reproduces the MS. entry: House of Lords, Lords' Journals, i, ff.224, 681. Sandys attended parliament in the reigns of Edward VI and Mary.

[102] D. E. Hoak, *The King's Council in the Reign of Edward VI* (Cambridge, 1976), ch. 2, passim.

ment in the reign of Henry VIII indicates their readiness to play a greater part in central government if they were offered the chance.

The house of lords could act as a forum for the politically ambitious. What did it have to offer noblemen who were content to be leaders of their localities? For some, perhaps, a meeting of parliament was primarily a social occasion. John lord Zouche never in any session achieved a daily attendance which reached double figures: he, presumably, found better things to do with his time in London. Zouche was not typical, but when parliament met noblemen from all over the kingdom were conveniently brought together for business or pleasure. On 3 July 1536 – during the parliament, but a day on which the house of lords did not sit – the earl of Rutland's residence in Shoreditch was the scene of a magnificent triple wedding reception. Rutland's eldest son and daughter married the daughter and eldest son of the earl of Westmorland, and another of Westmorland's daughters married the son and heir of the earl of Oxford. The celebrations were attended by 'all the greate estates of the realme' and Henry VIII himself rode over from York Place after dinner, disguised as a Turk, to join in the dancing and feasting.[103] Yet the assembly of parliament created many more sober opportunities, seized by noblemen as much concerned with advancing their own interests as with making new laws for the kingdom. In almost every session Henry VIII gave his assent to private bills for individual noblemen and their families. For the reversal of an attainder there was no alternative to an act of parliament until 1523, when 'th'acte of auctorite' authorized Henry VIII to reverse Buckingham's attainder and earlier attainders by letters patent.[104] In other cases a private act was not essential, but it provided the best safeguard for property rights. It could deal with the consequences of the breakdown of a marriage: in 1543 William lord Parr obtained an act to bastardize his wife's children after she had eloped with another man.[105] A bill in parliament might be seen as the way to the settlement of a dispute: in March 1512 the house of lords read a bill put in by Buckingham against Thomas Lucas, called for and read the response of Lucas, read Buckingham's replication, received another reply from Lucas, read Buckingham's rejoinder and finally sent the case to arbitration.[106] More often a statute confirmed a settlement already reached: in the last session of the Reformation parliament, for example, an act confirmed the terms of a settlement between Suffolk and

[103] Wriothesley, Chronicle, i, 50–1.

[104] 14 & 15 Henry VIII, c.21.

[105] House of Lords, Original Acts, 34 & 35 Henry VIII, no. 39.

[106] LJ, i, 14–17. For Buckingham's disputes with Sir Thomas Lucas see Carole Rawcliffe, The Staffords, Earls of Stafford and Dukes of Buckingham 1394–1521 (Cambridge, 1978), pp. 171–3.

Sir Christopher Willoughby – reached through the mediation of Henry VIII – which divided between them the inheritance of William lord Willoughby de Eresby.[107] Marriage settlements were occasionally confirmed. The indenture for the marriage of Oxford's son to Westmorland's daughter, only agreed a few days before the opening of parliament in June 1536, was at once confirmed by act of parliament, as was another indenture, agreed during the session between lord Ferrers and the earl of Huntingdon, for the marriage of their son and daughter.[108] But grants of land, land sales and exchanges were the transactions most often confirmed by statute.[109]

The Howard family was particularly careful to obtain such confirmations. The elder Thomas Howard had learned the importance of statute early in the reign of Henry VII. In 1491, while he was in the north on the king's business, parliament 'at the unresonable sute' (as he saw it) of the marquess of Berkeley excluded him from lands to which he claimed to be the legal heir; in 1512 he obtained a private act annulling the previous statute.[110] In 1514, after Henry VIII's grant to him of lands to support his new title of duke, Norfolk had the king's letters patent confirmed by statute; if he had not done so, legal opinion held that the grant of the manor of East Wickham in Kent would have been void, since Henry VIII had (it turned out) no more than the reversion to the manor.[111] The younger Thomas Howard, when he was duke of Norfolk, surrendered his office of admiral at the king's request in 1525 and was recompensed with a grant of land.[112] By indenture of June 1526 it was agreed between him and Henry VIII that the exchange should be made sure by act of parliament or otherwise at the duke's request, and when parliament next met, in 1529, it was confirmed by a private act.[113] Henry VIII's own land transactions were often confirmed by statute. In 1540, for example, a bill to add to the honour of Hampton Court the royal palace of Nonsuch, with the manor of Wimbledon and other manors in Surrey recently bought from lord Cromwell, received the royal assent.[114] In the same session a bill for an exchange of lands between the king and Cromwell was passed by both houses before the recess.[115] The manors

[107] 27 Henry VIII, c.40.
[108] 28 Henry VIII, cc.37, 48.
[109] For many examples see below, chapter 7.
[110] 4 Henry VIII, c.13.
[111] 5 Henry VIII, c.9; *The Reports of Sir John Spelman*, i, 149.
[112] See below, pp. 217–18.
[113] C54/395; 21 Henry VIII, c.22.
[114] House of Lords, Original Acts, 32 Henry VIII, no. 61.
[115] *LJ*, i, 136–7. The bill was evidently drafted before Cromwell's creation as earl since in its title he was called lord Cromwell.

in Surrey probably formed part of this exchange, which was almost certainly agreed by the (missing) indenture of 1 March 1540 cited in Henry VIII's last grant of lands to Cromwell, a week before his creation as earl of Essex in April 1540.[116] Cromwell's attainder later in the session made the bill superfluous and it was not presented for the royal assent.

As Surrey had discovered 'it was not only the initiators of private bills who might have a legitimate interest in them. Early in 1536, when Shrewsbury, ill at Handsworth, heard that a bill was before parliament to confirm the sale of lands by Northumberland to Henry VIII, he wrote to the king to ask him not to approve it until provision had been made for his daughter, the countess of Northumberland, and sent his son, lord Talbot, to see Cromwell. As a member of the house of lords, Talbot no doubt helped to ensure that the act did indeed protect his sister's rights to dower and jointure.[117] Presence, of course, was no guarantee of success: in 1542 a bill for the earl of Derby – a regular attender in this session – was read in the upper house but never emerged as an act.[118] Yet absence was clearly a risk, especially in the late 1530s when many estates were changing hands in the wake of the dissolution of the monasteries. Indeed, the high attendance in the lords in the parliamentary sessions of June 1536 and 1539 may have owed something to the exceptional need for vigilance. Even a bill confirming a previous grant by letters patent could come as a surprise to other property-owners. Quick action was necessary to ensure the full protection of their rights, either by amendments to the text of the bill or, more commonly, by the addition of provisos. If they were alert, noblemen might actually turn a bill – public or private – to their own advantage, as Norfolk and Cobham did when they secured provisos to the act of dissolution of 1539 confirming their acquisition of church lands under licences from Henry VIII given only by word of mouth.[119] Arthur Plantagenet, viscount Lisle, unable to leave Calais, tried without success to frustrate a comparable move by his enemy, Sir Richard Whethill, to add a proviso to the bill for Calais in 1536 to confirm his son's title to a spear's place in the retinue.[120] In May 1536 Lisle thought of obtaining a proviso himself in the new parliament to prevent lord Daubeney from selling lands which should descend to Lisle's stepson, but his counsel advised against it, preferring less

[116] See below, p. 247.
[117] *LP*, x, 459, 460; 27 Henry VIII, c.47. Talbot is known to have attended this session: BL, Harl. 158, f.143.
[118] *LJ*, i, 180.
[119] See below, p. 241.
[120] *The Lisle Letters*, iii, 669, 669a, 684, 719; 27 Henry VIII, c.63.

forceful tactics.[121] Lisle accepted the advice, but he was still anxious to attend parliament himself. In 1539 Husee suggested that, if he intended to apply again to the king for a licence to come over, he should keep the letter short: 'the fewer lynes the better, for I have herde say that his grace lovythe not to rede long lettres'.[122] But it was not until the following year that Lisle received permission to leave his post to attend parliament. He was present in the house of lords every day from 27 April 1540 until the recess; when parliament reassembled he was a prisoner in the Tower.[123]

Henry VIII occasionally dealt directly with the nobility, as he did in the parliamentary session of 1529. The king was determined to end the evasion of feudal dues by the device of the use, which transferred the legal ownership of land to feoffees. The intention was to proceed by statute, but as the first move Henry made an agreement with a number of noblemen which bound them, in advance of any legislation, to pay the feudal incidents on one-third of an estate covered by a use or devised by will in return for recognition of their right to make such settlements. The agreement was signed in December by Henry VIII, the chancellor and 30 noblemen, including six of the seven barons created earlier in the month and two of the three men promoted in the peerage on 8 December.[124] These noblemen were hardly in a position to oppose the king's wishes, but the compromise was not necessarily harmful to the interests of the owners of large estates. However, when a bill was eventually introduced into parliament, in 1532, it provoked great opposition from the commons. Henry VIII fought back with ruthless energy, putting pressure on the judges to find for him in a test case over the will of Thomas Fiennes, lord Dacre, ingeniously framed to deprive the king of all his feudal rights. The judges duly declared the will fraudulent. Parliament then had no alternative but to accept in 1536 a statute of uses so restrictive that it became a major grievance of landowners in the pilgrimage of grace. Henry VIII had overplayed his hand and in 1540 the statute of wills repealed much of the act of 1536 and restored the right to devise land by will, reinstating the main lines of the agreement with the nobles in 1529.[125]

The nobility was called upon to support another royal initiative in 1530, when parliament was not sitting. Henry VIII summoned the nobles to court in June to sign a letter to the pope asking him in the strongest terms to nullify the king's marriage to Katherine of Aragon.

---

[121] *The Lisle Letters*, v, 703, 703a.
[122] SP1/144, f.91 (*LP*, xiv(1), 505), printed ibid., 1366.
[123] See above, p. 69.
[124] *LP*, iv(3), 6044.
[125] E. W. Ives, 'The genesis of the statute of uses', *EHR*, lxxxii (1967), 673–97.

When a number of noblemen – and leading churchmen – had signed, commissioners were sent round the kingdom to collect more signatures and the letter was sent off in July signed and sealed by the two dukes, the two marquesses, 13 earls (including the Irish earl of Kildare, not a member of the English house of lords) and 26 barons (including George Boleyn under his courtesy title of lord Rochford, probably representing his father, the earl of Wiltshire, who was on embassy abroad).[126] With such numbers signing, the exercise, though fruitless, was a triumph of organization. When a second letter to the pope was mooted early in December 1533, Cromwell nevertheless noted that it could not well be done 'before the parlyament' – due to reassemble in January 1534 – and the project was abandoned.[127] Cromwell was no doubt unsympathetic to the idea itself and perhaps also to the practice of consulting the nobility in this way. Henry VIII discussed the problem created by Elizabeth Barton with a large number of noblemen in November 1533, another meeting of lords was expected in January 1534 – although there is no evidence that it ever took place – and there was talk early in 1537 of an assembly of peers or a more general council of the kingdom to consider the state of the north.[128] But that was the last heard of an assembly of notables. The role of the nobility as advisers of the crown now lay within parliament, not apart from it.

The Reformation parliament had extended the scope of statute – to the dismay of Darcy and others, but to the benefit of the institution, its authority effectively freed from constitutional constraints. Henry VIII showed that he understood and accepted the legislative sovereignty of king-in-parliament when he declared in 1542: 'We be informed by our iudges that we at no time stand so highlie in our estate roiall as in the time of parlement, wherein we as head and you as members are conioined and knit together into one bodie politike.'[129] Noblemen who were unwilling to compete for the offices which would bring membership of the privy council, or unable to obtain them, had more incentive to take part in political life as members of the house of lords. Some of them, as owners of parliamentary boroughs or as local magnates, could influence elections to the house of commons, and the growing number of men seeking election enhanced the value of their patronage. Moreover, the majority of the noblemen created by Henry VIII

---

[126] *CSPSp.*, iv(1), 354, 366; *LP*, iv(3), 6513. The barons numbered 27 with the prior of St John of Jerusalem.

[127] *SP*, i, 411–15.

[128] *CSPSp.*, iv(2), 1153, v, 8; *The Lisle Letters*, iv, 910, 915, 923; *LP*, xiv(1), 463.

[129] *Holinshed's Chronicles of England, Scotland, and Ireland*, 6 vols (London, 1807–8), iii, 826.

between 1529 and the end of the reign had themselves been members of the house of commons: Thomas and Gregory Cromwell, FitzWilliam, Audley, Paulet, Russell, Parr (of Horton), Dudley, Wriothesley and Wharton, besides the four sitting members ennobled in 1529. They took to the upper house their different parliamentary experience to complement that of the old nobility and further strengthened the links between lords and commons.[130] Parliament was increasingly seen to be the chief 'point of contact' between the crown and the political nation.[131] It was not the centre of politics – the court was the scene of the continuous struggle for power – although the action might on occasion be moved into parliament.[132] Yet parliament could offer the nobility both involvement in contemporary events and, with the consent of king and commons, the furtherance of family interests.

The reform of the council forced a shift in the role of the nobility affecting above all the older noble families and those of higher rank. But the noblemen who lost a place on the council were not excluded from an institution which they could have continued to attend in their former manner; the service expected of a privy councillor was not geared to their style of life. Parliament, on the other hand, was by its nature suited to their needs. It demanded a certain amount of time – more than some were willing to give – but parliamentary sessions were limited in number and in length. Lords and commons assembled to make laws and to grant taxes in response to individual writs of summons or as elected representatives of the nation, combining the local and particular with the national in a way which reflected and reinforced the power of the nobility. The owners of great estates especially could translate wealth and social dominance into a recognized importance at Westminster. Every nobleman who attended parliament had the opportunity to express his views on any policy to be implemented by statute. Membership of the house of lords was more than the distinguishing mark of the nobility; it had the potential to become its greatest political asset.

[130] Helen Miller, 'Lords and commons: relations between the two houses of parliament, 1509–1558', *Parliamentary History: A Yearbook*, 1 (1982), 14–15, 18–22.

[131] G. R. Elton, 'Tudor government: the points of contact, i. Parliament', *TRHS*, 5th series, 24 (1974), 196–200.

[132] G. R. Elton, 'Parliament in the sixteenth century: functions and fortunes', *HJ*, xxii (1979), 257.

CHAPTER 5

Attendance in War

Henry VIII had to be informed by his judges that in parliament his royal estate was at its greatest. He needed no one to tell him that he was at the height of his power when he led his kingdom in war. In his old age he turned to an invasion of France as a distraction from the problems of government. In his youth his overriding ambition was to win glory on the field of battle. Henry VIII saw himself as a second Henry V, a role that he was begged to play by the translator of *Vita Henrici Quinti*, published in English for the first time in 1513.[1] His aim seems genuinely to have been the conquest of France, the recovery of the lost dominions to which the Tudor dynasty was heir.

His father had proclaimed the same intention when he appealed to his subjects for funds in 1491.[2] But Henry VII was never the victim of his own propaganda and the true purpose of that campaign was only to exert pressure on France. Nevertheless, it still needed a show of strength for its realization and in 1492 the king recruited an army by indenture, retaining his leading magnates to serve him with specified numbers of soldiers for at least one year.[3] The obligation of personal military service was given penal backing when parliament next met, in 1495. 'Whereas every subgette', the preamble of the act declared, 'by the dutie of his alleigeaunce is bounden to serve and assiste his prince and sovereign lorde at all seasons when nede shall requyre, and most specially suche persones as have by hym promocion or avauncement, as grauntes and giftes of offices, fees and annuyties, which owe and verily be bounden of reason to gif their attendaunce upon his roiall persone to defend the same, when he shall fortune to goo in his persone in werres for the defence of the realme or ageynst his rebelles and

---

[1] Scarisbrick, *Henry VIII*, p. 23n.
[2] *CPR, Henry VII*, i, 353.
[3] *Foedera*, v(4), 43–4; E101/72/6.

ennemyes', anyone having such grants and gifts and not attending the king to war – unless ill, or licensed not to come – would forfeit his office, fee or annuity.[4] In 1504 the act was extended to cover all those who held lands of the king's gift – 'by reason wherof they ar more bounden to give ther attendaunce upon the kinges moste royall persone in his seid warres then other rehersed persones havyng but fees, offices and annuyties for terme of lyffe' – who had 'by overseght' been omitted from the earlier act: they too would lose their grants if, without sufficient reason, they failed to attend upon the king 'when he shall fortune to goo in werres, within this his realme or elswher'. Provisos ensured the payment of wages from the time of leaving home, extended the list of exempted persons to include those under 21 or over 60, and declared that the act did not apply to those who had bought their lands from the king.[5]

Henry VIII did not explicitly invoke these acts in 1513, although he was to do so in 1544. But he began his preparations for war in 1511 with signet letters to a number of landowners and office-holders calling upon them to send in certificates of the number of able men they could recruit within their 'landes, auctorities, rowmes and offices'. In 1512 Sir Henry Willoughby, a recipient of this letter, was retained by indenture to serve the king under Thomas Grey, marquess of Dorset, the commander of the expedition to Guienne, taking with him 835 able men, to be paid as laid down in Henry VIII's indenture with Dorset.[6] However, such indentures were uncommon, even in the early years of the reign, and Henry VIII never used them after 1512. The army raised by signet letters was not recruited for any specified time and it was based, so far as the ordinary soldier was concerned, not on contract but on tenurial relationship.[7] The dangers of such a quasi-feudal system were obvious: the noblemen who led the largest retinues in time of war were apt to be the men who in peacetime fell foul of the law against retaining.[8] Nevertheless, it served Henry VIII well enough in 1513. Not the least of its merits was its power to rouse the nobles to active service. Their 'honour' was at risk as well as the king's if they failed to appear with adequate retinues.

Some, perhaps, approached at any rate this war in the same spirit as Henry VIII. Service in an 'army royal' could be viewed as an extension of the ceremonial role of the nobility, designed to reproduce

[4] 11 Henry VII, c.18. Certain office-holders, including the captains of Berwick and Carlisle, were exempted.

[5] 19 Henry VII, c.1.

[6] *HMC, Middleton*, pp. 126–8.

[7] J. J. Goring, 'The military obligations of the English people, 1511–1558', Ph.D. thesis (London, 1955), pp. 16–17.

[8] See above, pp. 108–10.

in France as much as possible of the splendour of the court. The king relied on his intimate servants and friends to lead the action. The army was divided into three 'battles' on the traditional plan – foreward, middleward or king's ward, rearward – and Henry chose to command the foreward and rearward two noblemen of his household, the lord steward, George Talbot, earl of Shrewsbury, and the lord chamberlain, Charles Somerset, lord Herbert. His favourite of the early years of the reign, Charles Brandon, having been created viscount Lisle was appointed high marshal, second in command of the whole army.[9] When Henry VIII met the emperor near Thérouanne in the middle of August, the nobility attended upon him in sumptuous dress, the duke of Buckingham being particularly memorable in purple satin.[10] Even in the absence of the king men were conscious of the opportunity for display offered by a military expedition, especially since on active service they were exempt from the sumptuary laws.[11] Sailing for Spain in 1512 the higher officers had been 'richly appareled in clothes of gold, and of silver, and velvettes of sundery colours, pounsed and embroudered', while the petty captains had worn 'satin and damaske of white and grene', the royal colours. The reality of the experience had sadly belied the hopeful expectations with which the army had embarked. It had landed in June and waited in vain for the support promised by Ferdinand of Aragon. After a long summer of delay and disorder, the troops mutinied on hearing that Henry VIII meant them to stay for the winter. Dorset, with his second-in-command, the younger Thomas Howard, and the rest of the captains, including William lord Willoughby de Eresby and Robert lord Willoughby de Broke, had to make an ignominious return to England with their men.[12] The events of 1512 had been little improvement on those of 1511, when Thomas lord Darcy, eager to fight the Moors, had within a fortnight of landing in Spain been asked by Ferdinand to take his men home.[13] In warfare reputations were at stake, and the two successive failures only made those involved in them the more determined to excel when their chance came again. In France, in 1513, Darcy was reluctant even to be out of sight of Henry VIII. Ordered to look after the treasure and ordnance, he 'was lothe to goo from hys master but by streyte commaundemente'.[14] The sentiment may appear conventional,

[9] *LP*, i(2), 1948 gg.62, 93, 2053(7).

[10] *Hall's Chronicle*, p. 544. For a German account of the meeting which also commented on the rich clothing of Henry VIII's entourage see *LP*, i(2), App.25.

[11] The act of apparell of 1510 exempted anyone in the king's service in wartime: 1 Henry VIII, c.14.

[12] *Hall's Chronicle*, pp. 527–32.

[13] ibid., pp. 521–2.

[14] ibid., p. 550.

even the routine embellishment of the chronicler, but in Darcy's case it was in character. The following year, afraid that he was not going to be summoned for the expected campaign, he wrote to Wolsey insisting on his desire to serve – 'if the kingis grace in his own person kepe his purpoos to procede in his moost noble werres ayenst Frenchemen'. He had already spent £4,000 on his expeditions to Spain and France, but to be left out, when the king went to war, appeared as a slight to Darcy, who had been vice-chamberlain and captain of the guard to Henry VII and felt himself, as he told Wolsey, 'mooste specially bownde' to serve – although, as captain of Berwick, he was in fact exempt under the statute of 1495.[15] Duty and honour were surely reinforced by hope: the influence which had slipped from him since he left the court might be retrieved by personal service to the king in war.

Motives may have been mixed in 1513, but the force behind them was Henry VIII's own enthusiasm, with its implicit assurance that this was a service acceptable to him, and the explicit command in his second signet letter, 'ffaile ye not . . . as ye tender the honour and suertie of us and this our realme'. These letters went out early in the year, announcing Henry's intention 'personally to procede into ffraunce with an armye roiall this next somer' and informing the recipient that he had been appointed to attend the king with a specified number of soldiers: Robert Radcliffe, lord FitzWalter, was to bring 50 archers and 50 bills on foot, 'sufficiently harneysed and appointed for the warres'.[16] In April further signet letters were sent out with the final instructions: George lord Hastings was told that he had been assigned to serve in the foreward under the earl of Shrewsbury and should assemble at the port of embarkation with his men by 8 May: shipping would be provided for his whole retinue of 60 archers and 40 bills and the horses and carriages which he was to bring with him.[17] Most noblemen were assigned to the 'army royal': 23 served in France and another three (all in their fifties) were represented on the French expedition by their eldest sons. One nobleman served at sea and nine fought against the Scots.[18] The Scottish campaign produced by far the greatest victory, but the earl of Surrey, commander of the northern army, saying farewell to the king at Dover, correctly gauged the

[15] SP1/7, ff.80–1 (*LP*, i(2), 2576).

[16] C82/387 (*LP*, i(1), 1662 g.50).

[17] C82/389 (*LP*, i(1), 1804 g.28).

[18] Figures from sources cited below, n. 25 (army against France), n. 43 (army by sea), n. 49 (army against Scotland). Mountjoy did not muster with the rest: he was commissioned in May to see to the shipment of the army to France (*LP*, i(2), 1948 g.69) and in September 1513 himself left for Calais with 500 men (*Original Letters*, 3rd series, i, 152–4).

situation if he was indeed (as Hall related) overcome with emotion at leaving his prince and 'the floure of all the nobilitie'.[19] Of the noblemen aged 19 or more in the summer of 1513, only four were neither on active service themselves nor represented by their heirs. Lord Ormond was at least 70 years old, well past the age limit for military service;[20] the earl of Arundel was over 60;[21] and lord Stourton, aged about 55, had been pardoned in 1505 from attending any parliament or council and was probably incapacitated.[22] Only for lord FitzWarin's absence is there no obvious explanation. He had been appointed early in 1513 to lead the defence of Somerset and Dorset against an expected French invasion, but lord Daubeney, appointed with him, and lord Audley, similarly commissioned in Hampshire, both went to France with the rest of the army in the summer, when the invasion threat was over.[23] Nevertheless, FitzWarin was the exception in the general call to arms. Not since the battle of Agincourt had the nobility been so totally engaged in war.[24]

Moreover, the muster records show that even the absentees provided soldiers in 1513.[25] The minimum size of retinue was generally the company of 100 demanded of FitzWalter and Hastings. All officers and men were paid, on a sliding scale: captains according to status (noblemen 6s 8d a day, others 4s), petty captains 2s, horsemen 9d and footmen 6d a day. Receipts for wages survive for the rearward only.[26] Charles Somerset, lord Herbert, its captain-general, was paid 40s a day for himself, and the appropriate wages for 10 captains, 10 petty captains, 153 demilances – light cavalry – and 883 footmen.[27] Other

---

[19] *Hall's Chronicle*, p. 555.

[20] He had probably been at the battle of Towton in 1461.

[21] His son and heir, styled lord Mautravers, was included with his retinue in the rearward in a herald's list of captains (College of Arms, L.12, ff.18v–24), but there is no other reference to him.

[22] *CPR, Henry VII*, ii, 451. GEC supposed that Stourton was appointed to serve at sea, but the references cited show that he only provided men.

[23] *LP*, i(1), 1662 g.27. FitzWarin was 42 years old and cannot have been exempted on grounds of age. *The Chronicle of Calais*, p. 13 refers to his arrival in Calais with Henry VIII, but there is no supporting evidence.

[24] Every active baron had been present in France in 1415: Michael Powicke, *Military Obligation in Medieval England. A Study in Liberty and Duty* (Oxford, 1962), p. 171.

[25] Foreward in E101/62/14 (*LP*, i(2), 2052); king's ward in E101/62/11 (*LP*, i(2), 2053(2)); rearward in SP1/5, ff.52–4 (*LP*, i(2), 2053(7), total 'of the rerwarde' wrongly given as 'of the retinue').

[26] SP1/4, f.143, SP1/5, f.16 (*LP*, i(2), 2130(1, 2), 31 July misprinted 1 July); SP1/6, ff.1–259 (*LP*, i(2), 2414).

[27] The receipts signed by Herbert cover payments in advance for three months (of 28 days), 31 July – 22 October 1513, but the drummers and fifers were paid from 3 July and there must be a missing indenture for the whole retinue for 3–30 July. Payments for the rearward before it left England have not survived.

noble retinues paid wages for the period 3 July – 22 October were those led by Henry Stafford, earl of Wiltshire (20 demilances, 586 foot), John Sutton, son and heir of lord Dudley (194 footmen), John Tuchet, lord Audley (123 footmen), Richard Grey, earl of Kent (100 to 105 footmen), Thomas Fiennes, lord Dacre (121 or 122 footmen), John Zouche, son and heir of lord Zouche (100 footmen), and Sir Thomas West, son and heir of Thomas lord La Warre (53 footmen).[28] Henry Percy, earl of Northumberland, received wages for an odd 17 days from 14 July, but was then paid with the others for himself and his 103 demilances and 400 foot. Robert lord Willoughby de Broke also entered into wages during the course of an accounting month. He was paid by the treasurer of the rearward from 7 July for 300 footmen, but he and his men had received wages for the period 19 May – 6 July when they had assembled under Lisle at Southampton as part of an army originally intended for a landing in Brittany.[29] All the retinues included a captain, a petty captain and a chaplain for each company of 100 men. The numbers paid in most cases tally exactly with those recorded at the muster of the rearward, and in no instance is there a discrepancy of more than three men. But it was clearly the general practice to claim – and to receive – wages for the original number each month throughout the campaign, which hardly suggests very tight control by the treasurer, although casualties in France were low.

There is a greater differential between the numbers mustered in the king's ward and the retinues receiving conduct money home again in October and November 1513.[30] Two noblemen received conduct money for more than their mustered retinue – the duke of Buckingham for 50 more and lord Bergavenny for 12 – and some for less, the largest discrepancy here being 169 men mustered under the earl of Essex for whom no journey money was paid when his retinue went home. Some of the missing men were presumably dead, but some soldiers stayed on as garrison in the captured city of Tournai.[31] And it seems reasonable to assume a certain mingling of the retinues as men hurried to join any captain going in their direction. Nevertheless, the payment of conduct money to the captains and their retinues of the king's ward 'from Dover home to their mansion places' provides substantial evidence for

---

[28] *Hall's Chronicle*, p. 537 mentions lords Dudley and La Warre among the rearward and *The Chronicle of Calais*, pp. 10–11 the arrival at Calais of lords Dudley and Zouche; in each case the reference should be to the heir to the title.

[29] BL, Cotton Faustina E.VII, ff.4–5 (*LP*, i(2), 2575).

[30] E101/56/25 (*LP*, i(2), 2480); E101/56/13 (*LP*, i(2), 2480(2)); SP1/230, f.83 (*LP*, i(2), 2427).

[31] C. G. Cruickshank, *Army Royal. Henry VIII's Invasion of France, 1513* (Oxford, 1969), p. 153.

the places of origin of these retinues of the nobility.[32]

The two captains, one petty captain, nine demilances and 130 footmen under William lord Willoughby returned to Belleau, Lincolnshire, a manor granted to him in March 1511.[33] George Manners, lord Ros, recruited his men from four counties: the captain went back to Nottingham, his petty captain and 23 footmen to Godalming, where lady Ros had inherited lands, another 40 footmen to his manor of Helmsley, Yorkshire, and the nine demilances to Etal, Northumberland, the ancestral home of the Manners family. Lord Ros did not return. He had fallen ill while in France and died soon after making his will on 26 October, probably in London, where he was buried.[34] Henry Bourchier, earl of Essex, also had men from Helmsley in his retinue – 55 footmen – but he returned 200 footmen to Halstead, Essex, where he had a house, 10 archers on horseback to Bildeston, Suffolk, where he was tenant of the manor, and another 10 mounted archers and 30 demilances to other places in Suffolk. John Bourchier, lord Berners, was commanded by Henry VIII to stay behind in Calais to supervise the return of the ordnance, but after being left without wages for ten days he crossed over to Dover on 13 November with 15 men of his retinue, which had mustered 50 beside himself at the start of the campaign. He received conduct money for the return of one petty captain to Hull and 14 footmen to Haughton, one of his manors in Staffordshire. Henry lord Daubeney's captain, petty captain and 100 footmen went back to his manors of Heanton Punchardon in Devon and South Perrott in Dorset. The conduct money was paid to John More, servant to lord Bergavenny, in whose retinue Daubeney was to muster at Canterbury in May 1514, when Bergavenny was appointed chief captain of a relief force for the defence of Guisnes.[35]

John More also collected the conduct money of lord Bergavenny's own retinue, one of the largest in France in 1513. His ten officers and 27 demilances returned either to Abergavenny, the lordship from which his title derived, or to Birling, his residence in Kent; 287 of his footmen went back to Abergavenny, 59 to Birling, 40 to Lewes, where he owned the moiety of the barony, and 40 to Bury St Edmunds, where he was lord of the manor. The remaining 60 footmen were evidently

[32] Quotation from heading to the account in E101/56/25.

[33] See below, p. 211.

[34] *The Itinerary of John Leland in or about the years 1535–1543*, ed. Lucy Toulmin Smith, 5 vols (London, 1907–10), i, 93 mentions his illness in France and burial at Holywell priory, although his final resting place was in St George's chapel, Windsor.

[35] SP1/10, ff.177–83 (*LP*, i(2), 2912 and, more fully, ii(1), 471); SP1/230, f.182 (*LP*, i(2), 2937). Daubeney married a daughter of lord Bergavenny.

town retinues: they returned in groups of 20 to Walsingham, Colchester and Ipswich. The possession of an estate in Wales clearly helped Bergavenny to mobilize a retinue comparable with those of the higher nobility. On this occasion it easily outnumbered that of Thomas Grey, marquess of Dorset, whose five officers together with 233 footmen returned to Groby, Leicester, and Stoke upon Tern, Shropshire, two of the family's manors; the remainder of his retinue – 20 footmen – went back to Lynn, Norfolk. Indeed, Bergavenny's numbers fell very little short of those of the highest nobleman of all, in 1513 the only duke, Edward Stafford, duke of Buckingham. He returned from France with ten officers, 20 spears and 520 footmen. Nearly one-third went back to Thornbury in Gloucestershire, his chief residence, or to Newport and Brecon in South Wales, to Stafford or to Maxstoke, Warwickshire, the core of his estates in the west. The remainder returned to scattered destinations in 13 counties, including Penshurst, Kent, and Bletchingley, Surrey, or to London. Darcy was the only baron besides Bergavenny to have a retinue of 500 men. Although this was the number which he could provide out of his own household and lands, he could call upon over twice as many out of his offices.[36] In 1513 his retinue was largely recruited through his office-holding. Four captains and four petty captains and 88 of his footmen returned with him to Temple Newsam, Yorkshire, but all his 100 demilances (including their two officers) went back either to Berwick or to Keswick, Cumberland, and the rest of his footmen – over 300 men – to Bamburgh, Northumberland, where as the king's officer he had command of men, or to Knaresborough, Pontefract, Snaith and Selby, Yorkshire, where he was steward.

The nobleman with the largest retinue in the king's ward was Charles Brandon, viscount Lisle. As joint constable of Caernarfon castle, chief justice of North Wales and steward of the lordships of Holt, Bromfield and Yale, and of Chirk, he had access to a vital source of manpower. Even his English captains made use of it. Sir Richard Cavendish, for example, received conduct money home for himself and his petty captain to Suffolk, but his 70 footmen went back to Holyhead, which was also the destination of 78 footmen who had served under Sir Lewis Orell, who with his petty captain and remaining 22 footmen returned to Wisbech, Cambridgeshire. Indeed, apart from 100 men supplied by lord FitzWarin, who went back to Devon and Cornwall, and 100 footmen led by Sir Edward Chamberlain and Sir William Essex who returned to Woodstock, Oxfordshire, every one of the remaining officers and men in Lisle's retinue for whom conduct money receipts survive went back to Holyhead – in all, over 1,500 footmen, 39 demilances, 14 petty captains and 14 captains. The Welsh captains included John Puleston of Caernarfon and Sir William Griffith of Penrhyn, near Bangor, but they were all paid to conduct their men to Holyhead, wherever they lived themselves. The small port cannot have nurtured so many troops. Either the captains unscrupulously claimed conduct money to the furthest corner of North Wales or the men were not Welsh at all, but Irishmen recruited in Wales.

George Talbot, earl of Shrewsbury, captain-general of the foreward, had in his retinue at the muster 43 captains, 43 petty captains and 4,335 foot soldiers. No record survives of payment of either wages or conduct money to this ward, but the names of the captains are known: they were noted on a separate schedule of Shrewsbury's retinue, divided into companies of 90–100 men. The companies were listed under counties: Shropshire (12 companies), Derbyshire (11), Staffordshire (9), Nottinghamshire (7), Worcestershire (2), Oxfordshire (1), with one company each from 'my lordes household' and his guard, reflecting the commission to Shrewsbury in February 1513 to retain as many men as he could get, under the degree of baron, in Derbyshire, Staffordshire, Shropshire, or elsewhere.[37] The foreward included four other noblemen, who mustered separately: Thomas Stanley, earl of Derby, had with him 10 officers, 60 demilances and 440 footmen, while lords Cobham, FitzWalter and Hastings each had between 100 and 112 footmen. The retinues of the nobility in this ward therefore accounted for over 5,000 men, almost half the contingent under Shrewsbury. In the rearward, too, noblemen's retinues, with some 3,200 men, formed nearly half the total. But in the king's ward the proportion was smaller: even with Lisle's retinue the nobility contributed under 5,000 men to a force, including the king's guard and the ordnance, some 14,000 strong.[38]

Although all the captains in the army were mounted, only ten noblemen brought cavalry in their retinues, providing in all just under 560 demilances.[39] The Venetian ambassador was correct in reporting that the real strength of the English army was the infantry, and that men at arms – the heavy cavalry – were almost impossible to find.[40] The footsoldiers recruited by the nobility were predominantly billmen

[37] SP1/231, ff.193–4 (*LP, Addenda*, i, 108, some names misprinted); *LP*, i(1), 1662 g.57.
[38] Total number of the three wards from Cruickshank, *Army Royal*, pp. 28–9.
[39] The foreward and rearward muster lists distinguish between horse and foot; the list of the king's ward does not, but the number of horsemen in each retinue is given in the conduct money receipts.
[40] *CSPVen.*, ii, 1287.

and archers (a few of them mounted for travelling); some men with morris-pikes appeared in their contingents, but no handgunners. Henry VIII himself was interested in the new firearms and both handguns and the more powerful arquebuses were bought for distribution in France, but fundamentally the 'army royal' was an old-fashioned force, raised by quasi-feudal methods, fighting with out-of-date weapons for an anachronistic cause. But it was well led and well disciplined, with the morale of its troops higher than at any other time in the sixteenth century. It was not despised by continental observers.[41] And for all its lack of real military success it fulfilled at least one of the aims of its creator: it enabled Henry VIII to appear upon the European stage as a warrior king. His sheer enjoyment of the campaign shines through the contemporary descriptions from the moment of his landing at Calais, greeted by a deafening salvo of guns, to the return in October, the fighting and the jousting, the receptions and triumphal entries of the summer season now for the moment ended.[42] He had established himself as a ruler whose dynastic ambitions would have to be taken seriously in future.

The impression of ordered power at the disposal of the English king was deepened by the knowledge that the army in France was but one part of the total force mobilized by Henry VIII in 1513. The 'army by sea' was provided by a number of individuals and by cities and towns. Noble families unable to serve themselves mostly contributed men to this force. The earl of Oxford – a boy of 13 – supplied 150 men, the earl of Arundel 140, the mother of the young earl of Devon 100 and lord Stourton 50. The one nobleman to sail in the fleet was Walter Devereux, lord Ferrers, who had 420 men of his retinue with him on board the *Trinity Sovereign*.[43] As a ship's captain Ferrers's pay was only 18d a day until it was raised by the king's gift to the 6s 8d a day paid to the noblemen captains in France. His 300 morris-pikes, 100 archers and seven billmen, like the mariners, were paid only 5s a month.[44] Yet service at sea proved far more hazardous. The lord admiral, Sir Edward Howard, was killed in action on 25 April and Ferrers, who had lost 25 men in the same engagement, took temporary command of the fleet; but when Surrey's eldest son arrived to take over as admiral

---

[41] Cruickshank, *Army Royal*, pp. 78, 205.

[42] E.g. the account (in Latin) by John Taylor, clerk of the parliaments, who went with the army to France: BL, Cotton Cleo. C.V, ff.65–97 (*LP*, i(2), 2391).

[43] E101/62/17 (*LP*, i(1), 1661(4)). Other lists give slightly different figures. One includes 100 men of the lord chamberlain's retinue and 50 men supplied by lord Ormond: SP1/3, ff.181–4 (*LP*, i(1), 1661(3)).

[44] E315/315, ff.1–2 (*LP*, i(2), 2304(3)). *LP*, i(1), 1176(3) gives the details of Ferrers's retinue; on this list Oxford's men numbered 200.

he found 'the worst ordered armye and furthest owte of rewle that ever I saw'.[45] Many of Ferrers's men had deserted: as Howard reported to the council, Ferrers was sure that there were more than 100 missing and was 'as angrie therwith as ever was man', swearing that Hereford gaol was 'full of his men that be ron away'.[46] Ferrers eventually received conduct money from Portsmouth to Hereford for himself and 388 men and mariners from his ship; another 36 mariners from the *Trinity Sovereign* were paid for their journey home to Cromer and Sheringham in Norfolk.[47]

In August the lord admiral sailed to Newcastle to help his father against the Scots, taking with him men who had been in his retinue at sea. Surrey had mustered 500 men in his retinue at Lambeth in July and set off for the north.[48] After sending letters to all those with power to make men, he ordered the army to assemble at Newcastle on 1 September. The younger Thomas Howard arrived on 4 September and six northern barons were assigned to the foreward under his command. Surrey was to lead the rearward himself, with lord Scrope of Bolton under him; lord Dacre of the north was appointed captain of his right wing.[49] Since Dacre, as he reported afterwards, was 'not of sufficient power be my countrey folkes to be a wynge' to the earl at Flodden, Surrey assigned to him the men of Bamburgh and Tyne-mouth – 'whiche at the furst shott of the Scottishe gonnys fledd from me and taryed noo lenger'. Nevertheless, Dacre killed many Scotsmen and at the end was the one to find the body of James IV 'slayne in the felde' and convey it to Berwick.[50] Thomas Ruthal, bishop of Durham, advised Henry VIII to send a special letter of thanks to Dacre as well as to Surrey and his son and to Sir Edward Stanley.[51] Surrey himself knighted a number of men, including lord Scrope of Upsall, lord Ogle and lord Lumley. In France, as he prepared to return to England, Henry VIII knighted rather more of his captains, but only two barons, Audley and Cobham.[52]

The triumphs of the war brought advancement to some individuals but no lasting gain to the kingdom. The Scottish threat was not

[45] Alfred Spont, *Letters and Papers relating to the War with France 1512–1513*, Navy Records Soc., x (London, 1897), no. 76–8.

[46] SP1/229, ff.187–8 (*LP*, i(2), 1978).

[47] E101/56/29 (*LP*, i(2), 2304(5)).

[48] E101/56/27 (*LP*, i(2), 2651).

[49] *Hall's Chronicle*, pp. 555–8.

[50] BL, Cotton Calig. B.VI, ff.47–8, B.II, ff.200–2 (*LP*, i(2), 2386, 2913).

[51] *LP*, i(2), 2284.

[52] ibid., 2246(4ii), 2301.

removed by the accession of an infant king, Henry VIII's nephew, and Tournai, Henry's conquest in France, eventually had to be returned to the French. Yet the treaty of universal peace signed in 1518 could not long suppress the urge to war. In 1521 Wolsey made preparations to raise a force of 6,000 archers for a new expedition against France: none of the captains recruited was a nobleman, but 17 peers were expected to provide from 10 to 100 men each.[53] The selection of a commander preoccupied the king in July, as Wolsey was on his way to Calais to negotiate with Charles V. Henry VIII sent him word by Richard Pace that one of three noblemen 'must be generall capitane': Thomas Grey, marquess of Dorset, the lord steward, Shrewsbury, or the lord chamberlain, Worcester. Wolsey did not agree. He had already put forward the name of Sir William Sandys, the treasurer of Calais, who had taken part in Dorset's abortive expedition in 1512 and served in the king's retinue in 1513. Henry VIII would not accept such an unorthodox choice. Pace reported the king's conviction that 'itt can not stonde with hys honor to sende ony personage off lower degree than an erle owt off hys realme wyth the sayde army'. Moreover, other knights would 'disdayne' to serve under Sandys, 'beynge but a knyghte, as theye be, thoghe he be of the Garter'. Wolsey did not give up easily. He thought Shrewsbury should be kept to lead the army which would have to be raised to counter the likely invasion from Scotland. He gave his opinion of the other noblemen as tactfully as he could. The 'experience and activenes' of the aged Worcester certainly made him a suitable commander, but it would be better to keep him, too, in reserve. Dorset was 'a right valiaunt and active capitain', but he would have to be paid more than a man of lower rank, and for other respects – 'whiche I coude declare unto your grace, if I were with you' – he 'mought be well forbourne at this tyme'. As for men being unwilling to serve under Sandys, 'summe of the best knyghtes' chosen for the expedition, including Sir John Hussey, 'were the more benevolently mynded to goo, bycause that Mr Sandes was named to be their chefetain'. Henry still refused to appoint Sandys, arguing that anyway he could not be spared from Calais. But he withdrew his first three nominations and named instead the former captain of the spears, Henry Bourchier, earl of Essex, thinking him, as Wolsey noted, 'for hys hardinesse to be ryght mete for that purpose', with suitable men to advise him. Wolsey replied by making one more attempt to obtain the appointment of Sandys: he saw 'none such immynent perill, by siege or otherwyse', in store for Calais, since the French, faced by the

[53] BL, Cotton Otho E.XI, ff.34–40.

English archers and the emperor's power, would be in no state to attack the town.[54]

In the event, no army was sent abroad in 1521. The treaty agreed with Charles V on 25 August bound Henry VIII to lead a full-scale invasion of France, but not until 1523.[55] However, Henry VIII broke off relations with the French king during the emperor's visit to England in 1522, and ordered his men to engage the enemy. As Charles V prepared to leave for Spain the English navy assembled at Southampton under the lord admiral, created earl of Surrey for his part in the battle of Flodden. Robert Radcliffe, lord FitzWalter, was the only other nobleman in the fleet: he was paid 6s 8d a day as 'graunde capiteign' of *The Make Glory*, having with him 200 soldiers and their captains.[56] Surrey led an attack on the Breton port of Morlaix, which was plundered and fired before the landing party withdrew. Once disembarked at Calais, he took charge of the middle-ward and FitzWalter – who, according to Hall, 'kept his men in very good order' – commanded the foreward of the army which crossed into France; Sir William Sandys was given a joint command of the rear-ward and showed himself a resourceful leader. Surrey's invasion amounted to no more than a spoiling raid, but it helped to confirm Sandys's military prowess. Charles Brandon, duke of Suffolk, chosen to lead a new attack in 1523, appointed the recently ennobled Sandys as high marshal, second in command of the army – the post he himself had held as a new peer in 1513.[57] The king maintained his honour by entrusting the power of his kingdom to a nobleman of the highest degree, but the man so persistently recommended by Wolsey two years before was also advanced in rank and authority.

Sandys could not contribute many soldiers, as he had already explained to Wolsey.[58] However, Suffolk still had his major offices in Wales, and in July 1523 he was commissioned to recruit the king's tenants and other men in Anglesey, Caernarfonshire and Merioneth and in the lordships of which he was steward, as well as in his borough of Southwark.[59] In the list of the 'army royal' under his command his own retinue included 1,028 footmen, 200 demilances and 116 archers on horseback, out of a total force of some 10,000 men. Few noblemen served in France in 1523. As Surrey had been in 1522, Suffolk was the

[54] *SP*, i, 23–4, 29–36.
[55] *LP*, iii(2), 1508.
[56] BL, Royal 14 B.XXV.
[57] *Hall's Chronicle*, pp. 642–3, 646–8, 662.
[58] *LP*, iii(2), 2238.
[59] ibid., 3197.

sole representative of the higher nobility. He had under him retinues supplied by the earl of Arundel and a number of barons, but – on the evidence of this list – the only other nobleman to lead his own men, apart from lord Sandys, was Walter Devereux, lord Ferrers, who brought with him 476 footmen, 10 demilances and 14 mounted archers.[60] Edward Hall described a somewhat bigger army – of 13,100 men besides Suffolk's retinue – which also included the lieutenant of Calais castle, the newly ennobled lord Berkeley (who died on 12 September 1523, a week before the invasion was launched), lord Marney (presumably the son of the first baron, who had died in May) and the young lord Grey of Powis, who was knighted by Suffolk at Mondidier on 1 November with the lord chamberlain's son and heir, styled lord Herbert.[61] The army proved hard to control, particularly the Welshmen, some of whom rioted at Calais soon after they arrived; according to Hall, Ferrers was 'straightly commaunded to appese their rage, for with hym thei came thether'. In November they 'muttered and grudged more and more' and, when the frost began to grip, openly cried 'home, home'. The Welsh were an easy target for an English chronicler's criticism. The blame for the collapse of morale lay with the commander. Suffolk's military reputation fell sharply. His army broke up as Henry VIII was about to send lord Mountjoy to France with reinforcements and Suffolk was unable to get it together again. He had to wait in Calais for permission to come home, and when he was allowed to return the king at first refused to see him, although in time the old familiarity revived.[62]

In contrast to the pattern of Henry VIII's first war, the nobility in the 1520s played a greater part on the Scottish frontier than in France. As Wolsey had suggested the previous year, Shrewsbury was appointed lieutenant-general of the army against the Scots in 1522.[63] The earl of Northumberland and his eldest son were chosen to be of his 'secrete counsaile', along with lords Dacre, Darcy, Latimer and Conyers; all of them except Dacre met him on his arrival at York.[64] Shrewsbury recruited his own men in Shropshire, Staffordshire and Derbyshire, the three counties which had provided the bulk of his retinue in France

---

[60] SP1/28, ff.193–210 (*LP*, iii(2), 3288).

[61] *Hall's Chronicle*, pp. 661–2, 670. *The Chronicle of Calais*, p. 33 named only Suffolk, Sandys and Ferrers, with Worcester's son, in an invasion force of 15,000. Besides Grey of Powis and Herbert Suffolk knighted three men later ennobled by Henry VIII, Thomas Wentworth, Edward Seymour and John Dudley: ibid., p. 100.

[62] *Hall's Chronicle*, pp. 662, 671–2.

[63] *Foedera*, vi(1), 206.

[64] SP49/1, ff.140–2 (*LP*, iii(2), 2412); BL, Cotton Calig. B.II, f.104, B.III, f.156 (*LP*, iii(2), 2503, 2523).

in 1513. Northumberland, who had also been with Henry VIII in France in 1513, now provided 559 men for the northern army. Lord Conyers served with 2,601 soldiers, 200 of them, mainly from his manors of Hornby and Brompton in Yorkshire, being captained by his son and heir; lord Scrope also came with men, and lord Clifford, who was unwell, sent 100 soldiers from Skipton under his eldest son.[65] Thomas Manners, lord Ros, whose father had been taken ill in France in 1513, was appointed warden of the east and middle marches and served with a contingent which included men from Sherwood and Nottingham; 56 of his household servants returned with him to London in October.[66] The 24-year-old earl of Westmorland in his first military action suffered crippling pain in his knee and led his 'power' from a horse litter in an impressive display of endurance, but lord Lumley refused to serve and kept his servants and tenants at home.[67] He was not, it seems, the only one. In Carlisle the warden of the west march, lord Dacre, had to leave his only son to face a Scottish army – which Dacre estimated at 80,000 men, well equipped with artillery, arquebuses and countless handguns – with 16,000 unwilling soldiers; 'and some grete men there is, that wald not com forward, worthie punishment.'[68] On his own authority Dacre negotiated a truce, where-upon Shrewsbury, diseased and weary, disbanded his troops and went home.[69]

In 1523 the high command was transferred to Surrey and the northern noblemen were reinforced by the marquess of Dorset, the new warden of the east and middle marches.[70] Leading members of the king's household were to go north with Dorset, who was admitted a member of the privy chamber as he set out, a gesture which emphasized Henry VIII's special trust in him.[71] It was not, appar-ently, misplaced, despite Wolsey's lack of enthusiasm for him as a war leader. At all events, Surrey commended him as a 'noble, valiante and paynefull man' in a raid in May, in which Westmorland – evidently recovered – also fought well, as did lord Lumley, redeeming his inactivity of the previous year. But Dorset then returned to the court.[72] He left his retinue of 537 men to serve under his brother in another

[65] SP1/26, ff.10–13, 29–32 (*LP*, iii(2), 2524(2), 2545).
[66] E36/254, ff.231–41 (*LP*, iii(2), 2613).
[67] BL, Cotton Calig. B.III. ff.301–2 (*LP*, iii(2), 2546).
[68] BL, Cotton Calig. B.II, ff.326–8 (*LP*, iii(2), 2536).
[69] *SP*, i, 107–10.
[70] *Foedera*, vi(1), 209–10.
[71] See above, pp. 84–5.
[72] BL, Cotton Calig. B.II, ff.156–9 (*LP*, iii(2), 3039); SP49/2, ff.15–16 (*LP*, iii(2), 3040).

raid, in June, in which lord Ogle took part and lord Dacre led the rearward.[73] Dacre had agreed to defend the west march at his own expense while the war lasted 'and at the ending therof to abyde the reward of his highnes', and acted throughout with great energy. In September he brought as many as 4,000 men to a raid, but refused to accept the place in the camp next to the earl of Westmorland allocated to him. Lodged outside, his horses broke loose and some 800 were lost. There was, wrote Surrey, no hardier knight than Dacre, but he paid dearly for his neglect of order.[74] Nevertheless, the offensive seemed to be going well until suddenly, at the end of September, a Scottish counter-attack appeared imminent, perhaps to be combined with an invasion by Richard de la Pole, who claimed to be duke of Suffolk.[75] Dorset's men and those brought by his fellows of the privy chamber had already departed, and Surrey wrote to Wolsey on 8 October to ask for some noblemen and gentlemen of the king's household to be sent to his aid. Even if they brought no great numbers, the news of their departure for the front would stir others to follow suit – or should do so: the king would not be well served if he looked equally favourably on those 'that wolbe but dauncers, disers and carders'.[76] Surrey soon heard from Wolsey that Henry VIII 'for his comforte' was sending him the marquess of Dorset and others 'oute of thise parties'.[77] Dorset 'with all the gentilmen of the kingis hous' arrived at Newcastle within ten days, at the same time as the earl of Northumberland and lords Darcy and Latimer, Clifford and Scrope.[78] Darcy's retinue totalled 1,751 and included 100 men of his household as well as men from his offices.[79] Northumberland came with 732 men, including 64 household servants; six days later at Alnwick his retinue had increased to 876 men.[80] Surrey's own retinue had amounted to only 211 men at the muster on 7 October and he was understandably relieved as more soldiers came in, especially as they were 'the beste willed men unyversally fro the higheste to the loweste that ever I sawe'. Yet his thoughts turned to the danger ahead, and he begged Wolsey's help for his children if he should be killed; 'I have spent so moch to serve the kyngs hyghnes that, iff God do now his plesure off me, I shall leve them the pourest noblemannys childerne that died in this realme thes

---

[73] BL, Add. 24, 965, ff.164–5 (*LP*, iii(2), 3135).
[74] BL, Add. 24, 965, f.154 (*LP*, iii(2), 3106); *Original Letters*, 1st series, i, 214–18.
[75] *SP*, iv, 37–9.
[76] *LP*, iii(2), 3360; *Original Letters*, 1st series, i, 224–7.
[77] BL, Cotton Calig. B.VI, ff.376–8 (*LP*, iii(2), 3421).
[78] *Original Letters*, 1st series, i, 228–32.
[79] E36/43 (*LP*, iii(2), 3432).
[80] E101/531/34; SP1/28, ff.322–36 (*LP*, iii(2), 3475).

xl yers.'[81] As it turned out, the show of force proved enough to discourage the Scots. Wark castle managed to hold out against a fierce attack and the Scottish army withdrew as Surrey moved up in support.[82] Richard de la Pole failed to materialize and the crisis subsided.

In 1536 the military machine was tested under a different kind of pressure, the uncertainties of war magnified by a conflict of loyalties. On 5 October, four days after the start of the rising in Lincolnshire, it was reported that the rebels numbered over 20,000. Instructions for dealing with the insurrection were on their way to lord Hussey at Sleaford in Lincolnshire and to the earls of Huntingdon and Shrewsbury.[83] Shrewsbury had taken action on his own initiative the previous day, writing from his lodge in Sheffield park to call upon a number of his friends to join him in his advance against the rebels with 'as manny able men as ye can make, well horsed and harnesed'.[84] Some of those who were with him recalled years after how the earl had taken this decisive step in spite of his knowledge that to muster men without the king's commission was 'in substance' treason.[85] George Hastings, earl of Huntingdon, also had misgivings. He received Shrewsbury's letter at Ashby de la Zouch early on 6 October, before the king's letter reached him. No doubt remembering his trouble over illegal retaining in 1516, he wrote anxiously to Henry VIII to seek his authority to raise men, that 'neithur I nor thay that shall goo with me incurr the daunger of your lawes which is to hevy to anny of us to bere'.[86] Later that day Shrewsbury, by then at Hardwick in Sherwood forest, received the king's letters missive – which he cautiously noted were sealed but not signed – commanding him to assemble his servants, tenants and friends and to move with the gentlemen of the locality against the rebels. He appointed Nottingham as the place of rendezvous, to which everyone should come by 9 October; the earl of Rutland was one of the first to arrive.[87] Hussey, having received the king's letter, reported to Shrewsbury on 6 October that for the moment he could not join him: 'I am so environyd so that I dare not come owte of my house.' But the next day he slipped out disguised as a priest to make his way to Nottingham.[88] Darcy sent a message to Henry VIII from Temple Hirst announcing his intention to go to his post at Pontefract – 'after

---

[81] SP1/28, ff.248–9 (*LP*, iii(2), 3401); *Original Letters*, 1st series, i, 228–32.
[82] *Original Letters*, 1st series, i, 232–5.
[83] *LP*, xi, 552, 553.
[84] BL, Egerton 2603, f.20 (*LP*, xi, 537).
[85] *Holinshed's Chronicles*, iii, 800.
[86] SP1/106, f.282 (*LP*, xi, 560).
[87] *LP*, xi, 562, 581.
[88] SP1/106, f.283 (*LP*, xi, 561); *LP*, xi, 852.

the olde custome specially in tymes of busynes'.[89] The young Edward lord Clinton, who had fled from the rebels, made himself useful by delivering fresh letters from Henry VIII to the earl of Huntingdon at Ashby on 6 October and to Shrewsbury at Hardwick early on 7 October and went on his way with a letter to lord Burgh, who had also been put to flight.[90] Shrewsbury told Hussey that he expected the army at Nottingham to number 40,000 men, made up of 'all the kynges hoole subiectes of the counties of Derby, Stafford, Salop, Worcetter, Leycetter and Northampton', but in fact, although his own retinue eventually amounted to just over 4,000 men, all on horseback, his total force still numbered little more than 7,000 ten days later.[91] For immediate action in Lincolnshire Henry VIII gave the command to the duke of Suffolk, since by his recent marriage to the Willoughby heiress he held many lands in the county.[92]

Preparations were also in hand to assemble forces from the rest of the kingdom. Letters missive dated at Windsor castle on 6 October and signed with a stamp set out the king's instructions for the reserve army. One addressed to lord Montagu commanded him immediately he received it 'to put all your ffreendes, servauntes, tenauntes and such other as ben under your rule in suche a redynes as in case neede shall require ye may within a dayes warenyng' advance to any place which might be designated. 'And herof faile ye not as we specially trust and as ye will for the contrary answere at your perilles.' A similar letter was addressed to lord Scrope of Bolton.[93] The next day fresh letters were got ready, signed with a stamp, in which Henry VIII declared that he intended himself to proceed against the rebels, or at the least to send 'some grete and notable personage to encountre with them'. The recipients were to prepare specified numbers of able men and horses 'and with the same in cace ye be not gretely diseased to cum your self, or elles to send them with some substanciall leder'.[94] In response to such a letter Walter Devereux, lord Ferrers, raised 3,215 men: his 31 captains, 31 petty captains, 680 demilances and 2,473 bowmen and billmen set out from Wales and the marches, Herefordshire, Gloucestershire and Warwickshire to confront the Lincolnshire rebels.[95]

In the midst of all this activity Norfolk was shocked to receive an

[89] SP1/106, f.287 (*LP*, xi, 563(2)).

[90] *LP*, xi, 533, 590.

[91] SP1/107, f.71 (*LP*, xi, 589); *LP*, xi, 758, 930.

[92] *LP*, xi, 656.

[93] SP1/106, ff.273–4 (*LP*, xi, 556).

[94] SP1/107, ff.5–37 (*LP*, xi, 579).

[95] SP1/110, f.80 (*LP*, xi, 938). The contingent was countermanded before it reached Lincolnshire.

order from Henry VIII 'to tary at home to stay the contry'. He had been at Kenninghall, out of favour at court, until the outbreak of the rising, but Henry had recalled him then and he had appeared in London, looking overjoyed. On 7 October he left for Kenninghall in order to raise men. The next day, when the king's 'discomfortable' letter arrived, he wrote back to Henry in immediate protest. 'Alas, sir, shal every noble man save I only eyther come to your parson or els go towardes your enemys? Shall I now sit still lyk a man of law? Alas, sir, my hert is nere ded as wold to God it wer.' Unless he heard again from the king within two days he intended to set off against the rebels rather than 'to remayne at home with so moche shame as I shall do'.[96] He wrote a similar letter to Cromwell and two others, signing it 'the unhappy T. Norffolk', and, in the evening, one to Cromwell and the council, withdrawing his threat to go to Lincolnshire but still complaining at his treatment.[97] The next morning he wrote again to Henry VIII. He had arranged to have some 1,500 tall men on horseback ready in Suffolk at an hour's warning and expected to recruit a good company from Norfolk as well; as the duke of Suffolk had been appointed the king's lieutenant, he would gladly serve under him.[98] Then at last he heard that the decision to keep him at home had been reversed and he was to go to the king at once.[99] The army of reinforcements was to assemble at Ampthill and Norfolk was named at the head of a list of 21 noblemen from the southern half of the kingdom 'to attende upon the kinges owne parson' with their retinues.[100] They had been picked from a longer list of noblemen and retinues which shows that practically the entire peerage was considered for military service, or at least the provision of men. The only noblemen omitted were Daubeney, Latimer, Mountjoy (who was 20 years old) and Mordaunt (who was later called on to provide men). The size of retinue was not entered in every case but, apart from Latimer, the noblemen who later joined the northern rebellion were all listed with the number of men they were to bring: Lumley 100, Scrope of Bolton 300 and Darcy 500.[101]

As news came in of the rising in Yorkshire, the king decided to send Norfolk with 5,000 men from Ampthill and make him joint lieutenant with Shrewsbury. He also instructed Derby to prepare to join Shrewsbury, but soon had to divert him to put down a rising in Lancashire:

[96] *CSPSp.*, v(2), 104; SP1/107, ff.81–2 (*LP*, xi, 601).
[97] SP1/107, ff.83–4 (*LP*, xi, 602, 603).
[98] SP1/107, f.118 (*LP*, xi, 625).
[99] SP1/107, f.120 (*LP*, xi, 626).
[100] SP1/107, ff.41–5 (*LP*, xi, 580(2)).
[101] E36/118, ff.160–4 (*LP*, xi, 580(5)). The order to Mordaunt is in *LP*, xi, 844.

Derby advanced with 8,000 men, including 97 from his own household and 616 supplied by Thomas Stanley, lord Monteagle.[102] Norfolk and Exeter took the musters at Ampthill, where the army still numbered 19,000 men despite the premature dismissal of many contingents when the Lincolnshire rising collapsed. The two commanders moved off, each leading a company of 2,000 picked men, with another 1,000 men from Gloucestershire, all on horseback. The rest of the army was discharged, apart from 560 horsemen under Sir Anthony Browne, sent to support Suffolk.[103] Norfolk's own company had been halted at Cambridge. It was even bigger than he had expected since his friends and servants had brought two or three times the number assigned to them in the king's letters. But it was short of equipment and when he caught up with it on 20 October Norfolk reacted indignantly to orders to send artillery and munitions to the duke of Suffolk to complete the reduction of Lincolnshire and ten pieces of ordnance to Sir Anthony Browne: 'I can do no les then judge that som be desirous to have a greter company more for glory then for necessite.'[104] Secure in the knowledge that he was going to the centre of the action, Norfolk wrote to Shrewsbury, Rutland and Huntingdon to report that he was on his way and ready to treat Shrewsbury 'as my father and governour most worthie', although given an equal authority with him.[105]

The niceties observed, Norfolk on the same day sent to the king his suggested plan of campaign: the line of the Trent should be held to contain the rebels in Yorkshire and Shrewsbury should take no offensive action until he arrived. Henry VIII expressed complete approval.[106] But before he could reach him, Norfolk heard that Shrewsbury had, after all, crossed the Trent. He complained to the king that the earl's advance had jeopardized his strategy, but promised that, whatever happened, he would not spare his 'litle poure carkes'. He assured Henry VIII that he had no intention of keeping any promise he might make to the rebels: 'none oth nor promes made for polecy to serve you myn only master and soverayne can destayne me, who shall rather be torne in a myllion of peces then to shew one poynt of cowardise or untrouth to your maieste.' He asked the king to be good to his sons and daughter 'if it chaunse me to myscary'.[107]

---

[102] *LP*, xi, 716, 719, 806, 1251.

[103] ibid., 750, 765, 803.

[104] SP1/108, ff.116, 230 (*LP*, xi, 727, 800).

[105] SP1/108, f.234 (*LP*, xi, 802).

[106] *LP*, xi, 816.

[107] SP1/109, f.96 (*LP*, xi, 864), printed Madeleine Hope Dodds and Ruth Dodds, *The Pilgrimage of Grace 1536–1537 and the Exeter Conspiracy 1538*, 2 vols (Cambridge, 1915), i, 259–60.

Henry's draft reply contained a promise of favour to Norfolk's children, 'being your lyvely ymages', and authorized him to proceed with the 'politique devise' of his Cambridge letter.[108] When he reached Doncaster, Norfolk, with Shrewsbury, Rutland and Huntingdon, met the representatives of the opposing army headed by Darcy, Latimer and Lumley. (Lord Scrope remained with the rearguard at Pontefract, ceded to the rebels by Darcy.) Norfolk effectively halted the pilgrimage of grace by arranging a truce while the king considered a petition of grievances.[109] He was soon on his way back to Henry VIII, describing his heart as 'nere bresten' at having had to 'appoynt' with rebels as a result of Shrewsbury's rash advance: 'wo, wo, wo worth the tyme that my lord steward went so far forth.'[110] In truth, a negotiated settlement left open the possibility of concessions to the rebels, an outcome which could only have favoured Norfolk and the conservative peers if the king had been willing to consider it. As it was, Cromwell remained in power, but Norfolk had re-established himself, at least as a military leader, by his relentless self-promotion. He headed the list of those commissioned to make a final agreement with the leaders of the pilgrims at Doncaster and when rebellion flared briefly again, early in 1537, he was the natural choice for lieutenant of the north.[111] Shrewsbury, trying to be conciliatory, informed the king of Darcy's offer to serve against the new rebels, which moved Henry to send what he described as a gentle letter to Darcy in reply.[112] But Norfolk had already prejudged Darcy in his letter to Henry VIII after making the truce as 'the most arraunt traytor that ever was lyvyng', and his savage repression of the north continued until he had secured his indictment.[113]

Early in November 1536 the king had sent to his ambassadors in the Netherlands the official version of events: his armies could have devoured the rebels of Lincolnshire and Yorkshire and still given battle to the greatest prince christened.[114] Norfolk had in fact just reported to the council that the men in his company and in Exeter's could be trusted, 'and the noblemen of the rest, but I feare what th'oders wold'.[115] The loyalty of the nobility was indeed crucial. Whatever they thought of the aims of the rebellion, most noblemen

---

[108] *SP*, i, 493–5.
[109] Dodds, *The Pilgrimage of Grace*, i, 262, 265–8.
[110] SP1/110, ff.6–7 (*LP*, xi, 909), printed ibid., 268–9.
[111] *LP*, xi, 1205–6, xii(1), 97–8.
[112] ibid., 169, 170, 208, 226.
[113] See above, pp. 61–2.
[114] *LP*, xi, 984.
[115] As above, n. 110.

had rallied to the king. Shrewsbury's immediate response had given the lead; Henry VIII rewarded him by reducing the price of a wardship sold to him by 1,000 marks. Cumberland and Westmorland had kept the king informed of the danger they had been in from the rebels around them and he had promised to recompense them both; Cumberland was elected Knight of the Garter for his services during the rebellion, but Westmorland apparently received nothing.[116] Robert Radcliffe, earl of Sussex, was the only other nobleman to be rewarded for his services against the rebels – fittingly enough, with a gift of monastic land.[117] His main contribution had been made after he had been commissioned with Derby in February 1537 to restore order in Lancashire, which was outside Norfolk's jurisdiction. By inducing the abbot of Furness to surrender his abbey, too rich to be dissolved by the act of 1536, Sussex created the precedent for the piecemeal dissolution of the larger monasteries.[118]

Leadership in war demanded more than the agility in arms learned on the tournament field and the power to raise men. An observer on behalf of the papacy in 1538 noted the qualities of the high nobility of England with special reference to the military power of each man. His report is obviously biased – he probably wanted to prove that an invading force would meet little effective opposition – but, even so, it is a reminder that the nobility at any time contained men of varying ages, experience and natural ability. Norfolk was described as the chief and best captain, Suffolk as a good captain but sickly and half lame. The old earl of Shrewsbury was dead; his son was young, strong, of great power – but with little wit and no experience. Oxford was of great power but little experience, Arundel of great power, with little wit and less experience, although his son was of good wit and likely to do well. Derby was the greatest nobleman in terms of power and land, but a child in wisdom, half a fool. Huntingdon, Rutland and Cumberland were all powerful but with little or no discretion, Westmorland had power without wit or knowledge. The aged earl of Essex had little wit, less experience and no power. The earl of Bath was old and foolish, the earl of Worcester young and foolish and of great power in Wales. Wiltshire and Sussex were both of small power; the former was wise, though of little experience, the latter a man of many words and little discretion. Only four high noblemen besides Norfolk were commended. Henry Courtenay, marquess of Exeter, was described as the man nearest the crown, powerful, loved and gouty. The young Henry

---

[116] WARD9/149, f.68v; *LP*, xi, 1002–3.
[117] See below, p. 237.
[118] *LP*, xii(1), 302, 840; G. W. O. Woodward, *The Dissolution of the Monasteries* (London, 1966), p. 101.

Grey, marquess of Dorset, was strong but poor, since his great possessions were out of his hands, with little or no experience but well learned and a great wit. Edward Seymour, earl of Hertford, was young and wise, but of small power. William FitzWilliam, earl of Southampton – made by the king – was wise, active and of good experience, one of the best captains in England.[119] Given his reluctance to commit the command of his armies to any but high noblemen, it was from these men, or from others he might raise to their rank, that Henry VIII had to choose his war leaders.

Yet even within this small group he was slow to give a chance to younger men. For the war against Scotland in 1542 he again appointed Norfolk lieutenant of the north, supported by Suffolk and Southampton.[120] Only when Southampton died at Newcastle as the army prepared to move up to Berwick did Henry VIII turn to a man in his early forties, the earl of Hertford. He arrived in time to join a raid across the border to burn the town and abbey of Kelso. Norfolk soon heard that Henry was far from satisfied with this achievement; but the counter-attack of James V saved the day as the Scots at Solway Moss were destroyed by 3,000 borderers under the command of the deputy warden of the west march, Sir Thomas Wharton.[121] When Henry VIII came to nominate a new lieutenant of the north, early in 1543, he chose Suffolk.[122] In September 1543, after the failure of the peace treaty signed in July, Suffolk himself expressed some misgiving and asked for a replacement to be named in case he proved unable to command the army 'by sycknes or other wyse'. But when he was told that it was not 'expedyent' for him, as lord lieutenant, to risk his life in an attack on Edinburgh, he took it as a personal slight: 'I dowt not to sustaigne not oonly that jornaye, but I trust many worse then that, as well as they that arr more yonger then I.' However, eight days later he advised a truce and recommended his own recall.[123] The council replied that the king had long had it in mind to call Suffolk to his presence – 'if he might ones have brought his matiers in Scotland to some certayn poynt'.[124] Suffolk remained as lieutenant of the north until 1544, when Henry VIII, having agreed with Charles V on an invasion of France, decided to replace him by Hertford so that he could join the expedition. Even then, he assured Suffolk, in consideration of his long service, 'if youe shall thinke this enterprise faisible, and that there is honour to be gotten by the same', he could lead the

[119] *LP*, xiii(2), 732.
[120] *LP*, xvii, 714 g.19.
[121] *The Hamilton Papers*, i, 209–14, 221, 226, 231, 240, 244.
[122] *APC*, i, 71.
[123] *The Hamilton Papers*, ii, 7, 37, 40, 78.
[124] ibid., 80.

invasion of Scotland before getting ready for the French campaign.[125] But in the event it was left to Hertford to burn the town of Edinburgh and leave it as a 'perpetuel memory of the vengeaunce of God'.[126] Supported by 4,000 horsemen who had ridden in under lord Eure, Hertford's army by sea landed at Leith and burned Edinburgh and Holyrood before returning; on the way back he made a number of knights, including lords Clinton and Conyers. In his first independent command Hertford had had under him 12,000 men, with John Dudley, viscount Lisle, as captain of the foreward and Francis Talbot, earl of Shrewsbury – soon to be appointed lieutenant of the north – as captain of the rearward.[127] At last a new generation of military leaders had been given their opportunity by Henry VIII.

But it was only on the Scottish front that they were appointed to the highest posts. For the French campaign – always the more interesting to Henry VIII – the king still preferred the two veteran dukes: Norfolk was captain of the foreward and Suffolk captain of the middleward under the king. Russell, about the same age as Suffolk and one of Henry's closest friends, was captain of the rearward. However, Henry VIII appointed as marshal of the army the 32-year-old Henry FitzAlan, earl of Arundel, who had been deputy of Calais before succeeding to the earldom in January 1544.[128] Musters taken in preparation for the campaign had shown that every adult nobleman in the southern half of the kingdom was ready to provide men for France except Hertford, otherwise engaged, lord Parr of Horton, who was to be left to attend upon Katherine Parr, and lord Grey of Wilton, already on active service at Hammes. Most of the noblemen who were privy councillors certified that they had 100 horse prepared: between them they accounted for over half the horsemen returned by the nobility. (Russell had 1,200 foot as well, the rest generally between 300 and 500 foot.) Only lord Wriothesley had no more than 40 horse, but he had 20 demihakes among his footmen. The earl of Oxford, with no horsemen, had 50 demihakes on foot. The only other nobleman to return any firearms in his certificate was Charles Blount, lord Mountjoy, who had ten hackbuts. As in 1513, archers and billmen on foot formed the majority of the troops available.[129] The three wards of the army were made up from the muster book.[130] Most of the noblemen on the list crossed to France, with the addition of the northern lord Latimer,

[125] ibid., 159.
[126] ibid., 207.
[127] ibid., 227, 230, 232–3; *LP*, xix(1), 531. Narratives of the campaign ibid., 533–4.
[128] ibid., 273(5). Reference to Arundel as marshal in *Foedera*, vi(3), 119–21.
[129] SP1/184, ff.85–221 (*LP*, xix(1), 273).
[130] *LP*, xix(1), 273–5.

stepson of Katherine Parr, and the 17-year-old earl of Rutland; Stourton, who had taken part in the Scottish campaign, did not go, but Cobham and Clinton, who had served under Lisle, and Lisle himself, transferred to the French expedition. Henry VIII instructed Wriothesley, as lord chancellor, and Hertford to remain at court to advise the queen-regent – although Hertford was later allowed to proceed to France.[131] There were a few others who also stayed in England. Two were over 60 – Audley and La Warre – and four – Burgh, Mordaunt, Morley and Zouche – in their late fifties, if not older: all were probably excused on grounds of age. Morley, it is true, was still exceptionally active in civilian life, following up his attendance at every trial by peers with an outstanding record of regular attendance in parliament; he was even present in the house of lords for each reading of the bill passed in 1542 to attaint his daughter, lady Rochford, and Katherine Howard.[132] He was represented by his son in France in 1544. Three noblemen may have been left out on purpose. Lady Bridgwater had been attainted of misprision by the same act of parliament for concealing the queen's treason. Her husband, Henry Daubeney, earl of Bridgwater, aged 50 in 1544, did not go to France. Vaux and Sandys, in their thirties, also remained at home; neither took any part in political life, even as a justice of the peace, during the last years of Henry VIII's reign.[133] The only peer to sue out an exemption from attending the king to France was Gregory lord Cromwell. He had lands of Henry's gift in Leicestershire and Monmouth which brought him within the scope of the statutes of 1495 and 1504 and paid £66 13s 4d for his 'composicion' with the king.[134]

The retinues of the nobility constituted a smaller proportion of the whole than they had done in 1513. This expeditionary force was almost certainly the largest English army yet to have been sent abroad – or to be sent until the reign of William III.[135] However, Henry's military thinking did little to justify such a concentration of manpower. A few days after arriving at the camp Russell complained to the king that they were wandering about in a 'wylde warre'. Boulogne and Ardres should be their targets. To Sir Anthony Browne he was more explicit: in spite of so much campaigning Henry VIII had not one foot

[131] *Foedera*, vi(3), 114–15. Hertford was in France by 13 August.

[132] *LJ*, i, 168, 174–5; 33 Henry VIII, c.21.

[133] See above, pp. 125–6 and below, p. 204. However, Sandys raised men to resist a French invasion of the Isle of Wight in 1545: *LP*, xx(1), 1329.

[134] *LP*, xix(2), 340 g.58; E315/337, f.128.

[135] C. S. L. Davies, 'The English people and war in the early sixteenth century' in *Britain and the Netherlands*, vi, *War and Society*, ed. A. C. Duke and C. A. Tamse (The Hague, 1977), p. 2.

more land in France than he had had at the start of his reign. If so noble a king, 'the father of all Christendom in this worlde', should go home without any conquest, the French would never again respect an English army. Within ten days Suffolk had received orders to besiege Boulogne.[136] Henry VIII arrived at Calais four days later, on 14 July, and went to view Boulogne, but the town was not taken until mid-September. After the king's triumphant entry he made a number of knights – including the young earl of Rutland and lord Bray – before sailing back to England.[137] Henry VIII was immensely pleased with the victory although Boulogne was to prove no more tenable than Tournai. Charles V made a separate peace with France before the end of September and, until Henry could negotiate a peace treaty which recognized his right to remain in temporary occupation of Boulogne, England lived under threat of a French invasion. To meet it, Henry VIII appointed the three commanders of 1544 – Norfolk, Suffolk and Russell – to command three armies raised in 1545 to defend the southern half of the kingdom.[138] When a foray from Boulogne seemed necessary, Suffolk was chosen to lead it, but died a few days later.[139] Henry maintained to the end his predilection for men he had known since his youth, in war as at court. Yet the military skills of Hertford and Lisle could not be ignored. The lord admiral, Lisle, governor of Boulogne after its capture, was recalled in 1545 to take charge of the navy, while Hertford was busy in France or on the Scottish borders during most of 1545 and 1546. When they eventually returned to court in the last weeks of the reign they had established their reputations as leaders in war and given credibility to their aspirations to political power.

The armies which the nobility led and helped to raise were rarely pitted against the full force of the French army since Henry VIII never went to war except in alliance with the king of Spain or the emperor. In each of the three major continental expeditions of the reign he had the support of auxiliary troops furnished by his ally as well as foreign mercenaries. Auxiliaries and mercenaries together made up more than one-fifth of his total army in the field in 1513 and nearly one-quarter in 1544, while in 1523 they amounted to almost one-third of Suffolk's army. The withdrawal of Charles V's auxiliaries in 1544 was followed

[136] SP1/189, ff.151–2, 153–4, 251–2 (LP, xix(1), 816, 817, 882).

[137] LP, xix(2), 334. Narratives of the campaign in Foedera, vi(3), 119–21 and 'A diary of the expedition of 1544', EHR, xvi (1901), 503–7.

[138] LP, xx(1), 958. This despite the unauthorized withdrawal from Boulogne of Norfolk and Suffolk after the king's departure in 1544: Scarisbrick, Henry VIII, pp. 449–50.

[139] See above, p. 117.

by the retirement of most of the mercenaries; Henry VIII was forced to recruit large numbers of replacements from all over Europe to support the English army as for once it faced the enemy alone. By March 1546, when Hertford at last took command of the army in France, almost half the 30,000 soldiers were foreigners, some of them men who had served with him on the northern front in 1545 when for the first time mercenaries were used against the Scots. It was these professional soldiers who provided the heavy cavalry which England lacked and most of the pikemen and arquebusiers, besides supplementing the light cavalry brought by some of the nobility and gentry.[140] The quasi-feudal English army, incapable of modernization, fell progressively further behind the rising standards of the continent during the reign of Henry VIII.

The gap between the image and the reality of war had to be experienced afresh in each generation. For old hands such as Russell the futility of Henry VIII's wars might be apparent, but not to the young Charles Blount, lord Mountjoy, who before going to France in 1544 set down in his will the epitaph he wanted on his grave, if he should be killed, to remind his children to 'kepe themselfes wordye of so moche honour as to be called hereafter to dye for ther maister and countrey'.[141] (Mountjoy died in October 1544 in Dorset, aged 28, probably of illness contracted during the campaign, always a greater risk than death in action, which claimed no nobleman in Henry VIII's reign, although lord Ogle may have died of wounds inflicted by the Scots in 1545.) Nevertheless, whatever the individual judgement on the king's policies, the nobility accepted without question its duty of military service. For some, a military command served a personal ambition: success in arms would always win renown. For most, perhaps, it was no more than a duty, but one which enabled them, as well as the king, to appear at the height of their power as they led their men to war. Yet in September 1544, almost casually, Henry VIII took a decision which was to transform the role of the nobility in war. He summoned to France 4,000 militiamen to reinforce the army. Every able man between the ages of 16 and 60 was bound to serve in the militia when needed, but by ancient tradition, reinforced by statute, these county levies could not be sent abroad. Henry VIII simply ignored the limitation. His motive was probably mere convenience. The nobility and leading gentry were still in action in France and could not easily recruit more men; the militia was ready to hand.

---

[140] Gilbert John Millar, *Tudor Mercenaries and Auxiliaries 1485–1547* (Charlottesville, Va, 1980), pp. 25–7, 43–8, 161–2, 168.
[141] PROB11/30/45.

Although there is no sign that Henry VIII intended it, his action heralded the end of the quasi-feudal system. Within 15 years, armies were normally recruited on a county basis by muster-masters appointed by commission, not raised by royal letters to noblemen and others. The feudal army had virtually ceased to exist.[142] Individual noblemen, no longer called upon to serve with their men, might still see active service overseas, but the mass involvement of the nobility in foreign war was a thing of the past. No doubt the accession of a minor and two women would anyway have altered the nature of an obligation founded on personal attendance on the monarch; but the direction of the change was determined in 1544. The development of a national system of recruitment left the reign of Henry VIII as the last in which military service was the nobility's most conspicuous duty.

In the eyes of Henry VIII it was also its most important service. Noblemen called to a great ceremony at court were informed that their presence would do the king 'very acceptable pleasure'; attendance at parliament might be excused on grounds of personal inconvenience; but the summons to war went out with the command 'fail ye not'. The need to recruit large numbers of men at the same time not infrequently led to disputes between rival landowners. In October 1523, for example, Dacre remonstrated with Clifford for calling up men whose service Dacre claimed.[143] Lumley's refusal to turn out in 1522 apparently stemmed from a quarrel with the bishop of Durham, whose tenants in the forest of Weardale were under Lumley's rule.[144] Even a nobleman with many able men at his command might find the requirement to provide soldiers somewhat irksome. 'Cartthorsses lakes noo callying uppon' was Darcy's wry comment to Hussey in August 1523 when he was ordered to send a further 300 men to raid Scotland.[145] Other noblemen were burdened with wider responsibilities. The struggle to pay for the later campaigns drove the lord chancellor, Wriothesley, near to distraction. 'You write to me styll, pay, pay', he complained to the privy council in September 1545; 'consider it is your partes to remember the state of thinges with me and, by your wisedomes, to ponder what may be doon.' A month later he told Sir William Paget that he was at his wit's end to know 'howe we shal possibly shift for thre monethes folowing'. Yet he swore fervent loyalty to the king: 'God is my judge, I wold I, and all myn, were bounde to drynk water twies in a weke, whilles we lyved, upon condition that his majeste might

---

[142] Goring, 'The military obligations of the English people', pp. 270–3, 279–80; C. G. Cruickshank, *Elizabeth's Army*, 2nd edn (Oxford, 1966), p. 12.

[143] *LP*, iii(2), 3427.

[144] BL, Cotton Calig. B.III, ff.301–2 (*LP*, iii(2), 2546); *LP*, iii(2), 2806.

[145] SP1/28, f.177 (*LP*, iii(2), 3276).

compasse all thinges to his hartes ease.'[146] Wriothesley perhaps hoped
that his fantasy of self-denial would reach Henry's ear, but many of the
king's subjects had to make real sacrifices. Although Henry VIII
eventually made peace with France, he died with the kingdom at war
with the Scots. It was his royal prerogative to decide whether the
hoped-for gains were worth all the effort and expense. Henry's priorities were not those of the common people, who had, it seems, lost any
illusions about the glory of war by the 1520s, but they were easier for
noblemen to understand. Honour was their standard, too, even if, in
the field, discretion sometimes appeared the better part of valour. The
defence of the realm against the king's enemies was the traditional role
of the nobleman, the justification of his life of privilege. The nobility in
the reign of Henry VIII was still a military elite.

---

[146] *SP*, i, 830–1, 839–40.

PART III

The King's Rewards

CHAPTER 6

Grants of Office

Office conferred status and, in many cases, wealth, patronage and power. It might also entail much hard work. The grant of office was not reward pure and simple, therefore, but – in the words of the statute of 1495 for the enforcement of military service – 'promocion or avauncement', creating a less lasting obligation of service than the gift of land but still, while the office was held, binding the office-holder to the king. Office was a more realistic aim for most noblemen than land, at least until the dissolution of the monasteries. The workings of the patronage system are for the most part hidden, but the appointments made by the king, the highest patron of all, give some indication of his approach to this aspect of government.

In a few cases his choice was limited by the inherited rights of certain noble families. There were five great offices of state which were, or might be, hereditary.[1] They were almost entirely monopolized by the high nobility in the reign of Henry VIII. The office of high steward, merged in the crown with the accession of Henry IV, was filled by royal commission for special occasions only – coronations and the trials of peers. All those whom Henry VIII appointed were of the rank of earl or above except lord Audley of Walden, created a baron and named high steward for the trials of Exeter and Montagu in 1538. The duties of the hereditary butler were only performed at coronation banquets. Successive earls of Arundel exercised the office at the coronations of Henry VIII and Anne Boleyn, but the title of chief butler was used at other times by the holder of the duplicate office, who was responsible for the prisage of wines. The office of great chamberlain, lost by the de Veres in 1399, was recovered by them in

[1] J. H. Round, 'The great offices of state' in GEC, ii, Appendix D and *The King's Serjeants and Officers of State with their Coronation Services* (London, 1911).

1485, and on the accession of Henry VIII the earl of Oxford quickly
obtained confirmation of his hereditary right to it.[2] Oxford acted as
great chamberlain at Henry's coronation and when he died the office
descended to his heir, his 13-year-old nephew; it was granted in 1514
to the duke of Norfolk, his father-in-law, during the boy's minority.[3]
Oxford came of age in 1520, but died in 1526 leaving no children. The
landed inheritance was disputed between the heir male and the heirs
general, but all the family agreed that the hereditary office should go
with the earldom to the heir male. However, the terms of the original
grant meant that by law it should descend to the heir general or – if, as
in this case, there was no one heir general – revert to the crown.
Oxford enlisted the help of Wolsey to try to forestall this disaster.
Wolsey wrote to the king to ask him 'to be good and gracious lord' to
'your old trusty servaunt Sir John Veer, nowe erle of Oxford', who was
coming to see him. 'Your highnes shal finde him true, humble,
constant, and faythful, without leaning to any man, save oonly to your
grace . . . and, to my supposal, he shal furnish that rome as wel as any
of his predecessours hath doon in tymes past, to your honnour and
good contentacion.' Henry VIII responded so far as to grant the office
to Oxford for life.[4] In the 1530s the earl resumed the quest for the
'offyceys of myn inherytauns' – which also included the offices of
constable of Colchester castle and keeper of the forest of Waltham,
Essex – and, after suing to the king for two years, sought the aid of
Thomas Cromwell. As he explained, he had received 'good and
comfortabyll wordes of hys grace at alle tymes of my sewtt, how be yt
as yet I am at no poynt'. He had also sued to 'the quenys grace that
now ys', who had taken charge of the bills he had prepared for the
grant of each office and promised to 'move the kyng for me and to gett
me my bylles assyngned'.[5] But Henry VIII, if not Anne Boleyn, had
had years in which to perfect the courteous display of sympathy
towards subjects with a grievance, and Oxford died in 1540 without
having gained his desire. It would not have been in Cromwell's own
interest to persuade the king to be more generous: on 18 April 1540,
the day of his investiture as earl of Essex, he was appointed great
chamberlain for life, the office in all likelihood securing him the
earldom.[6] It also gave him the opportunity to complete his reform of
the household, to establish his authority over the king's chamber as
well as the privy chamber and transform the formerly honorific title

[2] GEC, x, Appendix F; *LP*, i(1), 54 g.56.
[3] *LP*, i(2), 2964 g.80.
[4] *SP*, i, 169; C82/581 (*LP*, iv(2), 2713).
[5] SP1/83, f.203 (*LP*, vii, 594).
[6] C82/765 (*LP*, xv, 611 g.38); see above, p. 32.

into an effective head of the household 'above stairs'.[7] But Cromwell's fall meant that he held the office for only a few weeks. He was succeeded in turn by Robert Radcliffe, earl of Sussex, and Edward Seymour, earl of Hertford, each appointed for life.[8] Henry VIII had converted the office of great chamberlain into a valuable item in his patronage, a gift suitable for men at the top of the political hierarchy.

The two other hereditary offices had military antecedents. Richard III had recognized Henry Stafford, duke of Buckingham, as hereditary great constable as heir to the Bohuns. Buckingham's attainder later in 1483 was reversed in favour of his son in the first parliament of Henry VII's reign, but Edward Stafford, duke of Buckingham, did not thereby recover the hereditary office, and for the coronation of Henry VIII he was only appointed great constable for the preceding day (as well as high steward for the day itself). In June 1510 Buckingham petitioned the king and council to be restored to the office which he claimed was rightfully his. He was instructed to produce his evidence, which he did two days later, when his claim was discussed by the council. Early in July the attorney-general put forward the king's answer to Buckingham's bill and the duke was given until Michaelmas to prepare his response.[9] Four years later Buckingham at last won his legal battle when the judges accepted his argument that he held two manors in Gloucestershire by service of being constable of England and decided that the king must be able, at his pleasure, to compel the duke to exercise the office, since otherwise the manors would be held without service. But the king's pleasure had been, and still was, that Buckingham should not be hereditary constable. When the chief justices reported their findings to him Henry VIII refused to call upon the duke for this service on the grounds that the office was 'very high and dangerous, and also very chargeable to the king in fees'.[10] Buckingham had gained a hollow victory, and one that may have aroused Henry's fear of his ambition. His attainder removed any hereditary claim to the office and thereafter it was bestowed only for coronations. By contrast, the Howards made good their claim to the office of earl marshal or marshal of England, ranked next below that of great constable. Richard III had granted it to John Howard, duke of Norfolk, as heir to the Mowbrays. It was lost by Norfolk's attainder in 1485 and granted the next year to the other

[7] Starkey, 'From feud to faction', 20.

[8] C82/771, 805 (*LP*, xv, 1027 g.12, xviii(1), 226 g.58).

[9] BL, Lansdowne 639, ff.34v–5; Huntington Library, Ellesmere 2655, f.8v.

[10] *Reports of Cases in the Reigns of Henry VIII, Edward VI, Queen Mary and Queen Elizabeth taken and collected by Sir James Dyer*, ed. John Vaillant, 3 vols (London, 1794), iii, 285b.

coheir to the Mowbray inheritance, William Berkeley, earl of Nottingham, in tail male. After his death without male heir the office was
granted to Prince Henry, but on his accession Henry VIII appointed
Thomas Howard, earl of Surrey, earl marshal for the coronation and
then, in 1510, made him earl marshal for life, with £20 p.a. backdated
to the previous Michaelmas, from which date, it was said, he had
exercised the office by the king's command.[11] This partial recovery
was checked in July 1523, when Henry VIII gave the reversion to
Charles Brandon, duke of Suffolk.[12] Suffolk was about to lead an army
into France and was in a strong position to demand a favour. Ten
years later the tables were turned. In April 1533 the next duke of
Norfolk, uncle to Anne Boleyn, was preparing to go on embassy to
Francis I to make sure of his support for Henry VIII's marriage.
Pressure was put on Suffolk and before the end of the month Cromwell
was able to draft a letter telling him that the king, being 'assuredlie
advertised' that he was content to surrender his patent, had granted it
to Norfolk, whose ancestors had held it 'untill nowe of late'. In
recompense Suffolk would be given for life the office of chief justice of
the royal forests south of the Trent. Cromwell assured Suffolk that
Henry was pleased with him for being ready to give up the great state
office, showing thereby more 'zele to norisshe kyndenes and love'
between Norfolk and himself than 'to thatt or any other office'.[13]
Suffolk's grant was vacated on 20 May 1533 and on 28 May Henry
VIII formally granted Norfolk the name, style and title of earl marshal
of England in tail male, with an annuity of £20.[14] The politeness with
which the transaction was officially handled can hardly have mollified
Suffolk, deprived of the title which since 1524 had been part of his
style, used to give him a comparable status to that of the duke of
Norfolk, treasurer of England. Moreover, the grant was clearly made
with an eye to Anne Boleyn's coronation on 1 June, although Norfolk
would not be able to be there. Suffolk lost his one opportunity of acting
as earl marshal at a coronation. His appointment as great constable
and high steward for the occasion temporarily softened the blow by
giving him an alternative role in the proceedings commensurate with
his rank.

The office of admiral of England, unlike the offices of constable and
marshal, was never hereditary. It also entailed services which were
more than ceremonial, although they might be performed by deputy.

---

[11] *LP*, i(1), 546 g.42.
[12] *LP*, iii(2), 3161.
[13] SP1/75, ff.245–6 (*LP*, vi, 415).
[14] *LP*, vi, 578 g.50.

But it, too, generally went to a nobleman in the reign of Henry VIII. In 1485 Henry VII had appointed John de Vere, earl of Oxford, admiral of England, Ireland and Acquitaine for life; Henry VIII on his accession renewed the grant.[15] When Oxford died on 10 March 1513 preparations for an invasion of France were nearly complete and Henry VIII immediately made Sir Edward Howard lord admiral for life. After he was killed in action on 25 April his brother, Norfolk's son and heir, was appointed to succeed him, again for term of life.[16] Twelve years later Henry VIII went back on this decision. He wanted his young son, Henry FitzRoy, to be admiral of England, and he requested Thomas Howard, now duke of Norfolk, to return his patent. Norfolk's compliance enabled the king to give the office to FitzRoy for life in July 1525, a month after he had created him duke of Richmond.[17] (Norfolk was recompensed with a generous grant of lands.)[18] Arthur Plantagenet, viscount Lisle, acted as vice-admiral under Richmond from 1525 until he went to Calais as deputy in 1533, but it was Sir William FitzWilliam, the treasurer of the household, who had been a vice-admiral in the early 1520s, who was appointed lord admiral when Richmond died in July 1536.[19] His appointment was, as usual, for life, but the fall of Cromwell released a number of offices and FitzWilliam, by then earl of Southampton, gave up the admiralty on becoming lord privy seal and was succeeded as lord admiral in turn by John lord Russell, Edward Seymour, earl of Hertford, and John Dudley, viscount Lisle.[20] For Russell and Hertford it also proved the ladder to further promotion, while to Lisle it brought entrance to the privy council, the first rung on his ascent to power in the reign of Edward VI.

The act of 1539 for placing the lords in council and parliament listed the offices of great chamberlain, constable, marshal and admiral in this order of precedence. Four offices were ranked above them.[21] The highest of all was not the preserve of the nobility. In October 1529 Chapuys, the newly arrived imperial ambassador, reported that there had been talk of the duke of Suffolk becoming lord chancellor and giving up his office of marshal to Anne Boleyn's father, a move which it was believed had been blocked by Norfolk's opposition.[22] In the aftermath of Wolsey's fall anything may have seemed possible, but

[15] *CPR, Henry VII*, i, 22; *LP*, i(1), 54 g.11.
[16] C82/392 (*LP*, i(2), 1948 g.13).
[17] *LP*, iv(1), 1500, 1576.
[18] See below, pp. 217–18.
[19] C82/715 (*LP*, xi, 385 g.15).
[20] *LP*, xv, 942 g.117; *APC*, i, 68; *LP*, xviii(1), 19, 100 g.27.
[21] See above, pp. 113–14.
[22] *CPSp.*, iv(1), 211.

once Henry VIII had made up his mind to break the succession of clerical chancellors he turned instead to men trained in the common law. When Sir Thomas More in May 1532 resigned the office of lord chancellor to which he had been appointed in 1529, the king ordered Thomas Audley to exercise all the functions of the chancellor in chancery, star chamber and council, but only to be called keeper of the great seal. At the same time he gave him a knighthood.[23] The lesser title had in the past been given to men holding the office temporarily, and it may have been that Audley's was initially considered a short-term appointment; but he was made lord chancellor in January 1533, ten days before parliament reassembled.[24] For over five years he held the office as a commoner, and if Henry VIII had not wanted him to preside over the trials of Exeter and Montagu he would probably have died a commoner. As it was, he surrendered the great seal as lord Audley of Walden on 21 April 1544, too ill to continue in office. The next day Henry VIII delivered it to another nobleman, albeit one of less than four months' standing: Thomas lord Wriothesley, created a baron on 1 January 1544. Henry at first named him, too, lord keeper, but only out of respect for his ailing predecessor. On 3 May, with Audley now dead, Wriothesley gave up the great seal and received it again from the king's hands on his appointment as chancellor.[25] The social pattern set in the reign of Henry VIII has lasted to this day: numerous peers have held the office of lord chancellor but in every instance they have been men ennobled by the crown before or after their appointment.[26]

Lord Audley of Walden in 1539 described the office of lord chancellor as high and honourable but 'chargeable', pointedly reminding Cromwell that he held no other.[27] However, it was also well paid. Audley's fees (as More's had been) were £542 15s 0d p.a. for himself and the masters in chancery, with £200 p.a. for his attendance in star chamber and an allowance of £80 p.a. for wine and wax, £822 15s 0d p.a. in all; Wriothesley was in addition given an annuity of

[23] *Foedera*, vi(2), 171.

[24] ibid., 176.

[25] ibid., vi(3), 106–8.

[26] List of chancellors to 1954 in *Handbook of British Chronology*, ed. Sir F. Maurice Powicke and E. B. Fryde, Royal Historical Soc. Guides and Handbooks, no. 2, 2nd edn (London, 1961). The 2nd lord Hailsham would have been the exception had he not disclaimed his hereditary titles some years before his appointment as lord chancellor in 1970, when he was created a life peer.

[27] BL, Cotton Cleo. E.IV, ff.231–2 (*LP*, xiv(2), 36), printed *Three Chapters of Letters*, pp. 239–41 and (abbreviated) John Strype, *Ecclesiastical Memorials, relating chiefly to religion . . . under King Henry VIII, King Edward VI, and Queen Mary I*, 3 vols (Oxford, 1822), i(1), 407–8.

£300.[28] Audley had in fact told Cromwell that he had suffered no
financial loss from his appointment as lord keeper. He had incurred
debts through the purchase of a suitable house, with 'stuff' and plate,
but they were after all his own property 'to make shift therwith
ageyn'.[29] It was only later than he discovered that his fees 'wil skant
ffynde my howse kepyng, vitayle ys so dere', especially in London; by
then he was more conscious of the insignificance of his landed estate,
worth no more than £40 p.a. He offered Cromwell a couple of geldings
– 'and my hert wile I liff' – if he would get the king's signature to a bill
he had prepared for a grant of property. He had only accepted the
office 'upon the comfort of the kynges grace, and, if ye remembir,
moche ye advysed me to yt'. A royal gift now would demonstrate that
the king was his good lord 'and entendyth to putt me in a certente of
lyvyng, wherby I shal have no cause resonabill to declyne from justice
nor be afreyd of eny person'.[30] Audley's suits for land were successful
enough to bring his income from office and his income from land into
rough balance by 1539.[31] Even so, the office was still financially
important to him. It also gave him much patronage, although Audley
had some difficulty in making use of it. Cromwell made a number of
successful attempts to fill posts supposedly in the chancellor's gift.[32] 'I
thynke never chauncelor lesse sett by', Audley protested in 1535.[33]
Offices could indeed vary in status with the quality and interests of the
office-holder, but the lord chancellor of England would always rank
first in the order of precedence of the king's ministers, except during
the few years when Cromwell exercised the royal supremacy as
vicegerent in spirituals.

Next below the chancellor was the lord treasurer. Henry VII had
appointed Thomas Howard, earl of Surrey, to the office during pleasure,
with a fee of £365 p.a., and Henry VIII renewed the grant on his
accession and again in 1514, after Surrey became duke of Norfolk. In
1522 Norfolk surrendered his patent at his manor of Horsham and the
king granted the office the following day on the same terms to his son
and heir, who retained it until his attainder in 1547.[34] Throughout
the reign, therefore, the two Howards monopolized this high office
without enjoying any formal security of tenure. Father and son followed the tradition of their predecessors in giving no more than

---

[28] *LP*, xix(1), 610 gg.31, 41; Guy, *More*, pp. 32–3.
[29] *SP*, i, 388–9.
[30] SP1/78, ff.69–70 (*LP*, vi, 927).
[31] BL, Cotton Cleo. E.IV, ff.222–3 (*LP*, xiv(2), 775).
[32] Lehmberg, 'Sir Thomas Audley', pp. 11–14.
[33] BL, Cotton Titus B.I, f.365 (*LP*, ix, 528).
[34] *CPR, Henry VII*, ii, 239; *LP*, i(1), 132 g.98, i(2), 2772 g.4, ii(1), 2736, iii(2), 2700.

nominal attendance to their charge, the supervision of the exchequer.[35] The son, by his own account, made but modest use even of the patronage of the office, claiming in 1540 that he had never accepted any gift or reward, as all his predecessors had done 'right largely', to appoint customs officials: 'I thank God I have kepte my handes clene therefrom.' Furthermore, he.had put in only two of his servants as customer or comptroller, leaving the rest to be named by Henry VIII at the suit of others.[36]

Two of the higher offices in the exchequer were sought after even by noblemen. The chancellor of the exchequer was not yet an important official and received only the comparatively small annual fee of £26 13s 4d, but in May 1514 John Bourchier, lord Berners, secured the reversion after the death or surrender of Sir Thomas Lovell, whom Henry VII had appointed for life in 1485. Two years later, Berners had a fresh grant of the reversion enrolled and when Lovell died he was admitted to the office.[37] Robert Radcliffe, viscount FitzWalter, was granted the reversion to Berners in 1527, but when Berners died in 1533 it was Thomas Cromwell who replaced him as chancellor of the exchequer.[38] Unlike his predecessor and his rival for the office – for both of whom it was a desirable sinecure – Cromwell wanted it in order to achieve greater control of the financial administration.[39] He had not become a chamberlain of the receipt of the exchequer, whose salary was £52 3s 4d p.a., when a vacancy had occurred the previous year. One of the two chamberlains was George Talbot, earl of Shrewsbury, appointed for life by Henry VII and reappointed by Henry VIII at his accession. In 1522 Sir William Sandys obtained the reversion, but if he hoped to come to an agreement with the earl for a transfer of the office he was disappointed. In July 1527 Shrewsbury indeed surrendered his patent, but only to receive a new grant to himself and his son and heir in survivorship, which enabled the Talbots to see out the reign in the office.[40] The other chamberlain of the receipt was a commoner until Robert Radcliffe, by then earl of Sussex, was appointed for life in 1532; after his death he was succeeded by Sir Thomas, later lord Wriothesley.[41] Cromwell may have hoped for the post in 1532 – it had been held earlier in the reign by Sir John Heron,

[35] Elton, *Tudor Revolution*, pp. 23, 109, 121.
[36] *SP*, i, 650–2.
[37] *LP*, i(2), 2964 g.53, ii(1), 1946, 2736; J. C. Sainty, *Officers of the Exchequer*, List and Index Soc., special series, 18 (London, 1983), p. 38.
[38] *LP*, iv(2), 3540 g.19, vi, 417 g.22.
[39] Elton, *Tudor Revolution*, p. 118.
[40] *LP*, i(1), 54 g.10, ii(2), 2736, iii(2), 2145 g.14; C82/590 (*LP*, iv(2), 3324 g.17).
[41] C82/656 (*LP*, v, 1139 g.2); *LP*, xviii(1), 100 g.35.

as concerned as Cromwell himself to collect financial offices – but the appointment of Sussex made it easier to disregard his claim to the chancellorship of the exchequer and eased Cromwell's path into an office with more potential for development.

Cromwell's most important office (apart from the vicegerency) was that of lord privy seal, marked fourth in the order of precedence, immediately below the president of the council – the office re-established in 1529 for the benefit of Charles Brandon, duke of Suffolk.[42] It had been assumed for a time after Audley's appointment as chancellor that Cromwell would soon take over the great seal from him, but the privy seal, apart from being a traditional promotion for the secretary, had certain advantages. It gave Cromwell control over the clerks of the privy seal office as well as over the clerks of the signet, already his as secretary; and it brought him a barony, as it had done Marney in 1523.[43] The opportunity came with the fall of Anne Boleyn, itself engineered by Cromwell. Her father had been appointed lord privy seal in January 1530, to hold the office during the king's pleasure, with the customary fee of £365 p.a.[44] In June 1536 John Husee believed that he had been replaced by Edward Seymour, viscount Beauchamp, but on 2 July 1536 letters patent were issued appointing Cromwell to the office, his fee to be paid from 24 June, the day on which Wiltshire's tenure was said to have ended.[45] Cromwell's sucessor was William FitzWilliam, earl of Southampton, who was first called lord privy seal in the journal of the house of lords on 17 June 1540, the day of the first reading of the bill to attaint Cromwell, although the warrant for his appointment was not signed until August and the letters patent were not issued until October. He was succeeded in 1542 by John lord Russell. Each was appointed, like Cromwell, during pleasure, but each retained the office for the rest of his life.[46]

In the royal household the two highest offices were always held by noblemen. George Talbot, earl of Shrewsbury, was lord steward at the death of Henry VII and was continued in office by Henry VIII.[47] Although formally responsible for the household 'below stairs', the lord steward had ceded active control to the treasurer of the household in the fifteenth century.[48] Shrewsbury was at times reluctant even to

---

[42] See above, p. 111.

[43] Elton, *Tudor Revolution*, pp. 121–3.

[44] C82/623 (*LP*, iv(3), 6163).

[45] *The Lisle Letters*, iii, 734; *Feodera*, vi(3), 7.

[46] *LJ*, i, 145; C82/771 (*LP*, xvi, 220 g.38); *Foedera*, vi(3), 85. Russell was reappointed by Edward VI and Mary.

[47] Shrewsbury, like many household officers, held office without letters patent.

[48] Elton, *Tudor Revolution*, p. 42.

come to court; he gave more attention to his role as local magnate and military leader, exemplified above all in his immediate response to the rebellion in Lincolnshire in 1536. Shrewsbury was by then nearly 70, and Robert Radcliffe, earl of Sussex, a much more assiduous courtier, hoped to succeed him as lord steward. Sussex was a persistent seeker after office, which was no doubt one reason why he paid Cromwell a yearly fee of £6 13s 4d. When he sent the money in November 1534 or 1535 he wrote from his manor of Woodham Walter in Essex to remind Cromwell that when they had last been together in the council chamber 'ye shewed me how good lord the kynges highnes was unto me (by your sute) concernyng th'office of the lord stuard after my lord Shrewysbury', and that he had left with Cromwell a bill 'to be assigned for the same'. Sussex obtained the reversion, but not until June 1537.[49] On 1 August 1538, after news of Shrewsbury's death reached the court, he reminded Cromwell of this, confident that, with his help, the king would prove himself 'as goode and gracious lord unto me nowe as he was at the tyme of his graunte'.[50] But his confidence was misplaced. The office went to Charles Brandon, duke of Suffolk.

Plans were already on foot to upgrade the lord steward by making him great master of the household, as in France: in March 1538 Sir John Dudley had reported it among 'soche newes as be curraunt here with us that be of the courte and not of the counsayle'.[51] In 1539 it was 'the great maister or lorde stewarde' who was assigned a place in the order of precedence enacted by parliament, and in the second session of parliament, in April 1540, Suffolk introduced into the lords a bill announcing that the change had taken place and vesting in himself as great master and in his successors in the office all the authority which had belonged to the lord steward.[52] This part of Cromwell's reform of the household helped to establish the superiority of the great master over the lord chamberlain, originally the parallel officer charged with the supervision of the household 'above stairs', and when Suffolk died in August 1545 the office of great master went to William Paulet, lord St John, promoted from lord chamberlain.[53] But St John was soon seriously ill and the thoughts of John Dudley, now viscount Lisle, turned towards the office 'which was latly in a grete mans handes', if it should fall vacant again, 'which God forbyde'. After discussing it with

---

[49] SP1/87, f.41 (*LP*, vii, 1442, placed under 1534); *LP*, xii(2), 191 g.36.
[50] BL, Cotton Vesp. F.XIII, f.183 (*LP*, xiii(2), 5).
[51] SP3/3, f.18 (*LP*, xiii(1), 503), printed *The Lisle Letters*, v, 1123.
[52] *LJ*, i, 130, enacted as 32 Henry VIII, c.39.
[53] Elton, *Tudor Revolution*, pp. 371–2, 393–6.

Paget, Lisle wrote to him on 22 September 1545 noting that the office was 'no hier in dignyte' than the one he already held (he was lord admiral), 'yet the thinge beinge occupyed before by soche a personage, and in so great favour, wold gyve a more estimymation to the worlde'. He left it to Paget's discretion whether or not he should try for it: 'in case you thought yt a convenyent sute for your frend, and colde bring yt to passe, I mought then leave this which I have.' 'Take not this for ambition', Lisle insisted; 'I had moche rather for the quiet liffe to seke no promocion.'[54] However, St John himself, although he seemed in danger of death, rightly believed that he would be able to 'were yt out'; he took his seat in the privy council again on 18 November and appeared in the house of lords on 23 November, the first day of the parliament, as great master, his precedence in council and parliament showing that he had also succeeded Suffolk as president of the council.[55]

The treasurer and comptroller of the king's household – offices under the lord steward or great master – were never peers, but both offices were held by men who were later ennobled by Henry VIII. Sir Thomas Boleyn sued for one or other position in 1515, when he told the king that he wanted to serve him in the court all his life. On embassy to France in 1519 he heard from Wolsey that Sir Thomas Lovell intended to give up as treasurer on 29 May, the day of the St George's feast. But the long awaited news came with tidings less welcome. According to Wolsey, the king thought that, without discouraging Sir Edward Poynings – then comptroller of the household – he could do no less than promote him 'for a season'. Henry intended before long to create Poynings a baron, and would then 'ondoubtedly' make Boleyn his treasurer; meanwhile he would appoint as comptroller someone with whom he could work easily when the time came. Boleyn fought back. Henry VIII had many times promised him that when Lovell went Poynings would be treasurer and he would be comptroller; now the king wanted him merely 'to lyve in trust by promyse' of the higher office. It occurred to him that Wolsey himself now favoured another candidate; nevertheless, Boleyn asked him to support his claim to the comptrollership, 'for faythfuller promesse shall I never have of thing than I have had of this'.[56] His protests were effective. Poynings became treasurer, dying in office (still a commoner) in 1521; Boleyn succeeded him first as comptroller and then as treasurer of the household. After Boleyn's creation as viscount Rochford in 1525, Sir William FitzWilliam replaced him as treasurer. On

[54] SP1/208, ff.49–50 (LP, xx(2), 427).
[55] SP1/208, f.21 (LP, xx(2), 405); APC, i, 271; LJ, i, 268.
[56] SP1/18, ff.162–3 (LP, iii(1), 223).

FitzWilliam's creation as earl of Southampton in 1537 Sir William Paulet – then comptroller of the household – moved up to become treasurer, and Sir John Russell was appointed comptroller. These two remained in office until their creation as barons in 1539.

The chamberlain of Henry VIII's household was always a nobleman. The reign started with Charles Somerset, lord Herbert, as lord chamberlain and on 1 February 1514, when he was created earl of Worcester, Henry VIII formally granted him the office for life.[57] He was over 50 then, yet remained an active courtier and diplomat well into his sixties. But in the autumn of 1525 William lord Sandys, then treasurer of Calais, was offered instead the posts of lord chamberlain of the king's household and lieutenant of Guisnes. Sandys thanked the king at some length for the 'exaltacion of so mean, poore and unworthy person as I am unto the room of so high dignyte of lord chambrelayn with your grace where as I lack wisedom, knowledge and habylite to occupy the same, and also that to mayntayn it pleaseth your highnes that I shall have the place of Guysnes'. To his patron, Wolsey, he also sent fulsome thanks, promising to give him 'to the most extremyte' of his life 'as redy servyce as eny servaunt your grace hath'. However, he pointed out that FitzWilliam, the current lieutenant of Guisnes, had expected when he left on embassy to France to remain in office until April and that he himself would find it more convenient to stay on at Calais until then.[58] Nevertheless, in February 1526 letters patent were issued granting Sandys the office of lord chamberlain whenever the earl of Worcester gave it up.[59] But Worcester was evidently reluctant to step down. Henry VIII had to devise an order for the remaining weeks of his life, allowing him – when he was able to come to court – to resume his duties, and guaranteeing that his absence would not mean his loss of the title of lord chamberlain. All the same, the office had to be 'contynually excercised by a nobleman whiche may be alwais or for the most parte attendant in the kinges courte'. Lord Sandys was therefore instructed to carry out the earl's duties, but only when necessary and (inserted) without naming himself lord chamberlain. The agreement was signed by Henry VIII at the top and by Worcester and Sandys at the bottom, the two noblemen binding themselves to observe it 'withoute any grudge or contradiccion'.[60] Sandys was lord chamberlain from Worcester's death on 15 April 1526 until his own death in December 1540, although he, too, in his later years, was

[57] *LP*, i(2), 2684 g.4.
[58] SP1/36, ff.139–40, 141–2 (*LP*, iv(1), 1752, 1753).
[59] C82/569 (*LP*, iv(1), 1996).
[60] BL, Cotton Vesp. C.XIV, ff.295–7 (*LP*, iv(3), App.66).

frequently absent from court. The need for a chamberlain of the household, so pressing in the 1520s, had been reduced by Cromwell's reforms and no successor to Sandys was appointed while Sussex was great chamberlain. However, soon after Hertford's appointment to the higher office in 1543 William Paulet, lord St John, was made lord chamberlain.[61] When he became great master in 1545, the office was again left vacant, but for a shorter period: Henry FitzAlan, earl of Arundel, was appointed lord chamberlain on 25 July 1546.[62] The vice-chamberlain was normally a commoner. At the death of Henry VII Thomas lord Darcy held the post; he was quickly replaced by Sir Henry Marney.[63] Marney was eventually created a baron, but no nobleman was appointed to the office by Henry VIII.

The queen's chamberlain after the marriage of Henry and Katherine of Aragon was the aged Thomas lord Ormond; by May 1512 he had been replaced by William Blount, lord Mountjoy, who was then given an annuity of £66 13s 4d.[64] The office proved a heavy burden in the end to the man whose reputation as a humanist helped to sustain the favourable impression he himself had promoted of the youthful king's devotion to learning. In April 1533 Chapuys reported that the council had ordered Mountjoy to stay with Katherine to prevent her escaping from England.[65] Mountjoy next had to inform her that she was in future to be known as princess dowager, a title she utterly rejected. The last straw was Henry VIII's insistence on being given the names of those in Katherine's household who continued to call her queen. Mountjoy told Cromwell how he felt about it. 'Sir, what busynes I have had in this matter sens hyt firste beganne, as well in the cardinalles dayes as sythen, by the kynges commaundement, I have good cawse to have hit in remembraunce for the hiegh displeasour whiche I have had for the same ... I suppose hit shall not be well possible for me to be a reformer of folkes tongues in this matter; and for me to be a complayner and accuser of them whiche, as I veryly do thynke, bere their trewe hertes servyce and allegyaunce to the kynges grace, hit is not my parte, nor for me this often to vexe or unquyet her whom the kynges grace cawsed to be sworne unto and truly to serve her to my power ... And if hit be thought unto the kynges hieghnes that any other can serve hym in this rowme better than I have doon, as I dought not but there be many, I hertely requyer youe to be a meanys

[61] LJ, i, 219, 220. St John's new precedence shows that he had not been chamberlain before this.
[62] APC, i, 495.
[63] LP, i(1), 54 g.9.
[64] ibid., 82, 1221 g.29.
[65] CSPSp., iv(3), 1058.

on my behaulf to his grace, that I maye, without his graces displeasour, be discharged of the rowme of chamberlaine.'[66] Whether or
not Mountjoy was allowed to resign, when he died in November 1534
he was not replaced. John lord Hussey, who had been chamberlain to
Princess Mary, lost his office when her household was broken up in
1533.[67] Anne Boleyn's chamberlain was Thomas lord Burgh, a baron
of less than four years' standing when he attended on her at her
coronation.[68] Thomas Manners, earl of Rutland, was chamberlain to
Jane Seymour.[69] When Henry in 1539 showed signs of marrying again
the post of queen's chamberlain was sought by Arthur Plantagenet,
viscount Lisle, desperate to get away from Calais. He claimed indeed
that Cromwell had promised him the appointment, which Cromwell
categorically denied.[70] Rutland was kept on as chamberlain to both
Anne of Cleves and Katherine Howard.[71] William lord Parr of Horton,
who had been chamberlain to Henry Fitzroy, duke of Richmond, was
chamberlain to Katherine Parr.[72]

The distinction between appointments to high office for life and
during pleasure was less important in practice than in theory. Offices
granted for life might have to be surrendered – with due recompense –
and office-holders appointed during pleasure normally held their posts
until they died. Whatever the terms of the grant, office was generally
treated as a form of property. In 1509 Henry VIII reappointed almost
all the noblemen selected for high office by his father: only Darcy was
immediately discharged from his position at court, and he was at once
given offices in the north.[73] But by the 1530s the old nobility faced
competition from the growing number of new peers for vacancies in
the central administration and the royal household. Only three were
successful, all of them courtiers: the earls of Rutland, Sussex and
Arundel. Although Rutland was chamberlain to three queens in
succession, the appointment did not bring him membership of the
privy council. Sussex was already a councillor when he became great
chamberlain, but office brought council membership to Arundel: on
the day he took the oath as king's chamberlain he was also sworn of
the council. Offices which carried membership of the privy council
established an alternative, albeit transient order of precedence to the

[66] *SP*, i, 408–9.
[67] *LP*, vii, 38.
[68] *Hall's Chronicle*, p. 801.
[69] *LP*, xii(2), 1060.
[70] *The Lisle Letters*, v, 1593.
[71] ibid, vi, 1634; *LP*, xvi, 1088.
[72] *LP*, xx(2), App.2.
[73] See below, pp. 187, 200–1.

traditional order within the ranks of the nobility based on the date of creation of the peerage. It not only redefined the relationship between individual noblemen but also meshed together the hierarchies in different areas of government. Offices in the administration and in the household could be compared. Lisle was right to describe the office of great master as no higher than his own office of lord admiral: it came under his in the act of precedence. However, he may have known that it was to remain linked with the presidency of the council, which would indeed have been promotion. (In 1550, at the height of his power, he succeeded St John in both offices.) Moreover, once office – or a personal qualification – had brought membership of privy council, there was a better chance of further promotion.

Henry VIII, according to Hall, 'muche consulted with his counsaill' over the choice of a new chancellor in 1529.[74] If he sought the advice of the council on other appointments it is perhaps not surprising that he consistently chose men who were already councillors, taking in newcomers to fill the gaps left by these promotions. Most of the highest offices had few specific duties: it was therefore possible to treat them primarily as rewards. But turnover was slow. Thomas Boleyn, earl of Wiltshire, was the only nobleman to be dismissed from any of these offices by the mature Henry VIII apart from those who were also condemned as traitors. Death – natural or contrived – was the normal determinant of change. Noblemen could not afford to be squeamish about filling dead men's shoes even when they themselves had helped to make them available. By the exercise of his patronage at the highest level Henry VIII kept alive the hope of advancement among the small group of noblemen at the centre of power. It was a rational policy, although it was also the line of least resistance; any other would have aroused the resentment of the ruling elite. Even as it was, there were not enough offices to reward each one who might be held to deserve promotion and, inevitably, some noblemen were more successful than others. William Paulet, lord St John, was twice promoted within three years of his return to the privy council in 1542 on his appointment as master of the newly established court of wards and liveries. Robert Radcliffe, earl of Sussex, on the other hand, was passed over for office even when he held the reversion, although in the end, two years before his death, his patience was rewarded with an office high in the table of precedence.

Refusing to be bound by his grants of reversions unless it suited him, Henry VIII made his appointments in response to the needs of the

[74] *Hall's Chronicle*, p. 761.

moment as he saw them – or was persuaded to see them. Like any patron, he was subjected to pressure from those anxious to secure advancement for themselves or their clients. The number of offices in his gift throughout the kingdom meant that the king and those around him were besieged by suitors. Sometimes the petitioner had already arranged with the current holder for the transfer of an office; at other times a payment might compensate an office-holder replaced by a successful suitor. Offices were undoubtedly bought and sold by private individuals. Were they sold by the king? Henry VII had taken money in return for appointments in the judicial system and in local government, although his practice might (charitably) be seen as a tax on new office-holders rather than the outright sale of offices.[75] It was certainly supposed that the gift of money to Henry VIII might secure an appointment. In 1528, for example, Sir John Mordaunt sent Wolsey 500 marks and offered to give the king £100 if he might become under-treasurer.[76] His suit was unsuccessful, but failure is no proof of a mistaken strategy. In 1546 Hertford could bluntly declare that a 'well lerned' friend of his would not get the office he was seeking unless he gave Henry VIII some money.[77] Yet no evidence has been found of the direct sale of office by Henry VIII except in Calais and the marches; and even there it relates to appointments in the garrison rather than any higher office.

The importance of Calais in both diplomacy and war meant that traditionally it was the preserve of the king's familiar servants: in the 1470s the number of household men there had made it almost an 'outward office' of the king's chamber.[78] Henry VIII at first appointed non-noble household servants as lieutenant of Calais or as deputy, the title generally used in his reign. But in 1520 he gave the office to a courtier nobleman, making John Bourchier, lord Berners, deputy of Calais during pleasure.[79] In 1523 Berners published the first volume of his translation of Froissart's *Chronicles*, undertaken at Henry VIII's suggestion and dedicated to him; the second volume appeared in 1525. The next year, however, he was suddenly ousted from his post by a move apparently initiated by the new lord chamberlain, lord Sandys, or by Wolsey. In September 1526 Sandys wrote to inform Sir Robert Wingfield that Henry VIII had authorized him to appoint Wingfield as deputy of Calais and Sir William FitzWilliam as lieutenant of the

[75] Ives, *The Common Lawyers of Pre-Reformation England*, pp. 85–6.
[76] *LP*, iv(2), 4452.
[77] SP1/217, f.179 (*LP*, xxi(1), 743).
[78] D. A. L. Morgan, 'The king's affinity in the polity of Yorkist England', *TRHS*, 5th series, 23 (1973), 16.
[79] *LP*, iii(1), 1074.

castle of Calais in Wingfield's place. FitzWilliam also wrote to Wingfield enclosing a letter from the king ordering them to take up their new offices on 6 October, after which date no wages would be due to Berners as deputy.[80] Wingfield on receiving these letters wrote to Wolsey in some astonishment: considering that he held the office of lieutenant for life, he did not think he could surrender it without an explicit warrant, nor become deputy without a patent. After the arrival of a letter from Wolsey himself, and his patent, Wingfield calmed down and thanked Wolsey for his promotion.[81] The action was apparently designed less for Wingfield's benefit than for FitzWilliam's. Earlier in 1526 – most likely on 6 April, the other half-yearly date at which wages at Calais were paid – Sandys had taken over as lieutenant of Guisnes, an office to which FitzWilliam had been appointed in 1523 for 20 years. FitzWilliam had realized, when Henry VIII wanted him to become treasurer of the household in 1525, that he would be expected to give up Guisnes. The appointment as lieutenant of Calais seems to have been the recompense to him for the years of his grant that he had lost, giving him an alternative office to support him in his household service, in the same way as the Guisnes post supported Sandys in his.[82]

Berners, discomforted in 1526, returned to Calais as deputy in 1531, reappointed on Wingfield's surrender of his patent; but he had to agree to pay Wingfield 100 marks p.a. during his tenure of the office.[83] Berners died in Calais two years later. Sir John Russell, by his own account, could have become deputy of Calais, and it was probably in 1533 that the offer was made to him; he also gave some advice – evidently discouraging – to the man who was willing to go, Arthur Plantagenet, viscount Lisle, appointed on 24 March 1533 to serve during pleasure.[84] Russell's refusal was as beneficial to his career as Lisle's acceptance was disastrous to his. The post at Calais may have been a prize in earlier years, but by the mid-1530s it brought mainly trouble and expense. Lisle had had no experience to prepare him for the office. He had been a squire of the body to Henry VII and was sworn as a carver to Henry VIII early in his reign.[85] His service had been in the navy as well as at court, but he probably owed his selection for the deputyship less to his achievements than to his birth; a blood relative of the king could represent him in a more personal way than even the closest servant. Lisle soon regretted the honour. Within a

[80] *LP*, iv(2), 2518, 2519.
[81] ibid., 2546, 2597.
[82] *LP*, iii(2), 3027, iv(1), 2344 (misplaced under 1526), iv(3), 6490 g.23.
[83] *LP*, v, 166 g.48; *DNB* under Sir Robert Wingfield.
[84] *The Lisle Letters*, v, 1530; *Foedera*, vi(2), 178–9.
[85] *LP*, i(1), 20 (as Mr Arthur); E36/130, f.191.

year one of his Calais friends suggested that if Sandys – apparently on
the point of death – should die, he should apply to move to Guisnes in
his place, even if he had to give Henry VIII 1,000 marks for the
exchange. (John Husee later heard that if Sandys had died, George
Boleyn, lord Rochford, would have been appointed lieutenant of
Guisnes.)[86]

The chief perquisite of the office of deputy was the right to appoint
men to the retinue at Calais. Lisle soon received requests for soldiers'
places for their men from, among others, the duchess of Suffolk, the
marquess of Exeter and Henry Parker, lord Morley.[87] But Henry VIII
persisted in granting places himself to men who then put pressure on
the deputy. In September 1534 Lisle became so incensed by a dispute
over an office that he wrote to Henry Norris threatening to abandon
his post to go to see the king in London.[88] The act for Calais passed in
the last session of the Reformation parliament attempted a major
reform by prohibiting all sale of offices.[89] It did nothing to alleviate
Lisle's frustration. In November 1538 he declared to his wife, who
was on a visit to England, 'if I shuld be every mans dogbold, I had
leyther to be withoute myn office then yn yt'. When she met William
FitzWilliam, earl of Southampton, and Cromwell she was to tell them
that 'every man is master of his rome save I and surerly I wolbe at no
mans commaundment here but the kynges'.[90] Henry VIII himself was
exasperated by the continuous wrangling. When a soldier dismissed
from the retinue appealed to him in 1539, the king rounded on him: 'I
have more adoo with yow Cales men than with all my realme after.'[91]
Things were indeed going wrong there in more dangerous ways, with
the town disturbed by religious disputes and the council of Calais itself
divided. As Lisle could get no improvement, Henry VIII in March
1540 commissioned Sussex, St John and others to help him to restore
order and on 17 April he called Lisle to court to give his own report.[92]
Lady Lisle had visions of her husband's promotion to the great
chamberlainship, vacant by Oxford's death, even an earldom.[93] The
grant of both honours to Cromwell on 18 April was followed on 19
May by Lisle's arrest on suspicion of traitorous dealings with Cardinal
Pole.[94]

[86] *The Lisle Letters*, ii, 152, 155a.
[87] ibid., i, 5, 5b, 5c.
[88] ibid., ii, 260.
[89] 27 Henry VIII, c.63.
[90] SP3/1, ff.8, 1 (*LP*, xiii(2), 906, 909), printed *The Lisle Letters*, v, 1285, 1287.
[91] SP3/3, f.34 (*LP*, xiv(1), 1234), printed ibid., 1481.
[92] *LP*, xv, 436 g.30; *The Lisle Letters*, vi, 1673.
[93] *The Lisle Letters*, vi, p. 116.
[94] *LP*, xv, 697.

Lisle was neither tried nor attainted but remained a prisoner in the Tower until March 1542, when he died immediately after Henry VIII ordered his release. He had been replaced as deputy in 1540 by Henry's godson and future chamberlain, Henry FitzAlan, lord Mautravers, aged 28 and described by a Welshman in the garrison as a silent, reasoning, cunning man and a good judge, but melancholic.[95] The biography written by one of his household shortly after his death credited Mautravers with an unparalleled success as deputy, although he did not hold the office long: when he became earl of Arundel on the death of his father in January 1544 he returned to England 'with good contentment and favour of the kinge'.[96] If the deputyship was not thought suitable for an earl, it was by now in the hands of noblemen of less exalted rank. Mautravers had been given an annuity of £200 besides the usual fee of £100 p.a. out of lands in Calais and £104 'espial money', and the same additional sum was allocated to his successor, George Brooke, lord Cobham, appointed in June 1544. However, the £100 fee was reduced to 100 marks for Cobham.[97] He had heard that the annuity was to be diminished *by* 100 marks – double the actual reduction of his total payment – and drafted a letter to the king's secretary, Sir William Paget, asking for his help and the chancellor's, 'for without booth your helppes I shall be undone in this office, I perceave by the beginnyng', since he had had to sell land worth £30 p.a. 'to sett me forthwarde'.[98] But whatever the effect on his finances he remained deputy of Calais until 1550.

The threat to England's possessions on the continent ended the era when offices there could be treated as sinecures. When lord Sandys became chamberlain of the king's household and lieutenant of Guisnes he was evidently expected to remain in England most of the time. He exercised the office at Guisnes by deputy, making only one visit in the next ten years – although that was an extended one, a busy eight months in 1529 getting urgently needed repairs to the castle started, on which he had to spend his own money when government funds ran out.[99] Even the office of lord chamberlain seems to have become too much for him by the autumn of 1533 and Henry VIII, in consideration of his age and ill health, licensed him to stay at his Hampshire home until parliament assembled again.[100] But the act for Calais in 1536 insisted on the residence of office-holders unless they had the king's

[95] ibid., 942 g.10; *The Lisle Letters*, vi, p. 160.
[96] 'The life of Henrye FitzAllen', 12–13.
[97] *LP*, xix(1), 812 g.59.
[98] BL, Harl. 283, f.308 (*LP*, xix(1), 680).
[99] *LP*, iv(3), 5167, 5168, 5296, 5420, 5433, 5892.
[100] *LP*, vi, 1307, 1556.

licence to be absent. Sandys, in his mid-sixties, quickly obtained a licence to remain in England for two years, but was soon plagued by disputes at Guisnes which threatened his authority there. The difficulties persisted until eventually, in March 1537, he had to set off for Guisnes.[101] He stayed there for six months, arriving back in England shortly before the birth of Prince Edward; after reporting to the king and council he was allowed to go home, but had to return to the court in October to attend the funeral of Jane Seymour.[102] Still the shadow of Guisnes hung over him. In June 1538 he wrote twice to ask Wriothesley to get him a new licence of absence. Then in January 1539 the order went out for all governors of castles to repair at once to their charges, and by March Sandys was again in Guisnes; he returned to his home in October.[103] In June 1540 he was once more en route to Guisnes; by 7 November he was back, attending every meeting of the privy council at Windsor until 22 November; on 6 December he died.[104] A peaceful retirement without loss of office, such as Worcester had enjoyed in 1526, proved too much to hope for in more dangerous times.

The lieutenants of castles in Calais and the marches were not often noblemen in the reign of Henry VIII, although Sir Nicholas Vaux, lieutenant of Guisnes, was created a baron in 1523 at the same time as Sandys himself, then treasurer of Calais, and Sir Maurice Berkeley, lieutenant of the castle of Calais, were ennobled. But Henry VIII appointed William Blount, lord Mountjoy, lieutenant of Hammes for 20 years from 6 October 1509 and thereafter during pleasure.[105] After the capture of Tournai in 1513, Henry also made him in turn acting lieutenant, bailiff and, in January 1515, governor of the city. It was a difficult posting, with the garrison threatening to desert to Richard de la Pole if their wages were not paid, and the inhabitants understandably restive; early in 1516 Mountjoy confessed to Wolsey that he would be glad to be relieved of the office, but he was not replaced until January 1517.[106] Mountjoy more easily combined attendance at court as queen's chamberlain with periodic visits to Hammes, and he remained lieutenant there for the 20 years of his grant. After his years were up, however, and the office became his only during the king's

---

[101] C82/712 (*LP*, x, 1015 g.23); *LP*, xi, 241, 288, 313, 341, xii(1), 17, 151, 589, 750.

[102] *LP*, xii(2), 773, 802, 994, 1060.

[103] *LP*, xiii(1), 1141, 1230, xiv(1), 144, 630, xiv(2), 568.

[104] *LP*, xv, 754, 795, xvi, 315, 321; *PPC*, vii, 79–87.

[105] *LP*, i(1), 257, g.27. Mountjoy's father and uncle had been lieutenants of Hammes in the late fifteenth century.

[106] *LP*, i(2), 2617 g.22, ii(1), 41, 325, 891, 1510, ii(2), 2820 (misplaced under 1517), 2825.

pleasure, he soon retired. Henry VIII did not dismiss him without recompense, as he was entitled to do. Instead, he allowed one of his servants, William lord Grey of Wilton, a young man not long out of wardship, to buy the office from Mountjoy. On 6 April 1531 the incoming lieutenant made the usual indenture with the king setting out the terms of his appointment and Henry signed the warrant granting him the office in May, when Mountjoy surrendered his patent.[107] For Grey of Wilton it was the start of a military career of some distinction, although it included the surrender of Guisnes to the French in 1558. In April 1546 he was appointed governor of all the armies in Boulogne and the Boulonnais.[108] Boulogne, conquered in September 1544, had at first been put under the rule of John Dudley, viscount Lisle. He was anxious that it should not affect his other office, as he explained to the privy council: 'My truste ys that I shal have the kinges majesties ffavour t'enioye th'offyce of highe admyralltye of England ffor yt ys an offyce of honour, of estymation and profytt, and within the realme; and, haveing his gracious favour therunto, I maye occupye yt with a deputye, and serve in this natwithstanding.'[109] Lisle held both appointments for some months, but in January 1545 Henry VIII recalled him to prepare the naval defence of the kingdom. To replace him the king chose from the council of Boulogne Sir Thomas Poynings, because he 'hath ben longest acquaynted in the warres with the Frenchmen upon the frontyers, and best knoweth their natures, and speketh also their language, which is a thing very necessary for our service': he was created a baron the day before his appointment.[110] Poynings died in Boulogne in August 1545. His replacement by Grey of Wilton was announced by the privy council on 25 August, but within six days Henry VIII revoked his decision and appointed instead Norfolk's son, styled earl of Surrey. Surrey's aggressive policy angered his father, who thought him foolish for 'animating' the king to keep Boulogne, which could not be held with the resources available. Surrey should rather be content to become lieutenant of Guisnes or deputy of Calais, which Norfolk offered to try to arrange for him. Henry VIII himself grew to distrust Surrey and recalled him in March 1546. Grey of Wilton, taking over at Boulogne in April, was then replaced as lieutenant of Hammes.[111] In June 1546 William lord

[107] *LP*, i(1), 257 g.27, v, 318 g.41; *A Commentary of the Services and Charges of William Lord Grey of Wilton, K.G.*, ed. Sir Philip de M. G. Egerton, Camden Soc., xl (London, 1847), p. 1.
[108] *Foedera*, vi(3), 134–5.
[109] *LP*, xix(2), 337; SP1/193, f.15 (*LP*, xix(2), 338).
[110] *SP*, x, 250–3; *LP*, xx(1), 125 gg.29, 30.
[111] *APC*, i, 235, 238; *LP*, xx(2), 738, xxi(2), 200 g.42.

Stourton was put in charge of the fort built at Newhaven (Ambleteuse in the Boulonnais).[112]

Jersey was the only one of the Channel Islands sometimes to have a nobleman for governor. Henry VIII appointed Thomas lord Vaux of Harrowden to the office for life in January 1536 in succession to Sir Arthur Darcy. However, a proviso was added to his letters patent by order of the lord chancellor: Vaux would forfeit the office if he were to give, sell or in any way alienate it to anyone without special licence.[113] The grant to Vaux was at the request of Sir Arthur, who had bound himself by an indenture of 1 January 1536 to sell to Henry VIII the manor of Green's Norton and other manors in Northamptonshire, which he had bought from Vaux, in return for a money payment from the king, the promise of land and the appointment of Vaux as governor of Jersey for life. An act of parliament a few weeks later confirmed Henry VIII's possession of the lands. A second act cited a recognizance entered into by Vaux on 19 November 1535, after his sale of Green's Norton and other manors of his inheritance, binding him to sell no more land without the king's special licence. As various people had since bought lands from him 'upon condycion that the kynges highnes shuld be contentyd and pleased with suche bargaynes', the act announced that Henry VIII was 'not contented with such bargayns', and declared that the sales would be void on the death of Vaux.[114] In April Vaux wrote to Cromwell to beg for an interview before he had to see the lord chancellor, 'which ys nott myne indyfferant goode lord'; he feared he would be trodden underfoot and 'made a slave'.[115] Yet if, as Audley apparently suspected, Vaux valued office mainly as a saleable commodity, he reaped some benefit from his appointment as governor of Jersey, although he only held the post for a few months. In July 1536 Edward Seymour, recently created viscount Beauchamp, replaced him as governor, and in August paid him £150 for the office.[116]

In few other parts of his dominions was Henry VIII so free to appoint whom he liked to high office. In England and its marches and in Ireland the expectations of local magnates had generally to be remembered, if not invariably respected. Henry VIII, as many another, found a policy towards Ireland difficult to formulate and impossible to impose. He wavered between trusting an Irish lord as his deputy and appointing an Englishman to rule in his name. In 1529 he made his

---

[112] *LP*, xxi(1), 1092, 1133.
[113] C82/706 (*LP*, x, 226 g.12).
[114] E305/7/D 62; 27 Henry VIII, cc.29, 30.
[115] SP1/103, f.187 (*LP*, x, 744).
[116] *LP*, xi, 202 g.12; Anstruther, *Vaux of Harrowden*, p. 53.

son, the duke of Richmond, lieutenant of Ireland, but the only English nobleman actually sent over was Thomas Howard, earl of Surrey, appointed lieutenant of Ireland in March 1520.[117] Surrey, the first Englishman to be made deputy by Henry VIII, sent back his considered opinion that the Irish 'wol not bee brought to noo good order, onles it bee by compulsyon, which woll not bee doon without a great puissaunce of men, and great costis of money, and long contynuaunce of tyme'. He struggled with the problem for 18 months and then asked to be recalled, having 'spent all that I myght make' and being laid low with the flux. Henry VIII agreed to recall him, convinced that he was in danger of death.[118] Surrey never forgot his time in Ireland nor the effect it might have had on his career: as late as 1537 he heard rumours that the king 'wold send me incontinent into Irland and that I was out of favour'.[119] Ireland was worse then Calais in simultaneously removing a courtier from the king's presence and embroiling him in problems beyond his power to solve.

Henry VIII had in fact expressed no dissatisfaction with Surrey's service in Ireland, although it had been both costly and ineffective. In October 1521 he sent a message to Wolsey, then at Calais, asking him and the councillors with him to discuss 'wither itt schal be more expedient to have an Englysche man ruler there, and the kynge to be at the same chiarge he nowe berith, or els to make sum Irysche lorde hys deputie there, in suche forme and maner as the erle off Kyldare was, and so to save suche mony as he nowe exspendyth there all in wast'. Henry suggested two possible replacements for Surrey, although he stressed that he was committed to neither of them. Pace gave their names: 'the lorde Ferys (yff your grace can induce hym therunto) and the erle off Ormonde.' Wolsey replied by advising against Ferrers. He was 'a goode and right active gentilman, mete and hable to have the conduyting and leding of a good number of men in the werres (where other higher capitayns, having experience, shalbe governors above hym); yet to committ the hoole rule and governaunce of Irelande unto hym, as your lieutenaunt, not being experte in waightie matiers requiring sadd advise and good counsaile, specially amonges such brittle people as they bee, in whome is moche crafte, and litle or noo faithe and trouthe, it is thought daungerous.' As no Englishman was likely to do better than Surrey, Wolsey recommended the appointment of the earl of Ormond.[120] Henry accepted his advice.

The saving came from not having to send out an armed force from

[117] LP, iii(1), 669, 670.
[118] SP, i, 69–70, ii, 35–8, 84.
[119] SP1/115, f.10 (LP, xii(1), 198).
[120] SP, i, 69–70, 72–4.

England: an Irish lord was expected to recruit an army from his own tenants and followers. In the northern marches of England – also in need of constant military protection – the ability of the wardens to raise men was an important consideration. Thomas lord Dacre, although not as well endowed with land as some other northern noblemen, enjoyed the advantage of having a compact landholding in Cumberland, adjacent to the border with Scotland. He served as warden of the west march from early in Henry VII's reign until shortly before his death in 1525. Thomas lord Darcy, who had been warden of the east march for a time under Henry VII, was appointed again by Henry VIII in June 1509. Darcy's lands lay no further north than Yorkshire, and he was equipped for the wardenship – to which the middle march was added in July 1509 – by grants of office making him captain of Berwick during pleasure and steward of Bamburgh, Northumberland, for life, of Dunstanburgh, in the same county, during pleasure, of the lands of Sir Ralph Grey during his son's minority and of Raby and other lordships in the bishopric of Durham during the minority of Ralph Neville, earl of Westmorland.[121] But in December 1511, after returning from his expedition to Spain, Darcy refused to serve again as warden since it had been decided that, in view of the state of the borders, the warden must be resident in the marches until Easter. Dacre was prepared to reside and he was appointed warden of the east and middle marches until Easter, and then during pleasure. However, Darcy retained his other offices.[122] For over two years Dacre grappled with the mammoth task of being warden of all three marches. At last, in May 1514, faced by mounting criticism, he wrote to put his side of the case. Showing the insecurity typical of office-holders far from the court, unable to defend themselves in person, he reminded the council that he had only accepted the wardenship of the east and middle marches on condition that no report should be believed to his discredit until he could make his answer. He denied any secret conversations with the Scots, who 'love me worst of any Inglisheman living be reason that I founde the body of the king of Scottes slayne in the felde'. It was impossible for him, a poor baron, to keep all three marches secure, especially as in the east march Berwick, Bamburghshire and Dunstanburgh, with Sir Roger Grey's power, were in Darcy's hands, and Alnwick and Warkworth castles belonged to the earl of Northumberland. Dacre had been promised that Darcy, or someone else, would soon be sent to defend the

[121] *LP*, i(1), 94 gg.65, 66, 67, 69, 77, 132 g.38; Robert Somerville, *History of the Duchy of Lancaster*, i, *1265–1603* (London, 1953), p. 537.
[122] *LP*, i(1), 845, 984, 1003 gg.17, 23.

east march, but nobody had come.[123] Nobody came in 1514, nor for
years after. Neither was a solution found to Dacre's basic problem, the
lack of manpower available to him in the east march, although Darcy
was replaced as captain of Berwick by Sir Anthony Ughtred in June
1515. Darcy blamed Wolsey for this and for the earlier loss of the
wardenship, recording in July 1529 'how cularable and wrongfully he
voyded me from th' offices of captayn of Berwic and warden of the
marches', worth £1,000 p.a. Admittedly, he had refused to continue as
warden, but that was only because Wolsey would have compelled him
to be resident in the far north.[124] Darcy was willing enough to serve
Henry VIII, but on his own terms.

Only with the onset of war were Dacre's responsibilities reduced.
Early in 1522 Thomas Manners, lord Ros, was given a commission of
array and appointed warden of the east and middle marches.[125] His
grandfather had lived in Northumberland but the family estates were
now centred on Leicestershire and his chief qualification for the office
was his friendship with Henry VIII. In June Ros, already at Newcastle, went on to Alnwick to meet Dacre, who reported to Wolsey 'I
like hym right wele for he lakes nothing but experience of the countrie
which will com to hym dayly'.[126] But the lack could not be so easily
remedied. On 7 October Dacre reported that Ros, though as keen to
serve the king 'as any living man can be', wanted to be relieved of the
wardenship after experiencing the border gentry's reluctance to serve
under him against the Scots.[127] Before the end of the month Ros had
returned to court, leaving a deputy in the north, and been replaced as
warden by the earl of Northumberland's son and heir, lord Percy.
Percy was very young – hardly into his twenties – yet Dacre considered
him the best choice after Ros.[128] His own long stint as warden of all
three marches would not have been necessary if Henry VIII had been
willing to make use of Northumberland, the natural leader on the
eastern border, but the king refused to trust him.[129] However, if lord
Percy actually took up the appointment – which is doubtful – he was
superseded before the start of a new campaigning season. In February
1523 Thomas Grey, marquess of Dorset, was appointed warden of the
east and middle marches and given a commission of array.[130] Like Ros

[123] BL, Cotton Calig. B.II, ff.200–2 (LP, i(2), 2913).
[124] SP1/54, ff.234–41 (LP, iv(3), 5749); LP, xii(2), 186(62).
[125] LP, iii(2), 2213iv, v.
[126] ibid., 2328; SP49/1, f.139 (LP, iii(2), 2363).
[127] BL, Cotton Calig. B.I, f.23 (LP, iii(2), 2598).
[128] BL, Cotton Calig. B.II, ff.343–4 (LP, iii(2), 2636); SP, i, 107–10.
[129] M. E. James, A Tudor Magnate and the Tudor State: Henry 5th Earl of Northumberland,
Borthwick Papers, no. 30 (York, 1966), pp. 22–5.
[130] Foedera, vi(1), 209–10; LP, iii(2), 2875vi.

he was a courtier whose main residence was in Leicestershire; such lands as he had in the far north were in the west march. He was admitted to the privy chamber as he set out for the borders in an attempt to furnish him with extra authority as an intimate servant of the king.[131] Ros and Dorset held the office of warden as an adjunct to their military commands, each under the leadership of the king's lieutenant in the north, the earl of Shrewsbury in 1522, the earl of Surrey in 1523. Henry VIII did not expect either of them to stay long in the north and Dorset was away for less than three months. As the summer drew to an end, Surrey was also anxious to be off. He waited impatiently for a new warden to be appointed for the east and middle marches; when he heard in September that it was to be lord Percy he welcomed the news. Should Percy, as seemed likely, marry a daughter of the earl of Shrewsbury he could expect the active support of lord Dacre, already a son-in-law to Shrewsbury. Surrey soon realized that Percy's appointment was not so certain. He continued to support it but suggested that Dacre might serve as deputy for a time; the people would put up with him if they knew that Percy was coming. On 1 October he repeated his conviction that there was no alternative to Dacre until lord Percy came: not only was he a great worker, but he would be content with 40s a day instead of his own £5. Surrey was seriously worried since there was in reality one alternative: himself. In the same letter he was careful to explain to Wolsey how decayed in body he felt, as well as worn out in purse, by his continual war service of the past four years. He seems indeed to have been acting as warden of the east and middle marches as well as being lieutenant of the north, since Dacre addressed a letter to him as warden and lieutenant on 18 October, but Henry VIII had by then decided to recommission the marquess of Dorset as warden, to Surrey's great relief.[132] Once the threat of a Scottish invasion had receded, however, Dorset was allowed to return south. Wolsey then backed the appointment of Dacre, confident that he could persuade him to accept the office again.[133] The idea of appointing Percy was dropped and in November Surrey was able to forward to Dacre the king's commission as warden of the east and middle marches. The local gentry may have been unenthusiastic, but so was he. Dacre complained of his gout and his sore leg as well as of his expenses as warden of the west march and captain of Carlisle; however, as Surrey was not well and there was no one else suitable for the office, he agreed to take it on – but only until Easter.[134]

---

[131] See above, pp. 84–5.
[132] *LP*, iii(2), 3321, 3384, 3438, 3445; *SP*, iv, 37–9.
[133] *SP*, iv, 53–6.
[134] *LP*, iii(2), 3544.

If he expected any gratitude from the king he was disappointed. Henry VIII was infuriated by his inability to keep order in the marches and eventually threatened to compel him to make recompense out of his own lands and goods. Dacre wrote bitterly to Wolsey on 1 April 1524, pointing out that 'in tymes past' the king's second son was nearly always warden, or a great nobleman, and they were never expected to make restitution for the crimes of men they could not bring to justice. Considering all that he had done on the east and middle marches, he felt he deserved better thanks. Easter was already past; he would serve until the end of May but 'longer then May I may not indure nor it is not to me possible to contynue with the charge therof'. He begged to be allowed to be warden only in the west march, where he had friends and tenants about him.[135] On 25 April he heard from Wolsey that the borders must be put in better order before he could be discharged. Dacre assured him that the country was 'in as good order and rather better now' than it had been under Surrey. Since he had become the king's officer in the east and middle marches, 13 years ago, he had served with all possible diligence, without a penny wages for himself, as his indenture would confirm. He requested a commission of inquiry.[136] But the investigation went against him. Summoned to London, he confessed in February 1525 to negligence in punishing thieves and was committed to the Fleet by the council.[137] On 6 September he entered into two recognizances, one in 2,000 marks for the payment of three annual sums of 500 marks, the other in 5,000 marks to appear before the king and council at any time on 20 days' warning and to recompense anyone suffering damage during his administration of justice.[138] His long career was over.

Henry VIII no longer needed his service. In July 1525 the king had made his first major change of policy for the government of the borders. Following the precedent of his own appointment as a small boy, he made his young son, recently created duke of Richmond, warden-general of the marches. In October Richmond's council was still pressing for the formal appointment of the two deputy wardens selected to serve under him: Henry Clifford, earl of Cumberland, in the west march, and Ralph Neville, earl of Westmorland, in the east and middle marches.[139] Dacre refused to deliver Carlisle to his old rival, Cumberland, without an express order from the king or Wolsey, and died in October after a fall from his horse before he could be

[135] BL, Add. 24, 965, ff.236–8 (LP, iv(1), 220).
[136] BL, Add. 24, 965, ff.261–2 (LP, iv(1), 279(2)).
[137] See above, p. 110.
[138] LP, iv(2), 3022.
[139] LP, iv(1), 1510, 1727.

made to give up the keys of the castle and town. Cumberland was granted the stewardship of Penrith and other crown lands formerly held by Dacre, for which he had asked since he had 'nother lande nor men of myne own, of any reputation, ner the borders', and in January 1526 took delivery of Carlisle castle, although the representative of the new lord Dacre still refused to surrender the keys of the inner gates.[140] It was an inauspicious start which Cumberland did little to counter-act, seeming to suppose that the march could be ruled from his own castle of Skipton, in Yorkshire.[141] Nor was the earl of Westmorland, based at Raby, in Co. Durham, any more effective in his marches. The only surviving letter from him as warden dwells on his need to discover who exactly was meant to pay him his £1,000 p.a.[142] In 1526 instruc-tions for keeping the warden courts were sent to his two vice-wardens, and Sir Anthony Ughtred, from whom Westmorland had taken over as captain of Berwick, was put back in charge there. In November 1527 Richmond's council told Wolsey that the earl's deputy in the middle march, Sir William Eure, admitted that he could not keep order because he was not supported by the local gentry. The council could see no solution except by the 'powre of some nobleman lying continu-elly in Northumberlande'.[143] The death of the earl of Northumberland in May had opened the way for the traditional answer to the problem and there is no doubt that the council had in mind the former lord Percy, now earl. Richmond's nominal rule as warden-general of all three marches came to an end in December 1527 when the new earl of Northumberland was appointed warden-general of the east and middle marches. On the same day William lord Dacre was appointed warden of the west march, having already replaced Cumberland as steward of Penrith and, apparently, as governor of Carlisle, although the letters patent for that office were not issued until 1529.[144] For the first time in the reign – with the possible exception of a few months in the winter of 1522–3 – the borders were under the rule of the two families best placed by their local landownership to exercise authority.

The outlook seemed hopeful, but the power of both noblemen was destroyed in the 1530s. Dacre, acquitted in 1534 on the charge of treason laid by his enemies, was nevertheless heavily fined. Thus disgraced and distrusted by Henry VIII, he could not return to the

---

[140] *SP*, iv, 420–1, 437; *LP*, iv(1), 1700, 1727.

[141] M. E. James, 'The first earl of Cumberland (1493–1542) and the decline of northern feudalism', *Northern History*, i (1966), 46.

[142] *LP*, iv(2), 2441.

[143] *SP*, iv, 470–3 (misdated 1527); *LP*, iv(2), 2435; BL, Cotton App. XXIX, ff.68–9 (*LP*, iv(2), 3552).

[144] *LP*, iv(1), 1700ii, iv(2), 3628, iv(3), 5906 g.6.

north as warden. Cumberland was reappointed warden of the west
march, governor of Carlisle and steward of Penrith; but he was no
more able now than he had been before to rule in opposition to the
Dacre interest.[145] Northumberland survived longer, but with increasing difficulty. Although allotted the normal fee of £1,000 p.a., he
wanted in 1528 to be made constable of the castles of Wark – the 'stay
and ke off all thys contry' – and Dunstanburgh, should the illness of
the current holder of both posts prove fatal: 'yff I shall contenw thes
rooms I must ahave some thyng to ber houth my charges, and not all
way to oondo myselff and have no thank.'[146] Disappointed of these
offices, Northumberland in November 1535 wrote from Topcliffe 'in
hast', in his own 'rude and ragyd hand', to offer Cromwell 1,000 marks
for the captaincy of Berwick, Sir Thomas Clifford being judged
(wrongly, as it turned out) on the brink of death.[147] The earl's
problems – at root psychological rather than financial – led him
eventually to disinherit his brother and leave all his lands to the
king.[148] The involvement of his brothers in the pilgrimage of grace
finally made it impossible for Northumberland to continue as warden
of the east and middle marches. Cumberland's loyal but ineffective
resistance to the rebels in the west march suggested that he too should
go. Yet who could replace them?

Norfolk, appointed the king's lieutenant of the north, left the court
in the middle of January 1537 as Henry decided to make the earl of
Westmorland warden of the east and middle marches again. But
Westmorland no longer trusted his own people there and was doubtful
of his ability to rule the borders. He asked his uncle, lord Sandys, to
get Cromwell to explain his misgivings to the king. Henry VIII
approached his second choice, another nobleman with previous experience as warden, Thomas Manners, the former lord Ros, now earl
of Rutland. He also refused the appointment.[149] The king had to turn
to a more radical solution. He himself became warden-general and
appointed to serve under him two border gentlemen who had served
under Westmorland, Sir William Eure as deputy warden now of the
east march and Sir John Widdrington as deputy warden of the middle
march; at the same time the leading gentry of Tynedale and Reedsdale
were retained to the king's service. In choosing the deputy wardens,
the council told Norfolk, Henry VIII had called to mind that the duke

[145] *LP,* vii, 1217 gg.7, 8, 9; James, 'The first earl of Cumberland', 44 – 6.
[146] SP1/50, f.276 (*LP,* iv(2), 4907).
[147] *SP,* v, 34–5.
[148] J. M. W. Bean, *The Estates of the Percy Family 1416–1537* (Oxford, 1958), p. 157.
[149] *LP,* xii(1), 151, 291, 636, 667.

had 'sundry times' asserted that the king could well be served in the office by 'a meaner man'.[150] Henry VIII planned a similar change for the west march. On 31 January 1537 the council wrote to the earl of Cumberland to inform him, as he put it in his reply to the king, that 'ye have apoynted me to be advaunced to the ordre and honour of the Gartier and ... that your pleasour is I shuld not occupye the wardenship of the west marches'. Cumberland signified his readiness to take up or resign any office at the king's command.[151]

However, once in the north, Norfolk changed his mind. He now believed that the 'wylde people' of the marches could only be kept in order by men of 'good estimacion' and 'nobilitie'.[152] On 12 March the council relayed the king's displeasure at receiving such second thoughts. When Northumberland had been removed as warden the post had been offered to two noblemen, but 'they did both, as they might, refuse it'. The king was forced to take such as he could get. On the west borders the feud between Dacre and Cumberland meant that if Cumberland were replaced by Dacre the 'pyke' between them could only increase. Was not the king's authority sufficient to gain respect for the meanest man? With the king also retaining the leading gentlemen, all should be well; 'at the leaste we think it shal not be yvel that his majesty shall assay this way.'[153] As Norfolk still stood firm, Henry exploded with righteous indignation. This time the council reported his very words. 'When I wold, quoth his highness, have preferred to the wardenry of the est and middle marches my lord of Westmerland, like as he did utterly refuse it, so my lord of Norfolk noted him a man of such hete and hastines of nature that he could not think him mete for it; when we wold, quoth his grace, have conferred it to my lord of Rutland, he refused it also, and my lord of Norfolk noted him a man of to moche pusillanimitie to have doon us good service in it.' Who, then, was suitable? 'Now touching the west marches, my lord of Norfolk himself, quoth his grace, thought it not mete that th'erle of Cumbreland shuld be avoyded out of the wardenry therof and the lord Dacres eftsones therunto preferred, for that shuld but engendre mortal feude betwene their houses. Again we think, quoth his majesty, that it were unsemely to remove him, that hath so wel preserved himself from our rebells in this troublous time, and hath so wel kept our town and castle of Carlisle, and in his place to put him, that hath been taken as his enemy. If then, having determined for the withdrawing of hertburning

[150] *LP*, xii(1), 225; BL, Harl. 6989, f.63v (*LP*, xii(1), 291).
[151] *SP*, v, 64–5.
[152] SP1/116, f.215 (*LP*, xii(1), 594).
[153] BL, Harl. 6989, f.68 (*LP*, xii(1), 636).

from them both, to remove them both from that office', what other nobleman could Norfolk name? The council reiterated the king's belief that there was no man who would not as readily serve under himself and his deputies as under a nobleman.[154] On 12 April Norfolk replied to the council that he had no third choice of nobleman to offer for the east and middle marches: 'I knowe none in thiese parties, and if any shold come owte of the southe parties, ye knowe them all as well as I or better.' But later on the same day he revealed his mind in a private letter, to be shown only to the king. For the east and middle marches Rutland was after all his first choice because 'he is of kyn to all the jantlemen of Northumberland, a few wantyng, and for that he is a man that will here and folow counsell, and being alied with my lord of Westmerlond is sewer at all tymes to have all his powre at command-ment'. Westmorland would be the next best, although it was true that his household servants had refused to serve the king against the rebels. In the west march no man could do better than Dacre, but to reappoint him might make people say that in 1534 a quarrel had been picked with him for the sake of his fine. Sir Thomas Wharton would never serve the king well as warden, so Cumberland was the best choice there – but he should be told not to be so greedy in getting money from his tenants.[155] Norfolk failed to convince the king. Henry VIII took no immediate decision, but the two gentlemen already appointed deputy wardens in the east and middle marches remained in office and in June Sir Thomas Wharton was appointed deputy warden of the west march, assisted, as they were, by local fee'd men.[156] Henry VIII had implemented his decision to employ border gentry in place of noblemen.

Nevertheless, it is clear that the motive for the policy was plain necessity: the king indeed took such as he could get.[157] There was no master plan for the rule of the borders by lesser men in the wake of Henry VIII's acquisition of the Percy inheritance. It was an experi-ment forced upon the king; and eventually it had to be modified. The outbreak of war in August 1542 brought renewed active service for Norfolk as lieutenant of the north. At the same time Henry VIII retired as warden-general and sent Rutland to the borders as warden of all three marches. Rutland was in poor health but he arrived at Alnwick before the end of the month. Henry then decided that he should lead the rearward of the army about to raid Scotland, leaving

---

[154] BL, Harl. 6989, f.69 (*LP*, xii(1), 667).

[155] SP1/118, ff.148, 155–6 (*LP*, xii(1), 916, 919).

[156] *LP*, xii(2), 191 g.51.

[157] This is also the conclusion of M. L. Bush, 'The problem of the far north: a study of the crisis of 1537 and its consequences', *Northern History*, vi (1971), 40–63.

the duke of Suffolk to be warden in his stead.[158] However, Suffolk had no appetite for the office and within a few weeks obtained his discharge. On 29 October Edward Seymour, earl of Hertford, back from the Scottish raid, was shocked to receive the king's commission for the wardenship. He wrote at once to the privy council to explain that he could not 'do the service that my desire is t'accomplishe'. He had been sent north 'in post', assured that he would find on his arrival 'all thing necessary, where in dede I founde nor colde have anything, but only a bare tent', the sole item of the late earl of Southampton's possessions which had not already been stowed away in his ships. Moreover, 'he that shall serve here had neide to be bothe kyn and alied emong them of thies parties and suche oon that hathe and dothe bere rule in the countreye, by reason of his landes or otherwise; who may heraftre, occasion serving, consider and helpe them that shal serve under him according to theire doinges. And furdre it may engendre a grudge or ontowardnes emonge those noblemen here whose men if I shall remayn I must of necessite use to serve his grace under me, when they shall perceive me a straunger to have the charge comyttid to me.' He begged the council to solicit the king 'with expedicion'.[159] The next day he wrote again, 'haste, haste, haste post haste, haste', to send the council the names of men 'more meter to serve in this case than I'. They were 'my lorde of Comberlande by reason of his landes, kinred and aliance, my lord Parre beinge of greate possessions and kinred in thies parties, my lord Lisle who is alredy furnished for that he should have goon into France', and lord Dacre, 'if the kinges majestie did so accept him'. He recalled, too, another reason against his own tenure of the post – his recent appointment as lord admiral – but crossed out this relevant argument on the draft copy of his letter, perhaps for fear of losing the admiralty rather than the wardenship, although it had been granted him for life.[160]

In November the search was on again for a new lord warden. Henry VIII's initial impulse was to send Rutland back. As he reluctantly made ready, the decision was queried by Norfolk, Suffolk and the others waiting at York for Rutland to set out from Belvoir. The earl had 'suche diseases uppon hym', they wrote, that to return would kill him. They recommended instead the appointment of the new earl of Cumberland, 'considereng he hathe a great power of fresshe men nere at hande'. Henry agreed to discharge Rutland but thought Cumberland, who was in his mid-twenties, too young and inexperienced for

[158] *LP*, xvii, 713, 714 g.19, 764, 778.
[159] *The Hamilton Papers*, i, pp. lxii–lxiii.
[160] *HMC, Bath*, iv, 29.

the job. He therefore appointed John Dudley, viscount Lisle, as a man 'wel qualefied', although with 'but smal experience of the matyers of the bordres'; for his assistance and Cumberland's instruction the young earl was to be sworn one of the council with Lisle and remain with him on the east and middle marches.[161] Lisle served in the north only for the winter, returning to the court in April 1543. The king replaced him as warden by William lord Parr, soon to become his brother-in-law, the last man (apart from Dacre) on Hertford's list.[162] He was a northerner by birth, with his estates centred on Kendal in Westmorland, but his interests were at court and he was back there in less than a year. In March 1544 Henry VIII at last gave up the attempt to find a suitable warden-general. Instead he turned to Eure and Wharton, deputy wardens since 1537, and created them barons and full wardens of the east and west marches; at the same time he promoted Eure's son and heir from deputy to warden of the middle march.[163] Border gentry might serve as deputies to the king or a great nobleman; if they were to be wardens on their own they needed a patent of nobility.

It was above all in offices demanding military leadership that noblemen were deemed essential. Richmond's council, established in 1525 to provide more effective justice for the north, contained no noblemen. Lord Darcy in 1529 complained at the number of spiritual men among the commissioners, 'not meitt to governe us', who tried even cases of murder and felony.[164] The council was remodelled in 1530 under the presidency of Cuthbert Tunstal, bishop of Durham, but only after the pilgrimage of grace was it reorganized on a permanent basis, as an administrative and judicial body. Its members then included the earls of Westmorland and Cumberland and lord Dacre, three former wardens of the marches. All three remained on the council in 1538 under a new president, Robert Holgate, bishop of Llandaff.[165] However, it is unlikely that they attended very often. In 1544 or early in 1545, when Henry VIII prepared fresh instructions for the council in the north, he ordered that Westmorland and Dacre, with the current wardens, lords Eure and Wharton, among others, should 'gyve theyer attendaunce at theyre owen pleasure, that is to say, go and come when theyre will is, onelesse they shalbe otherwise by the saide presidente appoynted, savinge onelie at foure generall sittinges' each year; on reflection, the king considered even this obligation would

---

[161] *The Hamilton Papers*, i, 231, 232; *SP*, v, 216–19, 220–1.
[162] *LP*, xviii(1), 464.
[163] *The Hamilton Papers*, ii, 189.
[164] SP1/122, ff.48–57 (*LP*, xii(2), 186(38)).
[165] *LP*, xii(2), 102(2) and (3), xiii(1), 1269.

be 'teduous and chargeable' and reduced it to attendance at the general sitting nearest their own residences. Francis Talbot, earl of Shrewsbury, was the only other noble member of the council at that time; the new earl of Cumberland had been added by September 1545.[166] Shrewsbury was to become president of the council of the north in the reign of Edward VI, but the only nobleman to head a regional council in Henry VIII's reign was John lord Russell. He was appointed president of the newly established – and short-lived – council of the west in 1539, when the threat of invasion made the needs of defence paramount.[167] In the marches of Wales Princess Mary's council, set up in 1525 under the presidency of John Veysey, bishop of Exeter, included three noblemen. Thomas Grey, marquess of Dorset, was master, Walter Devereux, lord Ferrers (who had first been appointed to the council in the marches in 1513) steward and Edward Sutton, lord Dudley, chamberlain of the household. In March 1528 Mary was recalled and her household discharged. The council continued, but had little effective power. Darcy's complaint was echoed in the marches of Wales in 1533, when the ban on spiritual men condemning anyone to death was blamed for the prevalence of unpunished crime.[168] Rowland Lee, bishop of Coventry and Lichfield, appointed president of the council in 1534, seems to have obtained a dispensation to enable him to impose the death penalty and went about his work with a vigour that became legendary. But for all his efforts, and against his advice, the solution to the problem of disorder in Wales eventually adopted was the act of union, by which the independent jurisdiction of the marcher lords was sharply curtailed.[169]

Henry VIII by his grants of local office had himself built up the authority of the dominant nobleman of the marches in 1536 and the chief exemplar of tyranny and corruption, Henry Somerset, earl of Worcester. The earl's father had obtained a number of marcher lordships by his marriage to the Herbert heiress in 1492, but had failed in his attempts to persuade Henry VII to make him sheriff of Glamorgan, or to give him any office except during pleasure. Henry VIII – who gave no office to the duke of Buckingham, the greatest marcher lord at his accession – was generous to lord Herbert. He appointed him constable and steward of castles and lordships in Wales and the marches and sheriff of Glamorgan for life; in 1510 Herbert surrendered

---

[166] *SP*, v, 402–11, 529–33.

[167] Joyce Youings, 'The council of the west', *TRHS*, 5th series, 10 (1960), 41–2, 48–53.

[168] *LP*, i(2), 2222 g.9, iv(1), 2331(2), iv(2), 4096, vi, 210, *Addenda*, i, 458.

[169] Penry Williams, *The Council in the Marches of Wales under Elizabeth I* (Cardiff, 1958), pp. 16–22.

his patents for the king to make a new grant of these offices to him and his son and heir in survivorship.[170] Herbert had no intention of living in Wales and in fact seems to have visited it only once during the reign, in 1512.[171] But he clearly wanted the offices to build his power there through his deputies, which could have been to the king's advantage, and it suited Henry VIII to celebrate his accession with a show of munificence. But the king's liberality, hailed at the start of the reign as a welcome contrast to Henry VII's restraint, appeared in a different light in the aftermath of his first war. The time had come not merely to call a halt, but to annul some of the grants he had made. Acts of parliament to resume royal grants, especially of office, had been passed often enough in the fifteenth century. Henry VII had gone so far as to resume into his own hands all those offices granted not only by the Yorkists but also by himself in the first five months of his reign.[172] The act of resumption of 1515 explained the need to restore the king's revenues, 'so gretely mynysshed by reason of the manyfold giftes, grauntes and releases' approved since the beginning of Henry VIII's reign. The act resumed into the king's hands, besides annuities granted by letters patent, all grants of office in reversion, all regrants of office to a former patentee and another jointly with him (saving the rights of the first office-holder), all grants of office to two new men in survivorship, and all grants of office not requiring attendance even by deputy.[173] It was a sweeping indictment of the young king's exercise of patronage, but it restocked the reservoir of gifts. Moreover, Henry was free to make similar grants in the future, if he chose. He continued to favour his lord chamberlain, now earl of Worcester, and in 1518 granted the reversion to most of the earl's offices in Wales to his son. When Henry Somerset succeeded to the earldom in 1526 he took possession of lands valued at no more than £636 6s 8d clear p.a. His fees from royal offices in the marches (including some granted to him alone), amounting to nearly £300 p.a., provided a vital supplement to his income.[174]

The second earl was not an absentee, like his father, but he showed no interest in his offices except as sources of revenue and took no

---

[170] W. R. B. Robinson, 'Early Tudor policy towards Wales [Part 1]: the acquisition of lands and offices in Wales by Charles Somerset, earl of Worcester', *The Bulletin of the Board of Celtic Studies*, xx, pt 4 (1964), 422–7 and appendix.

[171] W. R. B. Robinson, 'Early Tudor policy towards Wales, Part 2: the Welsh offices held by Henry earl of Worcester (1526–1549)', *The Bulletin of the Board of Celtic Studies*, xxi, pt 1 (1964), 44n.

[172] Michael Hicks, 'Attainder, resumption and coercion 1461–1529', *Parliamentary History: A Yearbook*, 3 (1984), 23–5.

[173] 6 Henry VIII, c.25.

[174] Robinson, 'Early Tudor policy, Part 2', 44–6.

effective action to stop the oppressive misconduct of his deputies.[175] Nevertheless the act of union specifically safeguarded his exercise of 'the office of the justice of the hole countie of Glamorgan'.[176] The office of sheriff in the medieval lordship of Glamorgan had been a judicial, not an administrative one, and the proviso was evidently intended to allow Worcester – at least in the short term – judicial authority in the new county of Glamorgan, which was to include his own lordships of Gower and Kilvey. However, in 1540 another statute annulled all existing life-grants of the office of sheriff in Wales, now roundly declared to have been obtained by 'sinistre and subtill meanes'. After a long fight Worcester secured the fees of the office for his lifetime, but he lost its powers.[177] A proviso to the act of union also protected Walter Devereux, lord Ferrers, in his offices as chief justice of South Wales and chamberlain of South Wales and of Carmarthen and Cardigan, granted him in the mid-1520s. But for him, too, the concession was short-lived so far as it concerned his office of justice. The old judicial system was ended in 1541 by the appointment of four new justices, one for each of the circuits for the great sessions to be established in Wales.[178] The chanceries and exchequers in Wales survived the act of union and Henry FitzRoy, duke of Richmond, was appointed chancellor and chamberlain of North Wales in succession to Henry Norris in 1536. After Richmond's death a few weeks later the offices went jointly to Edward Seymour, newly created viscount Beauchamp, and Sir Richard Bulkeley of Beaumaris.[179]

Appointment as sheriff of an English county for a single year did not attract noblemen, but a longer tenure of the office was prized. The Cliffords were and remained hereditary sheriffs of Westmorland. Henry VIII allowed no other noble family to acquire a right of inheritance, but at different times in his reign there were two other noble sheriffs. Lord Monteagle, as Sir Edward Stanley, had been appointed sheriff of the county palatine of Lancaster in 1485; on the accession of Henry VIII the grant was at first renewed only until Michaelmas, but in October 1509 Stanley was again appointed sheriff during pleasure. After his ennoblement he petitioned for a regrant of the shrievalty and other offices to himself and his heirs male, arguing that as he had lands in tail male of the gift of Henry VII and the

[175] W. R. B. Robinson, 'Early Tudor policy towards Wales, Part 3: Henry earl of Worcester and Henry VIII's legislation for Wales', *The Bulletin of the Board of Celtic Studies*, xxi, pt 4 (1966), 337–42.

[176] 27 Henry VIII, c.26.

[177] 32 Henry VIII, c.27; Robinson, 'Early Tudor policy, Part 3', 352–7.

[178] *LP*, iv(1), 1610 g.22, 2200; Robinson, 'Early Tudor policy, Part 3', 351–2.

[179] *The Lisle Letters*, iii, 695; *LP*, xi, 385 g.16.

'landes and offices lye soo joyned togedder', he could do the king better service if he had the offices as well in hereditary possession. He offered 'to compownd with the kyng and gif his grace suche a some of money as shalbe thought reasonable', but Henry VIII refused his request and Monteagle's son never became sheriff.[180] The other nobleman, Henry Percy, earl of Northumberland, negotiated for nearly two years over the terms of his appointment as sheriff of Northumberland and was eventually, in February 1534, appointed sheriff for life, paying £40 p.a. to the king.[181]

The nobility more often based its power in the localities on land and title than on office. Nevertheless, local office extended a nobleman's power, if only temporarily, and could be crucial to his predominance. Hundreds of offices were available on the crown estates in England and Wales. Fewer grants of office were enrolled than grants of land and a series of local and family studies would be necessary to fill out the picture of Henry VIII's grants to the nobility. The patent rolls and chancery warrants and the records of the duchy of Lancaster and the court of augmentations provide evidence for grants of local office on the crown lands to somewhat under half the adult noblemen during the reign. Among the high nobility the balance was reversed: considerably more received a grant than did not. But even during the early years of lavish giving few noblemen of any rank were conspicuously favoured, and Buckingham was not the only high nobleman to be passed over altogether. Indeed, Surrey was actually replaced in one of the most important offices in the administration of the crown lands, that of chief justice of the royal forests north of the Trent.[182] Yet he could more easily accept his loss since he retained his post of lord treasurer and was soon to become earl marshal for life – which may, in fact, have been his recompense.

The chief justices of the forests were nearly always noblemen in the reign of Henry VIII. The king appointed Darcy to the office vacated by Surrey in 1509, to hold for life; five years later he regranted the office to Darcy and his son and heir, George, in survivorship.[183] The act of resumption extinguished George Darcy's entitlement and it was not renewed. After Darcy's attainder the office was granted to Cromwell, who in his turn was succeeded by Rutland.[184] Only after

---

[180] Somerville, *Duchy of Lancaster*, i, 462; SP1/27, ff.210–11 (*LP*, iii(2), 2968).

[181] *LP*, v, 1008, vi, 1583, vii, 262 g.22.

[182] *LP*, i(1), 438(3), m.1.

[183] *LP*, i(1), 94 g.64, ii(1), 355.

[184] *LP*, xii(2), 1311 g.39, xv, 1027 g.22.

Rutland's death was a commoner appointed: Sir Anthony Browne, master of the horse. The treasurer of the household, Sir Thomas Lovell, was chief justice of the forests south of Trent in the early years of the reign; in June 1523, when Dorset was serving in the north, Henry VIII granted the office to him and Lovell in survivorship.[185] Although Lovell died in 1524 and Dorset in 1530 no further grant was made until November 1534, when the king kept the promise he had made to Suffolk 18 months earlier and recompensed him with the office for surrendering his patent as earl marshal.[186] (The duke had been granted the wardship of Henry Grey, marquess of Dorset, in March 1533.[187] Either that link or Surrey's earlier experience presumably suggested this answer to the problem of compensation.) Suffolk certainly got the worse of the bargain in terms of prestige, although his new title was sufficiently elevated to be included in his style proclaimed by the heralds.[188] After his death William Paulet, lord St John, his successor as great master, was appointed chief justice of the forests south of Trent at the same fee, £100 p.a.[189] When the monastic lands began to come into the king's hands, two new offices were created which Henry VIII also gave to leading noblemen. Norfolk – although he would have preferred to hold the combined appointment – became chief steward of the lands of suppressed monasteries south of Trent in May 1536, with a fee of £100 p.a. Cromwell was appointed to the parallel office north of Trent two years later, being succeeded in turn by Audley of Walden, Suffolk and Wriothesley.[190]

Noblemen had to compete with the king's friends and household servants and with local gentry to become stewards and constables, bailiffs, foresters and keepers of parks. Only a few saw their local power widely enhanced by such appointments. Like Herbert, they were all noblemen close to Henry VIII. Beside his other offices in the north, Darcy in 1509 was granted duchy of Lancaster offices in Yorkshire which transformed him from a moderately wealthy baron in the West Riding into the dominant authority in the whole area around Pontefract.[191] In 1509 the lord steward, Shrewsbury, was appointed

[185] *LP*, iii(2), 3113.

[186] *LP*, vi, 415, vii, 1498 g.37.

[187] *LP*, vi, 300 g.20.

[188] BL, Add. 6113, f.61 (*LP*, xv, 1026).

[189] *LP*, xx(2), 1068 g.34.

[190] SP1/103, f.60 (*LP*, x, 599); *LP*, xiii(1), 1520, xiv(1), 1355, xvi, 1500, xx(1), 1336, xxi(2), 775.

[191] Somerville, *Duchy of Lancaster*, i, 515, 516, 522, 525; R. B. Smith, *Land and Politics in the England of Henry VIII. The West Riding of Yorkshire: 1530–46* (Oxford, 1970), p. 139.

steward for life of the duchy of Lancaster honour of Tutbury, Staffordshire, constable of its castle and of Melbourne and High Peak in
Derbyshire; in 1523 he also became bailiff of the new liberty of the
duchy in Staffordshire and Derbyshire. Six years later he obtained a
regrant of all his duchy offices to himself and his heir in survivorship,
which kept them in the family without further grant until 1560. Henry
VIII also made the earl and his son marcher lords by his grant to them
in survivorship in 1525 of the offices of constable of Radnor and
Wigmore castles as well as stewardships in the earldom of March.[192]
The power of Walter Devereux, lord Ferrers, was extended in the
1520s not only by his appointments in South Wales but also by the
grant of the stewardship of lands forfeited by Buckingham in the
marches of Wales.[193] In the west country the landed power of Henry
Courtenay, earl of Devon, was reinforced by his appointment in 1523
as steward of the duchy of Cornwall and of lands belonging to the
former duchies of Exeter and Somerset, offices which he held until his
attainder in 1538.[194] Finally, in July 1539, John lord Russell was
named as the new steward of the duchy of Cornwall and on the same
day given a long list of monastic lands in Devon.[195]

The double grant was unique: no other nobleman was so deliberately
created a local magnate. Moreover, the package put together for
Russell – which was soon to include a further grant of stewardships
forfeited by Courtenay[196] – followed his appointment as president of
the council in the west. Two contrasted ways of tackling the problems
of the less accessible parts of the kingdom were thus combined. Up to
the mid-1520s Henry VIII made large grants of offices to a handful of
specially trusted noblemen; after the re-establishment of the councils
of the north and in the marches of Wales he never again, except in
1539, gave local offices on such a scale to any peer. Regional councils
had the potential to become vehicles for the expression of noble power,
but it would then be exercised within an institutional framework,
under more effective royal control.

Although Henry VIII, even in the first half of his reign, confined his
major grants of offices on the crown lands to a favoured few, the
myriad offices at his disposal included many which would be a
welcome gift to any nobleman. To be constable of a castle, in particular, conferred great prestige. The most attractive appointments,

[192] Somerville, *Duchy of Lancaster*, i, 541; *LP*, iv(1), 1533 g.10, itemized in Robinson,
'Early Tudor policy, Part 3', 336.
[193] *LP*, iii(2), 2145 g.29.
[194] ibid., 2992 g.3, 3062 g.26.
[195] *LP*, xiv(1), 1354 gg.12, 13.
[196] *LP*, xiv(2), 264 g.17.

especially in the south-east of England, tended to go to courtiers. John de Vere, earl of Oxford, was constable of the Tower of London for life by grant of Henry VII, confirmed by Henry VIII.[197] After his death the office went to non-noble members of the king's household. Sir Thomas Bourchier, knight for the body, was constable of Windsor castle at Henry VIII's accession; in 1511 he surrendered his patent for a grant of the office to himself and Henry Bourchier, earl of Essex, in survivorship. However, in 1525 Essex made way for Henry Courtenay, soon to be created marquess of Exeter; in his turn and much to his distress, Exeter had to surrender the office at the end of 1536 and accept monastic land in recompense.[198] The constable of Dover and warden of the cinque ports was always a household servant: George Boleyn, lord Rochford, appointed in 1534, was the only nobleman to hold the offices during the reign of Henry VIII.[199] Even Thomas Cromwell – for all his accumulation of offices, local as well as central – was pleased to be appointed constable of Leeds castle, Kent, in January 1539; after some repairs the castle made a splendid home for his son Gregory.[200] But noblemen without direct access to the king might still obtain local offices which met their special needs. Thomas lord Berkeley, for example, whose great-uncle had surrendered the family castle at Berkeley, Gloucestershire, to Henry VII, managed at least to become its constable in 1533.[201] Noblemen, like Berkeley, created by Henry VIII were indeed more likely than not to receive at least one grant of local office, which no doubt made any lack of success harder to bear for those who were passed over. John lord Mordaunt, who had failed to buy his way into the under-treasureship in 1528, before his ennoblement, in 1539 explained his situation to Cromwell in a profusion of negatives: 'I have no office or ffee of the kynges grace, nor his grace never gave me nothyng.'[202] It was a state familiar to many noblemen by birth.

Only the unpaid office of justice of the peace was a near certainty for all noblemen. No commissions of the peace survive for the county palatine of Lancaster, issued under the seal of the duchy of Lancaster. It may be assumed that the earls of Derby, the greatest landowners in the county, were always included in the commission. For the other English counties commissions of the peace are to be found in varying

[197] *LP*, i(1), 54 g.14.

[198] *LP*, i(1), 857 g.5, iv(1), 1298, xiii(2), 453, 804. Exeter was paid his fee up to Michaelmas 1537.

[199] *LP*, vii, 922 g.16.

[200] *LP*, xiv(1), 191 g.2; Bindoff, *House of Commons*, i, 727–8.

[201] *LP*, vi, 300 g.7.

[202] SP1/150, f.191 (*LP*, xiv(1), 845).

numbers on the patent rolls and on the originalia rolls in the exchequer. There is also extant a *liber pacis*, for the 24th year of the reign,
which fills one of the gaps in the record.[203] New commissions were
necessary to register each change in a county's list of justices, but there
was no consistent practice governing enrolment in the reign of Henry
VIII. Yet the surviving evidence presents a fairly coherent picture.
Some noblemen lived for too short a time to be included in any known
commission. A few others were omitted for no obvious cause, such as
Ralph lord Ogle, who died in 1513, the Scropes of Upsall, whose
family died out in 1517, and John lord Zouche, who lived until 1526
without ever becoming a JP. Richard Grey, earl of Kent, a JP for
Bedfordshire in the commissions of 1512 and February 1514, was
dropped in October 1514 and remained off the commission for the rest
of his life, probably as a consequence of his financial difficulties.
Justices of the peace were appointed by the king, although normally
chosen by the lord chancellor. From December 1515, when Wolsey
became chancellor, until his disgrace in 1529 every adult nobleman,
apart from Zouche and Kent, is known to have been a justice of the
peace, except those resident in counties for which no commission was
enrolled.[204] Only one was removed: Thomas lord Dacre of the north,
dropped from the commissions for Cumberland, Westmorland and
Northumberland in August 1525 when he was dismissed as warden-
general.

After the Reformation, two noblemen seem to have been kept out by
a too open commitment to Roman Catholicism. Thomas lord Sandys,
although he was in his thirties, was omitted from the commissions of
1541 and 1542 for Hampshire – the only commissions of the peace of
Henry VIII's reign to be enrolled after his succession to the barony –
and Edward VI's commission, and was first appointed as a justice in
the county by Mary. Thomas lord Vaux, who had been made a JP for
Northamptonshire in 1531 at the age of 21, was removed from the
commission issued in July 1536, the month in which he had to give up
the governorship of Jersey. Henry VIII may have been angered by
that episode, but Vaux too had to wait to be restored to the commission until Mary came to the throne. The aftermath of a political crisis
best explains the treatment of two other peers. When Thomas Boleyn,

[203] Commissions from the patent rolls in *LP*, from the originalia rolls (E371) listed in
A. S. Bevan, 'Justices of the peace, 1509–47: an additional source', *Bull.IHR*, lviii
(1985); *liber pacis* in *LP*, v, 1694. I am grateful to Dr Bevan for allowing me to make use
of her list before publication.
[204] John lord Lumley (Durham), Thomas Stanley, lord Monteagle (Lancashire) and
Henry Somerset, earl of Worcester (Monmouth).

earl of Wiltshire, lost high office in 1536 he was naturally dropped from the commission in all those counties to which he had been added as lord privy seal. But he was also removed in Norfolk, where he had been in the commission since the beginning of the reign and still owned many lands. Only in Kent, the county of his residence, was he allowed to continue as a JP. Gregory Cromwell, in the commission of the peace for Sussex in 1538, was never appointed to the bench as a nobleman until the accession of Edward VI. Even in Leicestershire, where he was then living, he was not included in the commissions of 1541 and 1544, the only ones for the county to be enrolled in the last seven years of Henry VIII's reign. Yet the history of the Parr family warns against the assumption that non-appointment or removal, even in the 1530s and 1540s, was necessarily a sign of disfavour. Sir William Parr, created lord Parr of Horton in 1543, was no longer a JP in Northamptonshire or any other county after 1538. His nephew, lord Parr from 1539 and earl of Essex from 1543, was never a justice of the peace in Henry VIII's reign, even in Essex, where he was a commissioner to collect the benevolence in 1544.[205]

Many noblemen were justices of the peace in one county only, and fewer than one-third appeared in the commission of more than four counties or parts of counties. Neighbouring families, and successive generations of the same family, might be treated very differently while still remaining as justices. In Leicestershire, for example, George lord Hastings, created earl of Huntingdon in 1529, was regularly named in the commission from 1509; his son joined him when he was about 30 years old. Neither was a JP in any other county. On the other hand, Thomas Manners, lord Ros, created earl of Rutland in 1525, appeared in no commission of the peace until 1524, when he was over 30, but then within a few years was named in a dozen commissions besides that for Leicestershire. The two generations of the Howards displayed a marked contrast. The elder, as earl of Surrey and then duke of Norfolk, was in four commissions of the peace from the start of the reign: for Norfolk, Suffolk, Surrey and Sussex. The younger Thomas Howard was also a JP in Norfolk and Suffolk from 1509 or 1510 and, in addition, was named in the commissions for the three parts of Lincolnshire from 1514. But within two years of inheriting the dukedom in 1524 he had been added to the commissions for every county, although he held no higher office than his father had done. The explanation appears to lie in a change of policy inaugurated by Wolsey. From May 1519 Wolsey was added to every new commission of the peace as it was issued from chancery. The intention was no doubt to reinforce his

[205] *LP*, xx(1), 623 viii.

message on the need for law and order by taking the personal authority of the lord chancellor, at least notionally, to every corner of the kingdom. Norfolk, as lord treasurer second to the chancellor in order of precedence, perhaps sought the same distinction for reasons of prestige. His pre-eminence in turn seems to have stirred the envy of Suffolk, appointed president of the council in 1529. He had been a JP in Norfolk, Suffolk and Surrey from 1511 or 1512; he was added to the commission for Middlesex in 1524, for Berkshire in 1525 and for Oxfordshire in 1526; and then between December 1529 and the compilation of the *liber pacis* he too was named on every known commission of the peace. He was followed by Thomas Boleyn, earl of Wiltshire, who was put on all the commissions of the peace when he became lord privy seal in 1530, an honour accorded to none of his predecessors. This precedent, like that set by Wolsey, was followed for Wiltshire's successors – but only after an initial hesitation. Cromwell was not included in every commission issued during his first year as lord privy seal. However, from June 1537 he was added to each new commission of the peace, with the single exception of the commission of July 1539 for the bishop of Durham's liberty, from which the two dukes were also omitted. But it is unlikely that high officers of state often acted as justices of the peace even within their own counties. Office could be as important for what it symbolized as for the actual power which it conferred.

The large number of local offices in the king's gift may suggest that few of them could have been filled on his personal initiative, although his approval was necessary for every grant. Yet Henry VIII's grants of offices in the localities fall into a pattern very similar to that formed by his grants of office at the centre. The range of recipients was wider, but the offices of most estimation still went to the noblemen who were closest to the king and the men ennobled by him. Henry VIII made no effort to bind the nobility as a whole to him through office, even at the local level, if the majority of noblemen were never office-holders in receipt of fees. It remains to be seen whether he had a more expansive view of his role as patron when he came to make grants of that even more desirable commodity, land.

CHAPTER 7

Grants of Land

After the exuberant early years of the reign it was time not only to monitor grants of office but also to survey the state of the king's revenues. How much had his landed income been reduced by gifts of lands and leases, of fees and annuities? How much land had been restored by the king to his subjects or recovered against him? The general surveyors drew up a roll of the estates no longer – at Michaelmas 1515 – yielding the revenues they had produced in the last year of the reign of Henry VII.[1] The clerks made a few mistakes and did not always bother to find out the date of the letters patent or statute authorizing the disposal of crown assets, but their survey reveals the official valuation of most of the grants made by Henry VIII in the first seven years of his reign. Even taking into account his other grants, of land which had not been held by Henry VII, it is clear that if the young king had been guilty of extravagance, it had not been for the benefit of his nobility.

There was, indeed, no incentive for Henry VIII to make lavish gifts to noblemen. They would naturally rejoice at his accession if they were only released from the fear – or the reality – of burdens imposed upon them by his father.[2] Henry VIII ordered the cancellation of all the bonds and recognizances made to Henry VII by George Nevill, lord Bergavenny, or by others on his behalf, and released all his debts to the late king.[3] Bergavenny was thereby pardoned the residue of the fine of £100,000 'or thereabowtys' levied on him for illegal retaining and freed from the undertakings he had been made to give to Henry VII, including his promise never to enter Kent, Surrey,

[1] SC11/837, noted *LP*, ii(1),1795. Summary of roll's findings: SP1/12, ff.47–8 (*LP*, ii(1), 1363).
[2] Lander, 'Bonds, coercion, and fear', pp. 328–67.
[3] C82/338 (*LP*, i(1), 132 gg.69, 71).

Sussex or Hampshire without the king's licence.[4] Henry Percy, earl of Northumberland, was pardoned his fine of £10,000 for the abduction of a royal ward.[5] Other noblemen were saved smaller, but still substantial sums by the cancellation of their recognizances: Thomas West, lord La Warre, £400 remaining from a debt of £600,[6] Edward Stafford, duke of Buckingham, 1,000 marks from a debt of 1,500 marks,[7] and Buckingham's brother, created earl of Wiltshire by Henry VIII, the whole sum of £2,000 for which he was bound to Henry VII.[8] Robert lord Willoughby de Broke was released from a bond to pay £2,000 to the king at any time on two months' warning.[9] In April 1511 the estate of Giles late lord Daubeney was relieved from the obligation to pay £1,900 by annual instalments of £100 – of which Daubeney had paid one before his death – and in December 1512 the king ordered the cancellation of the six remaining recognizances entered into by William Blount, lord Mountjoy, his father-in-law and two others in 1506, saving them the 1,200 marks still owing of their debt of 2,300 marks. The executors of Henry VII's will, sitting with others of the king's council, had found these recognizances to have been unjustly obtained from Daubeney and Mountjoy: in the words of the signed bill in favour of Mountjoy – and the same formula was used for Daubeney's heirs – the recognizances had been made 'without any cause reasonable or lefull ... by the undue meanes of certain of the lerned counsaill' of Henry VII, so that the sums due 'may not be levyed without the evydent perill of our said late faders soule'.[10]

So far as is known, no money was refunded for the payments already made, although Edmund Dudley, in the Tower, had recalled that Henry VII had wanted restitution to be made to anyone wronged by him, and the king in his will had instructed his executors to make reparation where necessary. Dudley named among noblemen harshly treated in the previous reign not only the earl of Northumberland, lord Bergavenny and lord Daubeney, but others as well, who were not helped by Henry VIII on his accession: Edward Sutton, lord Dudley, and Thomas Howard, earl of Surrey, who had already paid their debts in full when Henry VII died, Henry lord Clifford, who was apparently expected to complete his payments, and Thomas Stanley, earl of Derby, whose debt was initially demanded by Henry VIII although

---

[4] *Select Cases in the Council of Henry VII*, p. cxxi; *CCR, Henry VII*, ii, 825; C54/373, quoted Richardson, *Tudor Chamber Administration*, p. 149.

[5] *LP*, i(1), 414 g.58; *CCR, Henry VII*, ii, 821(i).

[6] *LP*, i(1), 218 g.35; *CCR, Henry VII*, ii, 669.

[7] *LP*, i(1), 357 g.41; *CCR, Henry VII*, ii, 822.

[8] *LP*, i(1), 632 g.70; *CCR, Henry VII*, ii, 962(vi).

[9] *LP*, i(1), 749 g.26; *CCR, Henry VII*, ii, 955 (xii).

[10] C82/361, 385 (*LP*, i(1), 749 g.24, 1524 g.38); *CCR, Henry VII*, ii, 549, 686.

eventually substantially reduced.[11] However, a few noble families were restored to possessions they had lost. The financial entanglements of Richard Grey, earl of Kent, had by 1508 forced him to make over all his lands to the crown; no restitution was made to him, but Henry VIII, after the attainder of Empson and Dudley, restored to the countess of Kent – though for her lifetime only – two manors which the earl had sold to them.[12] Sir Thomas Darcy and his wife, widow of Sir Ralph Neville, had in 1500 agreed with Henry VII on a division of her jointure which gave the king the use of a considerable part of it throughout her life. On Henry VIII's accession Darcy, now lord Darcy, and his wife petitioned to be allowed to enjoy these lands, and the king in July 1509 granted their request, ordering the feoffees to make estate for lady Darcy's lifetime 'as right requireth', with the revenues from the death of Henry VII.[13] Yet Darcy never forgot that they had lost the income from the lands for nine years and, long afterwards, when his debts to Henry VIII brought him in danger of outlawry, he prepared a petition reminding the king that Henry VII had deprived him of 6,600 marks by retaining these lands.[14] Finally, George Nevill, lord Bergavenny, in December 1512 was given livery of the lordship of Abergavenny as heir to his grandmother, who had been disseised by Richard Neville, earl of Warwick. The estate had come to the crown in 1487 by assignment of the dowager countess of Warwick and was worth £253 7s 11½d p.a. at the end of Henry VII's reign. The restoration implied that Henry VIII recognized the injustice of Warwick's occupation and therefore of his own possession of the lordship, but the grant was described simply as 'de dono nostro' and Bergavenny was only to receive the profits from Michaelmas 1512.[15]

More immediately significant for the crown's revenues was Henry VIII's assent to the reversal of attainders. The royal income at the end of Henry VII's reign had included £545 17s 7d p.a. from lands which were restored to John Tuchet, lord Audley, by act of parliament in 1512; a general proviso protected the rights of those holding any lands for life or years by grant of Henry VII or Henry VIII. Audley had to

[11] Harrison, 'The petition of Edmund Dudley', 82–99 (text and footnotes); *LP*, i(1), 1. 'At the humble peticion' of Thomas earl of Derby 'and in consideracion of the good and acceptable servys that he hath don to hys grace', Henry VIII pardoned 2,500 marks of the earl's debt in 1517, when the earl assigned lands for the payment by instalments of the 5,000 marks still owing, as cited in his inquisition post mortem: C142/36/2.

[12] *CCR, Henry VII*, ii, 553, 763, 765, 784, 956; *LP*, i(1), 519 g.61. Bernard, 'The fortunes of the Greys, earls of Kent', argues that Henry VII may have been trying to protect the family inheritance against the earl's improvidence.

[13] *CCR, Henry VII*, i, 1192; C82/338 (*LP*, i(1), 132 g.115).

[14] *LP*, xii(2), 186(62).

[15] C82/385 (*LP*, i(1), 1524 g.36); SC11/837; *CCR, Henry VII*, i, 327.

pay 6,500 marks for his restitution, by yearly instalments of 250 marks; in spite of other pressing financial burdens he kept up the payments and by 1529 had paid 4,500 marks.[16] Katherine countess of Devon, daughter of Edward IV, was restored to a long list of Courtenay estates forfeited by her husband under the agreement which they had negotiated with Henry VIII in April 1511, renouncing in return any claim to lands belonging to the earldom of March and other lands of Edward IV. The grant was made in February 1512 and confirmed later the same year by an act of parliament which carried a proviso saving the rights of any private person claiming title to the lands.[17] Margaret Pole, daughter of George Plantagenet, duke of Clarence, although a lady of the chamber to Katherine of Aragon from the beginning of Henry VIII's reign, had to wait until October 1513 for the restoration of lands – valued at £1,599 19s 10½d p.a. – in the king's hands through the attainder of her brother, Edward earl of Warwick. This grant was made after she had assigned Wolsey an annuity of 100 marks and paid him £1,000 as the first instalment of 5,000 marks promised for the war in recognition of the king's 'hygh and great goodnes shewed unto her, as restorying her to the enherytaunce of her seid broder'.[18] In these restitutions Henry VIII was following the policy of his father, who had himself reversed the attainders of five of the noblemen attainted in his reign, in four cases without making full restitution of their estates.[19] The motive was to reconcile the noble family, but to leave fresh in its memory the penalties of treason.

The young Henry VIII very rarely made gifts of property to his nobles, but in July 1509 he gave the steward of his household, George Talbot, earl of Shrewsbury, the mansion of Coldharbour for life, rent free.[20] It was a fine house – Henry VII had given it to his mother for her lifetime – and Shrewsbury made it his London residence. In the same month Robert Radcliffe, lord FitzWalter, who had in 1505 obtained letters patent reversing his father's attainder, was permitted to lease three of the family manors in Norfolk, but he had to pay £100 p.a. rent and hold them only during the king's pleasure.[21] A third

---

[16] SC11/837; 3 Henry VIII, c.17; *LP,* iv(3), App.245.

[17] *LP,* i(1), 749 g.23, 1083 g.2; 4 Henry VIII, c.10.

[18] SC11/837; *LP,* i(2), 1987, 2422 g.11; BL, Cotton Titus B.IV, f.116 (*LP,* i(2), 1924).

[19] Lander, 'Bonds, coercion, and fear', p. 333.

[20] C82/338 (*LP,* i(1), 132 g.13).

[21] *CPR, Henry VII,* ii, 454; C82/338 (*LP,* i(1), 132 g.90). Henry VII issued these letters patent by virtue of 19 Henry VII, c.28, which authorized him, during his life, to reverse attainders by letters patent. FitzWalter obtained an act of Henry VIII's first parliament confirming the restitution and the arrangements made for the lands: 1 Henry VIII, c.19.

grant authorized in July 1509, although the letters patent were not issued until January 1510, gave to John Bourchier, lord FitzWarin, a 40-year lease of four manors in Somerset, paying nearly £45 p.a. rent; he already held the manors, at that rent, on a 20-year lease from Henry VII.[22] In April 1510 Thomas FitzAlan, earl of Arundel, and his son, styled lord Mautravers, were given the manor of Worldham, Hampshire, in survivorship, for their charges in the king's service. This grant, too, extended an earlier one from Henry VII, of a life interest in Worldham to the earl alone.[23] In March 1511 William lord Willoughby de Eresby received ahead of schedule the manor of Belleau, Lincolnshire, part of his share of an inheritance due to be divided by the crown after it had enjoyed the revenues for ten years.[24] These five grants were, it seems, the sum total of Henry VIII's land grants to the nobility at the start of his reign. Only in 1514 did he suddenly display himself as the bountiful prince to the two Howards, father and son, on their creation as duke of Norfolk and earl of Surrey, and (less spectacularly) to Charles Brandon on his creation as duke of Suffolk. No lands had been given to Henry Stafford when he was created earl of Wiltshire in 1510, although he was a courtier friend of the king, nor to Charles Brandon when he became viscount Lisle in 1513; neither was any land grant made to Charles Somerset, lord Herbert, on his creation as earl of Worcester early in 1514, at the same time as the Howards and Brandon received their new titles. No doubt the creation of two dukedoms called for a special celebration, but the treatment of the Howards indicates that it was above all their victory over the Scots – cited in their grants – that elicited the king's unprecedented generosity. Three months later Henry VIII again commemorated the great event by ennobling Sir Edward Stanley: he, too, was given land – the manor and park of Parlaunt, Buckinghamshire – but only for his lifetime.[25]

The younger Thomas Howard, the lord admiral, had in 1510 (under his courtesy title of lord Howard) been given a messuage in Stepney for his services to the king. On his creation as earl of Surrey he received lands which had belonged to viscount Beaumont, with an annual value of £333 6s 8d; although he was to hold them for his

---

[22] C82/338 (*LP*, i(1), 357 g.12); *CPR, Henry VII*, ii, 276.

[23] C66/611 (*LP*, i(1), 447 g.26); *CPR, Henry VII*, i, 121. Mautravers and his wife were granted four manors in 1511 and another four in 1514: *LP*, i(1), 709 g.60, i(2), 3049 g.11. They are not included in this survey since Mautravers was not a peer until he inherited his father's earldom in 1524.

[24] C82/360 (*LP*, i(1), 731 g.21).

[25] The grant was not enrolled, but Monteagle referred to it in a petition to Henry VIII: SP1/27, ff.210–11 (*LP*, iii(2), 2968).

lifetime only.[26] The new duke of Norfolk received in tail male manors in ten counties.[27] Both father and son obtained acts of the parliament then in session confirming their grants and ensuring that, if either suffered an eviction by law from any of these lands, the king would assign him other estates in recompense.[28] In fact, Henry VIII soon decided on a change in the grant to Norfolk. In 1515, by another act of parliament – not, as the earlier one had been, in the form of a petition – the manors in Derbyshire and Nottinghamshire given to the duke were taken back by the crown and others substituted for them, together with an annuity of £9 12s 6½d.[29] In all, the lands given to Norfolk had been worth £384 0s 2d p.a. at the end of Henry VII's reign.[30] In contrast, Charles Brandon was given only one estate, the castle, manor and park of Donnington, Berkshire, which had belonged to Edmund de la Pole, earl of Suffolk.[31]

However, Brandon's new honour was clearly intended to show that he had replaced the de la Pole earls of Suffolk and there were large estates of theirs still to be distributed if the king were to be so inclined. A year later Henry VIII made the duke of Suffolk a further gift of these lands in support of his title. This grant bestowed on him – without listing them – all the lands forfeited by Edmund de la Pole, earl of Suffolk, and John de la Pole, earl of Lincoln, including the reversion to those held for life by the queen or by Edmund's widow or by anyone else for life or years, excluding only two manors – Ewelme, Oxfordshire (held by Edmund's widow), and Worldham, Hampshire (already granted to the earl of Arundel and his son in survivorship).[32] The old countess of Suffolk died within a few days, so that the grant was immediately worth substantially more than the £500 p.a. at which the lands still in the possession of the crown were valued. The other reversions were potentially even more lucrative since they included lands worth £704 10s 2¼d p.a. held by Thomas Howard, earl of Surrey, for life as tenant by the courtesy, his first wife, Anne, having

[26] *LP*, i(1), 414 g.44; C82/401 (*LP*, i(2), 2684 g.2); SC11/837.

[27] C82/401 (*LP*, i(2), 2684 g.1).

[28] 5 Henry VIII, cc.9, 11. Norfolk's act had a proviso annexed to it, doubtless by the duke of Buckingham, saving the 'name, right, title, honour, dignitie, auctoritie, state, place, sete, prerogatif and preemynence' of Buckingham – now no longer the only duke.

[29] 6 Henry VIII, c.19.

[30] SC11/837.

[31] C82/401 (*LP*, i(2), 2684 g.5), letters patent recited in and confirmed by 5 Henry VIII, c.10; *VCH, Berkshire*, iv, 92–3.

[32] C82/415 (*LP*, ii(1), 94), letters patent recited in and confirmed by 6 Henry VIII, c.20. Ewelme was subsequently granted to Suffolk, with the profits from Michaelmas 1525: *LP, Addenda*, i, 477.

been assigned them as her jointure in 1510, in exchange for her inheritance from her father, Edward IV.[33]

Henry VIII authorized this magnificent gift early in 1515. The reason seems to have been his acceptance of Suffolk as his prospective brother-in-law. Before he had left for France in January to convey the king's congratulations to Francis I on his accession, Suffolk had spoken to Henry VIII of his wish to marry Henry's sister Mary, widowed by the death of Louis XII. Naturally, he had promised to do nothing without the king's knowledge and consent.[34] However, unwilling to wait while Henry VIII negotiated for the return of Mary's plate and jewels, Suffolk wrote to Wolsey on 5 March 1515 to confess that he had broken his promise: 'to by playn wyet you, I have mared her'.[35] Wolsey drafted a shocked letter in reply: Henry VIII had received the news with an incredulity shared by Wolsey himself, who had thought that 'wyld horsys' would not have induced Suffolk to fail the king 'wych hath browght yow up of nowgth' – amended to 'of low degre' – 'to be of thys gret honor'.[36] Nevertheless, Henry gave his assent to a private act of parliament, in the form of a petition from Suffolk, confirming the land grant and authorizing the duke to enter upon all the lands, not only those held by the king but also 'upon the possession of every other person and persons, and to be demed and juged in possession therof by th'auctoritie of this present parliament'. Any arrangements he had made or might make with existing patentees were confirmed.[37] With Wolsey ready to be helpful, the financial arrangements for the marriage were settled to the king's satisfaction in May and the couple celebrated a second wedding at Greenwich in the presence of the king and queen, which made it possible for Suffolk to claim, in his petition for an act of the autumn session of parliament assigning his wife's jointure, that it had pleased Princess Mary to marry him with 'your graciouse assent had and obteyned'.[38]

The terms of the gift to Suffolk, naming no manors except the two excluded from the grant, were at odds with letters patent issued on the same day, 1 February 1515, rewarding George Talbot, earl of Shrewsbury, for his services with the de la Pole manor of Walsham-le-Willows, Suffolk, in tail male.[39] Shrewsbury was already in possession

---

[33] SC11/837; *LP*, i(1), 520, 546 g.27, 632 g.63.

[34] SP1/10, f.77 (*LP*, ii(1), 224).

[35] SP1/10, f.71, BL, Cotton Calig. D.VI, ff.180–1 (*LP*, ii(1), 203, 222).

[36] SP1/10, f.77 (*LP*, ii(1), 224).

[37] 6 Henry VIII, c.20, introduced into the house of lords on 21 March 1515, already signed by the king: *LJ*, i, 36.

[38] *LP*, ii(1), 367, 436, 468; 7 Henry VIII, c.8.

[39] C82/415 (*LP*, ii(1), 93).

of this manor in Henry VII's reign, presumably holding for life or years, but by Michaelmas 1515 ownership had been transferred to the duke of Suffolk.[40] Henry VIII made one more grant to a nobleman in 1515: Thomas Grey, marquess of Dorset, received, for life, the reversion to the manors of Loughborough and Shepshed in Leicestershire, of viscount Beaumont's inheritance, part of the dowry assigned by the king to Beaumont's widow, the countess of Oxford.[41]

In the first seven years of his reign, therefore, Henry VIII restored some forfeited estates and gave lands for limited periods of time to a few noble families, but bestowed new estates of inheritance on two noblemen only, Suffolk, the friend who became his brother-in-law, and Norfolk, the victor of Flodden.

Estates of inheritance remained rare gifts for another 20 years, apart from a short period in the early 1520s. In 1516 William lord Willoughby de Eresby was rewarded for his services at the time of his marriage to one of the queen's Spanish attendants. He was given the reversion to three Lincolnshire manors of lady Oxford's dowry, to hold in tail.[42] The next year lord Dacre of the north, through Wolsey's influence, was granted nine tenements, including one in Carlisle, forfeited by Edward Skelton, and the lord chamberlain, Charles Somerset, earl of Worcester, received a messuage and lands in Kew, Surrey.[43] No more real property was given to any noblemen until February 1521, when Norfolk received for his services the manor of Sheldon, Warwickshire, with the revenues from Michaelmas 1513.[44] The manor (one of two in Sheldon) had descended for generations with the manor of Solihull, granted to the duke in 1514, and its allocation to Norfolk was evidently a supplement to the original gift.[45] Later in 1521 Henry Courtenay, earl of Devon, the king's cousin and a gentleman of the privy chamber, obtained his first grant: four manors in Middlesex to be held in tail male in reversion after Sir John and lady Peche.[46] The fall of the duke of Buckingham had by then opened the way to the second burst of liberality of the reign. Norfolk, who had presided over Buckingham's

---

[40] *The Field Book of Walsham-le-Willows 1577*, ed. K. M. Dodd, Suffolk Records Soc., xvii (Ipswich, 1974), pp. 15–16. BL, Harl. Ch. 56 G.52 records Shrewsbury's sale of the manor for 400 marks on 2 February 1515: information kindly provided by Mr Steven J. Gunn.

[41] C82/422 (*LP*, ii(1), 697).

[42] C82/436 (*LP*, ii(1), 2172).

[43] BL, Cotton Calig. B.II, f.347 (*LP*, ii(2), 3383); C82/451, 454 (*LP*, ii(2), 3563, 3769). Edward Skelton had been attainted in 1504: 19 Henry VII, c.34.

[44] C82/499 (*LP*, iii(1), 1164).

[45] *VCH, Warwickshire*, iv, 202–3.

[46] C82/510 (*LP*, iii(2), 1773). The lands were regranted to him as marquess of Exeter in April 1530 on his surrender of this patent: *LP*, iv(3), 6363 g.29.

trial, was given six of the duke's Norfolk manors for life in 1522, with
remainder to the earl of Surrey in tail male; the grant was rather oddly
said to be in consideration of the dangers which they had faced in
defence of the kingdom – presumably another reference back to
Flodden.[47] Surrey had not been on Buckingham's trial panel, but without exception the rest of the nobles gaining lands from his attainder at
common law had themselves pronounced him guilty of treason. Most
of the grants came in 1522. Charles Somerset, earl of Worcester, and
Henry Courtenay, earl of Devon, were granted one manor each
(Yalding, Kent, and Caliland, Cornwall, respectively).[48] Thomas
Grey, marquess of Dorset, received three manors in Warwickshire for
life, with remainder to his son for life – which the following year
he managed to get converted into a grant in tail male.[49] Charles
Brandon, duke of Suffolk, and his wife were granted five manors in
Suffolk in tail male.[50] Walter Devereux, lord Ferrers, benefited in-
directly from Buckingham's death when in 1524 he was rewarded for
his services with a manor which Henry Stafford, earl of Wiltshire, had
held of the duke.[51] Four years later he also received in tail male the
English manor of Penkelly, Brecon, forfeited by Buckingham, as a
reward for his services to Henry VIII and to Princess Mary, to whom
he was steward of the household.[52] Another noble beneficiary who had
sat in judgment on the duke of Buckingham was Henry Bourchier,
earl of Essex: he was given the manor of Bedminster, Somerset, in tail
male.[53]

Norfolk and Suffolk, Dorset, Worcester and Devon had all received
some form of land grant from Henry VIII before this. The king's
favour to them, being no new thing, may not have been entirely
unexpected in the aftermath of Buckingham's fall. Every nobleman on
the trial panel knew that the estates of convicted traitors provided the
crown with lands to keep or to distribute as it thought fit. No one
seems to have felt the procedure distasteful. The only concern of the
recipients of lands was to protect their legal title, should times change.
The outright gift of the de la Pole estates to the duke of Suffolk in 1515

[47] C82/520 (*LP*, iii(2), 2382).

[48] C82/515, 521 (*LP*, iii(2), 2214 g.12, 2482 g.1). The signed bill for the grant to
Worcester contains a deletion, suggesting that it originally included more than one
manor.

[49] C82/514, 533 (*LP*, iii(2), 2145 g.29, 3146 g.27).

[50] C82/534 (*LP*, iii(2), 3162). Charles Knyvet had hoped to obtain two of these
manors: *LP*, iii(1), 1289.

[51] C82/541 (*LP*, iv(1), 137 g.1).

[52] C82/602 (*LP*, iv(2), 4313 g.5).

[53] C82/514 (*LP*, iii(2), 2145 g.12).

had demonstrated Henry VIII's intention for that family: no reprieve was to be expected. The future of the Staffords was less clear. The parliament of 1523 which attainted the duke also authorized Henry VIII to reverse this and previous attainders by letters patent and restore those lands which at the time of restitution remained in the hands of the crown; only the heirs of Edmund de la Pole were excepted from this possible rehabilitation. The title of all those who had been granted any lands forfeited by attainder was specifically confirmed. Nevertheless, each nobleman who had received a grant of Buckingham's lands made doubly sure by attaching to the bill of attainder a separate proviso safeguarding it by name.[54] Henry VIII never restored Buckingham's son – his restoration (to a barony only) was left to the first parliament of Edward VI's reign – and by his land grants made it impossible for him to recover large parts of his inheritance. However, the king provided for him, his wife and mother by returning to them some of the duke's estates in a series of grants between 1522 and 1531.[55]

John Bourchier, lord Berners, the recently appointed deputy of Calais, took no part in Buckingham's trial. But when he heard that royal officials had entered upon lands which belonged to him under an exchange he had arranged with the duke years before, Berners appealed to the king by letter: 'withowtt your grase be good and grasyous lorde unto me yt shall be to myn undoynge . . . I trust I have nott deservyde nor never shall to lese eney part off my londe . . . I am her in your most grasious servys and can nott be ther wher as I myght speke and sew to your grase myselff.' However, he was ready to negotiate. Indeed, he made it clear that he would prefer to recover the lands which he had transferred to the duke in the exchange.[56] Berners made the last point again when he wrote to Wolsey for his support, and thanked the cardinal profusely when he was told that he was to have his own lands back again: 'withowtt your grasyous ffavore I shuld never [have] ateynyd therto.' Yet there remained one worry. 'I ensure your grase on my powr honeste that the londes that I had off the dukes ar better in valew then the londes that he had off myn.'[57] Berners further claimed that the exchange had been forced upon him by Buckingham and that the duke had not paid him the full sum agreed between them.[58] His

[54] 14 & 15 Henry VIII, cc.20, 21.

[55] LP, iii(2), 2554, recited in and confirmed by 14 & 15 Henry VIII, c.23; LP, v, 80 g.8, 364 g.29. Confirmation of the jointure assigned to the duchess by Wolsey's mediation: 14 & 15 Henry VIII, c.22.

[56] SP1/26, f.217 (LP, iii(2), 2730).

[57] SP1/24, ff.16, 114 (LP, iii(2), 2027, 2218).

[58] SP1/22, f.94 (LP, iii(1), 1288(7)).

persistence was eventually rewarded when, in 1528, he was also granted all the lands which Buckingham had assigned to him, with the revenues from September 1514, evidently the date of the exchange.[59]

Buckingham's attainder provided Henry VIII with a reservoir of land on which to draw but the spate of gifts was soon reduced once more to a trickle. The creation of Henry's illegitimate son as duke of Richmond in June 1525 was followed in August by a large grant to him.[60] But six other titles were bestowed on the same day, with only one land grant: Henry Courtenay, created marquess of Exeter, received the manor of Dartington, Devon, in support of his new dignity.[61] This was in addition to a favourable exchange which he made with the king. In March Courtenay had been assigned the reversion to the mansion of Coldharbour which Henry VIII now wanted for Richmond, presumably because the house had belonged to the king's grandmother, the countess of Richmond. Courtenay surrendered his patent in time for the grant to be made to Richmond in August 1525, and in return received in immediate possession the house in St Lawrence Poultney forfeited by the duke of Buckingham.[62] Thomas Howard, who had recently succeeded his father as duke of Norfolk, was also affected by Henry VIII's determination to provide for his son, in this case by the king's desire to make Richmond lord admiral, the office granted to Howard for life in 1513.[63] Norfolk duly surrendered his patent. At the same time he sold to the crown two manors which he had inherited from his father, Hunsdon and Eastwick in Hertfordshire. In return, Henry VIII gave him in tail male in July 1525 all the estates he had been granted in 1514 for his lifetime only.[64] The letters patent for the grant made no mention of the surrender and sale, but the terms of the agreement were set out in an indenture of 30 June 1526 between Henry VIII and Norfolk, in which the king also promised to confirm his grant of the previous year by act of parliament or otherwise at the duke's request.[65] When parliament met in 1529 this was done by a private act which rehearsed the whole transaction, stressing again a point made in the indenture, that the old duke had 'bestowed many great sommes of money uppon the

---

[59] C82/597 (LP, iv(2), 3991 g.15). For the manors exchanged see LP, iii(1), 1288(7) and Rawcliffe, The Staffords, p. 194.

[60] 22 Henry VIII, c.17, replacing letters patent, not enrolled, dated 11 August 1525.

[61] C66/647 (LP, iv(1), 1432).

[62] C82/563 (LP, iv(1), 1610 g.5), citing letters patent, not enrolled, dated 8 March 1525, giving Courtenay the reversion to Coldharbour.

[63] See above, p. 168.

[64] Foedera, vi(2), 19–20.

[65] C54/395.

buyldynges of the said manour of Hounesden'.[66] Norfolk was perhaps sorry to give up this manor, where he had sometimes lived, and may well have been reluctant to lose his office of lord admiral to a young boy, albeit the king's son; but he gained for his heirs an estate which he valued at £333 6s 8d p.a., the same amount that it had been worth when in the possession of the crown in the last year of Henry VII's reign.[67]

Exchanges so favourable as those with Exeter and Norfolk must be accounted as partial gifts, rewards for compliance with the king's wishes. From the 1520s exchanges became more common. One reason for this was the decision to reorganize the crown estates, grouping some of the lands into compact units and making them into honours.[68] It was for this purpose that Henry VIII had wanted Hunsdon. He enlarged the mansion to make it a royal palace to which he 'hathe great pleasure to resort for the helthe, comforte and preservacion of his moost royall person', as the act of parliament creating the honour of Hunsdon explained.[69] An exchange might be equally acceptable to both parties. Early in the reign, in March 1512, Thomas Grey, marquess of Dorset, acquired from the king the manor of Whitwick in Leicestershire which had belonged to viscount Beaumont, in return for three manors in Kent.[70] The reversion to two more of Beaumont's manors in Leicestershire (Loughborough and Shepshed), granted to the marquess for life in 1515, was converted in 1520 into a grant to the marquess and his wife in survivorship.[71] Finally, in 1527 these two manors were given to them in tail male, with Bardon park, in the same county, in exchange for the manors of Grafton and Hartwell, Northamptonshire, transferred to the king. Since the marquess could not enter at once on the Leicestershire manors, the king gave him an annuity of £82 out of the duchy of Lancaster until they became his either on the death of the countess of Oxford or upon Henry VIII somehow managing to 'gette the possession ... to the handes of the saied marques', when the annuity would go instead to the countess.[72]

[66] 21 Henry VIII, c.22.

[67] SP1/141, ff.86–9 (LP, xiii(2), 1215); SC11/837.

[68] The first sign of this policy was the act of 1523 annexing certain manors in Essex, forfeited by Buckingham, to the king's palace of Newhall, Essex, and establishing the combined estate as the honour of Beaulieu: 14 & 15 Henry VIII, c.18.

[69] The History of the King's Works, gen. ed. H. M. Colvin, 6 vols (London, 1963–82), iv(2), 154–6; 23 Henry VIII, c.30.

[70] LP, i(1), 1120, 1123 g.58.

[71] C82/422, 484 (LP, ii(1), 697, iii(1), 607).

[72] C82/589 (LP, iv(2), 3213 g.28); C54/396; DL42/22, f.95. This exchange replaced a more extensive one, agreed by indenture of 28 May 1525 (C54/394), which was annulled at the king's request.

The marquess of Dorset gained a full estate in two manors he was clearly anxious to obtain, in his home county; Henry VIII acquired Grafton, which he frequently visited and eventually converted into an honour, spending large sums of money on it in the early 1540s.[73]

Others were less fortunate. In a transaction confirmed by act of parliament in 1532 John lord Lumley agreed to give up five manors in Westmorland to the duke of Richmond and received in recompense not land, but an annuity of £50 from the abbot of Waltham which had been granted to Richmond the previous year.[74] The unwelcome news that Henry VIII wanted some of their property was forced upon two more noblemen early in 1532. Henry lord Scrope of Bolton was disturbed to learn that it was the king's pleasure to have the manor of Pisho, Hertfordshire, owned by his family since 1393, to add to the new honour of Hunsdon. Scrope inquired about suitable lands in exchange, but to his consternation was sent instead covenants for the sale of the manor. He followed up his immediate appeal to Cromwell by sending his servant to him with a secret promise of reward if Scrope obtained the lands he wanted in exchange.[75] Negotiations were still going on when Henry lord Scrope died in 1533, but his son continued the fight. As Edward Layton reported to Cromwell, John lord Scrope insisted that he had always understood that Pisho should only be surrendered in exchange for lands of equal value 'and as good, commodite for commodite'. He did not want to sell the manor 'for ony summe of money' since a 'greite summe off money withe hym wilbe shortely spennt and he and his heir hathe nothing to lyve apon butt only his inheritance'. However, according to Layton, he ended by proclaiming that he and all his possessions were 'att the kynges graces commawndement and pleissuire withe all his hartte'.[76] Although Cromwell's 'remembrances' included a note of lands appointed to lord Scrope for Pisho,[77] in the end Scrope had to accept the money. On 3 March 1534, probably on his arrival in London for the parliamentary session already under way, he signed an indenture selling Pisho and its park to the lord chancellor and others to the perpetual use of the king in return for the payment of £1,000. Because the feoffees were doubtful whether Scrope was yet 21, they insisted that he should do all that he could to get an immediate act of parliament confirming the sale.[78] A bill declaring the indenture as valid as it would have been had lord

---

[73] 33 Henry VIII, c.38; *The History of the King's Works*, iv(2), 92–4.
[74] 23 Henry VIII, c.28, amended by 25 Henry VIII, c.30.
[75] *LP*, v, 915, 916, 1015, vi, 43, 348.
[76] SP1/76, ff.30–1 (*LP*, vi, 453).
[77] *LP*, vii, 923 (xliii).
[78] E305/7/D64.

Scrope been of full age was introduced into the house of lords on 26 March and within two days had passed both houses; on 30 March Henry VIII gave it his assent.[79] The manor of Pisho was worth just over £46 p.a. in rents, so that the king obtained it for about the normal 20 years' purchase, although no valuation was made of the park – nearly 2 miles in compass – nor of the moated mansion and the stables for at least 20 horses.[80]

John Bourchier, lord Berners, got off comparatively lightly. He was only asked to give up a lease of Petty Calais, a property which Henry VIII had recently acquired by exchange with Westminster abbey.[81] Nevertheless, he, too, wrote in protest to Cromwell early in 1532. The house stood on marsh land and he had spent more than £100 on improving the drainage, as well as carrying out extensive repairs. Stationed in Calais, he might have made a profit of £10 p.a. by subletting the house, so great was the demand for accommodation in Westminster from lords spiritual and temporal and from merchants. He had chosen not to sublet; apart from the pleasure he took in the house with its gardens and grounds, without it, on his visits to London, 'I have never a howse to putt yn my hede'. All the same, like Scrope, he made the apparently necessary declaration of total sub-mission: 'the kynges grace may do as yt shall plese hym ffor all that I have ys and shall be at hys commandment.'[82] Some months later the terms had still not been agreed and Berners wrote again to Cromwell to know what recompense he should have. 'I ensure yow what so ever I shall have, yt woll do me mor goode now then twyse as mych at a longer leysure, and I know well by your good meanes I may the soner have an ende.' Cromwell had told him that he should be no loser. 'I know well all odyr that hath odyr londe or howssynge taken ffro them ar well rewardyd so that every man ys well content and I ensure yow ther ys no man that hath fforgoen so grett a plesure as I have done.'[83] Whether or not all those involved were as 'well content' as Berners chose to believe, Henry VIII by the end of 1532 had acquired the lands he wanted for his palaces of Whitehall and St James and for St James's park.[84]

The most extensive transfer of lands to the crown was, however, in a different category. In 1531 and 1535 the debts of Henry Percy, earl of

---

[79] *LJ*, i, 80–3; 25 Henry VIII, c.31.
[80] SC12/8/35.
[81] *LP*, v, 404.
[82] SP1/69, f.173 (*LP*, v, 857).
[83] SP1/70, f.209 (*LP*, v, 1219).
[84] *Survey of London*, xvi, *Charing Cross: The Parish of St Martin-in-the-Fields, Part 1* (London County Council, 1935), p. 1.

Northumberland, induced him to negotiate two sales to Henry VIII (the second amending the first) which left only his estates in Cumberland, Northumberland and Yorkshire in the earl's possession.[85] This should have ended his financial worries, but the character defects that had caused them remained to plague him and to undermine his relations with the king. Although his father was never allowed to become warden of the marches, he had been appointed warden of the east and middle marches as a very young man and later, as earl, held the office without a break between 1527 and 1537.[86] Henry VIII also made him sheriff of Northumberland for life in 1534.[87] The intention was evidently to underpin his authority as the natural leader of the region. It was frustrated by his wayward incompetence. The alternative policy was to remove his power altogether. Northumberland was persuaded to make Henry VIII the heir to all his lands. By act of parliament early in 1536 he assured his entire estate to the crown if he should die without heir of his body.[88] Childless and estranged from his wife, he died in June 1537 a few weeks after he had agreed to allow the king to take immediate possession of his inheritance. This final submission seems to have been forced upon him after the discovery of his acquiescence in Aske's takeover of Wressle castle during the pilgrimage of grace.[89] Robert Southwell soon sent Cromwell a lyrical report from Wressle. The Percy honours and castles 'purporten suche a maiestie in themselffes now beyng the kynges as they arr in maner as mirrors or glassez for the inhabitantes xx milez compasse every whay from them to loke yn and to direct themselffes by'.[90] Norfolk, more prosaically, pondered the future of the estates. Away in the north as the king's lieutenant he remarked early in May in letters to Cromwell and Henry VIII that he had no desire to stay there, even if he were to be given all Northumberland's lands. In July he reported that many had indeed urged him to ask for the lands so that he might reside there permanently.[91] If these were hints, they were ignored. In February 1538 Cromwell was appointed steward of all the lands north of the river Trent which had belonged to the earl.[92]

These sales to the crown came at a time when the king's grants to

[85] Bean, *The Estates of the Percy Family*, pp. 151–3.
[86] See above, pp. 188, 191–2.
[87] See above, p. 200.
[88] 27 Henry VIII, c.47.
[89] *LP*, xii(1), 1062, 1121, 1304 (misprinted 1804), xii(2), 19.
[90] SP1/24, ff.67–9 (*LP*, xii(2), 548).
[91] *LP*, xii(1), 1157, 1162, xii(2), 291.
[92] *LP*, xiii(1), 1520. As steward Cromwell had at his command 3,911 able men in Yorkshire, Northumberland and Cumberland: *LP*, xiv(2), 119.

the nobility were again concentrated on a very few families, as in the early years of the reign. Henry VIII made three grants in 1527, giving one manor each to George lord Hastings and Robert Radcliffe, viscount FitzWalter, two men he was to promote to earldoms in 1529, and the reversion to a hundred to the duke of Suffolk.[93] After that, until the dissolution of the monasteries in 1536, apart from his gift of one of Buckingham's manors to lord Ferrers, already mentioned, the king granted no land in tail to any noble families except to the beneficiaries of 1514–15, Howard and Brandon, and the new favourites, the Boleyns.

Norfolk was granted, in 1531, the priory of Felixstowe – which, with his formal consent, had been suppressed by Wolsey for his grammar school at Ipswich – and 15 manors in Suffolk, all forfeited by Wolsey.[94] Suffolk's grant came in 1535, ending 20 years of indebtedness to the crown. Two days before their second, public wedding at Greenwich, Mary and Charles Brandon had agreed to a bond for the payment of £24,000 to Henry VIII in annual instalments of £1,000. Eleven years later her debt still stood at nearly £20,000 while the duke owed the king more than £6,500 on his own account. It was agreed then that repayments should continue, but that Mary's debt would lapse on her death.[95] She died in 1533 and Suffolk claimed the remission of £20,000.[96] On 10 December 1535 Henry VIII released Suffolk from all his debts and granted him manors in Lincolnshire, which the king had just bought from the earl of Northumberland, and the reversion to the five manors in Suffolk granted to him and his wife in tail male in 1523, their son, the earl of Lincoln, having died in 1534.[97] However, the letters patent conceal the reality behind these grants: Suffolk paid for them (at least in part) in land, under the terms of two indentures made in July and December 1535.[98] He sold to the king a number of manors, mostly in Berkshire and Oxfordshire, including Donnington, granted to him in 1514, and Ewelme, another de la Pole manor, excluded from his grant of 1515 but granted to him later. The king was also to have the duke's London house, Suffolk Place in Southwark, after his death. In the event, Henry VIII was able to obtain the house early in 1536. The abbot of St Benet's, Hulme, about to be nominated bishop of Norwich, agreed to surrender all the lands of the bishopric to the

[93] C82/590, 594 (*LP*, iv(2), 3324 g.9, 3622 g.12); *LP*, iv(2), 3747 g.3.

[94] *LP*, iv(3), 5144; C66/656 (*LP*, v, 220 g.11).

[95] *LP*, ii(1), 436, iv(2), 2744.

[96] SP1/88, ff.103–4 (*LP*, vii, 1657).

[97] C82/705 (*LP*, ix, 1063 gg.5, 6, 7).

[98] Cited in act of parliament confirming the transactions: 27 Henry VIII, c.38. Original indenture of 10 December 1535: E305/7/D67.

crown.[99] The king assigned Suffolk the bishop's house, Norwich Place in the Strand, and took the duke's house for himself.[100] The complexity of the land exchanges makes it impossible to determine the balance of advantage. Henry VIII gained property which he found useful: he gave Suffolk Place to Jane Seymour on their marriage and made both Ewelme and Donnington into royal residences.[101] On the other hand, Suffolk was no doubt pleased to extend his landholding in Lincolnshire, a county opened to his dominance by his latest marriage, to his ward, the daughter and heiress of William lord Willoughby de Eresby.[102] The pardon of the duke's debts may have tipped the scales in his favour. The July indenture referred to the great sums of money which the king would forgo. No figure for the debt was mentioned, but Suffolk, when he petitioned for the pardon to be confirmed by act of parliament, made sure that it would be all-inclusive: under the terms of the act the duke and his heirs were released from all debts to the king 'from the begynnyng of the worlde'.[103]

The Boleyns were the family which advanced most rapidly in the early 1530s. Anne's father, Thomas Boleyn, earl of Wiltshire, received two grants in 1531. In February he was granted the manor and park of Henden alias Hethenden, Kent, which he already held for life by a grant of 1511.[104] In October he was granted 'le Posterne' and 'le Cage', two parks in Kent which had belonged to the duke of Buckingham; this grant was to the earl and his heirs male, with remainder to Anne.[105] In 1532 Henry VIII made his first land grants to Anne herself. As Dame Anne Rochford she was given two manors in Middlesex – Kempton and Hanworth – after Sir Richard Weston had surrendered his leases and Stephen Gardiner his reversionary interest.[106] As marchioness of Pembroke, the title bestowed on her in September 1532, she was given the earldom of Pembroke with five lordships or manors in Wales, one manor in Somerset, two in Essex and five in Hertfordshire, including Hunsdon and Eastwick.[107] Finally,

[99] 27 Henry VIII, c.45. The abbey's lands were transferred to the bishopric in replacement.

[100] 27 Henry VIII, c.39. Brandon's new house was renamed Suffolk Place.

[101] Grant to Jane Seymour cited in 28 Henry VIII, c.45. Ewelme was made into an honour by 32 Henry VIII, c.53, while 37 Henry VIII, c.18 authorized Henry to create the honour of Donnington, and other honours, by letters patent.

[102] Hodgett, *Tudor Lincolnshire*, p. 32.

[103] 27 Henry VIII, c.37.

[104] *LP*, i(1), 833 g.60; C82/638 (*LP*, v, 119 g.31).

[105] C82/648 (*LP*, v, 506 g.16). As Sir Thomas Boleyn he had been granted one of Buckingham's Essex manors in 1522: *LP*, iii(2), 2214 g.24.

[106] *LP*, v, 1139, g.32, 1207 g.7.

[107] C66/662 (*LP*, v, 1499 g.23).

as queen, she was in March 1534 allocated all the lands previously held by Katherine of Aragon and, in the following November, the manor of Pisho, recently bought by Henry VIII from the reluctant lord Scrope.[108] The next year Anne's brother, lord Rochford, was given the manor of South, Kent.[109]

Only one of the king's grants before 1536 was describe as a sale. In 1530 George Nevill, lord Bergavenny, was allowed to buy back, for 2,000 marks to be paid to the treasurer of the chamber, the manor of Birling, Kent, which he had been forced to sell to the king when he was under suspicion after the fall of the duke of Buckingham.[110] In July 1532 Norfolk also purchased land from the king, although the letters patent for the grant made no reference to any payment. Under an indenture of sale the duke of Norfolk bought the site of the suppressed priory of Snape, and four manors in Suffolk, forfeited by Wolsey.[111] Norfolk still owed £793 13s 5d for Snape in 1540, when the debt was taken into account in an exchange of lands between him and the king.[112] It may be that other noblemen, too, were expected to pay for the lands they received. Not all the grants were said to be in return for service, and even in the later 1530s payments for monastic lands were not invariably recorded in the letters patent making the grant.[113] No receipt book of the treasurer of the chamber survives which might include payments for land before the establishment of the court of augmentations.[114] But even if payment was sometimes made the distribution of Henry VIII's land grants in the years up to 1536 shows that any assignment of an estate of inheritance was an exceptional favour. Most of the recipients were close to the king. Not infrequently they had some pre-existing claim to the land – a reversionary interest, or a lease for years or life – which gave them the chance to press for a grant in fee. The relative abundance of letters of petition after the dissolution of the monasteries suggests that there had been little activity in pursuit of land grants before 1536, probably because for

[108] C82/680, 689 (*LP*, vii, 419 g.25, 1498 g.1).

[109] C82/692 (*LP*, viii, 632 g.13).

[110] C82/626 (*LP*, iv(3), 6363 g.1). Bergavenny had already paid half the purchase price.

[111] Grant to Norfolk and others to the sole use of Norfolk and his heirs: C66/661 (*LP*, v, 1207 g.37). Undated indenture on close roll for 24 Henry VIII (C54/401) and on patent roll, calendared among the undated grants: *LP*, vi, 418 g.3.

[112] E305/2/A42.

[113] Joyce Youings, *The Dissolution of the Monasteries*, Historical Problems: Studies and Documents, ed. G. R. Elton, no. 14 (London, 1971), p. 121.

[114] Richardson, *Tudor Chamber Administration*, Appendix iii lists the surviving account books. No payments were made into the exchequer: I am most grateful to Dr J. A. Alsop for this information, based on his study of all the tellers' rolls of the reign.

most noblemen there had been small hope of a successful suit. Arthur Plantagenet, viscount Lisle, was told by his London agent in November 1535 that he believed that there was nothing Lisle could ask of the king that would not be granted him – so long as it did not come out of the king's coffers. But he expected that, when Henry VIII proceeded to deal with the abbeys, Lisle would be granted one *in commendam*.[115]

Others besides John Husee appreciated the distinction between the crown estate and any new lands which might come into the king's hands, but few could read the king's mind with any certainty. Would he give away the lands or sell them, or keep them for his own use? In the four years from the beginning of 1536 to the end of 1539 a stream of letters revealed the lively interest of a number of noblemen. Petitioners for the lands supported their requests with persuasive reasons. Lisle himself felt aggrieved at having to foot the bill for entertaining official visitors to Calais. He made the point in a draft letter to Cromwell in May 1536, when his hopes turned momentarily towards the possessions of those now found guilty of 'most abhominable treasons'.[116] One of them, Henry Norris, had been Lisle's most helpful contact at court. It was through him – although he had also asked Cromwell's aid – that Lisle had in April obtained the king's licence to come over to Dover, which Henry VIII intended to visit early in May. The long desired permission seemed clear enough, although when Husee asked for it in writing the king replied that his word was sufficient: Norris could vouch for it.[117] The fall of Anne Boleyn put an end to the king's visit and to Lisle's planned meeting with him, which Husee had hoped would have enabled Lisle to make his own suit to the king for the grant of an abbey. So far, things had not gone well. Lisle had first suggested Beaulieu to Cromwell as a suitable abbey, sending the letter to William Popley, one of Cromwell's servants. Popley had replied on 22 February 1536 that no abbey of that size was likely to be suppressed; nevertheless, he promised that if the chance came he would act with diligence 'as your owne pore servaunt'. He thanked Lisle for the annuity he had sent him and added that he was sending back his letter to Cromwell: 'seyng no frute myght growe therby, me semethe best not to delyver the same.'[118] In March Lisle had written again to Cromwell 'to helpe me to sum olde abbey in myne olde days'. He explained that

[115] SP3/5, f.60, duplicate endorsed 19 November 1535, f.50 (*LP*, ix, 850), printed *The Lisle Letters*, ii, 483.
[116] SP3/2, f.113 (*LP*, x, 829), printed ibid., iii, 691a.
[117] SP3/2, f.132, SP3/4, f.39 (*LP*, x, 737, 738), printed ibid., 683, 684.
[118] SP3/6, f.110 (*LP*, x, 339), partially printed ibid., pp. 283–4.

he had written to the king 'to be good lorde unto me' and – taking up Husee's point – professed to be 'as lothe to axe any thinge oughte of his coffers as any creatures lyving . . . I have no trust but God, the kinge and you.'[119] In April he had instructed Husee to ask Henry Norris to offer £20 to the king for the gift of St Mary Magdalen's priory in Barnstaple for life: 'hit woll not be long owght of his graces handes.'[120] Whether or not Norris had had time to make the offer, it had come to nothing. Nor did Lisle have any success with his next request, handled by Sir John Russell. Although Russell claimed to have acted at once on receipt of Lisle's letter telling him of his suit to the king to remember him 'for somethyng lately in his handes by reason of these gentlemens deth', the king, reported Russell on 23 May, 'onswerd me that all thynges that were worthye for you were geven before he receyved your letters'.[121] A few weeks later one of lady Lisle's correspondents, Thomas Warley, advised her to come over to England on her own to sue for an abbey, as her husband could get no licence to leave his post. Although it would be expensive, 'it is a old sayeng, well is spent the peny that gettyth the pound'. He was convinced that 'now is the tyme to speke or never and the presence of a noble man or woman may do more then 1 xx[ti] ferefull solicitors'.[122]

Warley was right. It was not until Lisle himself was allowed a brief meeting with Henry VIII at Dover in July that he obtained the king's promise of a gift of lands worth 100 marks p.a.[123] Henry then 'hasted' him over to the chancellor of augmentations to arrange the details, a move which Lisle was later to regret.[124] Negotiations for the property – the priory of Frithelstock in Devon – were prolonged, with Rich insisting that the gift was to Lisle and his wife and the heirs of their bodies only (there were no children of the marriage).[125] 'He is full of dissimulacion', Husee exclaimed to lady Lisle in August 1536; 'he passyth all that ever I sywed unto'.[126] By September Husee was reminding lady Lisle of Rochford's words of warning about flatterers at court and recommending lord Lisle to write 'a gentill lettre' to Cromwell to get the priory granted to his heirs.[127] In February 1537

---

[119] SP3/2, f.133 (*LP*, x, 486), printed ibid., 653a.
[120] SP3/1, f.28 (*LP*, x, 708), printed ibid., 681.
[121] SP3/7, f.34 (*LP*, x, 943), printed ibid., 702.
[122] SP3/14, f.40 (*LP*, xi, 13), printed ibid., 737.
[123] SP1/240, f.38 (*LP*, *Addenda*, i, 1090), printed ibid., 753a.
[124] SP3/9, f.54 (*LP*, *Addenda*, i, 1142), printed ibid., 789.
[125] SP3/7, f.26 (*LP*, *Addenda*, i, 1152), printed ibid., 811.
[126] SP3/12, f.103 (*LP*, xi, 264), printed ibid., 753.
[127] SP3/11, f.79 (*LP*, xi, 467), printed ibid., 770; SP1/240, f.53 (*LP*, *Addenda*, i, 1100), printed ibid., 771.

Cromwell promised that Lisle's bill would be in the next batch of papers to be signed by the king.[128] But it was not until August 1537 that Husee was able to report that 'the best byll in ffee symple' had indeed been signed and Lisle was at last 'pryor and lorde' of Frithelstock.[129] Letters patent were issued in September rewarding Lisle for his service with a grant of the priory, worth some £10 p.a. more than the king's original gift, to be held by him and his wife with a remainder to his right heirs in perpetuity.[130]

After his initial disappointment over Beaulieu abbey, Lisle took no notice of Husee's advice to try for an abbey in Hampshire or Wiltshire or some such county near his home.[131] For other noblemen, however, the location of a monastic estate was of prime importance. Proximity often led to such close links with a religious house that a nobleman thought of himself as its 'founder' – a claim to a special relationship accepted by contemporaries, although it rarely accorded with the historical fact.[132] Thomas West, lord La Warre, was especially concerned about the fate of Boxgrove priory in Sussex, adjacent to his home at Halnaker. He was absent from the session of parliament that passed the act, but by 25 March 1536 he had heard that the smaller monasteries had been dissolved, although under the act the king might license some houses to continue. He wrote to Cromwell to ask for exemption for Boxgrove. He was its founder 'and there lyethe many of my aunsytorys and also my wyffys mother'. It housed his parish church and in it he had built 'a power chapell' to be buried in himself. He hoped that it might please the king, 'for the power servyce that I have doyn his highnes', to reprieve the house or to make it into a college. Nevertheless, if it was to be suppressed, he asked for the priory for himself.[133] Later, La Warre and his wife prepared a formal petition to Henry VIII for the church to remain 'unspoyled' as their parish church and the founder's lodging and other buildings to be allowed to stand. They offered to buy the church ornaments, the crops and cattle

---

[128] SP1/116, f.103 (*LP*, xii(1), 492), printed ibid., iv, 931.

[129] SP1/241, f.114 (*LP*, *Addenda*, i, 1245), printed ibid., 1000.

[130] C82/729 (*LP*, xii(2), 796 g.3), letters patent printed in translation ibid., iii, Appendix 4.

[131] SP1/104, f.49 (*LP*, x, 952), printed ibid., 703.

[132] Layton and Legh noted the founders of the religious houses they visited in the province of York and the bishopric of Coventry and Lichfield: *LP*, x, 364. The original founders, where known, are given in David Knowles and R. Neville Hadcock, *Medieval Religious Houses of England and Wales*, rev. edn (London, 1971).

[133] BL, Cotton Cleo. E.IV, f.280 (*LP*, x, 552), printed *Three Chapters of Letters*, pp. 119–20, and *Original Letters*, 2nd series, ii, 132–5. The church and La Warre's chantry are described in *VCH*, *Sussex*, iv, 146–7.

on the demesne lands and all the carts, ploughs and farm implements, and to pay the rent assessed by the king's surveyors for the demesne lands and four of the parsonages owned by the priory.[134] Cromwell wrote to the commissioners in La Warre's favour and when they dissolved the priory in March 1537 they sold him goods to the value of £125 13s 4d.[135] He was also allowed to buy the church and the founder's lodging and other houses for £10.[136] The following June the court of augmentations assigned him a 50-year lease of the house and site of the priory, together with the manor and rectory of Boxgrove, paying in rent the full £58 4s 5½d p.a. at which the commissioners had valued this part of the property.[137] Under the act setting up the court of augmentations leases for more than 21 years could only be granted by warrant from the king, so that this presumably represented the limit to which Henry VIII was prepared to go. But La Warre aspired to be the owner, not the lessee. He sought Cromwell's help in arranging an exchange. He offered to give Henry his moiety of the manor of Shepton Mallet, Somerset, to add to the moiety already held by the crown. Boxgrove was worth nearly £25 p.a. more than Shepton Mallet and he requested the king 'to geve the saide overplus to me and myn heires for the pore service I have don his grace'. But, if necessary, he was ready to make financial recompense for the difference in value or to add more lands to the exchange.[138]

In July 1538 La Warre prepared to entertain Henry VIII at Halnaker.[139] Whether or not he took the opportunity to discuss this matter with the king, by the end of the year any hope of royal favour was dashed. La Warre found himself being investigated for suspected involvement in a treasonable conspiracy with the marquess of Exeter and lord Montagu.[140] He was soon released from the Tower but had, on 22 December 1538, to give a bond of £3,000 (with help from friends) to appear before the king and council whenever called upon within the next year.[141] He prudently increased his annual fee to Cromwell a week later, raising it from £5 to £20.[142] It was Cromwell who obtained a warrant from the king for the cancellation of the bond

---

[134] SP1/113, f.191 (*LP*, xi, 1468).

[135] BL, Cotton Cleo. E.IV, f.281 (*LP*, xii(1), 747), printed *Three Chapters of Letters*, pp. 120–1.

[136] Reference in survey of 1539: SC12/15/54.

[137] E315/209, f.101 (*LP*, xiii(1), 1520). Valuation in SC11/647.

[138] SP1/114, f.1 (*LP*, xii(1), 2).

[139] *HMC, Third Report*, p. 217.

[140] See above, p. 132.

[141] *LP*, xiii(2), 1117.

[142] *LP*, xiv(2), 782 (pp. 320, 324–5, 327).

in November 1539.[143] But La Warre's troubles were not over. In the midst of the negotiations for the cancellation of the bond lady La Warre heard from Cromwell that the king wanted Halnaker. It was land of her inheritance, but she put up no resistance. She asked only that she and her husband might have reasonable time to depart, and that the land they would receive in exchange might be as good.[144] Lord La Warre understood that he was free to 'loke wher I cowde ffynde any land in any countre that lay mete for me'. He asked Cromwell to help him to obtain the nunnery of Wherwell in Hampshire, within 20 miles of his birth place; he had heard that it was 'but a resonable howse for to dwell in'. It was worth, he believed, £40 p.a. more than Halnaker, but he would make up the difference in land or money.[145] In March 1540 the exchange was agreed. La Warre was granted the nunnery of Wherwell and eight manors in Hampshire, paying an annual rent of £137 3s 8d, and gave up to Henry VIII his lease of Boxgrove priory as well as the manors of Halnaker and Walberton, the parks of Halnaker and Goodwood, and all his lands in this part of Sussex.[146] The exchange was confirmed by act of parliament later in 1540; another act of the same session created the honour of Petworth and annexed the king's newly acquired estates to it.[147]

The act of dissolution explicitly rejected any special claim to monastic property by 'suche as pretende to be foundours, patrons or donours' of religious houses, but the message fell on uncomprehending ears. Henry Bourchier, earl of Essex, like La Warre, wrote to Cromwell directly the act was passed. He asked Cromwell to remind the king that 'the lyttell house of Byleygh, wherof I was fownder, lyethe interly and hole within my lande'. He would give 1,000 marks to Henry VIII 'yf yt maye pleas the kynges grase to geve yt me as peassably as yt ys his', promising that it would never again be a house of religion. Cromwell's 'paynes' would be 'so lokkyd on that I truste ye schalbe pleasyde'. He hoped that his 'poure servys' to Henry VIII might be rewarded in this way.[148] He was disappointed. In January 1537 Beeleigh abbey in Essex was leased to John Gates; in 1540, four months after the earl's death, Gates was able to convert the lease into ownership, buying the house and site of the monastery for £300.[149]

---

[143] *LP*, xiv(2), 543, 619 g.45.

[144] SP1/154, f.142 (*LP*, xiv(2), 481).

[145] SP1/154, f.187, SP1/155, f.3 (*LP*, xiv(2), 544, 547).

[146] C82/764 (*LP*, xv, 436 g.72). Valuation in SC12/15/54.

[147] 32 Henry VIII, cc.74, 56 (*LP*, xv, 498).

[148] SP1/102, f.244 (*LP*, x, 531). The earl's grandparents were buried in the abbey: *VCH, Essex*, ii, 175.

[149] *LP*, xiii(1), 1520, xv, 942 g.71.

Edward Stanley, earl of Derby, turned not to Cromwell but to the treasurer of the household, Sir William FitzWilliam, for action to save the church at Burscough priory, Lancashire, founded by his ancestors, and their burial place. If possible, he also wanted FitzWilliam to get him the priory, which was adjacent to his manor of Lathom and already suppressed.[150] The church was not reprieved, and the king made no grant to Derby, who obtained only a lease of the lands from the duchy of Lancaster. It was not until after the death of Henry VIII that he was able to acquire the site and demesnes of the priory by purchase from Sir William Paget, to whom they were granted in May 1547.[151]

At least two noblemen had resorted to direct action before the act of dissolution was passed. Edward lord Grey of Powis bought the Cistercian abbey of Strata Marcella in Powisland, Montgomeryshire, from the abbot and convent. He sent the indenture of sale to Cromwell and obtained a promise of support. When he discovered, in October 1536, that officers of the court of augmentations were nevertheless coming to survey the abbey to the king's use, he wrote at once to Cromwell, who instructed the commissioners to permit him to occupy it since he had bought it and taken possession 'before the makyng of the act'.[152] William Stumpe, one of the commissioners, later reported to the chancellor of augmentations that 'the howse is gretly in dekey ... for the late abbott went away owt of his howse long before the howse was suppressid'. However, he added, 'the demeynes be the best in Walis ... ther is no better pastures'.[153] The act of dissolution invalidated grants fraudulently made by religious houses within the previous year, and Grey may have left his purchase too late, although he did, in 1540, produce a statement of receipts since Michaelmas 1534.[154] At all events, his claim to ownership was not in the end accepted and in December 1545 he was given a formal lease of the property for 21 years by the court of augmentations.[155] The duke of Norfolk occupied two religious houses before the act of dissolution, at Bungay and Woodbridge in Suffolk. The nuns of Bungay had all left, he recorded, and as founder he had taken over in November 1535; the following January

[150] *Correspondence of Edward, Third Earl of Derby, during the years 24 to 31 Henry VIII*, ed. T. N. Toller, Chetham Soc., new series 19 (Manchester, 1890), pp. 128–30.

[151] *VCH, Lancashire*, iii, 259.

[152] SP1/108, f.227, SP1/109, f.195 (*LP*, xi, 795, 875).

[153] E318/18/897.

[154] *LP*, xvi, 97.

[155] *LP*, xxi(1), 1538. For examples of formal leases granted long after the tenancy had begun see *Devon Monastic Lands: Calendar of Particulars for Grants 1536–1558*, ed. Joyce Youings, Devon and Cornwall Record Soc., new series, i (Torquay, 1955), p. xii.

the canons of Woodbridge surrendered their house to him.[156] But he had not moved early enough at either place, and was reduced to making the most of the fact that 'I never fownd fawte at the relacion of the seid act to the first day of Marche was xii[th] moneth, wiche hath plukked my lawfull interest clerely away'. Before the end of May 1536 he wrote to Cromwell to ask him to remind the king of this. He believed that Henry was about to 'appoynt suche howsis of religion as his plesure shalbe to appoynt to me' and appealed for Cromwell's help, 'if ye shalbe at the seyd appoyntyng'. Away from the court, he was at a disadvantage: 'wher other men spare not to speke for themselffes and I may not, I pray you be my sheld.'[157] He relied entirely on Cromwell. 'I have at no tyme laboured to the kynges maieste nor to none others but only to you, nor woll not', he declared in September. He was waiting for news of Cromwell's progress in the suit for Bungay and Woodbridge – waiting with growing impatience, 'for the tyme of sowyng is at hande, and every other noble man hath allredy his porcion'.[158] Norfolk was exaggerating but more was at stake than material possessions. His prestige was involved, and in another letter he reiterated his plea to Cromwell: 'I know no noble man but hath their desires, and if I shall now dawnse alone, my bak frends shall rejoyse therat.'[159]

Norfolk had in fact actually lost property to the crown in 1536. By an act of the last session of the Reformation parliament he had agreed to give up to Henry VIII his manor of Imworth alias Imbercourt, Surrey, which was near Hampton Court and 'very commodyous and pleasaunt' for the king. In return he received the advowsons of four parish churches in Suffolk which had been granted to the prior of Thetford in 1534 at his suit and on the understanding that the duke himself should make the presentation at every vacancy and receive all the issues of the property. Norfolk gained virtually nothing from the exchange, therefore, and now had to pay tenths to the crown.[160] In early summer his lands in Ireland, together with those of all absentee landlords, were confiscated by act of the Irish parliament.[161] Norfolk

---

[156] SP1/104, f.252 (*LP*, x, 1236).

[157] SP1/103, f.60 (*LP*, x, 599). The letter was written before Norfolk's appointment as chief steward of the lands of suppressed monasteries south of Trent on 26 May 1536.

[158] SP1/106, f.157 (*LP*, xi, 434).

[159] SP1/106, f.173 (*LP*, xi, 458).

[160] 27 Henry VIII, c.33. Norfolk had bought the manors of Imbercourt and Sheffield, Sussex, which together were worth £82 a year: SP1/141, ff.86–9 (*LP*, xiii(2), 1215).

[161] 28 Henry VIII, c.3 in *The Statutes at Large, passed in the Parliaments held in Ireland*, 8 vols (Dublin, 1765–99), i, *1310–1612*.

had to wait until 1537, but then he received three grants. In May he was granted the priory of Coxford, Norfolk, with lands in the county which had belonged to it or to other religious houses, valued in all at £230 14s 1½d p.a., with the issues since 4 February 1536. He was to pay an annual rent of £30 14s 1½d. Although no reason for the grant was given in the letters patent, Norfolk later included in a note of his income £200 p.a. 'of suppressed lands yevon by the kinges highnes'; it was almost certainly a gift in recompense for the loss of his Irish lands.[162] In December 1537, after a visit to court in October, when he attended the christening of Prince Edward, Norfolk received two separate grants: the nunnery of Bungay, its issues also backdated to the opening day of the parliamentary session which dissolved the monasteries, and the priory of Castleacre, Norfolk. The last grant differed from the others in being described as a reward for his service.[163] Unlike the others, too, it went through very rapidly, with Cromwell's help. Castleacre was a cell of the priory of Lewes, Sussex, which came into the king's hands on 22 November 1537, the first of the larger houses to be voluntarily surrendered to the crown.[164]

For all their anxiety, Norfolk and Lisle could in the end count themselves among the fortunate minority who were given lands. However, others nearer to the centre of power were favoured with more dispatch as the lands of the smaller monasteries were distributed in 1536 and 1537. The first nobleman to benefit was Sir Edward Seymour, rewarded for his services on 7 June 1536, two days after his creation as viscount Beauchamp. Henry VIII gave him some 18 monastic manors in Wiltshire and the priories of Easton and Farleigh in the same county. By another grant of the same date the king gave him three non-monastic manors in Wiltshire. No valuation was put on either grant, and Beauchamp got an act of the parliament which opened on 8 June declaring the letters patent to be as valid 'as though the certenty of the sayd manors and all other the premysses . . . hadde bene found by offyce or inquisicyon after the course and forme of the lawe of this realme, by verdytt of xii men'.[165] But the monastic grant had been unduly rushed. Two of the manors given to Beauchamp – Urchfont and All Cannings – were described in the letters patent as belonging to the abbey of St Mary, Winchester, lately dissolved. Two months later the abbey was exempted from suppression; however, the grant of the manors was again confirmed.[166] Another act of the

[162] C82/725 (*LP*, xii(1), 1330 g.26); SP1/141, ff.86–9 (*LP*, xiii(2), 1215).
[163] C82/733 (*LP*, xii(2), 1311 gg.24, 30).
[164] *LP*, xii(2), 1119. For Cromwell's help see below, p. 237.
[165] C82/713 (*LP*, x, 1256 gg.5, 6); 28 Henry VIII, c.25.
[166] *LP*, xi, 385 g.20.

parliament of June 1536 gave to Beauchamp a house with a garden and 8 acres of land at Kew, forfeited by Henry Norris.[167]

Two men were ennobled during this parliament – Walter Hungerford and Thomas Cromwell – and John Bourchier, lord FitzWarin, was raised to an earldom. Only Cromwell received a grant of lands. Created lord Cromwell in July, in his last weeks as a commoner he was given the manor of Wimbledon which came to form part of his title.[168] The manor had come into the king's hands early in 1536 by an act of parliament assuring to the crown the manors of Wimbledon and Mortlake, Surrey, surrendered by the archbishop of Canterbury in exchange for a dissolved priory in Kent.[169] An act of the new parliament extended the lands given up by the archbishop to include the manor of Burstow, Surrey, and gave all three manors – Wimbledon, Mortlake and Burstow – to 'Thomas Crumwell esquyre', together with the manors of North Elmham and Beetley, Norfolk, out of the former possessions of the bishopric of Norwich. Cromwell was to hold these lands by fealty only, free of tenths or any other charge.[170]

The celebration of the king's fresh start in matrimony was marked not only by the creation of peerage titles but also by gifts of land to three noblemen in reward for their services. The king's chamberlain, William lord Sandys, received a grant which was partly by gift and partly by exchange. He gave up his manor of Chelsea, valued at £53 p.a., and received the priory of Mottisfont, Hampshire, with 15 manors, valued in all at £171 2s 9d p.a., on which the rent reserved for tenths was £51 p.a.[171] The transaction had already been confirmed by act of the parliament then in session.[172] Sandys quickly visited the priory and acknowledged Cromwell's help in securing the gift from the king; work was soon in hand, under his supervision, to convert the house into a fine residence, which he apparently intended to make his home.[173] The great chamberlain, John de Vere, earl of Oxford, whose possessions included the honour of Castle Hedingham and the manor of Earls Colne, Essex, was given the two priories of Castle Hedingham

---

[167] 28 Henry VIII, c.26.

[168] Although the warrant under the privy seal of 8 July, delivered 9 July, gave Cromwell 'nomen et stilum baronis Crumwell', John Husee on 8 July reported his creation as lord Cromwell of Wimbledon and it was under this title that he took his seat in the lords on 18 July: C82/714 (*LP*, xi, 202 g.14); *The Lisle Letters*, iii, 742; College of Arms, 2 H.13, f.398v, printed GEC, ix, Appendix B.

[169] 27 Henry VIII, c.34.

[170] 28 Henry VIII, c.50.

[171] C82/714 (*LP*, xi, 202 g.29), privy seal dated 14 July.

[172] 28 Henry VIII, c.35, confirming the conveyance of Chelsea to the king by Sandys by deed dated 28 May and Henry VIII's grant to him by letters patent dated 27 June.

[173] SP1/105, f.253 (*LP*, xi, 241); SP3/10, f.3 (*LP*, xiii(2), 176), printed *The Lisle Letters*, v, 1209.

and Earls Colne – genuinely founded by his ancestors – and lands to the total value of £160 p.a. He was to pay £66 p.a. for tenths and rent.[174] Robert Radcliffe, earl of Sussex, received the priory of Little Dunmow – of which he was the patron – in his home county of Essex in a grant valued at £121 14s 0d. A reserved charge of £21 14s 0d p.a. for tenths reduced the annual value of the gift to £100.[175]

Henry VIII seems generally to have thought in terms of gifts worth a certain sum of money, often 100 marks or £100 a year. The recipient made the selection of the actual property, subject to the agreement of the court of augmentations whose officials worked out the 'tenth' payable on all monastic land alienated by the crown. This was frequently much more than the exact tenth part of the annual value of the land.[176] Any property could in this way be brought within the limits of the king's generosity. It was indeed to the advantage of the recipient to choose a valuable estate, even though it meant paying a large reserved rent. The rent might eventually be remitted: for example, the £51 p.a. charged on the grant to Sandys was given to him as an annuity in 1540.[177] Even if it were not, as the value of money fell the passage of time reduced the burden for the landowner. Naturally, noblemen knew best the properties with which they already had some connection. Thomas Manners, earl of Rutland, rewarded for his services in September 1536, chose the priory of St James, Warter, in Yorkshire, of which he was founder. It was valued at £187 14s 0d p.a.; the tenth was high, £121 2s 6d p.a., leaving him with a gift worth a few pence short of 100 marks p.a.[178] Two months later Henry Courtenay, marquess of Exeter, surrendered to the king an annuity of 100 marks which he and his wife had been granted in 1519. He accepted in exchange, and in reward for his services, the priory of Breamore, Hampshire, with all its possessions in England, paying for it an annual rent of £16 15s 7½d.[179] Breamore manor already belonged to him and the priory, valued in 1535 at nearly £155 p.a., was a convenient as well as a sizeable acquisition for the marquess and his heirs.[180] Nevertheless, the grant was something of an embarrassment. It was in response to the reproaches of his friends that Exeter apparently defended

[174] C82/714 (*LP*, xi, 202 g.45); *VCH, Essex*, ii, 102, 122.

[175] C82/714 (*LP*, xi, 202 g.36); *VCH, Essex*, ii, 153.

[176] Youings, *The Dissolution of the Monasteries*, pp. 118, 120–1.

[177] *LP*, xv, 1032. In May 1546 commissioners were authorized to sell the reserved rents on all grants made since 27 Henry VIII: *LP*, xxi(1), 970 g.4.

[178] C82/716 (*LP*, xi, 519 g.1); *LP*, x, 364.

[179] C82/718 (*LP*, xi, 1217 g.6).

[180] *VCH, Hampshire*, iv, 597; *Valor Ecclesiasticus* [ed. J. Caley and J. Hunter], 6 vols (London, 1810–34), ii, 18.

himself by declaring that he had only accepted church land in compensation for his forced surrender of the office of constable of Windsor.[181]

Henry VIII rewarded two noblemen with grants of land worth £100 p.a. in 1537. Henry Somerset, earl of Worcester, obtained Tintern abbey and lands in South Wales valued at £188 3s 10d p.a., paying an annual rent of £88 3s 10d.[182] Three months later he was in residence at Tintern.[183] Thomas lord Cromwell received the priory of Michelham and lands in Sussex valued at £171 4s 4½d p.a., paying an annual rent of £71 4s 4½d.[184] The king at the same time gave George Talbot, earl of Shrewsbury, lands worth £200 p.a. after payment of the reserved rent, but this grant – which brought Shrewsbury the abbey of Rufford, Nottinghamshire, and the lordship of Rotherham, Yorkshire – was in recompense for the earl's Irish lands, taken over by the crown.[185] Henry VIII rewarded Edward Seymour, viscount Beauchamp, in August 1537 with another gift of lands in Wiltshire, including the priory of Maiden Bradley. The grant was valued at £159 11s 11d p.a. and the annual rent demanded was only £16, the statutory tenth.[186] In October, when Seymour was created earl of Hertford, he surveyed his financial position and noted that Henry VIII had given him lands worth in all £604 p.a. – more than the value of the lands (£450 p.a.) which he had inherited from his father.[187] He received no further gift on his elevation to the earldom, but the lord admiral, Sir William FitzWilliam, was exceptionally well rewarded for his services the day before his creation as earl of Southampton. The king gave him lands valued at £264 16s 5d p.a., on which the rent was £28 4s 9d p.a. The grant included two religious houses in Sussex, the priory of Shulbred and the abbey of Durford.[188]

Henry VIII made a number of other grants in 1537 which were prefaced only by the unrevealing formula *de gratia nostra ac ex certa sciencia ac mero motu*. The two to Norfolk have already been mentioned. Charles Brandon, duke of Suffolk, also received two such grants, both in April: of the castle and lordship of Tattershall, Lincolnshire, which had escheated to the crown on Richmond's death, and the Suffolk monasteries of St Mary, Leiston, and St Peter, Eye. No valuation was put on either grant; the duke was to pay £136 8s 10d p.a., for the

[181] See above, p. 203.
[182] C82/722 (*LP*, xii(1), 795 g.16).
[183] Letter dated at Tintern: *LP*, xii(2), 158.
[184] C82/731 (*LP*, xii(2), 1008 g.3).
[185] C82/731 (*LP*, xii(2), 1008 g.9).
[186] C82/728 (*LP*, xii(2), 617 g.1).
[187] SP1/125, f.96 (*LP*, xii(2), 804).
[188] C82/731 (*LP*, xii(2), 1008 g.19).

monastic properties.[189] Tattershall became one of his chief residences, but he sold the monasteries to the crown in December 1538.[190] Henry VIII granted the abbey of Buildwas, Shropshire, with lands in Shropshire, Derbyshire and Staffordshire, to Edward lord Grey of Powis for an annual rent of £55 8s 8d.[191] The rent was remitted from April 1546 in return for his service and for the manor of Cottingham, Yorkshire, sold to the crown.[192] William lord Sandys received the manor of Empshott, Hampshire, forfeited by Robert Aske.[193] No evidence has been found suggesting that any one of these grants was in reality a sale. Admittedly, the early records of the treasurer of the augmentations were not kept with perfect accuracy. His first enrolled account supposedly recorded receipts from the sale of lands from the establishment of the court up to Michaelmas 1538; in fact, its three references to lands purchased by noblemen refer either to sales agreed after that date, in December 1538 and January 1539, or to a payment made in February 1539.[194] On the other hand, no items are known to be missing from this account. No discrepancy appears between the evidence of chancery warrants or letters patent and that of the record kept by augmentations. No receipt of money has been found for any grant not described as a sale. It seems reasonable to conclude that these grants, although ambiguously described, were in fact gifts.

As the larger monasteries began to fall and their lands to be distributed, the letters patent more consistently gave the reason for the grants to noblemen: for service, for money or in exchange, or for a combination of these.[195] From the beginning of 1538 to the end of the reign only two grants to noblemen – one to Cromwell, the other to his son – cited no specific reason. The first gave Thomas lord Cromwell in July 1538 lands which had never belonged to the church: the manor of Langham, Rutland, which Henry Norris had held for life, and the manor and castle of Oakham in the same county, with three manors in Northamptonshire and one in Leicestershire, which had returned to the crown on the natural expiry of a life-grant.[196] Cromwell had earlier in 1538 been rewarded for his services with a grant of the priory of Lewes, Sussex. Its many possessions, mostly in Sussex, and those of its

---

[189] C82/723 (*LP*, xii(1), 1103 gg.5, 11).

[190] *LP*, xiii(2), 1182 g.18.

[191] C82/728 (*LP*, xii(2), 411 g.13).

[192] C82/850 (*LP*, xxi(1), 716 g.12).

[193] C82/732 (*LP*, xii(2), 1150 g.1).

[194] E323/1/Pt 1, mm.5d, 6d, 7.

[195] The stated reasons are still not consistently included in the calendared entries in *LP*.

[196] C82/742 (*LP*, xiii(1), 1519 g.2).

cell, Castleacre, were all given to him, wherever they were – except those in Norfolk. No valuation was put upon the grant; the annual rent payable was nearly £78.[197] Cromwell and the duke of Norfolk therefore divided the possessions of Lewes priory between them. (At the partition, agreed between them on 1 December 1537, Norfolk was apparently expected to give Cromwell a Sussex manor and all his lands in Lewes.[198] This was presumably his payment for Cromwell's part in securing the grant for him.) Two other noblemen who, like Cromwell, had already been rewarded with land received further gifts in 1538. The king gave the abbey of Muchelney, Somerset, with all its lands in Somerset, Devon and Dorset to Edward Seymour, earl of Hertford, in January, when the abbot surrendered the property to the crown. The 'tenth' was set at £44 14s 6d p.a.[199] Robert Radcliffe, earl of Sussex, was rewarded for his services against the northern rebels with the manor of Cleeve, Somerset, including the rent from the abbey, which had already been leased out for 21 years. The grant was valued at £109 14s 8½d p.a. and the earl was to pay £33 14s 8½d p.a. for it.[200]

George Talbot, earl of Shrewsbury, also received an outright gift in 1538: the priory and chapel of Flanesford, Herefordshire, valued at £14 11s 4d p.a. The tenth was to be paid only until the earl had founded a chantry on the site of the priory.[201] Henry FitzAlan, lord Mautravers, son and heir of the earl of Arundel, was a peer in his own right since his summons to parliament in 1533. He was rewarded for his service by a grant of the priory of Tortington, Sussex, which he already held on a 21-year lease from the court of augmentations. In future he was to pay the crown a rent of £2 1s 4d p.a. instead of the £20 13s 4d p.a. due under the lease.[202] Ralph Neville, earl of Westmorland, was granted the manor of Rosedale, Yorkshire, which had belonged to Rosedale priory, and the priory of Keldholme, of which he was founder, in the same county. The property was valued at £90 15s 9d p.a. and the annual rent was £24 2s 5d. The earl was given the issues backdated to 25 March 1536.[203] Henry VIII had in fact promised him monastic lands worth 100 marks p.a. soon after the first act of dissolution; by July 1536 Westmorland was already reminding Cromwell that he had agreed to try to get the allocation raised to

---

[197] C82/735 (*LP*, xiii(1), 384 g.74).

[198] *LP*, xii(2), 1154.

[199] C82/734 (*LP*, xiii(1), 190 g.41).

[200] C82/733 (*LP*, xiii(1), 190 g.42). The patent was surrendered and a new one issued in March 1542: *LP*, xvii, 220 g.84.

[201] C82/741 (*LP*, xiii(1), 1309 g.12).

[202] C82/736 (*LP*, xiii(1), 646 g.68).

[203] C82/742 (*LP*, xiii(1), 1519 g.29).

£100 p.a.[204] On 7 November 1536 Henry had written to the earl
promising that his loyalty in face of the rebels would be kept 'in suche
wise in our remembrance that you shall have good cause to reioyse
therof'.[205] Lengthy negotiations followed to settle the details of the
grant, and Westmorland expressed his gratitude to Cromwell when his
'olde suyte' at last went through. He made no mention of the fact that
it was worth exactly 100 marks p.a. and no more.[206]

After this grant, issued in July 1538, the king's liberality suddenly
ceased. The fact did not go unremarked. John Husee, when the larger
monasteries had started to 'goo downe' late in 1537, had been hopeful
that something more would come his master's way; early in 1538 his
new year's wish for Lisle had been 'an abby *in commendam* to your
pryory'.[207] But by the end of September he had to advise Lisle that
there was no use suing to the king for any abbey, 'for his grace wylbe
the doer himselff in the suppresment, and wyll part ffrom none of
theym at anny sywt or otherwisse'.[208] Henry had even stopped giving
long leases to noblemen. In 1536 and 1537, besides assigning the lease
of Boxgrove priory to La Warre, he had rewarded the service of
Thomas lord Burgh with the gift of Louth Park abbey in Lincolnshire
for life, rent free, and leased Legbourne priory in the same county to
Cromwell for 80 years, manors in Suffolk which had belonged to the
see of Norwich to Charles duke of Suffolk for 40 years and St Agatha's
abbey in Yorkshire to John lord Scrope of Bolton for 30 years.[209] Then
the king had called a halt. But in March 1539 – at the same time as he
created three new peerages – Henry VIII resumed his gifts of land to
noblemen. He gave the duke of Suffolk Revesby abbey, Lincolnshire,
with lands in the county and the city of Lincoln which had belonged to
it; the duke noted later that it was worth nearly £350 p.a.[210] Besides a
life interest in other lands which were ultimately to go to Suffolk, the
duke of Norfolk was rewarded for his service with the Franciscan friary
in Norwich, to hold in free burgage and fealty, paying no rent.[211]
Norfolk had petitioned the king for this property before the surrender
of the house the previous autumn. He was its founder and the warden

[204] SP1/105, f.187 (*LP*, xi, 178).

[205] SP1/111, f.3 (*LP*, xi, 1003).

[206] SP1/130, f.143, SP1/134, f.188 (*LP*, xiii(1), 605, 1402).

[207] SP1/127, ff.61–2 (*LP*,xii(2), 1209), printed *The Lisle Letters*, iv, 1038; SP1/128, f.29
(*LP*, xiii(1), 24), printed ibid., v, 1086.

[208] SP3/4, f.94 (*LP*, xiii(2), 434), printed ibid., 1233.

[209] E315/209, ff.1v, 7, 101, E315/210, f.14v, E315/232, f.15 (*LP*, xiii(1), 1520).

[210] C82/750 (*LP*, xiv(1), 651 g.58); SP1/141, ff.192–3 (*LP*,xiii(2), 1269). Other
grants to Suffolk in March 1539 and in December 1538 were in return for lands sold to
the king: *LP*, xiii(2), 1182 g.18, xiv(1), 651 gg.45, 57.

[211] C82/750 (*LP*, xiv(1), 651 gg.31, 57).

had offered to give it up to him personally, but the duke had assured Cromwell that he meant to take the surrender to the king's use, not his own, to avoid giving a bad example to other founders. In the event, his son took the surrender, leaving Norfolk's servants in charge of the house.[212] A third nobleman received a gift described as a reward in March 1539, but in this instance the description is misleading. The lord chancellor, Thomas lord Audley of Walden, had as a commoner been generously rewarded for his service in May 1538 with Walden abbey, Essex, and all its possessions.[213] On 31 March 1539 the king added to this the manor of Walden, parcel of the duchy of Lancaster.[214] However, two days later, in recompense, Audley sold to the king two manors in Hertfordshire which he covenanted to be of the annual value of £98 7s 5½d.[215]

Of the three men ennobled in March 1539 – Paulet, Russell and Parr – only Russell was given lands. His grant was not issued until 4 July, the day on which he was appointed steward of the duchy of Cornwall in succession to the attainted marquess of Exeter. The gift – described as being for certain unspecified considerations and for his service – was exceptionally large and was clearly intended to fit him to replace the marquess as the leading landowner in the west country. It included Tavistock abbey, with the borough of Tavistock, Dunkeswell abbey and the Black Friars in Exeter, with much other property in Devon and some lands in Cornwall and Somerset. In all, the grant was worth about £1,000 p.a. For it Russell was to pay £284 5s 11d p.a. in rent.[216] In October 1539, and for the same stated reasons, Henry VIII gave him in addition the manor of Cary Fitzpaine, Somerset, which had belonged to the marquess of Exeter, but Russell obtained a licence to alienate it four months later.[217] In order to provide him with a house near the palace of Westminster, Henry also assented to an act of parliament asigning to Russell the bishop of Carlisle's place without Temple Bar in exchange for his mansion at Chiswick, which was to go to the bishop of Rochester.[218] Russell was pleased enough with his new house – it became his London residence, known as Russell house near Ivy bridge – but was evidently sorry to lose his old one. When Henry VIII granted him the late prior of St Swithin's house in Southwark, he asked the king to give it instead to the new bishop of Rochester on

---

[212] SP1/136, ff.174, 210 (*LP*, xiii(2), 365, 399).
[213] *LP*, xiii(1), 1115 g.23.
[214] C82/750 (*LP*, xiv(1), 651 g.59).
[215] E305/8/E6.
[216] C82/756 (*LP*, xiv(1), 1354 gg.12, 13). Draft valor in *Devon Monastic Lands*, no. 7.
[217] C82/759 (*LP*, xiv(2), 435 g.17); *LP*, xv, 282 g.1.
[218] House of Lords, Original Acts, 31 Henry VIII, no. 26.

condition that the bishop should return the house at Chiswick to him.
Henry VIII consented and the exchange was carried out by act of
parliament in 1542.[219]

Henry VIII made outright gifts to three more noblemen in 1539.
He rewarded the great chamberlain, Oxford, with the late prior of
Tortington's house in Candlewick street, London, which he already
held on lease from the court of augmentations.[220] He gave the lord
admiral, Southampton, the manor of South Cerney, near Gloucester,
which had belonged to Llanthony priory, with the issues from
Michaelmas 1537, paying only 47s a year in rent.[221] Since Southampton,
like Russell, had 'no convenient mansion and dwelling place of his
owne' near the palace of Westminster, by act of parliament Henry
VIII also made him a gift of the bishop of Bath's place in the Strand.
Renamed Southampton house, it became his town residence until his
death in 1542. (The duke of Norfolk then expressed the hope that it
might 'light on' him, since he had no house in London – Exeter Place,
where he stayed, was 'only of lendyng' – and 'all other noblemen be
well served save I only'. But he hoped in vain.) Henry VIII recompensed the bishop of Bath in 1539 by granting him the house just
surrendered by the Minoresses in London. The bill was introduced
first into the commons, perhaps to forestall opposition from the
bishops in the house of lords.[222] Henry VIII gave his assent as well to
a lords' bill in the form of a petition from the earl of Sussex giving to
him and his heirs male the house in St Lawrence Poultney – once
Buckingham's – which was again in the king's hands by the attainder
of the marquess of Exeter.[223] In this session of parliament, too, acts
confirmed earlier transfers of church property. In April 1537 Edward
Seymour, then viscount Beauchamp, had acquired from Rowland Lee,
bishop of Coventry and Lichfield, his house in the Strand known as
Chester Place. Although Henry VIII had no formal part in the
transaction, it had taken place with his support. The bishop had heard
from Cromwell that the king was 'myndyd' to have his London house;
he protested at the injury to his successors as well as himself, but
accepted the inevitable, only asking Cromwell to help him to an honest

[219] House of Lords, Original Acts, 33 Henry VIII, no. 41.
[220] C82/755 (LP, xiv(1), 1192 g.8).
[221] C82/753 (LP, xiv(1), 906 g.5).
[222] House of Lords, Original Acts, 31 Henry VIII, no. 25; The Hamilton Papers, i, 227.
Norfolk had acquired the site of Clerkenwell priory in 1540 in an exchange with the
crown, but it evidently failed to meet his needs. In 1543 he gave it up to Henry VIII in
return for a mansion in Lambeth: 32 Henry VIII, c.80, 34 & 35 Henry VIII, c.29 (LP,
xv, 498, xviii(1), 66).
[223] House of Lords, Original Acts, 31 Henry VIII, no. 17.

recompense. A fortnight later the cathedrals of Coventry and Lichfield agreed to the grant to Seymour, which in 1539 was confirmed by act of parliament.[224] The act concerning the dissolution of the larger monasteries confirmed all the king's grants of former monastic lands. A schedule annexed to it also protected the rights of the duke of Norfolk to Sibton abbey, Suffolk, and of George Brooke, lord Cobham, to the college of Cobham, Kent. Each had been authorized by the king – but only by word of mouth – to acquire these properties from their religious owners; the act made the king's permission a matter of record.[225]

The uncertainty surrounding the fate of the remaining religious houses in 1538 and 1539 was exploited by a number of noblemen. In April 1538 Thomas lord Wentworth informed Cromwell that he had bought the house of the Grey Friars in Ipswich, 'being their ffounder in blode', adding for good measure that he had done so in order to verify Christ's saying, 'Omnis plantatio quem non plantavit Pater meus, eradicabitur'. The Franciscan order he reckoned to be only 'a ipocriticall wede' of the bishop of Rome, not a true plant of God. The house was in financial straits since the people of Ipswich preferred to give alms to the poor and impotent than to 'such an idell neste of dranes'. The property he had acquired for himself and his heirs for ever was 'oonly the bare sete of the house with a garden or two inclosid within the walles' and he begged Cromwell's favour 'for the enyoing of the same'.[226] His ownership was not accepted, but he was allowed to occupy the site and at the end of the reign was still paying 10s a year for it to the court of augmentations.[227] John Tuchet, lord Audley, 'pouer baron', on the other hand, appealed first to Cromwell 'to be a meane for me to his highnes for sum of thes abbays that ys nowe leke to cum in to his grace his handes'.[228] But three months later, in November 1538, he too resorted to direct action. He sent his servant, the parson of Holford, to put pressure on the abbot of Athelney, Somerset. The parson was also an informant of Cromwell's and sent him a report of his proceedings. To the abbot's question, 'ys my lorde Audley a man off the new sett or arfter the olde sorte', he had answered 'he ys after the beste sorte . . . a good englysse man', and

---

[224] SP1/117, f.240 (*LP*, xii(1), 807); House of Lords, Original Acts, 31 Henry VIII, no. 18. Hertford gave the bishop in recompense the messuage in Kew that he had been granted in 1536.

[225] 31 Henry VIII, c.13.

[226] SP1/130, f.240 (*LP*, xiii(1), 651).

[227] SC6/Henry 8/3440, 3447.

[228] SP1/135, f.129 (*LP*, xiii(2), 140).

encouraged him to resign his house to the king.[229] When Athelney was surrendered, in February 1539, Audley was put in charge for the time being. He at once wrote to Cromwell for his help in obtaining the house, 'paying as it shall plese the kynges highnes and your lordshep to determen'.[230] Henry VIII granted him only a lease of the house and a life annuity of £20.[231]

Thomas lord Audley of Walden also persuaded an abbot to surrender his house. Having failed to get the king to turn two monasteries in Essex – St John's, Colchester, and St Osyth's, Chich – into colleges, Audley sent for the abbot of St Osyth's and, as he reported to Cromwell, 'inducyd hym to yelde the howse to the kynges mageste with his good wyll'. The king gave Audley permission to occupy the abbey during pleasure, and Audley wrote to Cromwell in August 1539 to ask him to further his 'litel sute' for a life-grant of the property.[232] But in April 1540 St Osyth's was granted to Cromwell himself in fee.[233] The other abbot, of St John's, Colchester, refused to surrender and was hanged on 1 December 1539. Audley was put in charge of this house too, but eventually heard to his dismay that the king intended to keep it in his own hands. Audley wrote again to Cromwell. To give up both St Osyth's and St John's 'shalbe no litell losse to my poor honeste and estymacion consideryng this to be in the contree where I was borne and most part browt up'. He asked for Cromwell's help. 'Sythen his mageste made me baron and sythen I maryed my wiff I never axyd eny thynge, and I am now abashed . . . I maryed at his magestes comandment . . . and yet I repent never a whytt my mariage, but have gret cause to thank the kinges mageste for enducyng me to it . . . And if God send us childern, whiche I desire, the kynges mageste hath made me a baron, and al my londes excedith not clerely £800, wherwith I am right wel content.' Audley's incoherent protest betrays a certain strain as he struggled to come to terms with the situation. However, there were other acceptable properties in Essex, including the manors of Chesterford and East Donyland. He gave Cromwell a note of his own lands that he was willing to offer in exchange, and promised him £40

[229] BL, Cotton Cleo. E.IV, f.135 (*LP*, xiii(2), 744).

[230] SP1/143, f.86 (*LP*, xiv(1), 300).

[231] SP1/157, f.61 (*LP*, xv, 71). The lease is confirmed by a later reference: *LP*, xix(1), 444 g.20. Audley, unable to pay his debts to the king in 1535, had been forced to sell him the manor of Wade, Hampshire, and other lordships and manors: *LP*, ix, 580, x, 370; C54/419; 27 Henry VIII, c.31.

[232] *SP*, i, 586–8, also printed *Three Chapters of Letters*, pp. 245–8; BL, Cotton Cleo. E.IV, ff.231–2 (*LP*, xiv(2), 36), printed ibid., pp. 239–41 and (abbreviated) Strype, *Ecclesiastical Memorials*, i(1), 407–8.

[233] See below, p. 247.

in ready money for his pains.[234] The transaction was not completed
until after Cromwell's fall. It went through in two stages, a sale by
Audley to the king in February 1541 being followed in March by a
grant to him described simply as for his service.[235]

Viscount Lisle, deputy of Calais, probably put pressure on the prior
of the Carmelite friary there as well as suing to Cromwell. Lisle was
beset by financial worries and in May 1538 described himself as living
'a worse lieff then the poorest soldier in Callis'.[236] He planned to visit
England but again, as in 1536, he had to wait for months for a licence.
Not until August was John Husee able to send it to him.[237] Lisle
quickly crossed the channel to forward his suit for an annuity as well
as church property. On 8 September he reported to lady Lisle that the
king had that day given him £400 p.a. for life; two days later Husee told
her that Cromwell – no mention of Henry VIII – had given Lisle the
friary in Calais for life.[238] Both items of news proved ill-founded.
When Husee saw Cromwell he was informed that the king had as yet
made no grant of the friary to Lisle and had assigned him an annuity
of no more than £200.[239] Cromwell had failed to get Henry VIII
to agree to a larger pension but undertook to try again for at least
400 marks, and assured Lisle that he would in time obtain the
friary 'accordyng unto his promesse'.[240] The crux of the matter was
Cromwell's wish to obtain Painswick, Gloucestershire, which belonged
to lady Lisle, and Lisle's insistence that she should not part with it at a
loss – 'you and I cannot lyve with fear wordes'.[241] By stages a solution
was hammered out. Lisle was given an annuity in December 1538, but
only for £200.[242] The prior of the White Friars in Calais – kept
informed of what was afoot – wrote to Lisle, offering to surrender the
house to him.[243] Lisle was in England again in September 1539, this
time on official business, and terms for the sale of Painswick to
Cromwell were agreed in October, when Lisle also obtained 'the
commmyssion ffor the frers'.[244] In March 1540 Lisle received a grant of
the priory of the Carmelite friars in Calais with all its possessions there

---

[234] BL, Cotton Cleo. E.IV, ff.222–3 (*LP*, xiv(2), 775).

[235] E305/2/A45; C82/778 (*LP*, xvi, 678 g.36).

[236] SP1/132, f.201 (*LP*, xiii(1), 1089), printed *The Lisle Letters*, v, 1170.

[237] SP1/135, f.233 (*LP*, xiii(2), 190), printed ibid., 1212.

[238] SP3/1, f.10, SP3/12, f.12 (*LP*, xiii(2), 302, 317), printed ibid., 1216, 1218.

[239] SP3/4, f.94 (*LP*, xiii(2), 434), printed ibid., 1233.

[240] SP3/5, f.7, SP3/4, f.66 (*LP*, xiii(2), 590, 781), printed ibid., 1248, 1265.

[241] SP3/1, f.7 (*LP*, xiii(2), 920), printed ibid., 1288.

[242] *LP*, xiv(1), 1355.

[243] SP3/3, f.12 (*LP*, xiii(2), 897), printed *The Lisle Letters*, v, 1305.

[244] SP3/1, f.18, SP3/12, f.85 (*LP*, xiv(2), 158, 302), printed ibid., 1536, 1562.

in reward for his service.[245] He sold it almost at once for 400 marks.[246]

There is no evidence that Walter lord Hungerford helped to procure the surrender of any religious house, but he intervened at the next stage. When the royal visitors arrived to take the surrender of Hinton priory, Somerset, of which he was steward, he bought the church and buildings from them. Unfortunately, he was away in London when Sir Thomas Arundell arrived to survey the priory, and discovered too late that a great part of the property he had bought had been demolished and carried away. He wrote to tell Cromwell about it in June 1539 and to ask him to move the king to grant him, in fee farm for ever, the house and demesnes of Hinton and its attached manors adjacent to his house at Farleigh.[247] Hungerford got no grant from the king, only a 21-year lease from the court of augmentations.[248] John lord Mordaunt was even less successful. He wrote to Cromwell in April 1539, asking him to speak to the king for permission to buy his house in London, which had belonged to the Charterhouse. No grant was issued, although Mordaunt had remarked rather pointedly that Henry VIII had never given him anything.[249] Ralph Neville, earl of Westmorland, could not make the same complaint, but he, too, wrote to Cromwell early in 1539 with a request. He wanted Blanchland abbey in Northumberland, adjoining one of his lordships, and begged to have it either for a quit-rent or to farm for years.[250] Blanchland was not surrendered until December 1539; one of the auditors of the court of augmentations was already after it, and it was he who obtained a 21-year lease of the abbey in May 1540, although Westmorland was accounted the founder of the house.[251]

The assignment of a lease to somebody else proved no obstacle to a nobleman with a longer record of service at court, the earl of Rutland. He wrote to Cromwell in September 1538, within days of the surrender of Croxton abbey, Leicestershire, asking him to move the king to grant it to him, either by purchase or exchange, since it lay very near his 'poore hous' at Belvoir; he also appealed to Wriothesley for his support.[252] Shortly afterwards Croxton was leased to Thomas Legh, who had been present at its surrender. Legh was soon persuaded to give up his lease and to accept the return of £64 he had paid for the

[245] C82/764 (*LP*, xv, 436 g.78).
[246] *LP*, xv, 738.
[247] SP1/152, ff.100–1 (*LP*, xiv(1), 1154).
[248] *LP*, xv, 1032.
[249] SP1/150, f.191 (*LP*, xiv(1), 845).
[250] SP1/143, f.141 (*LP*, xiv(1), 344).
[251] *LP*, x, 364, xiv(2), 482, 701, xvi, 1500.
[252] SP1/136, f.137, SP7/1, f.38 (*LP*, xiii(2), 331, 332).

buildings and implements belonging to the abbey.[253] In March 1539 Rutland received a grant from Henry VIII for his service and in exchange. He sold to the king the manor of Worcesters, Middlesex, the mansion called Elsings Hall in Enfield, in the same county, and the lordship and castle of Chilham, Kent. The king granted him Croxton abbey with 11 manors in Leicestershire, two in Northamptonshire and one in Lincolnshire, together with Rievaulx abbey in Yorkshire. The annual rent on his new possessions was to be £297 9s 4¾d.[254] Rutland was described as founder of Rievaulx, but he was evidently more interested in Croxton and moved into the abbey without delay: by the summer of 1540 his young son and heir, styled lord Ros, was in residence there.[255]

Henry VIII had had no house at Enfield other than lodges in the chase, and extensive repairs to Elsings were at once started to make it a suitable residence for him.[256] Nevertheless the balance of advantage in the exchange was clearly in Rutland's favour. Henry VIII made two grants in 1539 which were also described as partial gifts, although the gift-element in these cases is not so obvious. Edward lord Clinton, in consideration of his service and for £2,916 17s 1d (the sum inserted in the signed bill), was granted the Gilbertine priories of Haverholme and Sempringham in Lincolnshire, the priory of Folkestone, Kent, and the cell of Flitcham, Norfolk.[257] (Clinton already held Folkestone priory on a lease from the court of augmentations which he now surrendered.)[258] Andrew lord Windsor, for his service and for £1,055, obtained the priory of Ankerwyke and the manor of Alderbourne in Buckinghamshire, and Greenford Park in Stanwell, Middlesex, together with the rectory of Stanwell.[259] Neither had received any earlier grant of land; willingness to pay a substantial sum was crucial to their success. Other noblemen were ready by this time to opt for a straight purchase if the king would agree to it. The first to pay for monastic land after the dissolution was John Nevill, lord Latimer, in February 1538. His involvement in the pilgrimage of grace made him an unlikely candidate for any gift, and it is probable that he needed some help even to negotiate a purchase. At all events, before it went through he agreed to alienate his manor of Renhold, Bedfordshire, to

---

[253] *LP*, xiv(1), 1355, xiv(2), 236(7).

[254] C82/750 (*LP*, xiv(1), 651 g.43).

[255] *LP*, x, 364; *HMC, Rutland*, iv, 302–3.

[256] *The History of the King's Works*, iv(2), 87.

[257] C82/748 (*LP*, xiv(1), 191 g.10). Part payment: E323/1/Pt 1, m.6d. Sempringham became Clinton's residence: Hodgett, *Tudor Lincolnshire*, p. 52.

[258] *LP*, xiii(1), 1520, xiv(1), 1355.

[259] C82/757 (*LP*, xiv(2), 113 g.10). Part payment: E323/1/Pt 2, m.8.

John Gostwick – a sale that Gostwick had asked Cromwell to arrange for him at the lowest price he could get, promising him 100 marks for his pains. Latimer also sold the manor of Wingrave, Buckinghamshire, to Cromwell himself.[260] Latimer's grant from the king, which included the priory of Nun Monkton, Yorkshire, cost him £1,687 16s 8d as well as four manors in Yorkshire surrendered in exchange.[261] The following year George Brooke, lord Cobham, also obtained a grant for money and lands, while William Paulet, lord St John, agreed to pay £2,091 10s 10d for monastic lands, mostly in Hampshire, and the great messuage which he had built within the Austin Friars in London.[262]

Although gifts to noblemen were at their peak between June 1536 and the end of 1539, most noble families still received nothing. Of the high nobility, all those introduced into the peerage by Henry VIII received grants of land during these years, with one exception: for Thomas Boleyn, earl of Wiltshire, the dissolution of the monasteries came too late. Half the rest also received gifts of land. All the recipients were important office-holders or men well known to Henry VIII through their service at court. Moreover, high noblemen who received a grant were more likely to obtain several than to stick at one. By contrast, Sandys and Russell were the only barons, apart from Cromwell, to receive more than one grant during these years. Most barons, whether or not they had been ennobled by Henry VIII, obtained no gift of land of any sort. Russell seems to have been the sole nobleman of any rank to have been given land at this time in order to build up his territorial power in the interests of the crown. The grants inescapably altered the balance of power in the localities, but there is little sign that Henry VIII took this into account. The pattern of his giving – where it was not determined by his own desire to obtain an estate by exchange – reflected the structure of power at the centre. While every grant of monastic land and every lease for more than 21 years came from the king, he was put under increasing pressure. Much time had to be spent in dealing with the flood of requests, some of which were hard to refuse. Reputations were at stake, as Norfolk and Audley of Walden, among others, pointed out. Perhaps even the reputation of Henry himself was at risk. The lavish bestowal of lands could enhance the kingly role and add to the sense of munificence at court; what would be the effect of rejecting an eloquent case, pleaded in person? Yet suits

---

[260] *LP*, xiii(1), 190 g.19, 312, xv, 1029(27).

[261] C82/735 (*LP*, xiii(1), 384 g.54); E305/1/A9. Part payment: E323/1/Pt 1, m.5d.

[262] C82/756, 753 (*LP*, xiv(1), 1354 g.34, 906 g.1). Full payment from Cobham: E323/1/Pt 2, m.7d; reference to St John's debt, m.15.

had to be denied if all the lands were not to slip away. The readiness of many suitors to pay, if necessary, pointed the way out of the dilemma. Monastic lands could as well be sold as given away, and the king need not be personally involved in their dispersal. In December 1539 Henry commissioned Cromwell and Rich to sell lands up to an annual value of £6,000 for ready money at 20 years' purchase. Only where an individual item was worth more than £64 p.a. was the king's consent to be necessary.[263] From that time on, the acquisition of land from the crown was no longer indissolubly linked with influence at court. Noblemen, as other men, bought what they could afford, where it suited them: all the former monastic lands which were still in the hands of the crown were potentially on the market.[264]

For the rest of the reign sales and exchanges outnumbered gifts and part-gifts. In 1540, besides giving Lisle the friary in Calais, Henry VIII rewarded the service of Walter Devereux, lord Ferrers, with Merevale abbey, Warwickshire.[265] Thomas lord Cromwell was the only other peer to receive a gift or part-gift of land in 1540. In April, one week before his promotion to the earldom of Essex, he was given – in consideration of an indenture of 1 March 1540 and for his services – the monastery of St Osyth's, Chich, with 16 manors in Essex belonging to it, 13 other monastic properties in the county, the Grey Friars in Yarmouth, and three manors (two in Essex and one in Suffolk) which the king had lately acquired from the duke of Suffolk. The indenture was not enrolled and appears not to have survived, but it almost certainly recorded an exchange by which Cromwell sold to the king the manors of Wimbledon, Mortlake and Burstow in Surrey, granted to him in 1536, in return for this grant of lands centred on Essex, a county whose titular earl was an old man with no son to succeed him – although no one could have foreseen his accidental death 12 days after the making of the indenture between Cromwell and the king. The last section of Cromwell's grant was a part-gift. For his services and the sum of £1,446 10s 0d he was granted the priory of Launde, Leicestershire, with two manors there, and three gardens in the parish of St Stephen, Coleman street, adjoining his London house.[266] After Cromwell's fall and the creation of his son, Gregory, as baron, Henry VIII made his second grant of these years described only as proceeding *de gratia nostra speciali*, giving Launde priory to Gregory in February

[263] *LP*, xiv(2), 780 g.36. Subsequent commissions varied the value of individual items needing the king's consent.
[264] Youings, *The Dissolution of the Monasteries*, p. 118.
[265] C82/774 (*LP*, xvi, 379 g.4); E318/10/429.
[266] C82/765 (*LP*, xv, 611 g.8). Full payment: E323/1/Pt 2, m.11. For Cromwell's sale of lands to the king see above, pp. 128–9.

1541.[267] Two other noblemen received gifts of land in 1541. The king rewarded Edward lord Clinton with Bridge End in the parish of Horbling, Lincolnshire, which had been a cell of Sempringham priory, and the manor of Aslackby in the same county, formerly the possession of the hospital of St John of Jerusalem, dissolved by act of parliament the previous year. The particulars of the grant show it to have been worth over £33 p.a.[268] William FitzWilliam, earl of Southampton, who owned the manor of Cowdray in Midhurst, Sussex, was given, for his services, the other manor in Midhurst, known as St John's from its possession by the knights hospitallers.[269] In 1542, a few weeks before Southampton died leaving no heir, Henry made him a further gift of the two manors – Chalton, Hampshire, and Crookham, Berkshire – which he held on a lease granted after their forfeiture by the countess of Salisbury. He was now to hold them in tail male with remainder to William Somerset, styled lord Herbert, son and heir of the earl of Worcester and his wife, Southampton's half-sister.[270] The only other grant of 1542 described as a reward for service was in reality an exchange. For the third time the recipient was Thomas lord Audley of Walden. Henry VIII gave him Tilty abbey, Essex, the house of the Crossed Friars in Colchester, and the manor of Herringswell, Suffolk, which had belonged to Bury St Edmunds abbey, together with two manors in Essex, parcel of the duchy of Lancaster, worth in all £100 16s 10d p.a. Audley at once sold to the king other properties in Essex and Middlesex valued at £98 6s ¾d p.a. and paid £50 15s 5d to the treasurer of augmentations to make up the difference.[271]

One more nobleman joined the sad ranks of those forced to give up land to Henry VIII. The manor of Stanwell, Middlesex, had belonged to the Windsor family even longer than Pisho had to the Scropes. William FitzOther, constable of Windsor castle, held the manor when Domesday Book was compiled, and his descendants, taking the name of Windsor, continued to live there. Andrew lord Windsor, through his purchase and royal gift of 1539, had added to the manor the park and rectory of Stanwell, but in 1542 he surrendered the whole estate to Henry VIII. Family tradition related that the king, having dined at Stanwell, told his host that he liked the place so much that he must

[267] C82/777 (*LP*, xvi, 580 g.49). Gregory Cromwell also retained the manor of Rumney, Monmouthshire, granted to his father and himself in survivorship in 1532: *LP*, v, 1065 g.33.

[268] C82/783 (*LP*, xvi, 947 g.32); E318/24/1308.

[269] C82/783 (*LP*, xvi, 947 g.56); *VCH, Sussex*, iv, 75–8.

[270] C82/800 (*LP*, xvii, 881 g.19).

[271] C82/795 (*LP*, xvii, 285 g.2); E305/5/C58; E318/2/57. Full payment: E323/2B/Pt 1, m.30.

have it. The deed of exchange, ready drawn, duly arrived and – the final touch of pathos – lord Windsor was made to leave his home straight away, although he had already laid in his provisions for Christmas.[272] It is clear that the initiative was indeed the king's. An act of parliament of 1540 had annexed to Windsor castle the lands of various religious houses.[273] The reorganization of the estate was in Henry's mind, and in March 1542 Windsor formally agreed to sell him the manor of Stanwell with the issues since the previous Michaelmas. In exchange he was to have manors in Middlesex, Surrey and Gloucestershire, a hospital near Rye in Sussex and Bordesley abbey, Worcestershire, and other property, worth in all more than he was giving up; but he had to pay £2,197 5s 8d to balance the exchange. Windsor was evidently reluctant to leave Stanwell and obtained the king's consent to continue there until Michaelmas 1542, paying the clear annual value as one year's rent.[274] The exchange and sale went through in April 1542.[275] The particulars show that Henry VIII allowed Windsor, by way of gift, £13 6s 8d for the mansion and an annuity of £40, presumably in recompense for his enforced removal.[276]

Grants which were part-gifts went to a few other noblemen in the early 1540s. In 1541 Henry VIII gave Edward Seymour, earl of Hertford, lands worth £17 17s ½d p.a. within an extensive exchange which brought to the king the manor of Twickenham, Middlesex, and three manors in Hampshire and to the earl a nunnery in Amesbury, Wiltshire, and the Carthusian priory at Sheen, Surrey.[277] In 1542 Henry Clifford, earl of Cumberland, one of Henry's oldest friends, was granted the priory of Bolton in Craven, founded by his family, with 12 manors in Yorkshire, in consideration of his service and for £2,490 1s 1d.[278] The particulars for the grant show that the purchase price had been reduced by £1,000, deducted 'for the kinges gifte'.[279] Another former courtier, Henry lord Mautravers, the deputy of Calais, offered Henry VIII £1,000 in 1542 for the college of Arundel, of his family's foundation, confident that with the king's blessing he would be able to obtain the goodwill of the master and fellows and his father's consent. The college was not surrendered for another two years, by

---

[272] VCH, Middlesex, iii, 36–7; William Dugdale, The Baronage of England, 2 vols (London, 1675–6), ii, 307–8.

[273] 32 Henry VIII, c.54 (LP, xv, 498).

[274] BL, Harl. 1880, ff.1–7 (LP, xvii, 276).

[275] C82/795 (LP, xvii, 285 g.18); E305/4/C22. Part payment: E323/2B/Pt 1, m.30d.

[276] E318/22/1235.

[277] C82/779 (LP, xvi, 779 g.7); E305/4/C18; E318/13/572.

[278] C82/793 (LP, xvii, 283 g.11); LP, x, 364.

[279] E318/8/335. Part payment: E323/2B/Pt 1, m.29d.

which time Mautravers had succeeded to the earldom of Arundel; Henry VIII granted it to him then, with all its possessions, for his service and 1,000 marks.[280] Charles Blount, lord Mountjoy, jointly with his mother, in 1543 received a grant for his service, in exchange, and for £864 12s 2¼d. The surviving particulars are incomplete, but it seems that the gift element was small: when Mountjoy made his will in the following year, as he set off for the French campaign, he referred to the grant simply as a sale and exchange.[281]

With the kingdom again at war with Scotland and France, Henry reverted to the pattern of his early years and made outright gifts of land only to noblemen deeply involved in the war or related to himself by marriage. He created three barons in 1544 and gave each of them lands, either at once or within 12 months. Thomas lord Wriothesley, the principal secretary who was acting as treasurer for the wars, on his creation received manors and rectories in Hampshire and the London house of the former abbot of St Mary's, York.[282] Thomas lord Wharton, engaged in the war against the Scots, was given property which included the abbey of Shap in Westmorland, founded by the Cliffords, the family eclipsed by his rise to power. The grant carried a reserved rent calculated to bring the annual value down to £200, the gift stipulated by the king.[283] William lord Eure, the other new northern peer, also active on the northern front, received a gift of lands in Northumberland, Durham and Yorkshire and paid £428 10s 10d for additional property to be included in the grant.[284] Henry VIII also rewarded the service of the lord admiral, John Dudley, viscount Lisle, in May 1544 with the gift of the hospitals of Burton Lazars, Leicestershire, and St Giles in the Fields, London.[285] The following year Lisle sued to the king for another grant, offering him 3,000 marks in ready money for a college worth £400 p.a. 'and to fynde a free scole for ever in his majestes name'. Henry VIII remarked that it was a lot of money for him to spend and that he would do better to obtain 'a portion of lande'. Lisle expected a grant worth £200 p.a. and sent Sir William Paget a list of lands roughly to that value, asking him to remind the king of the matter.[286] Henry VIII made the grant to Lisle in December

[280] SP1/173, f.68 (*LP*, xvii, 861); C82/832 (*LP*, xix(2), 800 g.35).

[281] C82/812 (*LP*, xviii(2), 449 g.1); PROB 11/30/45. Surviving particulars refer only to the lands transferred to the king: E318/16/792. Full payment: E323/2B/Pt 2, m.22.

[282] C82/818 (*LP*, xix(1), 80 g.42).

[283] C82/832 (*LP*, xix(2), 800 g.5); E318/22/1203; *LP*, x, 364.

[284] C82/833 (*LP*, xx(1), 125 g.23); E318/10/417. Full payment: E323/3, m.43d.

[285] C82/824 (*LP*, xix(1), 610 g.8).

[286] SP1/208, ff.33–4 (*LP*, xx(2), 412, where Lisle's offer is wrongly given as 1,000 marks).

1545 for his services and £69 2s ½d. The particulars show that it was in fact a free gift of lands valued in all at £200 p.a. and that Lisle rounded out the grant by buying in addition an advowson and a pension he would otherwise have had to pay.[287] The last military commander to receive an outright gift of lands was William lord Grey of Wilton. In March 1546 Henry VIII gave him, for his service, the manor of Brampton, Herefordshire, valued at £22 14s 5d p.a.[288] Grey hoped as well for Beaulieu abbey in the Boulonnais. Indeed, he had supposed that he had been given it until Sir Thomas Heneage, the chief gentleman of the privy chamber, sent to tell him in June that the king had changed his mind. Invited to name an alternative property, Grey suggested the nearby priory of Waste. The gift was apparently intended as the fulfilment of a promise of reward for a 'pretie exploytt' against the French by Grey, but no grant was issued before Henry VIII's death.[289] Three relatives of the king received gifts of land in the last years of the reign. In 1546 Henry VIII gave to Henry Grey, marquess of Dorset, and his wife, Frances, daughter of the king's sister, Mary, the college of Astley, Warwickshire, valued at just under £40 p.a. It was the burial place of the Grey family.[290] The queen's uncle, created lord Parr of Horton in December 1543, was given, early in 1544, the priory of Harrold, Bedfordshire, and seven manors in Northamptonshire and Huntingdonshire.[291] Her brother, promoted to the earldom of Essex at the same time, waited over three years for any gift of land, but was eventually rewarded for his services in January 1547. Henry VIII, near to death, gave him the large estates in Westmorland and elsewhere which he already held from the crown on a lease due to expire in 1553; no further payment of the annual rent of £340 was to be collected from the earl or his heirs.[292]

The number of part-gifts rose sharply in 1545 and 1546, but all the recipients were men who also received at least one free gift from Henry VIII. There was therefore no extension in the range of the king's giving. Dudley and Seymour were especially concerned to obtain something more from the king before he died. In March 1546 Lisle made a formal request to have 'by waye of gift' the hospital of St John of Jerusalem in Clerkenwell, with the mansion place, gardens and courts, the prior's lodging and other houses, and the church. Henry

---

[287] C82/846 (*LP*, xx(2), 1068 g.41); E318/9/393.

[288] C82/849 (*LP*, xxi(1), 504 g.30); E318/11/509.

[289] SP1/221, f.15 (*LP*, xxi(1), 1142); *A Commentary of the Services and Charges of William Lord Grey of Wilton*, pp. 3–9.

[290] C66/798 (*LP*, xxi(1), 1537 g.7); E318/9/383; *VCH, Warwickshire*, ii, 119.

[291] C82/819 (*LP*, xix(1), 141 g.75).

[292] C82/861 (*LP*, xxi(2), 771 g.12); E318/10/414.

VIII gave him all the property except the church for his 'good and faithfull service' by land and sea against the French and Scots – and for £1,000 paid to himself and £6 13s 4d paid to the court of augmentations.[293] The price was no doubt a disappointment, but Lisle did markedly better in the 1540s than Hertford. There is indeed some evidence that Henry VIII disliked Seymour's sharp dealing even in the 1530s.[294] In 1545 the king was reluctant to put pressure on the bishop of Salisbury to grant Hertford two of the bishopric's Wiltshire manors, although he was eventually persuaded by Paget to allow the appropriate letter to be sent.[295] Yet Hertford had a double claim on the king as military leader and royal kinsman and could hardly be denied some further sign of favour.[296] In 1545 Henry VIII agreed to grant him the college of Ottery St Mary, Devon. But Hertford soon discovered that the charges on it were so great that it would be of no immediate benefit to him. He was the king's lieutenant in the north and wrote to him from Darlington to ask instead for the college of Beverley, Yorkshire. It was more valuable by some £200 – it was worth about £500 p.a. over and above the tenth – and would be charged with £300 p.a. in pensions when it was surrendered. He offered to pay more for it and in this way provide himself with a base in the north. At the same time Hertford wrote to Paget, explaining his pressing need for financial help. When neither letter produced a favourable response Hertford sent Paget another offer: if the king would favour him with the new college of Leicester he would never again be a 'craver'. The attraction of this proposal was that the lands lay near his house in Wiltshire. Henry VIII refused to meet this request either, saying that he would not deface any of his great colleges. Hertford fell back on his original suit, merely urging Paget to try to get the purchase price reduced and the tenth released. He himself made one more attempt to improve the grant by asking for a college in Cornwall to be added to it, bringing the annual value to over £400.[297] At last, in December 1545, he put in a formal request to have 'by waye of gyfte and purchace' the college of Ottery St Mary and two rectories in Devon which the king 'of his moste bountefull goodnes' was pleased to grant him, and for

[293] E318/15/715; C82/853 (*LP*, xxi(1), 970 g.1).

[294] Bush, 'The Lisle-Seymour land disputes', 272–4.

[295] Felicity Heal, *Of Prelates and Princes. A Study of the Economic and Social Position of the Tudor Episcopate* (Cambridge, 1980), pp. 119–20.

[296] Hertford exchanged lands with the king in 1541 and 1542 and bought lands in 1544, but he had received no gift from Henry VIII since the small part-gift in the exchange of 1541.

[297] SP1/202, ff.182, 184, SP1/203, f.98, SP1/204, ff.55, 144 (*LP*, xx(1), 1031, 1032, 1121, 1222, 1284).

which the earl humbly desired him to accept 3,000 marks. The letters patent were not issued until May 1546, but the grant went through unchanged, as a part-gift. It brought Hertford lands in possession and reversion valued at £354 6s 8¾d p.a., but worth in the short term less than £20 p.a. clear of all charges.[298]

Hertford's own idea of a useful gift may be deduced from the progressive enhancement of the value of his land grant supposedly authorized by Henry VIII's will. Starting at lands with an annual value of 1,000 marks, it was soon increased to £800, with an additional £200 'of the next bishopes landes'; by the time that Paget made his statement to the council early in the reign of Edward VI the addition had grown to £300 of the next bishop's lands to fall vacant, making a grand total of lands worth £1,100 p.a. As his son later admitted, Hertford became 'his owne carver' after Henry VIII's death.[299] Henry's gifts of land generally went to those best placed to put pressure on him, but no nobleman, however powerful, was allowed to develop from a 'craver' into a 'carver' while he reigned.

Henry VIII's pressing need for money in the 1540s no doubt precluded any great display of generosity at the end of his reign, but his behaviour as a patron was remarkably consistent throughout. He was no more free with his gifts of lands to the nobility than with his grants of offices. Moreover, the chief beneficiaries in each instance were often the same men: concentration was the keynote of his patronage. The majority of noblemen, only intermittently at court, had few opportunities to present their petitions in person to the king. For his part, Henry VIII evidently did not judge it politically necessary to treat them with indulgence. The service of the nobility as a whole was at his command: it did not have to be recompensed with special favours.

---

[298] C66/768 (*LP*, xxi(1), 970 g.41); E318/13/575, calendared *Devon Monastic Lands*, no. 82.

[299] Miller, 'Henry VIII's unwritten will', pp. 88–90, 103–4.

Conclusion

The aristocratic reaction after Henry VIII's death reveals the judgement of the leading nobles on his reign. He had been too unyielding to allow them the power they wanted, too sparing of the resources of the monarchy for their liking. The political crises of Henry's reign certainly suggest a contrary view – of a king whose fears and desires made him alarmingly vulnerable to manipulation – but, taking the reign as a whole, Henry VIII established and sustained his authority over the nobility. The incipient moves towards political dominance by a few noblemen at the beginning of his reign and in 1529 were stopped by the advent to power of Wolsey and Cromwell; after 1540 no faction established itself in full control while Henry lived. In 1549 Russell described the late king as 'a prynce of moche wisdome and knowledge, yet he was veary suspicious and much given to suspection'.[1] Henry VIII was surprisingly tolerant in some aspects of government: his offers of appointment to offices which were seen as more onerous than profitable were genuine offers which might be refused. But he could not be relied upon to support those who accepted a post away from the court nor to weigh in the balance the years of service of any man who lost his trust. Even a friend such as lord Berners or an old servant such as lord Windsor gave up their property rather than oppose his wishes. The terrible sequence of attainders and executions, if the sign of an intermittent loss of control, also proclaimed the overwhelming strength of a king able to carry the nobility with him against each designated victim.

By the mid-1540s Henry had learned to recognize the formula used by court factions to remove their rivals; he blocked the attempt to destroy Cranmer, whose enemies made the mistake of allowing him to

---

[1] Quoted Willen, *John Russell*, p. 32.

appeal to the king in person.[2] But he never saw so clearly when his own interests were more intimately involved. The nobility might have served him better if it had been less respectful of his majesty. As it was, noblemen, with few exceptions, did what he expected of them, attended on him at court for the great ceremonial occasions, led their men to war when he called upon them and, in the 1530s, responded in greater numbers to the summons to parliament. They even allowed themselves, it seems, to be assessed to the subsidy at something approaching their true incomes. (After Henry VIII's death, John Dudley and Wriothesley, both now promoted to earldoms, lord Russell and the earl of Arundel at once reduced their tax assessments.)[3] The king accepted their service as his due and was sparing with his rewards. Major offices and gifts of land were bestowed, for the most part, on a small inner circle of courtiers and administrators. Among them were the noblemen who led the reaction in 1547: gratitude for what they had received was no stronger in them than it was in Henry VIII.

The hope of gain and the fear of incurring the king's displeasure were powerful forces inducing noblemen to co-operate with Henry VIII. They were reinforced by Henry's conventional view of the role of the nobility. The concentration of patronage in the hands of the crown made it necessary for suitors to find a friend at court, where noblemen faced formidable competition. But no one could challenge them in other areas of activity where the essential qualification was simply noble rank. Moreover, ceremonial duties and military leadership came naturally to men whose status, wealth and power over men needed the opportunities for display which they provided. Certain offices, too, were the preserve of the nobility, although Henry VIII did not restrict his choice of men to fill them to those who were already noble. Only in its formal duty to advise the king did the nobility find its privilege curtailed during the reign of Henry VIII. The reform of the council in the mid-1530s substantially reduced the number of noble councillors. Even so, their exclusion was not an arbitrary act of discrimination: the establishment of a working privy council in itself made membership incompatible with their normal way of life. The few noblemen who wanted a career at the centre of government could still try to achieve their ambition. For the nobility as a whole membership of the house of lords came to offer a more acceptable way of participating in the political process.

---

[2] E. W. Ives, *Faction in Tudor England*, Historical Association Appreciations in History, no. 6 (London, 1979), pp. 26–7.

[3] Helen Miller, 'Subsidy assessments of the peerage in the sixteenth century', *Bull.IHR*, xxviii (1955), 16–21, 30–1.

Parliament was also important for the opportunity which it gave to further private interests. For many noblemen the struggle to build or maintain a local predominance was more engrossing than national politics. Henry VIII showed some concern for the effect of his appointments to local offices on the distribution of power, and may at times have had it in mind when selecting men for ennoblement or promotion in the peerage, but when it came to disposing of the former monastic lands he rarely took much account of the impact of his gifts and sales on the pattern of landownership. He himself never even visited the more distant parts of his kingdom. His summer 'giests' usually took the form of prolonged, itinerant hunting parties within a radius of 100 miles of London. He occasionally accepted the hospitality of a nobleman, but more often chose to stay at one of his own, increasingly numerous residences in the home counties.[1] For all his admiration of the French court, he evidently saw no need to emulate Francis I's practice of making systematic progresses through the provinces.[5] Henry ruled over a more centralized kingdom than Francis, yet the relationship between the centre and the regions still needed attention. The English nobility had as yet no official control over the institutions of local government: in the reign of Henry VIII the presidents of the councils of the north and in the marches of Wales were always bishops, not noblemen, and the office of lord lieutenant was no more than a temporary appointment in time of war. Nevertheless, extensive areas of England and Wales were dominated by noble families. They were the informal agents of the crown in the localities, the personal link between Henry VIII and his subjects. The fall and rise of families shifted the individual pieces in the mosaic without destroying the underlying structure of power.

By the end of the reign over half the surviving noblemen owed their titles to Henry VIII: his creations and promotions had transformed the composition of the peerage. Yet the newly created noble families were no more secure than the old. Indeed, a higher percentage of the new families than of the old foundered in the course of the reign, extinguished by the failure of male heirs or by attainder. Henry VIII's choice of men to ennoble was often determined less by a desire to reward past service than to pave the way for services still to come. He not infrequently used a parliamentary session as an opportune moment to create new peers and some of his creations were evidently designed to reinforce the lay members of the house of lords. More usually, however, a grant of nobility was the preparation for tenure of high

---

[1] *The King's Works*, iv(2), 1–5.
[5] R. J. Knecht, *Francis I* (Cambridge, 1982), p. 93.

office or appointment to a military command. Henry VIII had implicit faith in his power to confer an instant nobility which would elicit the willing subservience of lesser men. Noblemen by birth may have found it harder to accept that the newcomers were their equals or superiors. Nevertheless, every new creation in their own rank moved them up the table of precedence based on date of creation, so that noble families created in the fifteenth century soon appeared to be of ancient lineage. Noble pride was undoubtedly hurt by the king's reliance, for much of his reign, on two low-born ministers, but Henry VIII never doubted the importance of the nobility, never tried to rule without its support. He increased its numbers, which his father had allowed to fall, and confirmed it in its traditional roles. In a hierarchical society, the king needed a nobility as much as the nobility needed the king. But it was a nobility that he needed, not any individual nobleman.

Appendix

List of the English Nobility of the Reign of Henry VIII
(with dates during which titles were in use)

AUDLEY

Thomas lord Audley of Walden
1538–44

BERKELEY

Maurice lord Berkeley 1523
(April–September)
Thomas lord Berkeley 1523–33
Thomas lord Berkeley 1533–4
Henry lord Berkeley 1534–1613

BLOUNT

William lord Mountjoy 1485–1534
Charles lord Mountjoy 1534–44
James lord Mountjoy 1544–81

BOLEYN

Thomas viscount Rochford 1525–9
    earl of Wiltshire 1529–39
Anne marchioness of Pembroke
    1532–6
George lord Rochford 1533–6

BOURCHIER I

John lord Berners 1474–1533

BOURCHIER II

Henry earl of Essex 1483–1540

BOURCHIER III

John lord FitzWarin 1479–1536
    earl of Bath 1536–9
John earl of Bath 1539–61

BRANDON

Charles viscount Lisle 1513–14
    duke of Suffolk 1514–45
Henry earl of Lincoln 1525–34
Henry duke of Suffolk 1545–51

BRAY

Edmund lord Bray 1529–39
John lord Bray 1539–57

BROOKE

John lord Cobham 1464–1512
Thomas lord Cobham 1512–29
George lord Cobham 1529–58

BURGH

Thomas lord Burgh 1529–50

CLIFFORD

Henry lord Clifford 1485–1523
Henry lord Clifford 1523–5
    earl of Cumberland 1525–42
Henry earl of Cumberland 1542–70

CLINTON (or FIENNES)

John lord Clinton 1488–1514
Thomas lord Clinton 1514–17
Edward lord Clinton 1517–72
     earl of Lincoln 1572–85

CONYERS

William lord Conyers 1506?–24
Christopher lord Conyers 1524–38
John lord Conyers 1538–57

COURTENAY

Edward earl of Devon 1485–1509
William earl of Devon 1511
  (May–June)
Henry earl of Devon 1511–25
     marquess of Exeter 1525–38

CROMWELL

Thomas lord Cromwell 1536–40
     earl of Essex 1540
     (April–July)
Gregory lord Cromwell 1540–51

DACRE

Thomas lord Dacre of the north
  1485–1525
William lord Dacre of the north
  1525–63

DARCY

Thomas lord Darcy 1504–37

DAUBENEY

Henry lord Daubeney 1508–38
     earl of Bridgwater 1538–48

DEVEREUX

Walter lord Ferrers 1501–50
     viscount Hereford 1550–8

DUDLEY

John viscount Lisle 1542–7
     earl of Warwick 1547–51
     duke of Northumberland
     1551–3

EURE

William lord Eure 1544–8

FIENNES

Thomas lord Dacre of the south
  1483–1533
Thomas lord Dacre of the south
  1533–41

FITZALAN

Thomas lord Mautravers 1471?–87
     earl of Arundel 1487–1524
William earl of Arundel 1524–44
Henry lord Mautravers 1533–44
     earl of Arundel 1544–80

FITZHUGH

George lord FitzHugh 1487–1513

FITZROY

Henry earl of Nottingham,
     duke of Richmond and
     Somerset 1525–36

FITZWILLIAM

William earl of Southampton
  1537–42

GREY I

Thomas marquess of Dorset 1501–30
Henry marquess of Dorset 1530–51
     duke of Suffolk 1551–4

GREY II

Richard earl of Kent 1503–24

GREY III

Edward lord Grey of Powis 1504–51

GREY IV

Edmund lord Grey of Wilton
  1499–1511
George lord Grey of Wilton 1511–14?
Thomas lord Grey of Wilton
  1514?–17
Richard lord Grey of Wilton 1517–21
William lord Grey of Wilton 1521–62

HASTINGS

George lord Hastings 1506–29
    earl of Huntingdon 1529–44
Francis earl of Huntingdon 1544–60

HOWARD

Thomas earl of Surrey 1483–5,
    1489–1514
    duke of Norfolk 1514–24
Thomas earl of Surrey 1514–24
    duke of Norfolk 1524–47,
    1553–4

HUNGERFORD

Walter lord Hungerford 1536–40

HUSSEY

John lord Hussey 1529–37

LUMLEY

Richard lord Lumley 1507–10
John lord Lumley 1510–44/5

MANNERS

George lord Ros 1512–13
Thomas lord Ros 1513–25
    earl of Rutland 1525–43
Henry earl of Rutland 1543–63

MARNEY

Henry lord Marney 1523
  (April–May)
John lord Marney 1523–5

MORDAUNT

John lord Mordaunt 1532–62

NEVILL I

George lord Bergavenny 1492–1535
Henry lord Bergavenny 1535–87

NEVILL II

Richard lord Latimer 1469–1530
John lord Latimer 1530–43
John lord Latimer 1543–77

NEVILLE

Ralph earl of Westmorland
  1499–1549

OGLE

Ralph lord Ogle 1486–1513
Robert lord Ogle 1513–30/2
Robert lord Ogle 1530/2–45
Robert lord Ogle 1545–62

ORMOND

Thomas lord Ormond 1488?–1515

PARKER

Henry lord Morley 1518–56

PARR I

William lord Parr 1539–43
    earl of Essex 1543–7
    marquess of Northampton
    1547–53, 1559–71

PARR II

William lord Parr of Horton 1543–7

PAULET

William lord St John 1539–50
    earl of Wiltshire 1550–1
    marquess of Winchester
    1551–72

PERCY

Henry earl of Northumberland
  1489–1527
Henry earl of Northumberland
  1527–37

PLANTAGENET

Arthur viscount Lisle 1523–42

POLE

Henry lord Montagu 1529–38

POYNINGS

Thomas lord Poynings 1545
  (January–August)

RADCLIFFE

Robert lord FitzWalter 1505–25
    viscount FitzWalter 1525–9
    earl of Sussex 1529–42
Henry earl of Sussex 1542–57

RUSSELL

John lord Russell 1539–50
    earl of Bedford 1550–5

SANDYS

William lord Sandys 1523–40
Thomas lord Sandys 1540–59/60

SCROPE I

Henry lord Scrope of Bolton 1506–33
    lord Scrope of Bolton and
    Upsall 1506–12
John lord Scrope of Bolton 1533–49

SCROPE II

Ralph lord Scrope of Upsall 1512–15
Geoffrey lord Scrope of Upsall
    1515–17

SEYMOUR

Edward viscount Beauchamp 1536–7
    earl of Hertford 1537–47
    duke of Somerset 1547–52

SOMERSET

Charles lord Herbert 1504–14
    earl of Worcester 1514–26
Henry earl of Worcester 1526–49

STAFFORD I

Edward duke of Buckingham
    1485–1521

STAFFORD II

Henry earl of Wiltshire 1510–23

STANLEY I

Thomas earl of Derby 1504–21
Edward earl of Derby 1521–72

STANLEY II

Edward lord Monteagle 1514–23
Thomas lord Monteagle 1523–60

STOURTON

William lord Stourton 1487–1524
Edward lord Stourton 1524–35
William lord Stourton 1535–48

SUTTON (or DUDLEY)

Edward lord Dudley 1487–1532
John lord Dudley 1532–53

TAILBOYS

Gilbert lord Tailboys 1529–30
George lord Tailboys 1530–40
Robert lord Tailboys 1540–1

TALBOT

George earl of Shrewsbury
    1473–1538
Francis lord Talbot 1533–8
        earl of Shrewsbury 1538–60

TUCHET

John lord Audley 1512–57?

VAUX

Nicholas lord Vaux of Harrowden
    1523 (April–May)
Thomas lord Vaux of Harrowden
    1523–56

de VERE

John earl of Oxford 1462–75,
    1485–1513
John earl of Oxford 1513–26
John earl of Oxford 1526–40
John earl of Oxford 1540–62

WENTWORTH

Thomas lord Wentworth 1529–51

WEST

Thomas lord La Warre 1475–1525
Thomas lord La Warre 1525–54

WHARTON

Thomas lord Wharton 1544–68

WILLOUGHBY I

Robert lord Willoughby de Broke
    1502–21

WILLOUGHBY II

William lord Willoughby de Eresby
    1499–1526

WINDSOR

Andrew lord Windsor 1529–43
William lord Windsor 1543–58

WRIOTHESLEY

Thomas lord Wriothesley 1544–7
   earl of Southampton
   1547–50

ZOUCHE

John lord Zouche 1468–85,
   1495–1526
John lord Zouche 1526–50

Bibliography

I Manuscript sources

LONDON

British Library
  Additional Manuscripts
  Cotton Manuscripts
  Egerton Manuscripts
  Harleian Charters
  Harleian Manuscripts
  Lansdowne Manuscripts
  Reserved Photocopies
  Royal Manuscripts
House of Lords' Record Office
  Lords' Journals
  Original Acts
Lambeth Palace Library
  Talbot Papers (MSS. 3192, 3206)
Public Record Office, Chancery Lane
  C1   Chancery, Early Chancery Proceedings
  C54   Chancery, Close Rolls
  C66   Chancery, Patent Rolls
  C82   Chancery, Warrants for the Great Seal, Series II
  C142   Chancery, Inquisitions Post Mortem
  C218   Chancery, Petty Bag Office, Parliament Pawns
  CP40   Court of Common Pleas, Plea Rolls
  DUR3   Palatinate of Durham, Cursitor's Records
  DL42   Duchy of Lancaster, Miscellaneous Books
  E36   Exchequer, Treasury of Receipt, Books
  E101   Exchequer, King's Remembrancer, Various Accounts
  E179   Exchequer, King's Remembrancer, Subsidy Rolls
  E305   Exchequer, Augmentation Office, Deeds of Purchase and Exchange

E315   Exchequer, Augmentation Office, Miscellaneous Books
E318   Exchequer, Augmentation Office, Particulars for Grants of
            Crown Lands
E323   Exchequer, Augmentation Office, Treasurers' Accounts
E371   Exchequer, Lord Treasurer's Remembrancer, Originalia Rolls
KB8   Court of King's Bench, Baga de Secretis
KB27   Court of King's Bench, Coram Rege Rolls
OBS1   Obsolete Indexes
PROBII   Prerogative Court of Canterbury, Wills
SC6   Special Collections, Ministers' and Receivers' Accounts
SC10   Special Collections, Parliamentary Proxies
SC11   Special Collections, Rentals and Surveys, Rolls
SC12   Special Collections, Rentals and Surveys, Portfolios
SP1   State Papers, Henry VIII, General Series
SP2   State Papers, Henry VIII, Folios
SP3   Lisle Papers
SP7   Wriothesley Papers
SP10   State Papers, Domestic, Edward VI
SP11   State Papers, Domestic, Mary
SP49   State Papers, Scotland, Henry VIII
STAC2   Court of Star Chamber, Proceedings, Henry VIII
STAC10   Court of Star Chamber, Miscellanea
WARD9   Court of Wards, Miscellaneous Books
The College of Arms
Heralds' Books 2 H.13, I.11, I.18, L.12, M.8, Vincent 25
Garter's Roll Muniment Room 6/41

SAN MARINO, CALIFORNIA

Huntington Library
Ellesmere Manuscripts 2654, 2655

II   Printed books and articles

A Collection of Ordinances and Regulations for the Government of the Royal Household
    (London, 1790)
A Commentary of the Services and Charges of William Lord Grey of Wilton, K.G., ed.
    Sir Philip de M. G. Egerton, Camden Soc., xl (London, 1847)
'A diary of the expedition of 1544', *The English Historical Review*, xvi (1901)
Acts of the Privy Council of England, i and ii, ed. J. R. Dasent (London, 1890)
Anglo, Sydney, *The Great Tournament Roll of Westminster* (Oxford, 1968)
    Spectacle, Pageantry and Early Tudor Policy (Oxford, 1969)
Anstruther, Godfrey, *Vaux of Harrowden. A Recusant Family* (Newport, Mon.,
    1953)
'Aske's examination', ed. Mary Bateson, *The English Historical Review*, v (1890)
Bean, J. M. W., *The Estates of the Percy Family 1416–1537* (Oxford, 1958)

Bellamy, John, *The Tudor Law of Treason. An Introduction* (London and Toronto, 1979)

Bernard, G. W., *The Power of the Early Tudor Nobility. A Study of the Fourth and Fifth Earls of Shrewsbury* (Brighton, 1985)

'The fortunes of the Greys, earls of Kent, in the early sixteenth century', *The Historical Journal*, xxv (1982)

Bevan, A. S., 'Justices of the peace, 1509–47: an additional source', *Bulletin of the Institute of Historical Research*, lviii (1985)

Bindoff, S. T., *The House of Commons 1509–1558*, The History of Parliament, 3 vols (London, 1982)

Burnet, Gilbert, *The History of the Reformation of the Church of England*, ed. Nicholas Pocock, 7 vols (Oxford, 1865)

Bush, M. L., 'The Lisle-Seymour land disputes: a study of power and influence in the 1530s', *The Historical Journal*, ix (1966)

'The problem of the far north: a study of the crisis of 1537 and its consequences', *Northern History*, vi (1971)

Calendar of the Close Rolls preserved in the Public Record Office: Henry VII, 2 vols (London, 1955, 1963)

Calendar of the Patent Rolls preserved in the Public Record Office: Henry VII, 2 vols (London, 1914, 1916)

Calendar of Letters, Despatches, and State Papers, relating to the negotiations between England and Spain, ii–viii, with *Supplements*, ed. G. A. Bergenroth and others (London, 1866–1940)

Calendar of State Papers and Manuscripts relating to English affairs, existing in the archives and collections of Venice, ii–v, ed. Rawdon Brown (London, 1867–73)

Chronicles of London, ed. C. L. Kingsford (Oxford, 1905)

Coke, Sir Edward, *The Third Part of the Institutes of the Laws of England*, 4th edn (London, 1669)

The Fourth Part of the Institutes of the Laws of England, 5th edn (London, 1671)

Collected Works of Erasmus, ii, *The Correspondence of Erasmus. Letters 142 to 297: 1501 to 1514*, trans. R. A. B. Mynors and D. F. S. Thomson, annotated W. K. Ferguson (Toronto, 1975)

Condon, Margaret, 'Ruling elites in the reign of Henry VII' in *Patronage, Pedigree and Power in Later Medieval England*, ed. Charles Ross (Gloucester, 1979)

Correspondence of Edward, Third Earl of Derby, during the years 24 to 31 Henry VIII, ed. T. N. Toller, Chetham Soc., new series, 19 (Manchester, 1890)

Coward, Barry, *The Stanleys Lords Stanley and Earls of Derby 1385–1672. The Origins, Wealth and Power of a Landowning Family*, Chetham Soc., 3rd series, xxx (Manchester, 1983)

Cruickshank, C. G., *Elizabeth's Army*, 2nd edn (Oxford, 1966)

Army Royal. Henry VIII's Invasion of France, 1513 (Oxford, 1969)

Davies, C. S. L., 'The English people and war in the early sixteenth century' in *Britain and the Netherlands*, vi, *War and Society*, ed. A. C. Duke and C. A. Tamse (The Hague, 1977)

Devon Monastic Lands: Calendar of Particulars for Grants 1536–1558, ed. Joyce Youings, Devon and Cornwall Record Soc., new series, i (Torquay, 1955)

Dictionary of National Biography

Dodds, Madeleine Hope and Ruth, *The Pilgrimage of Grace 1536–1537 and the Exeter Conspiracy 1538*, 2 vols (Cambridge, 1915)

Dugdale, Sir William, *The Baronage of England*, 2 vols (London, 1675–6)

A Perfect Copy of all Summons of the Nobility to the Great Councils and Parliaments of this Realm (London, 1685)

Dunham, W. H., 'The members of Henry VIII's whole council, 1509–1527', *The English Historical Review*, lix (1944)

Elton, G. R., *The Tudor Revolution in Government. Administrative Changes in the Reign of Henry VIII* (Cambridge, 1953)

Policy and Police. The Enforcement of the Reformation in the Age of Thomas Cromwell (Cambridge, 1972)

Studies in Tudor and Stuart Politics and Government. Papers and Reviews, 3 vols (Cambridge, 1974–83)

'Thomas Cromwell's decline and fall', *Cambridge Historical Journal*, x (1951), reprinted *Studies*, i

'The law of treason in the early Reformation', *The Historical Journal*, xi (1968)

'Thomas More, councillor (1517–1529)' in *St. Thomas More: Action and Contemplation*, ed. R. S. Sylvester (New Haven, Conn., and London, 1972), reprinted *Studies*, i

'The early journals of the house of lords', *The English Historical Review*, lxxxix (1974), reprinted *Studies*, iii

'Tudor government: the points of contact. i, Parliament, ii, The council, iii, The court', *Transactions of the Royal Historical Society*, 5th series, 24–6 (1974–6), reprinted *Studies*, iii

'Parliament in the sixteenth century: functions and fortunes', *The Historical Journal*, xxii (1979), reprinted *Studies*, iii

'Politics and the pilgrimage of grace' in *After the Reformation: Essays in Honor of J. H. Hexter*, ed. Barbara C. Malament (Manchester, 1980), reprinted *Studies*, iii

'Excerpts from the manuscript of William Dunche, no. 3', ed. A. G. W. Murray and E. F. Bosenquet, *The Genealogist*, new series, xxx (1914)

Foedera, Conventiones, Literae [etc.], ed. Thomas Rymer, 3rd edn, 10 vols (The Hague, 1735–45)

Fortescue, Sir John, *The Governance of England*, ed. Charles Plummer (Oxford, 1885)

Fox, Alistair, *Thomas More. History and Providence* (Oxford, 1982)

Goring, J. J., 'The military obligations of the English people, 1511–1558', Ph.D. thesis (London, 1955)

Graves, Michael A. R., *The House of Lords in the Parliaments of Edward VI and Mary I. An Institutional Study* (Cambridge, 1981)

'The two lords' journals of 1542', *Bulletin of the Institute of Historical Research*, xliii (1970)

Guy, J. A., 'The court of star chamber during Wolsey's ascendancy', Ph.D. thesis (Cambridge, 1973)

The Cardinal's Court. The Impact of Thomas Wolsey in Star Chamber (Hassocks, 1977)

The Public Career of Sir Thomas More (Brighton, 1980)

Haigh, Christopher, 'Anticlericalism and the English Reformation', *History*, 68 (1983)

Hall's Chronicle, [ed. Henry Ellis] (London, 1809)

Halstead, Robert, *Succinct Genealogies of the Noble and Ancient Houses of . . . Mordaunt of Turvey* (London, 1685)

Handbook of British Chronology, ed. Sir F. Maurice Powicke and E. B. Fryde, Royal Historical Soc. Guides and Handbooks, no. 2, 2nd edn (London, 1961)

Harcourt, L. W. Vernon, *His Grace the Steward and Trial of Peers* (London, 1907)

Harrison, C. J., 'The petition of Edmund Dudley', *The English Historical Review*, lxxxvii (1972)

Hawarde, John, *Les Reportes del Cases in Camera Stellata 1593 to 1609*, ed. W. B. Baildon (London, 1894)

Heal, Felicity, *Of Prelates and Princes. A Study of the Economic and Social Position of the Tudor Episcopate* (Cambridge, 1980)

Herbert of Cherbury, Edward lord, *The Life and Reign of King Henry the Eighth* (London, 1672)

Hicks, Michael, 'Attainder, resumption and coercion 1461–1529', *Parliamentary History: A Yearbook*, 3 (1984)

Historical Manuscripts Commission: Third Report of the Royal Commission on Historical Manuscripts (London, 1872)

Seventh Report of the Royal Commission on Historical Manuscripts (London, 1879)

Report on Manuscripts in Various Collections, ii (London, 1903)

The Manuscripts of His Grace the Duke of Rutland, iv (London, 1905)

Report on the Manuscripts of Lord Middleton, ed. W. H. Stevenson (London, 1911)

Report on the Manuscripts of the late Reginald Rawdon Hastings, i, ed. Francis Bickley (London, 1928)

Report on the Manuscripts of the Most Honourable the Marquess of Bath, iv, ed. Marjorie Blatcher (London, 1968)

Hoak, D. E., *The King's Council in the Reign of Edward VI* (Cambridge, 1976)

Hodgett, G. A. J., *Tudor Lincolnshire*, History of Lincolnshire, ed. Joan Thirsk, vi (Lincoln, 1975)

Holinshed's Chronicles of England, Scotland, and Ireland, 6 vols (London, 1807–8)

Illustrations of British History, Biography, and Manners, in the Reigns of Henry VIII, Edward VI, Mary, Elizabeth, and James I, ed. Edmund Lodge, 3 vols, 2nd edn (London, 1838)

Ingulph's Chronicle of the Abbey of Croyland with the continuations by Peter of Blois and anonymous writers, trans. Henry T. Riley (London, 1854)

Ives, E. W., *The Common Lawyers of Pre-Reformation England. Thomas Kebell: A Case Study*, Cambridge Studies in English Legal History, ed. D. E. C. Yale (Cambridge, 1983)

'The genesis of the statute of uses', *The English Historical Review*, lxxxii (1967)

'Faction at the court of Henry VIII: the fall of Anne Boleyn', *History*, 57 (1972)

Faction in Tudor England, Historical Association Appreciations in History, no. 6 (London, 1979)

James, M. E., *Change and Continuity in the Tudor North. The Rise of Thomas first Lord Wharton*, Borthwick Papers, no. 27 (York, 1965)

A Tudor Magnate and the Tudor State: Henry 5th Earl of Northumberland, Borthwick Papers, no. 30 (York, 1966)

'The first earl of Cumberland (1493–1542) and the decline of northern feudalism', *Northern History*, i (1966)

'Obedience and dissent in Henrician England: the Lincolnshire rebellion 1536', *Past and Present*, 48 (1970)

English Politics and the Concept of Honour 1485–1642, Past & Present Supplement 3 (1978)

Journals of the House of Lords Beginning Anno Primo Henrici Octavi, i (no date or place of publication)

Keen, Maurice (M. H.), *Chivalry* (New Haven, Conn., and London, 1984)

'Treason trials under the law of arms', *Transactions of the Royal Historical Society*, 5th series, 12 (1962)

Kelly, Henry Ansgar, *The Matrimonial Trials of Henry VIII* (Stanford, Calif., 1976)

Knecht, R. J., *Francis I* (Cambridge, 1982)

Knowles, David, and Hadcock, R. Neville, *Medieval Religious Houses of England and Wales*, rev. edn (London, 1971)

Lander, J. R., 'Bonds, coercion, and fear: Henry VII and the peerage' in *Florilegium Historiale: Essays Presented to Wallace K. Ferguson*, ed. J. G. Rowe and W. H. Stockdale (Toronto, 1971), reprinted J. R. Lander, *Crown and Nobility 1450–1509* (London, 1976)

Lehmberg, S. E., *The Reformation Parliament 1529–1536* (Cambridge, 1970)

The Later Parliaments of Henry VIII 1536–1547 (Cambridge, 1977)

'Sir Thomas Audley: a soul as black as marble?' in *Tudor Men and Institutions. Studies in English Law and Government*, ed. A. J. Slavin (Baton Rouge, La, 1972)

'Parliamentary attainder in the reign of Henry VIII', *The Historical Journal*, xviii (1975)

Les Reports des Cases en les Ans des Roys Edward V, Richard III, Henrie VII et Henrie VIII, touts qui par cy devant ont este publies (London, 1679)

Letters and Papers, Foreign and Domestic, of the Reign of Henry VIII, ed. J. S. Brewer and others, 21 vols and *Addenda* (London, 1864–1932)

Letters and Papers Illustrative of the Reigns of Richard III and Henry VII, ed. James Gairdner, Rolls Series 24, 2 vols (London, 1861, 1863)

Levine, Mortimer, 'The fall of Edward, duke of Buckingham' in *Tudor Men and Institutions. Studies in English Law and Government*, ed. A. J. Slavin (Baton Rouge, La, 1972)

Literary Remains of King Edward the Sixth, ed. J. G. Nichols, 2 vols, Roxburghe Club (London, 1857)

McFarlane, K. B., *The Nobility of Later Medieval England* (Oxford, 1973)

'Memorial from George Constantyne to Thomas lord Cromwell', ed. Thomas Amyot, *Archaeologia*, xxiii (1831)

Millar, Gilbert John, *Tudor Mercenaries and Auxiliaries 1485–1547* (Charlottesville, Va, 1980)

Miller, Helen, 'Subsidy assessments of the peerage in the sixteenth century', *Bulletin of the Institute of Historical Research*, xxviii (1955)

'London and parliament in the reign of Henry VIII', ibid., xxxv (1962)

'Attendance in the house of lords during the reign of Henry VIII', *The Historical Journal*, x (1967)

'Henry VIII's unwritten will: grants of lands and honours in 1547' in *Wealth and Power in Tudor England: Essays Presented to S. T. Bindoff*, ed. E. W. Ives, R.J. Knecht and J.J. Scarisbrick (London, 1978)

'Lords and commons: relations between the two houses of parliament, 1509–1558', *Parliamentary History: A Yearbook*, 1 (1982)

Morgan, D. A. L., 'The king's affinity in the polity of Yorkist England', *Transactions of the Royal Historical Society*, 5th series, 23 (1973)

Nicolas, N. H. (Sir Harris), *Report of Proceedings on Claims to the Barony of L'Isle* (London, 1829)

Report of Proceedings on the Claim to the Earldom of Devon (London, 1832)

Original Letters Illustrative of English History, ed. Henry Ellis, 11 vols in 3 series (London, 1824–46)

Pike, L. Owen, 'The trial of peers', *The Law Quarterly Review*, xxiii (1907)

Powell, J. Enoch, and Wallis, Keith, *The House of Lords in the Middle Ages. A History of the English House of Lords to 1540* (London, 1968)

Powicke, Michael, *Military Obligation in Medieval England. A Study in Liberty and Duty* (Oxford, 1962)

Proceedings and Ordinances of the Privy Council of England, vii, *1540–1542*, ed. Sir Harris Nicolas (London, 1837)

Rawcliffe, Carole, *The Staffords, Earls of Stafford and Dukes of Buckingham 1394–1521* (Cambridge, 1978)

Reports of Cases in the Reigns of Henry VIII, Edward VI, Queen Mary and Queen Elizabeth taken and collected by Sir James Dyer, ed. John Vaillant, 3 vols (London, 1794)

Reports of the Deputy Keeper of the Public Records, iii (London, 1842)

Richardson, W.C., *Tudor Chamber Administration 1485–1547* (Baton Rouge, La, 1952)

Robinson, W. R. B., 'Early Tudor policy towards Wales [Part 1]: the acquisition of lands and offices in Wales by Charles Somerset, earl of Worcester', *The Bulletin of the Board of Celtic Studies*, xx, pt 4 (1964)

'Early Tudor policy towards Wales, Part 2: the Welsh offices held by Henry earl of Worcester (1526–1549)', ibid., xxi, pt 1 (1964)

'Early Tudor policy towards Wales, Part 3: Henry earl of Worcester and Henry VIII's legislation for Wales', ibid., xxi, pt 4 (1966)

Rosenthal, Joel T., *Nobles and the Noble Life 1295–1500*, Historical Problems: Studies and Documents, ed. G. R. Elton, no. 25 (London, 1976)

Roskell, J. S., 'The problem of the attendance of the lords in medieval parliaments', *Bulletin of the Institute of Historical Research*, xxix (1956)

Rotuli Parliamentorum, iv–vi (no date or place of publication)

Round, J. H., *The King's Serjeants and Officers of State with their Coronation Services* (London, 1911)

Russell, Joyceleyne G., *The Field of Cloth of Gold. Men and Manners in 1520* (London, 1969)

Rutland Papers, ed. William Jerdan, Camden Soc., xxi (London, 1842)

Sainty, J. C., *Officers of the Exchequer*, List and Index Soc., special series, 18 (London, 1983)

Scarisbrick, J. J. *Henry VIII* (London, 1968)

Select Cases in the Council of Henry VII, ed. C. G. Bayne and W. H. Dunham, Selden Soc., 75 for 1956 (London, 1958)

Smith, R. B., *Land and Politics in the England of Henry VIII. The West Riding of Yorkshire: 1530–46* (Oxford, 1970)

Smyth, John, *The Lives of the Berkeleys*, 2 vols (Gloucester, 1883)

Somerville, Robert, *History of the Duchy of Lancaster*, i, *1265–1603* (London, 1953)

Spont, Alfred, *Letters and Papers relating to the War with France 1512–1513*, Navy Records Soc., x (London, 1897)

Squibb, G. D., *The High Court of Chivalry. A Study of the Civil Law in England* (Oxford, 1959)

Starkey, David R., 'Representation through intimacy: a study in the symbolism of monarchy and court office in early modern England' in *Symbols and Sentiments. Cross-Cultural Studies in Symbolism*, ed. Ioan Lewis (London, 1977) 'From feud to faction: English politics circa 1450–1550', *History Today*, xxxii (1982)

State Papers published under the Authority of His Majesty's Commission: Henry VIII, 11 vols (London, 1830–52)

Stow, John, *Annales*, ed. Edmund Howes (London, 1631)

Strype, John, *Ecclesiastical Memorials, relating chiefly to religion . . . under King Henry VIII, King Edward VI, and Queen Mary I*, 3 vols (Oxford, 1822)

Survey of London, xvi, *Charing Cross: The Parish of St Martin-in-the-Fields, Part 1* (London County Council, 1935)

The Anglica Historia of Polydore Vergil A.D. 1485–1537, ed. Denys Hay, Camden Soc., 3rd series, lxxiv (London, 1950)

The Chronicle of Calais, ed. J. G. Nichols, Camden Soc., xxxv (London, 1846)

The Complete Peerage by G.E.C., ed. Vicary Gibbs and others, 12 vols (London, 1910–59)

The Field Book of Walsham-le-Willows 1577, ed. K. M. Dodd, Suffolk Records Soc., xvii (Ipswich, 1974)

The Hamilton Papers, ed. Joseph Bain, 2 vols (Edinburgh, 1890, 1892)

The History of the King's Works, gen. ed. H. M. Colvin, 6 vols (London, 1963–82)

The Itinerary of John Leland in or about the years 1535–1543, ed. Lucy Toulmin Smith, 5 vols (London, 1907–10)

'The life of Henrye FitzAllen, last earle of Arundell of that name', [ed. J. G. Nichols], *The Gentleman's Magazine*, ciii, pt 2 (1833)

The Lisle Letters, ed. Muriel St Clare Byrne, 6 vols (Chicago and London, 1981)

The Marcher Lordships of South Wales, 1415–1536. Select Documents, ed. T. B. Pugh, Board of Celtic Studies, University of Wales, History and Law Series, xx (Cardiff, 1963)

The Noble Triumphant Coronation of Queen Anne (London, 1533), from reprint in Edward Arber, *An English Garner*, 8 vols (London, 1895–7)

The Priory of Hexham, ed. J. Raine, Surtees Soc., 44, 46 for 1863, 1864 (Durham, 1864, 1865)

The Register of the Most Noble Order of the Garter, ed. J. Anstis, 2 vols (London, 1724)

The Reports of Sir John Spelman, ed. J. H. Baker, Selden Soc., 93, 94 for 1976, 1977 (London, 1977, 1978)

The Statutes at Large, passed in the Parliaments held in Ireland, i, *1310–1612* (Dublin, 1765)

The Statutes of the Realm, ii and iii (London, 1816, 1817): cited by regnal year and chapter number

The Tree of Commonwealth. A Treatise written by Edmund Dudley, ed. D. M. Brodie (Cambridge, 1948)

The Victoria History of the Counties of England

Three Chapters of Letters relating to the Suppression of the Monasteries, ed. Thomas Wright, Camden Soc., xxvi (London, 1843)

Two Early Tudor Lives: The Life and Death of Cardinal Wolsey by George Cavendish, The Life of Sir Thomas More by William Roper, ed. Richard S. Sylvester and Davis P. Harding (New Haven, Conn., and London, 1962)

Valor Ecclesiasticus [ed. J. Caley and J. Hunter], 6 vols (London, 1810–34)

Wagner, Sir Anthony, and Sainty, J. C., 'The origin of the introduction of peers in the house of lords', *Archaeologia*, ci (1967)

Wedgwood, J. C., *History of Parliament: Biographies of the Members of the Commons House 1439–1509* (London, 1936)

History of Parliament: Register of the Ministers and of the Members of Both Houses 1439–1509 (London, 1938)

Willen, Diane, *John Russell, First Earl of Bedford. One of the King's Men*, Royal Historical Society Studies in History Series, no. 23 (London, 1981)

Williams, Penry, *The Council in the Marches of Wales under Elizabeth I* (Cardiff, 1958)

Wills from Doctors' Commons, ed. J. G. Nichols and J. Bruce, Camden Soc., lxxxiii (London, 1863)

Woodward, G. W. O., *The Dissolution of the Monasteries* (London, 1966)

Wriothesley, Charles, *A Chronicle of England during the Reigns of the Tudors from A.D. 1485 to 1559*, Camden Soc., new series, xi, xx (London, 1875, 1877)

Youings, Joyce, *The Dissolution of the Monasteries*, Historical Problems: Studies and Documents, ed. G. R. Elton, no. 14 (London, 1971)

'The council of the west', *Transactions of the Royal Historical Society*, 5th series, 10 (1960)

Index

Pavia, battle of, 20
Peche, Sir John and lady, 214
Pembroke, marchioness of, *see* Boleyn
Penkelly, Brecon, 215
Penshurst, Kent, 100, 140
Percy, Henry, earl of Northumberland
1489–1527, 6–7, 13, 17, 20, 21n,
46–8, 82, 93, 103–4, 108–9, 112, 138,
146–8, 187, 191, 208, 221
Percy, Henry, earl of Northumberland
1527–37, 52n, 53–6, 58–9, 62, 82, 90,
96, 98, 105, 111, 122–3, 129, 146,
188–9, 191–3, 200, 220–2; wife Mary
(Talbot), 52n, 129, 189
Percy, Sir Thomas, 63
Philip, archduke, Philip I of Castile, 7
pilgrimage of grace, 44, 60–1, 63, 66,
149–54, 192, 245
Pisho, Herts, 219–20, 224
Plantagenet, Arthur, viscount Lisle
1523–42, 14, 18–19, 28, 31–2, 39n,
40, 69, 71, 87, 89, 98–9, 103, 122,
125, 129–30, 168, 177, 180–2, 225–7,
232, 238, 243–4; 1st wife Elizabeth
(Grey), baroness Lisle, widow of
Edmund Dudley, 14, 18, 32; 2nd wife
Honor (Grenville), 28, 31, 181,
226–7, 243; stepson, 129
Plantagenet, Edward, earl of Warwick
1492–99, 9, 41–3, 45, 210
Plantagenet, George, duke of Clarence
1461–78, 40–1, 210
Pole, Edmund de la, duke of Suffolk
1492–3, earl of Suffolk
1493–1504, 6–7, 15, 212; widow
Margaret (Scrope), 212
Pole, Sir Geoffrey, 65–6
Pole, Henry, lord Montagu 1529–38, 9,
23, 29–30, 45–8, 57, 64–8, 75, 81,
96–8, 122, 150; son and heir Henry,
68
Pole, John de la, earl of Lincoln
1467–87, 21, 212
Pole, John de la, duke of Suffolk
1450–92, 93
Pole, Margaret (Plantagenet), countess of
Salisbury, 9, 42, 50, 66, 68, 210, 248
Pole, Reginald, cardinal, 65, 67–9, 181
Pole, Richard de la, 15, 20, 148–9, 183
Pontefract, Yorks, 61, 140, 149, 153, 201
Pope Clement VII, 96, 130–1, Julius II,

37, Leo X, 17, 37, 81 and his brother
(Giuliano de' Medici), 87
Popley, William, 225
Portugal, Manuel I of, 87
Poynings, Sir Edward, 12, 34, 174
Poynings, Thomas, lord Poynings 1545
(January–August), 34–5, 39n, 40, 184
Puleston, John, 141

Raby, Co. Durham, 187, 191
Radcliffe, Henry, earl of Sussex
1542–57, 89, 97, 123
Radcliffe, John, lord FitzWalter
1485–95, 41
Radcliffe, Robert, lord FitzWalter 1505,
viscount FitzWalter 1525, earl of
Sussex 1529–42, 18, 21, 24, 27–9,
45, 47, 58, 60, 70, 73, 80, 82, 89, 94,
96, 98, 103, 111–12, 114–16, 119–22,
136–7, 141, 145, 154, 166, 171–3,
176–8, 181, 210, 222, 234, 237, 240;
1st wife Elizabeth (Stafford), 13; 2nd
wife Margaret (Stanley), 24
Reading, abbot of, 68
Renhold, Beds, 245
Revesby, Lincs, abbey, 238
Rice, John ap, 51
Rich, Richard, 56, 226, 247
Richard III, 41, 109, 166
Richmond, duke of, *see* FitzRoy
Rievaulx, Yorks, abbey, 245
Rochester, bishops of, *see* Fisher; Heath;
Hilsey
Rochford, viscount, lord, *see* Boleyn
Rockcliff, Cumb, 53
Ros, Edmund, lord Ros 1485–1508, 11
Ros, lords, *see* Manners
Rosedale, Yorks, 237
Rotherham, Yorks, 235
Rufford, Notts, abbey, 235
Rumney, Mon, 248n
Russell, John, lord Russell 1539, earl of
Bedford 1550–5, 30, 32–4, 73, 83,
85–6, 90, 113–14, 118–19, 123, 132,
156–9, 168, 172, 175, 180, 197, 202,
226, 239, 246, 254–5
Ruthal, Thomas, bishop of Durham, 14,
143, 160
Rutland, earls of, *see* Manners
Rye, Sussex, hospital at Playden beside,
249